This book is one of a series of Studies in Spatial Analysis stimulated by the theoretical and applied research conducted within the Netherlands Economic Institute, Rotterdam, published by Gower. Titles in the series are:

INDUSTRIAL MOBILITY AND MIGRATION IN THE EUROPEAN COMMUNITY

Industrial Mobility and Migration in the European Community

Edited by
L. H. KLAASSEN
W. T. M. MOLLE
Netherlands Economic Institute,
Rotterdam

Gower

© Netherlands Economic Institute, 1983

Published by
Gower Publishing Company Limited,
Gower House, Croft Road, Aldershot, Hants. GU11 3HR

British Library Cataloguing in Publication Data

Industrial mobility and migration in the European Community
    1. Industries, Location of—European Economic
       Community countries—Social aspects
    2. Industries, Location of—European Economic
       Community countries—Economic aspects
    I. Klaassen, L.H.   II. Molle, W.T.M.
    338.6'042'094   HD58

    ISBN 0 566 00486 0

Printed in Great Britain by Biddles of Guildford

Contents

Contributors

Philippe Aydalot, Université de Paris, Panthéon Sorbonne, Paris (France).

Franz-Josef Bade, IIM Industrial Policy, Wissenschaftzentrum, Berlin, (FRG).

Roberto P. Camagni, Università Commerciale 'Luigi Bocconi', Milano (Italy).

Ulf Christiansen, Danish Building Research Institute (SBI), Kopenhagen, (Denmark).

Georgio A. Giannopoulos, Faculty of Technology, University of Thessaloniki, (Greece).

Maria Giaoutzis-Flytzanis, Faculty of Technology, University of Thessaloniki, (Greece).

Leo H. Klaassen, President of the Netherlands Economic Institute, Rotterdam, (Netherlands).

Willem Molle, Department of Location Studies, Netherlands Economic Institute, Rotterdam, (Netherlands).

Patrick O'Farrell, Department of Town Planning, UWIST, Cardiff, (UK).

Peter Townroe, Urban and Regional Economics Division, The World Bank, (USA).

Norbert Vanhove, College of Europe, Bruges, (Belgium).

Acknowledgements

The editors' initiative to compile the present book met with unanimous positive reactions from the contributors. They all subscribed to the objectives outlined for the book, and agreed to organise their contributions according to the editors' suggestions. That positive response from our friends and colleagues has been decisive for the successful realisation of the project.

The first drafts of all papers were discussed at a conference organised by the Netherlands Economic Institute in May 1981. Apart from the contributors, a number of qualified and interested persons from academic, industrial, and government circles in all countries of the European Community attended this conference. Their active participation in the exchange of views and their critical yet constructive comments on the papers have done much to improve the quality of the present book.

The conference brought out guidelines for adapting the papers into a well thought out collection. All those concerned have worked with the editors in a friendly atmosphere to make the country chapters of the book as comparable as possible, and to improve the coverage of the subject and the quality of the information. The co-operation has been very stimulating. We want to thank most particularly all contributors for their openness to discussion, and the amount of work they have done under sometimes very difficult circumstances, having to cope with absence of data, undisclosed information, etc.; their continuous efforts have made it possible to arrive at the present book.

But all this was not enough to guarantee the successful finalisation of the book. Without the help of numerous other persons the work could not have been done. We want to thank, in our own names as well as those of the contributors, all those who have helped by providing information, by reading and criticising drafts of the various chapters, and by supplying the resources needed to do the research involved. Thanks are also expressed to the staff members of Erasmus University and the Netherlands Economic Institute, who created the best possible conditions for the conference to succeed. Words of gratitude are further due to those who have contributed by typing and retyping parts of the text, by photocopying and duplicating, and in various other ways.

Most particularly, Mrs Elderson has earned our gratitude by constantly and conscientiously improving the text, polishing up the English of most of the chapters written by continental authors.

A word of thanks is due to W. Cristofoletti, who has skilfully executed the disproportionate amount of art work required for the present volume.

Rotterdam, January 1982

1 Introduction

To design effective urban, regional, industrial, and transport policies, governments need to know the causes and patterns of change in the spatial distribution of industry in their countries. The purpose of the present study is to present the results of empirical analyses of one component of the redistribution, i.e. industrial migration. The factors that determine migration, and the mobility of industry, will get ample attention too. The terms 'migration' and 'mobility' will be defined in the next chapter; they are used in this book along with the more general term 'movement'.

The movement of plants is only one form of spatial adaptation to new circumstances, others being the creation of new plants and the death, growth and decline of existing activities. Together they yield the net change of activity in a region.

Studies of regional development tend to be based on net-change data because these are most readily available. A much deeper insight into the basic elements of the adjustment process can be gained by studying the components of change; however, for lack of data that approach has been rare so far.

The present volume sets out to synthetise the results of the inquiries carried out into industrial movement; such information as is available on other components — creations, deaths, *in situ* growth, etc. — will be referred to only in passing.

Apart from UK and USA studies, investigations of industrial movement have hardly become known outside their countries of origin. But are the UK and USA findings specific to these countries, or generally applicable? Research that could provide the answer to that question has not yet been made, owing to the inaccessibility of most relevant studies. The present book tries to fill the gap by providing an international comparison of industrial movement in all the countries of the European Community. A chapter each has been devoted to the ten present members of the European Community (Chapters 3–12). Efforts have been made to recapitulate in these chapters as much as possible of the empirical work done and the knowledge gained on industrial movement in the countries involved, a loose pattern of subjects being followed to facilitate international comparison. These subjects comprise the relative importance of movement in quantitative terms, the characteristics of moving industries, the spatial patterns of movement, the motives for moving, and, finally, the socio-economic effects of industrial movement.

A general introductory chapter – Chapter 2 – has been written to place the country studies in their proper context; it discusses in general terms the theoretical aspects of industrial migration and mobility. In a final chapter – Chapter 13 – we have tried to compose an international super-synthesis of the national synthetic studies; moreover, we have compared the various aspects of the phenomenon in the ten countries in an attempt to identify the general characteristics on the one hand and those specific to particular situations, conditions, and time periods on the other.

The object of study has been the movement of industry; although in principle industry should be understood in a general sense, in practice the book is largely confined to manufacturing industry.

The study of the movement of manufacturing plants, interesting enough *per se*, has also important societal connotations. Indeed, such studies are often undertaken to find out why companies relocate, and thus to evolve effective ways and means to lead relocation decisions in a direction that seems desirable to policy makers, a direction that may be different from the one chosen when the market is free. However, policy makers' objectives tend to vary widely with the policy field envisaged. One objective could be to renovate old urban quarters; the motives for movements of plants within an urban area would then be essential to know. An insight into the future location of offices in an agglomeration would be required to design an urban-transportation strategy. Regional policy could dictate what factors determining interregional movements of plants one needs to know. An understanding of international movements of plants could serve the purpose of strengthening a nation's competitive position. To answer as well as possible policy questions on all spatial levels, in all national studies efforts have been made to respect the distinctions between those levels.

2

Thanks to the wealth of subjects discussed and the variety of area levels analysed, the book covers most aspects of the subject. Moreover, it encompasses all the present member countries of the European Community.

On one other point the book aspires to completeness, namely that it uses, and refers to, all studies carried out (or at any rate published) in the member countries since the Second World War. The editors express the hope that the features mentioned will make the book not only a source of scientific information for all those interested in industrial migration and mobility, but also a bibliography on that subject.

Finally, editors and contributors hope that this volume will improve policy makers' understanding of the dynamics of industrial movement as an element of the general and permanent process of plants adjusting to changing conditions in Europe, and to devise effective strategies to improve the spatial equilibrium in Europe.

2 General considerations
L. H. KLAASSEN and W. T. M. MOLLE

The spatial distribution of activities across a country is subject to continuous change. Changes arise from all manner of causes; entrepreneurs will take advantage of every opportunity to adjust to changed circumstances.

In what follows we will try to shed some light on the nature of spatial adjustment processes, on their theoretical background, their statistical measurement, as well as their actual outcome in terms of industry migration.

It appears useful to make a distinction between the mobility of industries, that is, the degree to which entrepreneurs are inclined to follow an impulse to move, and actual migration, the volume of which is the result of the propensity to move and the intensity of the impulse.

To picture the general framework within which industrial migration takes place, we shall first review the existing literature on location and migration. Next, we shall elaborate some theoretical distinctions that will lead to a discussion of the most relevant concepts to be used in the rest of the analysis and their measurement in day-to-day practice. Next we will present some examples of spatial adjustment and a discussion of the factors influencing industrial mobility. Knowledge of all these elements is, although interesting as such, not the ultimate objective of this study; it is rather a condition for the judicious conception and efficient implementation of regional and urban socioeconomic policy. Some aspects related to this are discussed in a final section.

Theory

Introduction

In the course of time, the disciplines of spatial economics and economic geography have tried to explain, by various theories, how economic activities came to be spatially distributed the way they are, and why regions show differences in economic growth. At first, they tended to stress the location trends of industries, which were supposed to depend on regional features; later the attention switched to ways and means of influencing these processes and of diverting growth to the less developed regions. At that state of the art, policy makers became interested in the elements of industry migration. The trouble is that, while general location theory is far advanced, migration or mobility theory has hardly begun to develop, some empirical knowledge being about all there is to build on. This empirical knowledge, however, does link up with recent developments in location theory. A few lines may be devoted, hereafter, to the rudiments of migration theory found in literature.

Because the migration of industries cannot be considered apart from their location, closure, etc., we propose first to touch upon a few aspects of general location theory before proceeding to some specific elements of migration. The discussion of location theory falls into two divisions, the first dealing with classical theory, the second with behaviouristic theory; the latter links up with the 'theory' of migration.

Classical location theory

From a survey presented by, among others, Greenhut (1956), three groups of theories have contributed to classical location theory: the least-cost theory of location; the interdependence theory of location; and the theory of maximum-profit location.

The German economists Launhardt (1882) and Weber (1909) stood at the cradle of classical location theory; they assumed individual companies, freely competing for raw materials, labour, and markets, each trying to achieve a minimum level of production costs. Their assumption of cost minimization later gave rise to this earliest location theory being called the least-cost approach. Later authors, completing and reacting to this least-cost approach, developed new points of view, which came to be known as market-oriented and locational-interdependence theories, being based on, respectively, sales maximization and the locational influence industries exert on one another. Market-oriented

5

theories were developed by Fetter (1924) and Hotelling (1929), locational-interdependence theories by Hoover (1948) and Lösch (1954). Lösch was the first to choose profit maximization for a starting point, in an endeavour to reconcile the least-cost and market-oriented approaches. Other authors, too, shifted their approaches from cost through return to profit.

The most recent contributions to classical location theory were made in the 1950s and 1960s by such scholars as Isard (1956), Hamilton (1967, 1974), and Haggett (1965), who on the one hand refined the various concepts, and on the other developed the theory to equip it for the solution of very complex location problems.

Gradually, more and more inroads came to be made into the concepts of classical theory. Webber (1972) pointed out the consequences of uncertainty on location in an, admittedly classical, diagram. Indeed, scholars began to think in terms of 'spatial margins of profitability' rather than in terms of a single optimum location (see, e.g., Smith, 1971).

Our review of classical location theory shows, then, that all theories are variations on one basic theme: the search for the *optimum location* for an industry or complex of industries, by the well-known list of locational criteria: prices of raw materials and energy, transportation distances, availability of land, capital and labour, situation of the sales market, and agglomeration economies. The common factor in all contributions to classical location theory is the assumption of rational man, who acts from economic principles, and is always fully informed of all aspects of the problem facing him, as well as of the consequences of his actions and choices.

The behaviouristic school

Empirical locational research (for instance the studies by Greenhut, 1956) had shown that the conditions of classical theory often failed to be met in practice, and that locational decisions tend to be governed by quite different mechanisms from those indicated in classical theory.

Against the classical concept of economic man, Simon (1952, 1957), precursor of behavioural location theory, put his concept of a decision-maker with bounded rationality: an individual (entrepreneur) who is as unable to collect all the information relevant to a decision as he is incapable of digesting such information. Pred (1967) introduced this concept into a so-called behavioural matrix, placing along its coordinates, respectively, informedness and the ability to digest information. With both at the maximum, the chance of an optimum choice is greatest; with both at the minimum, the chance of a flop is greatest.

On a wide band in the centre lie all the places that may be satisfactory, with plenty of opportunity to choose locations satisfying as well the so-called non-rational or personal criteria. Greenhut (1956) in particular pointed out the significance of such factors, which indeed may provide the entrepreneur or his staff with a psychical income that counts for a lot in the final weighing-up of a location's advantages and drawbacks.

The progress of the behaviouristic school has been largely governed by scholars who investigated decision-making within companies (especially location and investment decisions) (Stafford, 1972; Lloyd and Dicken, 1977; Townroe, 1969). They looked upon location problems as a part, sometimes a derivative, of total company policy, production, investments, labour, environment, etc.; no wonder that many elements from decision theory came to be integrated in location theory.

A general picture has emerged, but so far not been developed into a formal theory. Internal and external conditions permitting, entrepreneurs seem to decide along the following lines:

1 expansion policy is hardened into a product policy;
2 one examines how far present production facilities can cope;
3 once a new plant has been decided upon, the search for the appropriate location is set in motion;
4 the location is chosen and production facilities are installed;
5 the new production line has to be made operational and profitable in the context of the total corporate policy.

In the literature, the decision stages mentioned above have been given unequal attention. There is no need for us to dwell on all of them here; it suffices to concentrate on two main stages: (a) pressure on present situation; extend existing facilities, establish a new plant, or move integrally (push factors) — points 1 and 2; (b) choosing the new location (pull decision — point 3).

The behaviouristic school is empirical rather than theoretical in nature. Because we aim to summarise in the next chapters the results of more complete empirical studies of the subject than the few quoted in the — mostly UK and USA — literature on behaviouristic location ideas, we shall not now go into the specific factors associated with the various decision stages.

A theory of industrial movement

From the previous sections theorising on the phenomena attending the spatial adjustment of production units, a theoretical concept of insuf-

7

ficient reality content on the one hand has been produced, and an insufficiently formalised realistic concept on the other.

Another point is that classical location theory generally assumes a new plant that has to be located somewhere, while the behaviouristic school also recognises other possibilities, such as deciding against investment, transferring part of the production, adjusting the production to changed circumstances. That is not to say, however, that writers of this latter school are clear about typical mobility governing factors. The only bit of theory they present — still strongly vested in empirical findings — is that companies show less tendency to move as the distance to the envisaged new location is greater.

Rather than, as is suggested here, studying determining factors and their development over time to arrive at an expectation pattern of industrial growth, decline, and migration in the region relevant for a specific policy objective, many behaviouristic studies set out to derive more general conclusions about the factors that induced relocation from surveys among relocated plants. Provided the sample was representative of sectors and areas, they may be more or less successful.

While in the latter approach the theory is thus 'formulated by looking at the facts', in the former the theory is formulated first and then tested with the material available, a procedure that is more elegant and scientifically easier to justify. Every researcher knows, however, that in practice both roads are apt to be followed simultaneously, theories being reformulated on statistical evidence, and new statistical information being required to test a reformulated theory, until data and theory are in satisfactory agreement.

For want of a clear general concept of location theory, one naturally looks elsewhere for useful theoretical developments. The theories of regional growth are an obvious possibility. Some of them, like growth-pole theory, and cumulative causality theory (backwash and spread effects) contain all the elements of location, but imply moves rather than stating them clearly. The theory coming nearest to being explicit on moves is the 'filtering-down theory' (Thomson, 1968; Vernon, 1969). It combines factors exerting pressure on a company to move with a classification of location factors important for the new location of a given establishment; moreover, it indicates technological progress, which changes both the products and the conditions of production, as a general inducement to continuous migration. A short description of this theory is in order.

According to the theory of *filtering-down*, when a new production line is first started and the product as well as its production process are still very much in need of innovation, producers need to be in close contact with highly developed information and research networks; they also need a large concentrated market with great purchasing power, and innovation-minded consumers. Those things can only be found in one of the central urbanised areas. As the product gets better known, its outlet will expand and the best production process will emerge; however, at this stage the production, still tied by original advantages, will continue to be carried on mainly in central areas. At the next stage, however, drastic changes are apt to occur. By then the production processes will have matured, the product will be marketed in large quantities, and the producers' main concern has become to produce as cheaply as possible. That means, in locational terms, that production will be moved to areas offering cost advantages. Such areas have from of old been peripheral regions, where labour costs as well as other costs tend to be lower than in central parts.

Recently, a new stage has been added, in which the production of articles that are getting close to the end of their 'life cycle' is moved to countries of the Third World. The sectors most affected by this new development are those that in the recent past have 'filtered-down' to the more remote parts of Europe, such as textiles and ready-made clothing; automobiles and chemicals are showing signs of following the same path.

The 'filtering-down' theory does provide a neat framework for migration processes, but there is reason to doubt its general validity and thus its adequacy as the sole foundation for further research; empirical tests of the theory's reality content have brought to light quite a few other elements important enough to be taken into account.

To put the present study on a more secure footing, we have borrowed some theoretical concepts from the migration of people (see e.g. Klaassen and Drewe, 1973) in particular those concerned with the distinction between mobility-controlling and migration-controlling factors.

As a matter of fact these ideas have recently been generalised by Alonso (1976) to fit many aspects of movement, including that of industry. Alonso's model has been interpreted by Anselin and Isard (1979), who describe it as follows:

> The Alonso model pertains to a closed system, consisting of a number of mutually exclusive groups, which together cover the whole system. Each group consists of units, which can move from one group to another. The model is concerned with building a logical framework for the flow of units out of one particular group into another and for the total flow out and the total flow into each group. As a consequence, each group can be regarded as an origin for those units which move out, and as a destination for those units which move in.

When considered as an origin, each group has a number of unfavourable (push-out) characteristics which induce units to leave.

Alternatively, when considered as a destination, each group has a number of attractive (pull-in) characteristics. Some of these may be the same as those listed under 'repulsive' characteristics. The characteristics of a particular group are themselves important for understanding flow out and into that group; so also are the same characteristics of all other groups in the system.

With respect to units leaving a given group, it is important to know what attractive groups exist in the system and how their attractiveness is evaluated taking into account the friction of distance in the broadest sense. In other words how difficult is it for a member in the given group to reach and become a member of every other group having attractive properties. With respect to units joining a given group, it is important to know what 'repulsive' groups exist in the system and how their repulsiveness is evaluated by the attracting group, again taking into account the friction of distance.

A framework for measurement

Definition of components

To clarify our thoughts on industrial migration, movement, and mobility, we shall start from a definition equation of the changes in a region's industrial activity. This equation indicates the elements constituting the change from year $t-1$ to year t in the volume of economic activity in a certain region. The economic activity is measured here in employment.

$$W_t^i - W_{t-1}^i = IS_p^i + NC_p^i - CL_p^i + \sum_j I_{ji,p} - \sum_j E_{ij,p} \qquad (2.1)$$

where

W_t^i = employment in region i at point in time t;

IS_p^i = net employment growth in industries present at the beginning and end of the period (*in situ* growth);

10

NC_p^i = employment in industries newly settled in region i during period p (creations);

CL_p^i = employment in industries closed down in region i in period p (closures);

$I_{ji,p}$ = employment in an industry migrated from j to i during period p;

$E_{ij,p}$ = employment in an industry migrated from i to j during period p.

A matrix of change

For a set of regions, the above definition can be translated into a matrix similar in structure to the well known input—output table in economic analysis, or the origin (O)—destination (D) matrix in transport analysis, (see Figure 2.1).

The rows in the matrix indicate employment in plants that have moved from one region to all five regions (the original region included); TE indicates total emigration from that region, adding up with CL (closures) and ISD (*in situ* decline) to its total gross decline of employment. The columns indicate the employment created in a region by moves from other regions as well as within the region itself, adding up to total immigration (TI). Adding the employment in newly created establishments (NC) and employment growth in existing ones (ISG = *in situ* growth), we find the gross growth of employment in the regions.

The matrix calls for some comment. First, the figures on the main diagonal refer to migrations within a region which actually neither add to nor detract from that region's total employment. These figures might have been left out, were it not for the interest of comparing intra-regional with inter-regional moves.

Secondly, in contrast to the input—output table, the matrix has neither a column of 'exports' nor a row of 'imports', a closed system being supposed here. However, by defining for example region 5 as 'rest of the world', we could make it fit to deal with international aspects as well.

Finally, for a proper analysis of the origin—destination part of the matrix, we should need to know the distance between each pair of regions as well, the characteristics of the plants represented by each cell (size, kind of industry, type of organisation, type of labour, production facilities, etc.) and the characteristics of each region.

For the analysis of the patterns and causes of migration the following hypothesis may be made. Push factors induce plants to leave their location; the greater the discrepancy in a region between ideal and

11

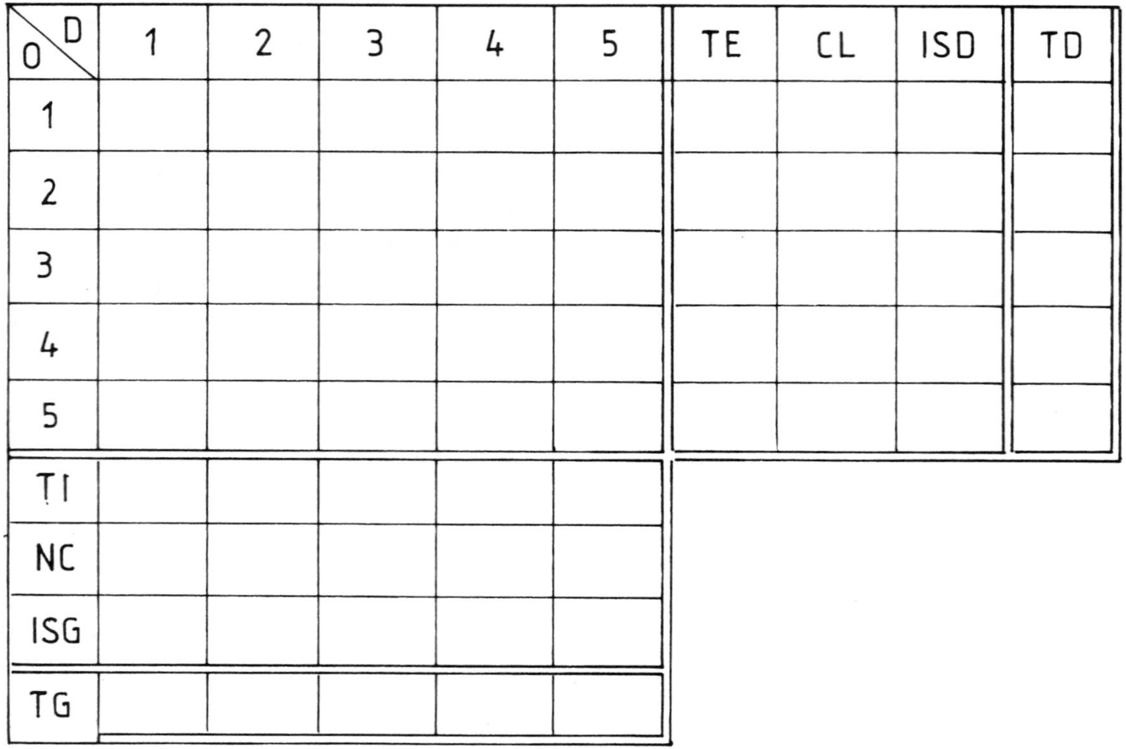

O\D	1	2	3	4	5		TE	CL	ISD	TD
1										
2										
3										
4										
5										
TI						
NC						
ISG						
TG						

Figure 2.1   A matrix conception of the components of change in economic activity in a system of regions

actual situation, the more plants are likely to move. On the other hand, pull factors tend to keep industries where they are and attract new ones; regions easily fulfilling the requirements of new plants will receive more income migration from industry than regions failing to do so. Of course the actual pattern of relocation as revealed by the matrix is the result of the combined effects of push and pull factors and distances. Naturally, if we filled in the matrix for several years and a set of regions, and if the pushing and pulling conditions of the regions as well as the characteristics of plants were known, we should have a good basis for the empirical analysis of industrial movement. It would indeed suffice for the application of certain methods, ranging from the simple ordering of data to such econometric tools as regression and probabilistic models.

The matrix gives rise to a few other remarks concerning particular data, concepts, and measurement problems that will be discussed in the following sections.

Definition of statistical units

If we try to fill in the matrix in practice the first thing that needs to be more clearly defined is the concept of a plant. Indeed, unlike human beings with which 'human' migration theory and practice deal, industrial migration is concerned with much more changing subjects, from a small single-person office to large extended factories.

For an international comparative study like the present one the concepts can best be borrowed from internationally accepted standard definitions. The best known international standard is the one developed by the United Nations (1968).

The United Nations distinguish four major units for the statistical measurement of economic activity, viz.: the establishment; the enterprise; technical and ancillary units.

The *establishment* is ideally defined as 'an economic unit which engages, under a single ownership or control (i.e. under a single legal entity) in one or predominantly one kind of economic activity at a single physical location (e.g. an individual farm, mine, factory, workshop, store or office)'.

The *technical unit* is defined as 'a section or a department of the establishment which engages directly in the production of a class of the goods made, or services rendered, by an establishment, or in a stage of the production of these goods and services'.

Ancillary units 'provide non-durable goods or services primarily or entirely for the use of parent producing units (e.g. central administrative offices, warehouses, garages)'.

13

Establishments may comprise one or more technical and ancillary units. Departments of a meat-packing plant which produce lard, cure bacon, or can meat, are examples of technical units horizontally integrated in an establishment; departments of a textile mill where yarn is spun, cloth woven, and cloth dyed, are technical units vertically integrated in an establishment.

An *enterprise,* or *legal entity,* 'may be a corporation, joint-stock company, co-operative association, incorporated non-profit association, partnership, individual proprietorship, or take some other form of association. It owns and manages the property of the organisation, enters into contracts, receives and disposes of all its income and maintains independent profit-and-loss and balance-sheet accounts and other records. It may consist of more than one establishment, though a large number of legal entities will own one establishment or kind of activity unit only'. If a legal entity comprises more than one establishment, these may be engaged in completely different areas of production, e.g. food and mechanical engineering — or be of the same type — the branch offices of banks.

Which of these concepts is most suited to spatial analysis? The enterprise, or legal entity, does not seem particularly suitable for spatial analysis on a fairly small scale, first because it need not be confined to one location, second because its various parts may be engaged in a variety of activities.

Establishments and technical or ancillary units can both be defined in a way that is spatially operational. The latter concept is not clear-cut however, for what is a mere stage in a long production line to some, will be looked upon by others as an independent technical unit.

That leaves the establishment as the most promising statistical unit, both for spatial analysis in general and for the envisaged analysis of industrial movement in particular. The concept of plant, much used in everyday life, had not got such a clear-cut definition. However, it seems that in practice the notion comes very close to the one of establishment insofar as manufacturing industry is concerned. We will consider the term, henceforward, as a synonym for manufacturing establishment as defined by the UN.

Some definitions of migration and movement

Classical analysis measures demographic growth in terms of individual persons by starting from the population stock at a given moment, adding births and subtracting deaths; for the spatial analysis of demographic growth, migration — that is the phenomenon of people physically moving from one area of residence to another — has to be taken into account as well.

The dynamics of economic activities can be described similarly, provided the economic activities are expressed in unequivocal units comparable to individual persons in demography. From the previous sub-section, the establishment has emerged as the unit best suited to such a regional account of activity change as we are envisaging.

Three types of changes in the distribution of activities can be defined:

1 The creation of a new establishment (comparable to a birth in demographic analysis). An establishment is created when an activity is started at a site where no such activity existed before.
2 The closure of an establishment (comparable to a death in demographic analysis). Closures occur when the activities carried on at a certain site are completely stopped there.
3 Migration (comparable with migration in demography). By migration is understood the complete transfer of economic activities from one site to another. Migration, sometimes referred to as 'complete move', always implies departure or emigration from the old region and arrival or immigration in the new region.

So long as we are keeping to 'integral' changes of one-establishment companies, the parallel with demographic phenomena is very neat. The picture becomes a bit blurred, however, as soon as we try to fathom what goes on in a multi-establishment concern, or what happens if establishments start splitting off and crossing over. Let us consider a few examples of spatial adjustment processes and the way they are likely to be registered. In giving these examples we will try to use both words and concepts that are used in day-to-day practice and try to define them in a somewhat systematic way.

1 Envisage a branch move or branch creation: a new establishment is created to which are transferred the activities hitherto carried on in one or two technical units of an existing plant. A move is made, but no migration is recorded; the movement is registered as a new creation and a contraction.
2 An establishment is closed down and its activities are transferred to another one already in existence. Once more, there is no migration in the strict sense, the whole operation being recorded as a closure here and an extension there.
3 Economic activities may be transferred without any record at all of migration, closure, or creation; this happens when part of the activities of one establishment are transferred to another existing establishment: in that case the record only gives evidence of a contraction and an extension.

15

4 To make things even more complicated, more than two establishments may be involved in the movement process. A group of establishments engaged in the same activity (say a group of general banks) may decide to concentrate one specialised function (say data processing) in one new specialised establishment (a computer centre). It is likely that this would only show up as a creation.

5 We might even think of the decline of one establishment and the simultaneous growth of another, competing, establishment as a de facto move of economic activity through space, without any creation, closure, or migration being recorded at all. Such a concept departs very far from the concrete physical relocation for which parallels can be found in demographic movements, however.

The five examples we have given will suffice to show that with all these partial transfers of economic activities there is no migration in the sense of the definition given above. So, to keep the issue clear, we shall in the following reserve the term 'migration' for the complete move of the activities of an establishment from one site to another, using the word 'movement' in a more general sense, that encompasses both branch plant creations as defined in examples 1 and 2. However, we will not use it in its widest sense suggested by example 5, that indeed is only concerned with expansion and contraction. In the following the term relocation will be used as a synonym for movement as well.

The examples given above will also have made it clear that an adequate study of the movement of economic activity should consider the creation, closure and migration of establishments as well as the growth and decline of existing plants. Indeed, restriction to migration alone would leave large portions of the total movement of industrial activities out of account.

The measurement of movement

As far as closures, creations, and migrations are concerned, industrial movement could be measured simply by the number of establishments involved. However, if one is not only interested in the number of plants involved but also in their relative importance, some indicator of the establishments' importance should be used. Production, value added, and/or employment could serve as indicators of size. Unfortunately, the first two indicators are mostly not on record for individual establishments, and are notably hard to get where a multi-plant enterprise is concerned. By contrast, the number of employees is practically always available on the establishment level, and so to keep things simple we shall measure establishments in terms of employment only.

To measure the movement of economic activity by number of jobs, we can use the theoretical accounting equation of the previous section. Total activity at time t−1 is equal to total activity at time t (by definition in existing establishments) plus creation, plus immigration, minus closure, minus outmigration, plus extension, minus contraction. Quite a satisfactory equation in theory; difficulties crop up, however, as soon as one tries to get hold of the elements statistically.

A first set of problems is related to the duration of the interval between two observations. A closure may come at the end of a long period of gradual contraction; thus, the closure of a once-important plant finally goes on record as the loss of just a few jobs with short registration periods. On the other hand, just a few 'quartermasters' may be employed at a new plant at the moment of creation, employment being stepped up at a high rate afterwards. So, for a fair appreciation of the weight of closures and creation, the developments before and after the recorded events should also be counted. Indeed, the total number of jobs involved in a closure tend to be the more accurately accounted for, the longer the interval between two registrations, all preliminary contractions being included in the total number of jobs involved. The same applies, of course, for creation and subsequent expansion.

These examples may suffice to show how different periods and manners of registration can affect the observed components of the spatial development of economic activity, contraction instead of closure, for example. However, for a proper appreciation of empirical data much more practical difficulties need to be overcome.

The first is that hardly anywhere in Europe do we find the kind of consistent statistical registration we assumed in the set-up of the matrix of Figure 2.1, for a sufficiently large set of regions and for an adequate period of time. On the contrary, registration practices vary widely not only among countries, but even among parts of one country, and among registration agencies. That makes it hard to distinguish between contraction and extension on the one hand and between extension, creation and closure on the other hand, as well as between creation, closure and migration. The closure of an establishment in a region will go on record as just a closure if its migration to another area is not reported at the same time. At the new location, the movement may be booked as a creation while by rights it should count as a migration because the origin of the establishment may stay unnoticed by the registration agency. In the case of partial moves, for instance of technical units, if they occur among European countries, or between them and countries outside Europe, the odds are that registration agencies record them only as creation of new establishments. Indeed, as the various registering agencies involved are not in the habit of consulting with one another to try and achieve consistent registration of migration cases, the measurement of migration can in practice only be an approximation. The best procedure seems to take the total of apparent creations and closures as a starting point and to try to find out how many of the establishments are indeed involved in actual migrations. To that end, an agency that has registered an establishment as newly created may be able to trace its origin, and also to find out whether a complete move has been accomplished, which should then be registered as a 'migration', or a 'partial move', (say, of a technical unit to form a new establishment) which at the new location should be registered as a new creation without migration aspects. If no origin is known, no migration can be assumed. In the same way, a registration agency may try to get hold of the destination of a plant checking out of its area; if the plant is found to have resettled elsewhere, 'migration' should be recorded, but not if its activities have been integrated in, or added to, an existing business at the new location. If the destination remains unknown, the move counts as a closure, without migration aspects.

The migration aspect is often further obscured by changes in the name and even the legal status of an establishment when it is moved; clearly such changes will increase the chance of migration being recorded a closure and a creation. Changes occurring at one location, only one registering agency being involved, may be obscured by legal aspects too. If an establishment stops its activities, and the premises are sold after some time to another legal entity which then starts production there, there is little doubt that the agency should register a closure and a creation. However, should the establishment change its name upon merging with another legal entity, the registration should remain as before. Those are clear-cut cases. Doubt as to the correct registration arises when a change of owner coincides with a change in name, and activities are temporarily suspended.

To make things even more complicated, most registers not only record total activity but also distinguish types of activity. Take, for example, the registration of manufacturing by branch. The classification of a new establishment at a new site is straightforward. However, should an establishment change the type of its activity from manufacturing to commerce, then it has to be deleted from the register; for the activity under consideration the establishment would count as closed down. Now while for broad industrial categories such a practice may be justified, for smaller categories it seems highly questionable. If an establishment that used to work in wood takes up plastics instead, should it be registered as closed down in the first and as created in the second category, or considered an existing plant? The latter solution is not satisfactory; the former, though correct in terms of statistics, increases the number of closures and creations in proportion to that of extensions and contractions as the sectoral detail becomes more refined.

Not even the 'existence' of an establishment can be determined beyond a doubt. Many registers contain a large number of establishments which exist on paper only, i.e. legal entities not engaged in any activity. A common procedure to assess whether or not such a legal entity is active at all, is to verify whether they have at least some staff regularly at work. But what to do about one-person establishments, with only the owner carrying on business? Many a perfectly genuine, active one-man shop might be disregarded until the moment someone is taken into employ, when they would show up as 'creations'. Should such a one-man business be normally registered, then it would count as 'created' at the moment of foundation, its proceeding to employ staff being registered as 'extension'.

Conclusions

The conclusion from the present section is that the results of studies quantitatively breaking down the components of activity growth should be cautiously interpreted, as even with the best practices a rather fluid border line exists between the various components in which the total change in economic activity in an area can be broken down. The analysis of the difficulties to be overcome if the movement of economic activity is to be measured in a consistent way, has clearly shown that total activity movement cannot be measured properly unless creation and closure are taken into account along with migration, and that their importance can only be judged adequately in relation to that of contractions and extensions.

Some examples of industrial characteristics and adjustment strategies

Enterprise strategies

An entrepreneur has a choice of strategies for adjusting his activities to changed external conditions. He may choose expansion in existing premises or open a branch plant, or he may migrate, or choose still another solution. The choice of the strategy will be largely dependent on the character of the change of external conditions on the one hand and the existing production circumstances on the other hand. Let us consider some alternative strategies in the light of external factors.

The first scenario we will point to is one of growth. This can be met by either *in situ* expansion or branch plant creations. Which strategy is chosen depends on the facilities offered by the present location and the degree to which it is expected that they may satisfy the demands of new production methods. Economies of scale (of production and management) will often make the present location preferable, the more so as in that case marginal decisions suffice and important risks can be decided on later. In practice, however, the decision is not only to be made by existing companies; newcomers, competing for a place on the market, will move in, leading to the creation of new establishments. This phenomenon will be the more likely to occur when existing companies choose to content themselves with their existing facilities.

Similar reasoning holds for a scenario of decline. Here one has notably to deal with closures and contractions. A company with only one plant faced with decline has no choice; it has to contract, ultimately perhaps close down. A concern producing at several locations has a choice of strategies: it may either concentrate production at fewer locations, closing down rather than contracting, or divide activities equally among its locations; which establishments are closed will depend on each one's current and expected cost/benefit ratios.

The strategies mentioned are not the only ones possible; indeed, a company may also decide to quit the old location and establish a completely new plant. A growing concern will choose that strategy if the advantages of setting up production at a new location are great enough not only to compensate for the costs and risks of migrating, but also to justify the total write-off of existing equipment. But migrating may also be the right strategy when the market is declining, namely, if a waiting attitude will presumably lead to the ultimate closure of the plant, while its migration to a location where production is still profitable, may save the firm even in a difficult market.

Anyway, a very important aspect that needs to be kept in mind is that a migration (complete move) or the opening of a branch plant (partial move) are discrete decisions that weigh very heavily in the cost and risk calculations of a firm. On the contrary, expansion and contraction can often be considered as marginal decisions involving much less risk. So firms are likely to have a preference for the adaptation strategies and adopt only the movement strategies if the need is very urgent.

Although this statement holds in general for all activities it needs to be refined for typical groups of industry. Indeed the characteristics of a company that determine its mobility, that is, its propensity to move, will determine too how often a migration strategy is adopted. Mobility varies among industries; whether it comes at all to migration depends moreover on the strength of the impulse (see Mobility- and migration-determining factors p. 24).

The above does no more than point to the options of migration and other adjustment strategies. We shall now try to shed some light on the phenomenon we are studying by working out a few practical examples. We have chosen to develop these cases, each one typical of an industry of a particular locational behaviour. The three categories chosen are, based on the decisive location factors: demand-oriented, supply-oriented, and labour-oriented industries. That trichotomy, though not perhaps encompassing all industries, is useful enough for us to give it some attention before discussing in some detail the relations among various kinds of industrial mutations.

Demand-oriented industries

We shall reason from the size of the relevant region. For the category of demand-oriented industries, the relevant region is defined as the area beyond whose borders the industry (or the industries) does (do) not export significant quantities.

Retail companies, small-scale technical firms, and various other service companies are typical establishments with relatively small relevant regions. They provide for their close environment and have at most a regional significance. The staff employed in this category of companies has no particularly high degree of skill, and supply factors are hardly relevant. Their relevant region being small, any moves will be short-distance ones as far as they wish to keep the same market. There can be all sorts of reasons for a move within their old market area, lack of space for expansion and diminishing accessibility because of traffic conditions, being two of them. Changes in the size, composition and spread of the population in large agglomerations may be the underlying causes; the population in the town centres is decreasing and containing a progressive proportion of people in the low-income brackets, while the reverse is happening in the outskirts of the same towns. As a result, the market in the inner cities is contracting, that in the suburbs expanding. Shops and services may then feel they ought to adjust to the changed circumstances. Whether they will do so on a large scale is another question. Moving costs a lot of money, and may lay a heavy burden on the budget available to a company whose turnover has been declining for some time. Moreover, other organisations with more capital behind them may well have recognised the changes earlier and may by now be safely ensconced in the 'new' market area. Such new establishments offer other advantages as well, such as easy parking and one-stop shopping; by which they attract customers from the old market areas, causing even greater turnover losses and decline of capital to the firms still struggling for life there, and entailing more and more business failures among them.

While it is true, then, that a new equilibrium can be achieved by migration, the same considerations can also result in old establishments in 'old' market areas being closed down while new establishments are created in 'new' market areas. To what extent establishments will be moved, closed down, or newly created depends on various conditions, local policy being one of them; when new shopping centres are created in new quarters, the local authorities can give priority to existing establishments 'expelled' from old town quarters. Be that as it may, when the market expands or contracts, when the purchasing power shifts, industry moves, closures, and creations will occur side by side.

Demand-oriented industries with a larger relevant region than the shops and small-scale services, can move over larger distances. In particular such emerging markets as the EC attracted such industries in the 1960s; many firms from countries outside the EC (the USA and the UK) set up activities there, moving their plants to EC countries. Still, they are limited in their movements, even within their relevant area. In spite of our assumption that these industries are not labour-oriented, they cannot entirely ignore the labour factor either. The costs of moving are high, and if a large portion of the staff has to be replaced (as is more probable as the new location is farther removed), the whole operation may become so costly that the management either drops the idea altogether, or chooses a location nearer to the original one. Staff may be averse to moving with the company from various motives. They are used to their place of residence, where they have their circle of friends, where the children go to school, where the shops are familiar and trusted. Moreover, a family often has more than one working member, and thus it is not for the one whose employer is moving to decide by himself, but for the family household as a whole, a fact that is too much overlooked in most personal migration analyses and in statistics.

Purely business economic considerations may not stop these demand-oriented companies from moving large distances, other considerations make such moves less probable as the distances increase.

Supply-oriented establishments

Industries can be tied down to a location because they depend on its natural deposits but also because they depend on local companies for their supplies. Examples of the latter category are industries based on perishable agricultural products, and industries processing outputs of basic industries (petrochemicals and carbochemicals for instance).

Relatively high transportation costs tend to keep these industries from moving too far from their suppliers. In this category, moves occur when the 'source' of the raw material shifts elsewhere. Thus, when new transportation techniques had made it possible for refineries to be established in the south of Federal Germany far from the large ports, petrochemical industries sprang up in the neighbourhood, owned in part by the same companies who so far had supplied the German market from coastal locations. Indeed, instead of expanding petrochemical activities *in situ*, large oil companies have often started up new activities elsewhere, a policy that in the end has made proper industry migration unnecessary. (Molle and Wever, 1983)

The faster the supply situation changes, the more probable industry moves become; more gradual changes are apt to be coped with by growth slowing down at one place and speeding up elsewhere. Again, industrial migration cannot be regarded in separation from changes in external conditions.

Labour-oriented establishments

The assumption is that labour-oriented industries are neither demand-oriented nor supply-oriented. The classical case of labour orientation is the 'trek' towards large pools of cheap labour. To cut costs, companies will consider leaving areas where labour is expensive and in short supply for areas where it is cheap and abundant. Recently, another type of labour orientation has emerged. It concerns mostly companies which have no goods to transport and maintain their outward contacts by telecommunication and/or letters. They are found mostly among the so-called 'basic' services. They rely in fact on highly skilled labour mostly, and tend to locate where such labour can be found. Now we know from recent developments in the regional demographic composition in western countries that young well-educated families prefer to live outside the large agglomerations. At first these families were mostly found in the suburbs of such agglomerations but now they are showing a marked and growing tendency to go and live in medium-sized towns not too far from the large cities; in these towns there is, consequently, a good supply of qualified labour. Several companies of

23

the labour-oriented kind have followed the trend, either by migration, moving their establishments from the large metropoles to the medium-sized towns, or locating their new settlements there. Of course, the speed at which the preference for new residences is realised, and the rate at which the sector involved is growing, will decide together (among still other factors) how far the adjustment to new conditions is achieved by migration, and how far by differential growth in large agglomerations and elsewhere.

Mobility- and migration-determining factors

Introduction

In the introduction to this chapter an explicit distinction was made between industrial mobility and industrial migration. Regrettably, common parlance has confused the issue by using both expressions for the same phenomenon, namely, for the actual moves of industry.

Nevertheless, for the present study it still makes sense to make the distinction, using mobility for the propensity to move, and migration for the actual movement of an establishment from one site to another. This can be seen in Figure 2.2.

We shall now first give attention to the external factors and impulses which could induce establishments to move. Next, we shall go into the basic features of establishments relevant to mobility.

External factors and impulses

In the previous sections some external factors have already been mentioned which could induce a company to consider relocation. The general aspects of 'filtering-down' theory have been pointed out; strategies to be adopted when sales decline or grow have been mentioned, etc.

There are other things, however, which may press companies to move; we mention just a few examples:

1 Shift of markets: owing to, for example, demographic movements, or changes of a technological (product) or institutional (EC, for example) nature, the market situation shifts, making the old location suboptimum.
2 Technological change: the use of forklift trucks (especially by

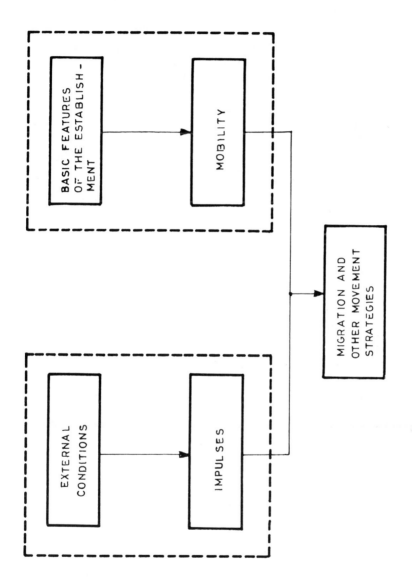

Figure 2.2   Migration-determining factors

25

wholesalers) calls for large flat ground-floor areas, which are often not available at old locations.

3 Social change: people have become very sensitive to pollution aspects lately, hence the pressure on polluting plants to leave residential areas.

4 Vehicle choice: when goods were conveyed by train and workers arrived on foot or by public transport, a central location was the best. As lorries became the general means of conveyance for goods, and private passenger cars for commuters, companies were put upon to leave for locations better accessible to lorries and cars.

5 Regional-policy intervention: governments, anxious to stimulate growth in developing regions, feel compelled to make existing activities move from concentration areas to peripheral zones.

6 Other government interventions: in places where a policy of town renovation is pursued, building plans in general leave little room for industries that used to be established there. Businesses that have to make space for road construction etc., mostly can not come back either.

7 Labour conditions: in regions with a troubled labour climate, productivity may be low in respect of other regions, in that case entrepreneurs will be inclined to move to regions with a good labour climate.

8 Labour availability: when an entrepreneur finds it very difficult to find suitable labour for his production, he will again be tempted to move elsewhere.

9 Changed international competitive conditions, for instance difference in effective wage level (that is the wage level corrected for differences in productivity), rate of exchange, political security, tax burden, etc.

10 High local rates for electricity, water, land tax, etc.

11 When a location becomes attractive for alternative uses, its rent will rise and hence the opportunity cost of continuing one's business there.

Other examples are easy to find, but these may suffice.

Basic characteristics of industries and their mobility

An industry's propensity to move is a direct function of the costs entailed. These costs in turn, are related to a number of basic characteristics, some of which we shall briefly discuss now.

Capital intensity is an important factor. Obviously a business which needs to provide only space for the staff to work in — space being in most cases abundant at the new location — will be cheaper to move than a plant, with extensive machinery, for which new factory halls must be erected, equipment transported and newly installed at great cost, etc. The objections to moving will be greater as the life-cycle of the capital stock is longer. With short-lived equipment new investments have to be decided upon at relatively short intervals, and a move to a new location might be considered at the same time.

Mobility is likely to be higher, the greater an industry's growth rate. Indeed, when a business grows fast and its replacement quota is high, the sum of replacement and new investment will be large. In that case the value of the remaining capital stock will be low enough in relation to gross investments to make moving to a new location a feasible proposition.

When the new location is far from the old one, the entrepreneur must reckon with a proportion of his manpower refusing to stay with the company. Particularly if he employs specialised staff that may entail considerable transition costs. Training new staff may take so long that the company suffers grievous losses. The management may decide not to move because the disadvantages of changing staff exceed the advantages of the new location.

When an industry is a profitable industry, which often coincides with growth of the industry, financial barriers to moving are less stringent than in the case of stagnation. Large profits may induce the firm to change location if conditions on the new location are more promising than at the existing one. This explains why the total number of movements in a period of high economic activity is significantly larger than in a time of recession.

Conclusions

An entrepreneur who is considering the prospects of moving to a new location, will have to make as accurate a cost/benefit analysis as possible, taking into account the characteristics of the industry and the external pressure exerted on it, as well as the reactions of competitors to the contemplated move.

More often than not the third element is overlooked in a cost/benefit analysis for an individual industry: yet one's competitors are just as likely to act as oneself. That is why a macro-approach should complete the micro-approach. Here we do in fact touch upon the border line between location theory, which is concerned with plants, and the theory of regional development, which is concerned with the spatial distribution of all activities.

Model

Although it will become apparent from the following chapters that only extremely simple models, if any, have been used in the analysis of industry migration, it seems appropriate to say at least a few words about the possible properties of a model that could serve as a background for such analysis. The following propositions, therefore, do not claim to be the last word in industry-migration models but rather some of the first. If more and more precise statistical data should become available it may become possible in the future to try and test this or any other kind of model that introduces at least some theoretical elements in the considerations.

A possible approach could be the following:

Assume that the attractivity of a location in a certain region i for an establishment of a given kind is determined by three elements:

(a) demand (size of the output market)
(b) supply (availability of inputs)
(c) labour (quality and quantity)

Define these three factors as potentials

(a) demand potential (Π_{iD})
(b) supply potential (Π_{iS})
(c) labour potential (Π_{iL})

In this definition

$$\Pi_{iD} = \sum_j D_j e^{-\alpha C_{ij}} \tag{2.2}$$

in which

D_j = demand for the products of the industry in region j
C_{ij} = communication costs (a function of distance)
α = influence or importance of communication costs for the establishment.

The absolute attractivity of region i for locating there can be written as:

$$A_i = \alpha_0 \, \Pi_{iD}^{\alpha_1} \, \Pi_{iS}^{\alpha_2} \, \Pi_{iL}^{\alpha_3} \qquad (0 \leqslant \alpha_1, \alpha_2, \alpha_3, \leqslant 1) \tag{2.3}$$

This function is written in a multiplicative form, since if there is no demand or no supply of inputs or no labour, the absolute attractivity of that region becomes zero. The coefficients represent the importance of demand, supply and labour availability.

However, it seems likely that a firm located in i and considering a move to j will not only look at the pull factors represented in (2.1) but also at the costs of such a move. Earlier it was assumed that such costs are a function of physical distance. So considering the attractiveness of a move from i to j, we should rewrite (2.3) as

$$a_{ij} = \alpha_0 \, \Pi_{iD}^{\alpha_1} \, \Pi_{iS}^{\alpha_2} \, \Pi_{iL}^{\alpha_3} \, e^{-\beta d_{ij}} \tag{2.4}$$

in which $1/\beta$ is the mobility coefficient.

It seems likely that the friction-coefficient β is inversely related to the total activity level in the country, frictions becoming less important if business goes well.

The establishment will, of course, not move after considering location in j only. It will compare the advantages of doing so with all other possible locations. If the ratio of j's attractiveness and the total attractiveness of moving to another location (including the present one) is high, the chances of moving towards j will also be higher. We therefore write:

$$\frac{a_{ij}}{a_i} = \frac{\Pi_{jD}^{\alpha_1} \, \Pi_{jS}^{\alpha_2} \, \Pi_{jL}^{\alpha_3} \, e^{-\beta d_{ij}}}{\sum_j \Pi_{jD}^{\alpha_1} \, \Pi_{jS}^{\alpha_2} \, \Pi_{jL}^{\alpha_3} \, e^{-\beta d_{ij}}} \tag{2.5}$$

Writing further:

$$m_{ij} = \frac{a_{ij}}{a_i} \qquad m_{i*} = p_{ij} m_{i*} \tag{2.6}$$

in which:

m_{ij} = number of establishments moving from i to j
m_{i*} = total number of establishments migrating including m_{ii} interpreted as establishments either migrating within i or not migrating at all
p_{ij} = probability of migration.

We arrive at a possible explanation of the migration of firms. Note that $m_{i*} = m_i$, the total number of existing establishments in i.

It may be remarked here that this model, simple as it is, contains a number of elements that were discussed in the previous sections and will come up in the following chapters. As such may be mentioned:

1 Demand factors (Π_{iD})
2 Supply factors (Π_{iS})
3 Labour market factors (Π_{iL})
4 Mobility factor(s) (β)
5 Total number of establishments (m_i)
6 Accessibility factors, entering into the analysis through low or decreasing values of all potentials.

A somewhat different version of this model, based on probabilities, attraction factors and so on was already presented in Molle (1977). A test using a maximum likelihood procedure gave promising results.

A factor not contained in the above model is the lack of space on the existing location (push factors). This could be introduced as a boundary condition on the number of workers in the establishment but it would maybe be better to consider firms moving for this reason separately.

Industrial migration and regional policy

The general objective of regional policy is to achieve a more acceptable or more favourable spatial distribution of activities, income, and employment than the present one. The investments used are often financial; they support the location of industries in certain regions mostly without discriminating between new creations, industries moved from elsewhere, and expansions.

Regional policy tends to focus on peripheral zones which, by their geographical situation, are unsuitable for the settlement of industries. Firms already considering a move and under pressure from rising costs in the central areas, are tempted by high premiums to settle in the zones selected for development by policy makers, where the necessary infrastructure is constructed at the same time.

The results of regional policy are rather obscure; they tend to be measured by the degree to which industries in the favoured regions profit from the schemes (Vanhove and Klaassen, 1979), without heeding the question of how these regions would have developed without the financial aids to extension and establishment. That becomes quite understandable if one considers how difficult it is to determine what would have happened if a certain policy had not been pursued; indeed that may often be harder even than to forecast the results of a certain policy if all other things remain constant (the notorious *ceteris paribus* clause).

There is, however, one part of regional policy that can be implemented without subtle financial inducements, namely, the migration of government agencies to peripheral regions. In principle, it needs no other effort than issuing the simple decree to move, although trade unions opposed to such moves may have considerable influence. The question is, however: is it beneficial, that is to say, is the net outcome of costs and benefits in the two zones concerned positive? The latest developments (in the Netherlands, for instance) make it doubtful. Investigations show widely different results, dependent on their being made from the point of view of a donor region (say, the Hague and surroundings) or from that of the recipient region (say, Groningen).

Some factors are very difficult to weigh. Donor regions tend to attach great weight to the social damage inflicted upon employees. Wives of transferring staff members wonder if their chances of finding a job (full- or part-time) will not be poorer in the peripheral area than in their present one, and are afraid of the social and financial consequences for their family. Children complain about leaving their friends behind, and the whole family is troubled by the idea of breaking up social ties.

The recipient authorities tend to quote former government statements, and try to support their point of view by calculating high multipliers of the 'stimulating unit' to be established in their region. Even researchers of the two regions fail to agree on the magnitude of the effects. The benefits and drawbacks of the operation were not conclusive in the case of transfers of government agencies. The same is true, in fact, of all transfers of industries.

A judgement of the use, or lack of use, of industry transfers is not easy, and neither is the answer to the question whether or not regional policy should stimulate the transfer of industries. The question has become even more complicated now that an increasing number of agglomerations are falling into a decline and a spontaneous decentralisation from these areas has begun (Klaassen, Molle and Paelinck, 1981). In particular the so-called labour-oriented tertiary activities are increasingly inclined to follow the outflow of the population from the large towns.

From the following chapters it will become clear that migration of establishments is high in periods of high economic activities and income and low in periods of recession. This seems to indicate that regional policy measures are more effective under favourable economic conditions than under unfavourable conditions. It will also become apparent which kind of establishments move more easily than others.

These indications seem relevant for regional policy makers. It cannot be denied, however, that more information on that score should become available before the results of industrial migration analysis could become an effective aid in the context of an overall regional policy.

Some conclusions

Some practical conclusions may be drawn from the previous sections.

The first conclusion is that the theoretical foundation for the study of industrial migration is weak; such a study has to rely on a few tentative concepts, either of empirical origin or borrowed from other disciplines.

The second conclusion is that migration is only one way of adjusting to changed conditions. Other adjustments as contraction, creation, etc. have their advantages and disadvantages and are weighed against each other in the firm's decision. That implies that the analysis of industrial movement should be placed in the total context of all the components of the dynamics of regional economic development.

The third conclusion is that an analysis of industrial movement should make a distinction between mobility-determining factors (in particular such features as size and capital intensity of the industry) and migration impulses (such as market shifts). These are different for different types of industries.

A fourth conclusion finally is that the move of an establishment has outside effects. Suppliers and customers, family members of the people employed, relatives and friends, they all are affected by the move. The question is whether government policy takes sufficient account of those factors.

References

Alonso, W. (1976), 'A theory of movement', *Conference on the dynamics of human settlement systems,* IIASA, Laxenburg.

Anselin, L. and Isard, W.V. (1979), 'On Alonso's General Theory of Movement', *Man Environment Space and Time,* vol. 1 no. 1.

Fetter, E. (1924), 'The Economic Law of Market Areas', *Quarterly Journal of Economics,* vol. 39, pp. 520–52.

Greenhut, M.E. (1956), *Plant location in Theory and Practise,* Chapel Hill, U.S.A.

Haggett, P. (1965), *Locational Analyses in Human Geography,* London.

Hamilton, F.E.I. (1967), 'Models of Industrial Location' in R.J. Chorley and P. Haggett (eds), *Models in Geography,* London.

Hamilton, F.E.I. (ed.) (1974), *Spatial Perspectives on Industrial Organisation and Decision Making',* London.

Hoover, E.M. (1948), *'The Location of Economic Activity',* New York.

Hotelling, H. (1929), 'Stability in competition', *Economic Journal,* vol. 39, pp. 41—57.

Isard, W. (1956), *Location and the Space Economy,* Cambridge Mass.

Klaassen, L.H. and Drewe, P. (1973), *Migration Policy in Europe,* Farnborough.

Klaassen, L.H., Molle, W.T.M. and Paelinck, J.H.P. (1981), *Dynamics of Urban Development,* Farnborough.

Launhardt, W. (1882), 'Die Bestimmung des Zweckmässigen Standorts einer gewerblichen Anlage', *Zeitschrift des Vereins deutscher Ingenieure,* no. 26, pp. 106—115.

Lloyd, P.E. and Dicken, P. (1977), *Location in Space,* London.

Lösch, A. (1954), *The Economics of Location,* New Haven.

Miller, E.W. and Miller, R.M.V. (1978), *Industrial location; a bibliography,* IGU/CIS, Pennsylvania.

Molle, W.T.M. (1977), 'Industrial mobility, a review of empirical studies and an alaysis of the migration of industry from the city of Amsterdam', *Regional Studies,* vol. 11, pp. 323—335.

Molle, W.T.M. and Wever, E. (1983), 'Oil refineries and petrochemical industries in Western Europe', Farnborough.

Pred, A. (1967), *'Behaviour and Location',* Lund.

Simon, H.A. (1952), 'A behavioural model of Rational Choice', *Quarterly Journal of Economics,* vol. 69, pp. 99—108.

Simon, H.A. (1957), *Models of Man,* New York.

Smith, D.M. (1971), *Industrial location: an economic geographical analysis,* New York.

Stafford, H.A. (1972), 'The anatomy of the location decision: content analyses of case studies', Hamilton (1974), pp. 169—187.

Stevens, B.H. and Brackett, C.A. (1967), *'Industrial location, a review and annotated bibliography of theoretical empirical and case studies',* RSRI Philadelphia.

Thompson, W.R. (1968), 'Internal and external factors in the development of urban economics' in H.S. Perloff and L. Wingo (eds), *Issues in urban economics,* Baltimore.

Townroe, P. (1969), 'Locational choice and the individual firm', *Regional Studies,* vol. 3, pp. 15—24.

Townroe, P. (1972), 'Some behavioural considerations in the industrial location decision', *Regional Studies,* vol. 6, pp. 261—272.

UN, (1968), 'International Standard Industrial Classification of All Economic Activities', *Statistical Papers Series M,* no. 4, rev. 2, New York.

Vanhove, N. and Klaassen, L.H. (1979), *Regional Policy, a European Approach*, Farnborough.

Vernon, R. (1969), 'International investment and international trade in the product cycle', *Quarterly Journal of Economics*, pp. 190–204.

Webber, M.J. (1972), *'Impact of uncertainty on location'*, Cambridge, USA.

Weber, A. (1909), *Über den Standort der Industrien*, Tübingen.

Wheeler, J.O. (1973), *Industrial location, a bibliography'*, 1966–1972, Illinois.

3 France
P. AYDALOT

General aspects

Economic and institutional setting

The post-war period, when so many industrial structures were shaken up and so many economic activities were on the move, offers an interesting field of study for location theorists. In that respect, France, whose widespread and fairly heterogeneous territory offers firms highly contrasting fields of activity, is a good example. Moreover, the country's rapid, post-war industrial growth (up to 1974 6 per cent yearly) was a driving force behind its policy of regional development. This growth accounted for (and was a product of) the structural transformations which left their own mark on space in this period. Since 1974, however, a new rupture has brought with it spatial implications that remain still largely unexplored.

Going back in time, one can easily see the result of a century of concentration: in the 1950s, one-sixth of the French population, a quarter of its industry, and one-third of its tertiary activity were concentrated in the metropolitan area of Paris. In fact, between 1850 and 1950 all French population growth was concentrated in Paris. Thus, studying the concept of space in France automatically leads to an examination of the underlying struggle of 'Paris versus the French wasteland'.

Since the 1950s much has changed, as can be seen from the figures of the population censuses contained in Table 3.1.

Table 3.1

Evolution of total population and total manufacturing employment, (× 1000) 1954–1962–1968–1975

Region	Population				Manufacturing employment			
	1954	1962	1968	1975	1954	1962	1968	1975
Île-de-France	7,317.1	8,469.9	9,250.7	9,878.5	1,316.8	1,418.0	1,335.9	1,287.9
Champagne	1,133.6	1,206.0	1,279.4	1,336.8	144.7	158.5	164.9	178.8
Picardie	1,386.5	1,482.4	1,579.4	1,678.6	157.8	188.8	209.9	243.5
Haute-Normandie	1,274.2	1,397.8	1,497.4	1,595.7	143.0	166.3	186.2	222.8
Centre	1,757.9	1,858.3	1,990.4	2,152.5	153.7	173.6	207.6	260.0
Basse-Normandie	1,164.7	1,208.2	1,260.2	1,306.2	68.5	82.5	102.5	134.6
Bourgogne	1,374.5	1,439.4	1,502.6	1,570.9	123.0	138.3	150.9	178.1
Nord	3,375.4	3,659.4	3,815.1	3,913.8	482.4	489.2	475.3	509.2
Lorraine	1,956.0	2,194.2	2,274.4	2,330.8	292.9	313.1	303.7	321.9
Alsace	1,217.6	1,318.1	1,412.4	1,517.3	185.9	194.6	193.7	222.8
Franche-Comté	856.1	928.4	992.5	1,060.3	132.7	149.3	161.2	186.8
Pays de la Loire	2,319.4	2,461.6	2,582.0	2,767.2	194.9	209.0	239.4	295.3
Bretagne	2,338.8	2,396.6	2,468.2	2,595.4	126.3	125.0	144.3	178.0
Poitou-Charentes	1,393.7	1,451.3	1,481.4	1,528.1	88.5	95.5	110.7	136.1
Aquitaine	2,208.9	2,312.5	2,460.2	2,550.3	186.1	182.7	191.2	208.2
Midi-Pyrénées	1,975.4	2,061.3	2,184.8	2,268.2	147.4	150.6	157.5	178.7
Limousin	739.9	734.0	736.3	738.7	56.5	58.3	62.2	68.4
Rhône-Alpes	3,629.7	4,018.6	4,423.0	4,780.7	572.1	634.5	639.0	690.0
Auvergne	1,246.7	1,273.2	1,311.9	1,330.5	117.4	123.6	131.6	148.2
Languedoc-Roussillon	1,449.1	1,554.6	1,707.5	1,789.5	75.5	78.7	85.2	90.9
Provence – Alpes – Côte d'Azur	2,415.0	2,819.0	3,298.8	3,675.7	} 199.6	} 208.7	} 217.4	} 241.0
Corse	247.0	275.5	269.8	289.8				
France (total area)	42,777.2	46,520.3	49,778.4	52,655.5	4,965.7	5,339.8	5,470.3	5,981.2

The table shows considerable spatial changes in the past 25 years. The capital has been losing its share of the total population since the beginning of the 1970s, mainly because the centennial migration trend towards Paris was reversed in this period; the outward trend has been accentuated since 1975. The second part of the table shows that the role of Paris in national industrial activity has also been steadily decreasing since the mid-1960s.

The beginnings of a regional policy in France in the 1950s were naturally associated with a policy of 'decentralisation', the major difficulty lying in the concentration patterns then prevailing. The theoretical framework for regional policy was provided by the then dominant theory of growth poles, and the general conviction was that France needed other growth poles beside Paris. But how were they to be created? Manufacturing was generally recognised as the proper driving force behind growth poles, so, decentralisation of manufacturing was looked upon as the most natural method of regional planning.

France is still a centralised country, which means that it was from Paris and by Parisians that a regional policy was to be formulated and put into practice. The DATAR (Délégation à l'aménagement du territoire et à l'action régionale), founded in 1963, and the principal regional-planning body in France, held on the whole a centralised view of decentralisation. The principle of regional prosperity was granted, but to limit the dominant role of Paris or to decentralise government remained unthinkable; even if the strengthening of regional administrative authority could be conceived, that did not mean that any real local autonomy would be allowed.

The industrialisation of Paris is a recent phenomenon: before the mid-1800s, Paris was a city whose political, cultural, and commercial functions greatly outnumbered its industrial ones. Now that its period of industrial leadership is over, de-industrialisation is found not to have hampered its growth; better still, it has actually enabled the city to rid itself of activities non-essential to its real power. Some figures may serve to illustrate the controlling power of Paris. The number of head offices in the capital is very important indeed: of the total number of 500 head offices of the largest French firms analysed by the inquiry Bureaux Provinces 1977, about 380 were in Paris. Their number even tended to a slight increase between 1953 and 1976 (from 375 to 388).

Moreover, initiatives for product and process innovation come to a very large extent from Paris; Paris, with 60 per cent of all research activities in France in 1973, is overwhelmingly dominant.

Map 3.1   The programming regions of France

Regional and urban policies

A short time after the end of the Second World War there was a growing concern with regional planning. During the 1950s certain institutions
and programmes which were to shape French regional policies were
set up: 21 regions were marked off (22 when Corsica was made into a
region) (see Map 3.1), a financial-assistance programme was worked
out, (Map 3.2), and links created between national and regional planning offices. DATAR was founded in 1963. The regional reform of
1972 provided regions with some means of action, a modest increase
in the authority of municipalities gradually widened local 'grass-roots'
possibilities.

Firm-oriented locational policies. These represented the most dramatic aspect of regional planning: bonuses, credits, and tax reductions
could be granted to firms to create jobs in peripheral or barely industrialised zones or in zones beset by specific reconversion problems.
These subsidies were given to industrial activities as well as to service and research activities; industry benefited most from the
schemes. Overall, 700–800 million francs were given out in bonuses
every year; the programme set up by the Fonds Spécial d'Adaptation
Industrielle enlarged these sums and made the system of bonus-giving
more flexible.

Map 3.2   Assisted zones of France

Urban-equipment policies. These represent urban decisions made
by public authorities. In keeping with the dominant growth pole
theory of the late 1950s, widely accepted views tended to favour
a small number of centres, which were considered influential
enough to spread industrial growth to the provinces. Eight so-called
'balanced' metropolises were proposed: Lyon—St Etienne—Grenoble,
Marseilles—Aix-en-Provence, Nantes—St Nazaire, Nancy—Metz—Thion-
ville, Strasbourg, Bordeaux, Toulouse, Lille—Roubaix—Tourcoing, urban units of from 500,000 to more than a million inhabitants. Giving
these metropolises the power to act as the polarising centres they were
designed to be, implied concentrating a considerable amount of public
equipment credits on them. The plans were to develop their infrastructures (airports, public transportation systems (subways)), decentralise
public services, and set up office blocks to encourage private tertiary
decentralisation.

As growth pole theory gradually lost ground later on, starting in the
early 1970s, urban policy began to include medium-sized cities (20—
200 thousand inhabitants), and then, from 1975 on, 'country areas'
(rural units set up around small cities and uniting the strong affinities
of a local area). There were also attempts to improve the equipment
of urban units so as to enable them to hold on to their populations,
attract activities, and make daily life easier.

Allocation of public credit. While numerous decisions were made in
accordance with certain norms which, determined by national priorities,
related public equipment to the size of population, authorities tried to
include regional planning criteria in their main distribution decisions
within the framework of the Sixth Plan (1971—75). To a certain extent,
credits were allocated in equal parts, that is, distributed according to
the national criteria for public investment following the increase in
regional population, corrected for the extra cost of equipment in urban
zones in the light of updated estimates of urban concentration; apart
from that, 'freely determined' credits could be granted for up to 20 per
cent of the total amount available, taking into account the objectives
of regional planning, along with such factors as industrialisation, con-
version, locations in a metropolis or in the Paris Basin; specific funds
being set aside for the West, the Massif Central, and Corsica. More cor-
rectives were introduced to grant extra credits to certain regions because of the specific cost they had to bear (notably, the Paris region).
Indeed, one might question the effectiveness of a policy which, using
the distribution grid described, appropriated 27.5 per cent of public
credits to the Paris region, which, after all, accounted for not more
than 18 per cent of the country's population, had a lower population
growth than the national average, and started off with a higher initial

equipment rate than the rest of France.

Local planning. While local planning seems to have taken on quite varied aspects, its importance for industrial movement lies mainly in the provision of industrial sites and accompanying services, such as electricity and water supply.

The information base

The analysis of industrial movement in France is based on four different elements: statistics, surveys, data files and studies. We will deal with them in succession.

Statistical sources. The available sources of statistics are not always adapted to the needs of researchers. First, because firms are promised confidential treatment of the information they provide: any information that can be traced back to a specific firm will be withheld from the public eye. For example, DATAR will not even publish a list of firms that were granted bonuses under its decentralisation policy. What is more, official surveys are often non-exhaustive and hampered by underestimations. In addition, some surveys do not cover a long enough period of time to be considered valid. There are, of course, private directories, but it takes a long time to analyse them, their information is incomplete which makes comparative studies unfeasible, and they are often not comprehensive and not kept up-to-date.

The following sources of statistical information are published by government authorities:

- files of establishments, not regularly updated, beset with many mistakes (unusable);
- files of large establishments (of more than 100 employees), updated since 1961; for each establishment of more than 100 salaried employees these files indicate location, number of salaried workers, and percentage of female employment (the last figure has been accurate for only a few years);
- the annual survey of firms, compulsory for all of them;
- the survey 'Employment Structures' from the Ministry of Labour;
- general population censuses.

Incidental surveys. Unlike their counterparts in most countries, French firms are often hesitant to fill out questionnaires sent to them, fearful that the information they provide will be used for public or private ends, and convinced that they have quite enough to do filling out compulsory surveys sent by government agencies, they indeed prevent French researchers from making general use of this direct way to collect data. Their response rate is most often quite low (between 10 and 25 per cent), which makes the job more complicated while reducing its accuracy.

Let us look at some surveys:

— a survey of large establishments founded between 1960 and 1970 (Hanoun and Templé, 1975); out of 1,103 forms sent out, there were 544 answers, of which 452 were usable;
— a survey conducted by the author of this chapter among 1,750 of the largest French industrial and tertiary sector firms: out of 260 answers, 220 could be used; in all, more than 2,000 establishments, employing more than 400,000 employees, were studied (Aydalot, 1978);
— a survey of firms with investments outside their own country was conducted in the late 1960s (Falise and Lepas, 1970); it provided information about location behaviour on an international level;
— a study of the Lorraine region in the same period, mainly focusing on the factors of industrial location.

Other studies on a more limited spatial scale concentrated on one region, an employment-attracting zone, or one city. For example, in the early 1970s, Ducreux conducted a survey of 4,000 industrial establishments in the industrial suburbs north of Paris, receiving 1,000 replies (we have used this study, notably in Aydalot, 1979).

Public and private files. An excellent source of information is provided by the files of the social security agencies, which, as far as a researcher has access to them, offer him almost exhaustive and very complete information about salaried employees.

Directories and private lists have already been referred to. Let us conclude with the files put together by researchers. First, set up in collaboration with DATAR, there is the AUREG (Association universitaire pour la recherche géographique) file on industrial decentralisation: though firms are not individually cited, it provides a framework for an analysis of 2,410 decentralisations which have taken place from 1952 onwards. We can also mention the files drawn up from several studies at the Centre Economie—Espace—Environnement of the University of Paris I: there is a list of industries set up in the Paris suburbs between 1967 and 1972, a study of moves of establishments from 1970 to 1974 in the cities of Reims, Epernay, Chalon sur Marne, another of moves of establishments in the Dijon area between 1965 and 1975, results of a survey of Dijon firms (200 answers out of a stock of 1,000 establishments of more than 10 salaried employees), and an on-the-spot survey conducted between 1977 and 1980 of the (re)location of 300 establishments in 25 French cities (Aydalot, 1981).

Specific studies. Drawing from the above references, several works have provided analyses of present-day patterns of location and movement of firms. For example, the 1971 study of the change in the departmental distribution of jobs and firms (Aydalot, Noël and Pottier, 1972), the works of Planque (1977) and the Centre d'Economie Régionale at Aixen-Provence, Durand's study (1975) of DATAR, the analyses being made at present by the Centre Economie—Espace—Environnement of the file on large establishments and the DAFSA files, the works of the Association Bureaux-Province (1977), an offshoot of DATAR, on the movement of tertiary activities, and more specifically, on the movement of decision-making functions of firms, and the study by Lojkine (1976) of location in bank and insurance sectors.

The structure of industrial movement

Some quantitative indications

Following the terminology set for this publication, we will make a distinction between kinds of 'movement' (migration, closure, creation, on the one hand, and contractions and expansions on the other). The relative importance of each category is given in Table 3.2, indicating the transformation of the stock (number of establishments, headquarters excluded, of 220 firms studied between 1965 and 1975).

Of the 1,585 establishments in 1965, only 946 (fewer than 60 per cent) were still in the same location, operating in nearly the same way, in 1975; of the 1,863 industries in 1975, 946 (50 per cent) had been in the same location and operating in a similar way 10 years before.

The following, more general figures measure several kinds of movements: over the ten-year period 1965—1975, out of 100 establishments in 1975, 6 closures, 8 migrations, 14 expansions, and 19 new establishments can be observed; overall, 47 per cent of the establishments came under a location decision. The relocation rate of headquarters reached 26 per cent, against a corresponding rate of 9.3 per cent for the other establishments.

Table 3.2

Some indications of the quantitative importance of
components of employment growth

	Abs. change 1965—75	in % of 1975 stock
creations	404	22
migrations	182	10
expansions	331	18
no change	946	50
deaths	126	

Source: Basic data from Survey 'Grandes Entreprises' used also in
         Aydalot (1978)

With no spatial distinctions made, these figures represent averages
for large firms. But their movements do not have the same degree of
intensity everywhere, as is evident from Table 3.3, which gives the
results of a number of surveys carried out in various regions.

On the whole, one is struck by two elements: rates vary widely from
one city to another (between 1 and 4 per cent a year); they tally fairly
well with the studies done in other countries.

To make these initial findings more detailed, one needs to distinguish the various types of establishments, the size of the firm, the size
of the establishments, and the sector of activity.

Type of establishment and sector

It seems useful to make a distinction between headquarters and other
establishments. First, headquarters can only be relocated, not closed or
newly set up (for the firms studied are old, and, by definition, have
not disappeared). For the 211 firms which provided information, in
the Survey 'Grandes Entreprises' (see Aydalot 1978) the following
rate of movement can be listed:

Table 3.3

Synoptic view of rates of movement
calculated from different studies
(in per cent)

	Reims 1970–4	Chalon 1970–4	Epernay 1970–4	Dijon 1964–74	France large firms 1965–75	Seine St. Denis 1967–72
Relocation rates	7.8	5.5	3.5	26.0	13.2	–
Birth rates	28.0	12.0	3.5	39.9	22.5	18.4
Death rates	9.7	3.6	4.1	8.6	7.0	–
Natural growth rates	18.3	8.4	−0.6	31.3	15.5	–
Expansion rates	–	–	–	–	18.0	–

Table 3.4

Average length of time of headquarters
on the same premises, by sector

Sector	Years
Steel	42
Mechanics	27
Chemical products	22
Electric	35
Farm and food industries	41
Textile	66
Glass, building materials	30
Bank, insurance	30
Tertiary	32

— from initial installation to 1955	24 movements
— from 1955 to 1965	31 movements
— from 1965 to 1975	56 movements

The rate of movement of headquarters is increasing and high (2.6 per cent a year during the most recent period); however, on the whole, almost half of the headquarters have not once relocated since their installation. The average number of years at the same location varies sharply with the sector of activity, as Table 3.4 shows.

Here there is a definite link between the age of the sector and its rate of movement. In the electric and mechanics industries, both expanding sectors, the rate of movement of their headquarters is higher than in the older sectors of the textile, food, and steel industries. Besides, as a whole, the tertiary sector has recently undergone changes which are reflected in the many headquarters moves. These changes are both technical (development of data processing) and economic (growing role of banks, transformation of commercial functions, setting up of new service sectors in firms). Overall, the tertiary sector shows higher rates of movement than manufacturing industry, but that is mainly due to its considerable expansion, for its relocation rates are not at all high. Natural growth is negative for steel and textiles, positive for the other sectors. In industry, relocation rates do not differ much among sectors (about 12 per cent), the main variances being due to the rate of setting up new establishments.

As for the other establishments, one notices a 'departure' rate (relocations and closures) of 16.8 per cent (in ten years' time), and an 'arrival' rate (relocations and creations) of 33.3 per cent (also in ten years' time).

In addition, a distinction can be made between factories on the one hand, and establishments whose main function is tertiary (laboratories, warehouses, commercial establishments) on the other. The differences in the rates of movement are given in Table 3.5.

The highest number of moves in the tertiary sector was in the banking and insurance sectors: 16,000 jobs were relocated or opened up directly in the provinces, making up 55 moves in all. Today these provincial relocations add 2,000—3,000 jobs a year, a fairly low figure compared to the 200,000 jobs created yearly by the tertiary sector. Map 3.3 shows the installation of 14 establishments relocated by the five largest French banks (BNP, Crédit Lyonnais, Société Générale, CIC, and CCF).

Tertiary growth in the provinces is seldom the result of direct movements. Of the 208 operations studied by the Association Bureaux-Province, 4 corresponded to movements out of Paris, only 1 was from one provincial city to another, while 175 were new operations (161 expansions, but only 14 new installations). Here the Aydalot (1978) study

Table 3.5

Rates of movement by category, period 1965—75
(in per cent)

Category	
Closures	
factories and workshops	6.5
other establishments	7.3
Creations	
factories and workshops	13.5
other establishments	19.1
Natural growth	
factories and workshops	7.0
other establishments	11.8
Expansions	
factories and workshops	17.8
other establishments	16.5

Map 3.3   Relocation pattern of banking establishments

Table 3.6

Rates of movement by size of firm

Establishments by firm	Firms	Establish- ments	Reloca- tions	Closures	Creations	Expan- sions	Total
1	51	51	3 (6)	4 (8)	–	6 (11)	13 (25)
2	43	86	25 (29)	10 (11)	10 (11)	16 (19)	61 (70)
3–5	52	196	26 (13)	11 (6)	20 (10)	50 (25)	107 (54)
6–10	36	277	39 (14)	13 (5)	32 (11)	38 (14)	122 (44)
more than 10	33	1519	105 (7)	77 (6)	338 (22)	205 (13)	725 (48)
Total	215	2129	198 (9)	115 (5)	400 (19)	315 (15)	1028 (48)

The figures in parentheses indicate the percentage in relation to the number of establishments.

mentioned earlier in the chapter is confirmed. It states that 'relocation' (the closing of a firm and the concomitant opening in another place of an establishment with the same function) is a fairly infrequent phenomenon; the movement of activities consists mainly of new operations which do not necessitate the closing of a pre-existing establishment.

Size of firms and establishments

The rate of movement also varies by category and size of the firm. The latter aspect can be measured by the number of establishments of any firm. Table 3.6 gives some details.

The table clearly shows that for medium-sized firms, relocation and extension of existing establishments are very important, while larger firms more frequently choose to add new establishments; this is hardly surprising, given the firms' financial resources. On the whole, a firm with two establishments can grow only by relocation (these firms are often located in urbanised zones where lack of space or city planning rules prohibit expansion); firms with three to five establishments have a wider choice, at least one or two of their establishments being able to expand. The largest companies, whose growth means both a considerable increase in production and a need to improve their commercial circuits, tend to set up new factories, business offices, and warehouses.

One can also analyse industrial movement in respect of the size of the establishments. From a survey conducted in the Seine Saint-Denis area, large establishments appear to be less mobile than small ones (the concept of mobility being approximated by the notion 'considers departure from present location'. In Dijon, on the contrary, small establishments appeared the least mobile among the establishments of more than 10 employees in the total agglomeration. Out of the category of establishments with 10–49 employed, 70 per cent had not moved during the period, out of the group with 50–199, 54 per cent had stayed put, and out of the group 200 and more, 43 per cent.

Distances covered during movements

The number of moves differs greatly by distance category. A first impression of that phenomenon is given by Table 3.7.

Table 3.7

Number*of moves by type of establishment
and category of distance bridged

Distances in km	Headquarters		Other establishments		Total
	intra-urban	inter-urban	intra-urban	inter-urban	
0–1	11	—	11	—	22
1–2	}27	—	14	—	}51
2–5		—	10	—	
5–10	33	—	22	—	55
10–20	27	—	37	8	72
20–50	}11	3	16	4	}36
50–100		—	1	1	
100–200	—	}21	—	4	}44
200–500	—		—	14	
over 500	—	—	—	5	5
Total	109	24	111	36	280

Source: Basic data of survey 'Grandes Entreprises' (Aydalot (1978))

---

*   All movements of headquarters have been recorded since their initial establishments; of other establishments only relocations in the ten-year period 1965–75 have been listed.

More than 75 per cent of the moves thus take on an intra-urban aspect, almost half referring to distances of under 10 km; only 15 per cent of the moves cover distances of more than 100 km from the initial location. Headquarters do not differ from other establishments in the distances over which they move. For establishments not including headquarters, the distances covered average 8.9 km for intra-urban moves, and 204 km for inter-urban ones. The distances of intra-urban moves differ with the size of the city: in Dijon, between 1964 and 1970, the average distance of intra-urban moves was 1 km, but 8 km was the average distance recorded for the 517 moves in the first ring of Paris suburbs in the period from 1969 to 1974. The 204 km figure found in the Aydalot study as an average distance of inter-urban moves is very close to the result of the AUREG investigations, where the reasoning is as follows. Because decentralising moves by definition start from the Paris region, their distance can be measured by identifying the new locations. Of 2,410 moves 58 per cent ended less than 200 km from Paris. Half of the establishments of fewer than 25 salaried employees are settled within a circle with a radius of 150 km, and half of the larger establishments employing more than 1,000 workers can be found within a radius of 215 km, (see Table 3.8).

Table 3.8

Distribution of decentralised establishments by
distance category and size of establishments
(in per cent)

Distance from Paris (km)	60/150	150/215	215/340	340/700
Establishments employing fewer than 25	48.0	13.1	23.8	14.9
Establishments employing more than 1,000	27.5	22.5	20.0	30.0

These findings seem to confirm that half the inter-urban moves are over more than 200 km and that large establishments move farther than smaller ones. The same fact can be illustrated in yet another way, namely, by measuring the average density of decentralised establishments (in numbers by km^2) classified by their distance from Paris. Table 3.9 shows how indeed this density decreases very rapidly as one gets farther away from Paris.

Table 3.9

Density (number of decentralised establishments
in an area of 1,000 km^2), by category
of distance to Paris

up to 100 km	28.0
100–200 km	12.0
200–300 km	4.3
300–400 km	1.7
400–500 km	2.0
more than 500 km	1.0

Mortality of establishments

Of a total of 2,100 establishments of the 220 large firms that responded to the 1975 survey, 6 per cent of those existing in 1965 had disappeared 10 years later. The rate of mortality of the 2,410 industrial decentralising moves in the period 1952–71 (analysed by AUREG) was 14.9 per cent (measured in 1971). Taking into account the distribution of settlements over this 20 year period, one may conclude that the mortality among new establishments is higher than average.

Now let us study the disappearance rate of decentralised establishments in relation to the distance of their moves, (see Table 3.10).

Table 3.10

Percentage rate of disappearance of establishments
by category of distance to Paris

Less than 100 km	12.9
100–200 km	16.7
200–300 km	11.8
300–400 km	15.3
400–500 km	13.1
500–600 km	18.3
600–700 km	28.6

Though a rigid conclusion would be premature, the risk of failure after relocation seems to increase with distance. That finding seems the more convincing as, on the whole, the establishments farthest away from Paris were also the largest, belonging to the largest companies, establishments which *a priori* had the best chance of success.

Spatial patterns

Industrial decentralisation

The most important feature of post industrial movement in France
is decentralisation. To describe the phenomenon of decentralisation,
noting its relative 'concentration' seems a good starting point. Out of
2,410 moves recorded by the AUREG researchers, 1,394 are concentrated between 60 and 200 km from the centre of Paris, 60 km marking the approximate boundary of the Paris region; the area involved
measures 100,000 km^2, as compared to the 540,000 square kilometers
that make up the whole of France minus the Paris region. In terms of
jobs, the ratio is somewhat lower (about 50 per cent). However, a closer
look at the larger companies (survey 'Grandes Entreprises', see also
Aydalot (1978)) gives a different picture. While 73 per cent of the
establishments employing fewer than 25 are found in the Paris Basin
(as defined by Maps 3.4 and 3.5), that area accounts for no more than
42 per cent of the new jobs and 23 per cent of the new non-Parisian
establishments of firms. No less true is the fact that the overriding
feature of industrial movement is the enormous share of the Paris Basin (roughly, the zones between 60 and 250 km from Paris) in the number of arrivals. Maps 3.4 and 3.5 give a good picture of the relative importance of the Paris Basin for the total decentralising moves (note
that the same aspect has already in a sense been highlighted by Table
3.7).

Foreign companies show a somewhat different decentralisation pattern. Map 3.6 shows the present location of headquarters, illustrating
the tremendous spatial concentration of supervisory establishments
first around Paris and second in the Midi around international airports.
The next, very different, Map 3.7 shows the spread of 222 foreign
establishments; a comparison of the two maps clearly shows how the
locational patterns deviate. An additional observation is that factories
set up with foreign capital are attracted more to border zones than
French firms, particularly in the north and east.

The destination of decentralised activities shows very distinct patterns across the French space. Within the Paris Basin, decentralising
industries tend to pick small communities as new locations, while
those that move farther afield mostly opt for the larger cities (see Map
3.8).

Regions close to Paris offer widespread locations for decentralised
industry; every city and all rural spaces receive new establishments.
Farther from Paris, rural spaces are hardly considered, much like many
peripheral agglomerations. On Map 3.9 the departments where not one

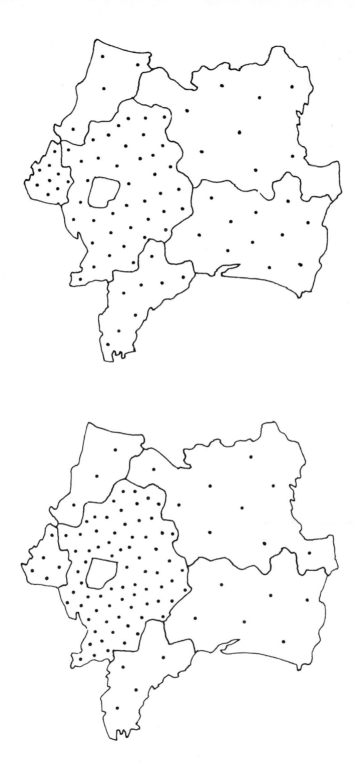

Map. 3.5 Pattern of movement of manufacturing establishments
(≥ 1,000 employees)

Map 3.4 Pattern of movement of manufacturing establishments
(≤ 25 employees)

53

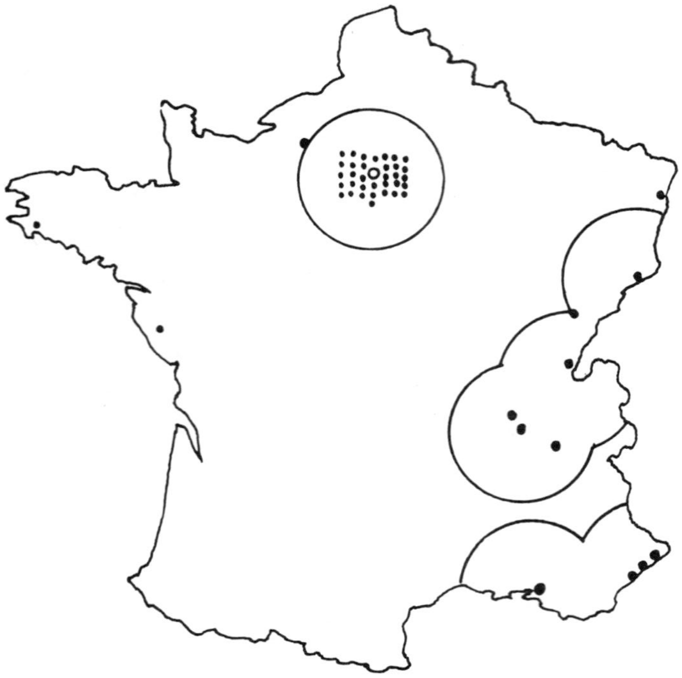

Map 3.7 Pattern of movement of 222 foreign firms

Map 3.6 Headquarters location of large foreign enterprises

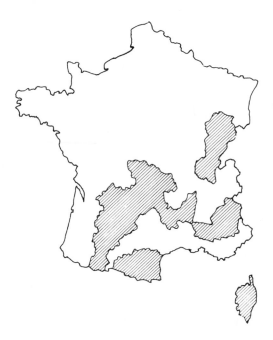

Map 3.8   Decentralisations in rural areas. Number of jobs created by decentralisations in rural communities and urban unities of less than 5,000 inhabitants. (As a proportion of all decentralised jobs).

city received decentralising firms (or at least no more than 20 decentralised jobs) have been marked; these zones are so far away from Paris that their small cities or rural spaces cannot attract industry, nor do they have large cities. On Map 3.10 five regions adjoining the Paris regions have been marked; these regions received 55.1 per cent of the jobs in the total of decentralised activities in France. Table 3.11 shows the difference in pattern of distribution across different size categories of towns between the five marked regions and the other fifteen regions of France.

A final remark: the dispersion of decentralising industries is limited to factories and does not include headquarters, as we have already seen.

Movements within the urban space

For both headquarters and other establishments, the pattern is clear-cut: of the 62 intra-urban moves of headquarters studied by the Aydalot survey, 38 are centrifugal, 6 have a centripetal tendency, while the

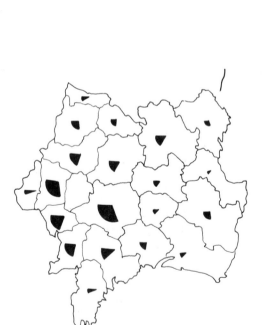

Map 3.9 Departments to which practically no industrial establishments migrated

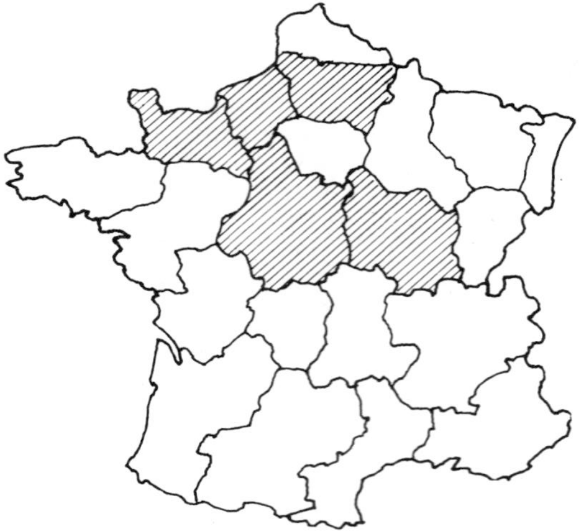

Map 3.10 Departments receiving together more than 55 per cent of total moves from Paris

Table 3.11

Percentage shares of three size classes of districts in total number of decentralised jobs

Group of regions	Size class of districts		
	<5,000	5—25,000	>100,000
The 5 marked regions	57.8	52.5	29.6
The remaining 15 regions	42.2	47.5	70.4

remaining 18 show no marked tendency. Among the 110 intra-urban movements of other establishments, 56 are away from the city, 5 have the opposite tendency, while 49 establishments remain at about the same distance from the centre.

The findings from the survey 'Grandes Entreprises', (see also Aydalot (1978)) conducted in the departments of the first suburban belt of the Paris region (1967—72) are similar: of 569 movements, 185 are within one municipality, 64 within a belt of municipalities around Paris, only 27 are towards a more central zone, and 293 go towards the periphery of the region.

The tendency is clear, then, and is confirmed by the study conducted in Seine Saint-Denis: the more central the establishments, the more they tend to change locations. Conversely, the more peripheral the belt that is analysed, the higher the ratio of recently installed establishments to establishments that consider moving away. It is a classic example of the de-industrialisation of urban zones, favouring the peripheral districts and bringing about the industrial demise of the more central areas.

While the phenomenon of de-industrialisation has most undoubtedly left its mark on the landscape and most clearly transformed urban structures, that does not mean that manufacturing industry is the activity in cities with the highest movement rate. We have measured the rates of movement of activities in the entire metropolitan area of Paris, taking into account both the level of responsibility and the function of each worker. The levels of responsibility were ranked from 1 for an unskilled worker to 5 for a firm's general manager; the functions considered were production, research, administration, commerce, and management. Through the period 1967—70 we measured the movement rates, defined not as the sum of the physical movements of particular jobs, but rather as the transformation of jobs within a spatial distribution. The total space was divided into 76 zones, with (fairly) homogeneous job structures, by the following formula:

$$M_j = \frac{1}{2} \frac{\Sigma_i |L_{ij_{t-1}} - L_{ij_t} (1 + g_i)|}{\Sigma_j L_{ij_t}}$$ (3.1)

The findings shown in Table 3.12 reveal that during this period of time relatively unskilled jobs and production appear more stable than most of the other categories.

Table 3.12

Job movement rates, 1967—70

Level of responsibility		Function in the firm	
Type	Rate%	Type	Rate%
1 Unskilled	4.2	production	4.3
2	5.6	research	18.6
3	5.8	administration	5.8
4	18.8	commerce	11.0
5 General Manager	9.1	management	9.8

On the whole, how do the various zones of urban space perform as to holding on to or attracting new activities? A preliminary overall approach included measuring the movement rates in the Paris region, with the above mentioned method of calculation. After marking off five concentric zones from the centre of Paris to the periphery of the region, the following rates could be calculated for 1969—70: 1: the central zone, rate insignificant, 2: 3.0 per cent, 3: 14.5 per cent, 4: 23.7 per cent, 5: 59.5 per cent. The more recently a zone has become urbanised, the less stabilised its structure appears to be. The most central zones are the ones where structures have been the least affected by change, while the developments in peripheral zones have been such as to transform their very nature in a couple of years.

Urban centres. Setting out to test the 'incubator' hypothesis, according to which urban centres are still irreplaceable as nurseries of new activities and young firms, which need the contacts and proximity that only such a centre can offer, we have discovered how weak its premises are. For example, the Aydalot survey shows that the city of Paris has a very low 'birth rate' of firms: in the study period, out of a total of 255 (for the whole of France), only 17 establishments were founded in the city of Paris, which is 6.7 per cent as compared to 15 per cent of existing establishments. For the urban area of Dijon similar results were obtained, as Table 3.13 shows. Comparing the proportion of newly created establishments in each of five concentric zones ranging from the historic centre to the periphery from 1964 to 1974 to their proportion in the stock of establishments in 1964, one finds that the ratio becomes higher as the zone is more peripheral.

Table 3.13

Birth rates of establishments by zone
(distance to the centre of Dijon)

Zone	Percentage share in the 1964 stock (1)	Percentage share in the 1964—74 new establishments (2)	(2)/(1)
1	28.0	16.5	0.59
2	25.5	16.5	0.64
3	16.5	10.8	0.65
4	21.5	40.4	1.88
5	8.0	15.5	1.94

What, then, is so special about an urban centre? What activities does it still attract, given a zero, even negative, overall growth of the economy?

In the greater Paris area, no one function tends towards the centre; what is more, production is still moving away relatively slowly, while research, management, and commercial functions are increasingly moving out. The most specialised functions (leisure activities, overall organisation of political, economic, and financial activities) are beyond a doubt still strongly concentrated in the central zones of Paris. Between 1967 and 1972, the number of jobs in all of the above categories decreased in the centre of Paris, except for commercial activities: even though the latter increased more rapidly in peripheral zones, the centre is still increasing its relative specialisation in commercial jobs as much as ever.

The same pattern prevails in all agglomerations of more than 100,000 inhabitants: while accounting for 40 per cent of the total number of establishments recorded, they only represent 28 per cent of those newly created. Thus, the theory of centres as growth incentives becomes less viable: most of the new creations, and most of the closures, take place in suburbs and small cities.

Suburbs. The location of establishments in the peripheral space of cities is related to the moment they first appear, the oldest specialisations having the most central locations. The study of five zones from the most to the least central in the north suburbs of the Paris region reveals a steadily decreasing proportion of mechanical industries: 43, 32, 26, 23, and 15 per cent, respectively. Likewise, the oldest establishments are found in zones close to the centre: the average life span steadily decreases from 24 to 16 years as one gets farther from the centre. Finally, the growth of establishments is most restricted in old suburbs near the centre: the proportion of establishments with a stationary or decreasing number of workers is 53 per cent near the centre, decreasing progressively to a mere 35 per cent in the periphery.

The spatial concentration of establishments is highest in old suburbs near the centre; in the zone called the Plaine Saint-Denis, at the entrance of the city of Paris, recently more than 30,000 salaried workers could still be counted in a zone of only 7 km^2, while land-use densities rapidly decrease as one moves toward the periphery.

'Mobility' measured by departure plans varies from 50 per cent in fairly central zones to only 18 per cent in peripheral spaces.

Where do establishments head for when they move away? From a study of the 569 moves in the three districts called the 'first belt' of the Paris region, most of the moves are short-distance ones; we have seen that 48 per cent of them are either within the same municipality or to an adjoining one, implying distances of less than 5 km. If moves starting from the city of Paris often head directly for the limits of the urban area (moves of about 20 km), most of those undertaken by establishments already installed in a suburb tend to remain fairly close to their initial premises.

The above information can be summed up by assessing the dynamism of each suburban zone. The findings are clear: if the farthest peripheries are still rapidly growing, the near suburbs are often rather sharply declining, while city centres are in an intermediate position. Table 3.14 presents a picture of five zones marked off from the centre of Dijon to the farthest periphery.

The same phenomenon can be pointed out in Paris: after marking off three belts in its suburbs, one can see how the number of industrial establishments has changed between 1967 and 1972 (see Table 3.15).

The old suburbs clearly appear to be the most vulnerable zones in the agglomerations, for one thing because their old specialisations no longer meet the needs of expanding activities, for another because the

Table 3.14

Dijon: Components of change by five zones
(from centre to periphery) (in per cent)

Zone	Variation between 1964 and 1974 in the number of establishments due to:		Variation in the number of workers in the establishments
	movements	new creations	
1	− 3.3	+ 23.0	+ 33.0
2	− 9.4	+ 19.0	+ 17.0
3	− 14.3	+ 4.5	+ 12.0
4	+ 141.0	+ 16.0	+ 93.0
5	+ 122.0	+ 33.0	+ 78.0

Table 3.15

Paris: number of moves by type of zone, 1967−72

	Arrivals	Departures	Difference
First belt	136	251	− 115
Second belt	219	125	+ 94
Third belt	214	94	+ 120

harmful secondary effects of these activities have prompted city planners to push industry even farther away.

The same phenomena can be observed, then, universally: an unchanging centre, decline in the first belts surrounding the central zone, enormous growth of new suburbs bordering a continuous urbanised area, and periodic spread of urbanisation into still largely rural zones (periurbanisation).

However, the above analysis is incomplete, not including any separate categories of firms. The movement behaviour of establishments is related to several factors: the small, often old, firm with only one establishment does not wish to change its location, and if forced to move by urbanisation, tries to find a new site as close as possible to its former one. By contrast, large firms readily leave a location that they have outgrown and which suffers from poor road transport facilities. They prefer to move to new sites on the outermost limits of existing agglomerations, where they are more accessible to a semi-rural labour supply and are able to secure a sizeable amount of land at a limited cost. There is indeed a dual pattern of location behaviour in urban space, large firms moving far away towards pre-established industrial zones, and small ones preferring to remain part and parcel of a dense urban space so as to hold on to their work force and clients. Thus it becomes understandable that the movements from one location to another, (decline of the suburbs nearby, rapid growth of distant peripheries) reflect the moves of different sets of concentrations of capital.

Peripheral moves

Movement towards the periphery pushes establishments ever farther away from the traditional centres of industry. It first becomes evident as an increasing distance of industrial locations from Paris. Let us look, for example, at the moves of large establishments in the western region. Maps 3.11 and 3.12 show that for three branches the centre of gravity for establishments and jobs has changed; in addition, one notices that establishments set up after 1961 are farther away from Paris than older ones, (see Table 3.16).

Table 3.16

Average distance from Paris of location of large
establishments that moved before and after 1961

Sector	before 1961	after 1961
Automobile	238	296
Electric engineering	252	321
Rubber, plastics	246	355

New establishments likewise head for smaller cities. Since 1961, again in the western region, 26 of the agglomerations which received establishments of more than 100 workers have fewer than 10,000 inhabitants.

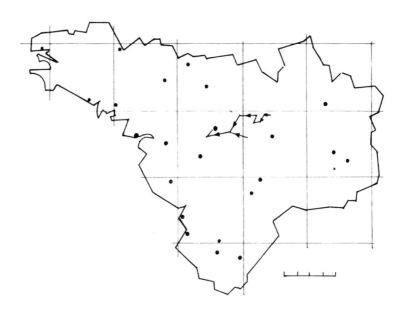

Map 3.11 Centre of gravity of establishments in the west of France
Source: Th. St Julien, Université de Paris I, 1982

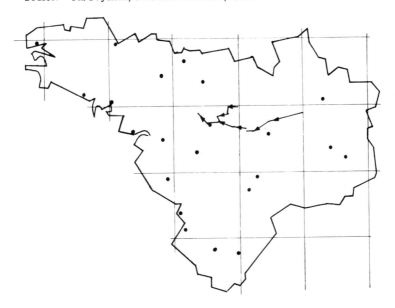

Map 3.12 Centre of gravity of employment in the west of France
Source: Th. St Julien, Université de Paris I, 1982

Location factors and firm-location policies

Motivations recorded in surveys

Several surveys have been conducted among firms to obtain more information about the specific nature of their location policies. Before they are analysed, it should be clear that the scope of their responses is often limited for the following reasons:

1 The choice of a location is more often than not an infrequent type of decision in that it is not systematically worked out by the firms in question.
2 Asking firms to rank various location factors often leads to misleading results: each factor operates on its own spatial scale, and it is of little use to add up or compare factors with different operational spheres of activity and of which the spatial variations are not symmetrical. For example, the fact that there is an equipped industrial zone or buildings available is taken into account in choosing a location within an urban space; in every fairly large city one can find both well and poorly equipped location sites. One may assess to what extent labour is drawn to a particular location by measuring its employment-attracting zone (the total labour-recruitment zone) and observing its inter-urban aspects. Likewise, the attraction of low salaries only becomes meaningful when one city is compared to another or one region to another. Tax differentials are linked to local policies, and therefore vary on a smaller scale (within the same agglomeration tax rates can be different). Moreover, the type of reception local authorities provide can be counted as a factor in comparisons between districts as well as regions. When firms rank their installation factors, they do not always answer the same questions, and so a comparison is often inconclusive.
3 Questioning a firm about its locational choice factors several years, sometimes more than 10 years, after its installation is necessarily misleading; a move decided on for a particular reason may have turned out a failure or quite a success for reasons of which the implications were not grasped at the time of decision. The head of the firm being questioned will respond by referring to the present situation of the location rather than to the original calculations which he does not know about or has forgotten.
4 Heads of firms hesitate to identify certain choice factors, such as low salaries, and prefer to give conventional answers which have little meaning.

5 Answers vary according to whether industrial managers are presented with a list of factors or left free to fill in their own reasons; similarly, respondents will answer differently dependent on whether the person making the decision is interviewed or someone in charge of carrying it out. Neither will the same answers be given if one sends a written questionnaire or conducts a personal interview.

6 Often industrial managers respond by citing the reason behind their final choice, involving a small number of pre-selected locations. Thus, the most important factors are already eliminated, only the secondary ones being mentioned, such as the amenities of the site, personal contacts, the kind of reception given the firm, etc.

A good idea of the factors associated with the movement of industry is given in the survey conducted by Hanoun and Templé (1975). The results of this survey among 442 large establishments set up in the provinces between 1960 and 1970 are summarised in Table 3.17.

An older study carried out by CETEC (1961) yields the following ranked list of locational factors.

1 labour force
2 cost and quality of the land or buildings
3 goods transportation
4 business contacts
5 pre-existing establishments
6 personal contacts
7 proximity of other establishments of the company
8 administrative or tax inducements
9 available housing for staff
10 existing university centre
11 energy-distribution network

A geographer, Chesnais (1975), submitted the responses given by the heads of 594 decentralising moves between 1954 and 1974 to a factor analysis. His findings largely correspond to the above ones: labour-related factors outrank the others, a large available workforce being factor 1. Decentralisation first and foremost expresses the will to change one's labour force, to avoid the expenses of the Paris region with its social and salary pressures. In that regard, the provinces appear to be less rigid, all the more so as their zones are still largely non-industrial. No matter what period of time, activity, establishment size, or region was chosen, the labour factor always ranked first. A pre-established industrial environment is seen as quite an important factor

65

Table 3.17

Factors interfering with the movement of industry in France

Determining factors	Role indicated as (in per cent of all responses)	
	strong	moderate
Labour-related factors		
recruitment of the work force	32.3	41.4
recruitment of unskilled labour	25.5	37.2
social climate	13.5	35.6
salaries	6.2	32.3
labour market competition	18.6	27.6
Distance-connected factors		
supplies	15.3	23.2
market links	21.0	13.5
links to other establishments		
of the same group	12.2	16.4
links to headquarters	9.7	19.2
Local-environment factors		
local industrial climate	8.2	25.0
subcontracting possibilities	3.5	14.6
available firm services	2.2	9.1
Personal factors		
pre-established local contacts	15.7	22.3
attractive location for executives	4.0	21.7
firm-owned land	12.6	9.7

Source: Hanoun and Templé, 1975

by small firms, as are easy contacts with Paris. The other factors listed are purely local considerations: road transportation, tax exemptions, dynamism of the municipality, available housing, equipped industrial zones, and bonuses. These factors play only a very minor role, as industrial zones (1,600 in France) or dynamic municipalities can be found just about anywhere.

The dynamism of municipalities especially concerns transactions that are far away, while the workforce factor clearly involves activities that take place between 100 and 250 km from Paris, which is quite normal: as extensive workforce-attracting zones are found less than 250 km from Paris, there is no reason to move any farther away, given that labour is the overriding factor.

In the survey 'Grandes Entreprises' (Aydalot (1978)) a list was made of the factors retained by firms according to the kind of operation they carried out: closures, relocations, or the setting up of branch plants. The results of 283 answers are shown in Table 3.18.

Table 3.18

Determining factors by type of move (frequency)

Determining factor	Closure	Relocation	Branch plants	Total
Urbanisation	1	9	0	10
Firm re-organisation	4	2	13	19
Technology	27	14	1	42
Technical availability	1	0	10	11
Economic availability	0	3	31	34
Commercial policy	11	8	81	100
Labour	1	2	8	11
Land/premises	0	26	20	46
Incentives	0	5	4	9

Oddly enough, one can see that the role of labour is eliminated. The distinctions based on the kind of operation are interesting: a firm primarily closes down because the establishment is too old and cannot be easily modernised: it relocates because it is pushed out by urbanisation programmes, its establishment is too run down, it is easier to build another one elsewhere, and another location would be better suited to its commercial undertakings. A new establishment is set up in a place chosen for both commercial and technical reasons.

Included in the same survey was a second 'closed' questionnaire which provided several reasons for locational decisions: availability and technical considerations were determinant factors here too (for 788 operations).

Finally, in the files set up of the 25 cities which received decentralised establishments (Aydalot, 1979), there was a survey of factory managers' reasons for deciding on a particular location. Labour connected reasons were found to play a leading role once again in that one is led to think that the decision was made in several steps, which implies a preliminary listing of locational factors. First, considerations connected with labour permit the selection of a group of possible zones and cities; then an analysis of technical concerns narrows down the sample and leads to a pre-selection of about half a dozen cities; lastly, a review of more personal factors (reception, personal acquaintances in the area) turns the tide in favour of one city. The value of these last mentioned surveys lies in their consisting of spoken interviews, which often provide more viable answers than written questionnaires.

At this point, it is desirable to go beyond the simple questioning of firm managers about the why and wherefore of their decisions, and proceed to assess the logic of their guiding principles in a study of firm moves.

Firm's labour force policies

Although labour is undoubtedly the dominant factor, it is still essential to analyse the differential aspects of the labour force in space to understand the logic behind the movement of firms. Workers, skills, social relations, and salaries are not the same everywhere; consequently firms tend to relocate establishments in the direction of the most adapted and (relatively) cheapest labour. Now it is clear that in the 25 year period from 1950 onwards, industrial processes based on standardised mass production developed along with the availability of several million workers 'freed' from agriculture, idleness, and declining industrial sectors. That liberation of the labour force did not take place just anywhere. What is more, one can wonder if that concern with finding a new type of labour (unskilled, ready to take on jobs requiring few skills at fairly low salaries) is not the result of company policies, companies adapting their production methods to new categories of workers so as to be able to 'mobilise' this much demanded labour force in industrial firms.

At this point it is interesting to note that there is a correspondence between the direction in which certain industrial sectors developed (in that of mass production), the type of labour corresponding to these sectors' needs, and the specific locations they chose. The sectors that have made the most progress and used the most standardised production methods are those that are the most decentralised (automobile, electric and electronics manufacturing, and mechanics). The various aspects: structural (concentration of capital), economic (contribution to mass consumption through mass production), technical (standardisation), and spatial (decentralisation towards the zones that have 'freed' formerly agricultural labour) are indeed all closely related.

68

Let us look more closely at this new labour force of decentralised establishments. The following figures from the surveys conducted by the Centre Economie—Espace—Environnement (Aydalot, 1981) provide us with more information. Using the analysis of a sampling done of 247 establishments in two dozen French cities that reaped the benefits of numerous decentralisation moves, one can measure the distribution of skills among the staff, a distinction being made between decentralised establishments, establishments of large firms installed for quite some time, establishments belonging to local firms, and the old establishments of the region (representative of old, declining industrialisation) being set apart, (see Table 3.19).

Table 3.19

Proportion of unskilled workers in the overall
labour force in groups of cities
(in per cent)

		Less than 40	40—50	50—60	60—70	70—80	more than 80
147	decentralised establishments	11	4	7	18	18	41
56	fixed ests.	39	8	11	12	9	20
32	local firms	34	15	12	3	6	28
12	ests. of the region	17	0	0	17	17	50

Two groups of establishments can be singled out: both the decentralised establishments and the old establishments of the region have a highly unskilled job structure; on the other hand, the fixed establishments (be they large or small-sized locally managed firms) have much more skilled workers. The evidence is clear: firms that have stayed in the location for a long time have — with few exceptions — a satisfactorily skilled labour force, while the relocation of others relates to their search for unskilled workers. One finds a dual structure among firms, connected with their dual spatial calculations.

These relocating firms — which have been the prime influence in industrial movements these last few decades — towards which workers are they heading? Whom are they offering their non-skilled jobs to? Various corresponding findings reveal that four categories of labour have dominated the new labour market: women, rural workers, youth, and immigrants. Generally speaking, the non-industrial background of these new workers in expanding sectors is their most striking feature. Various studies, comparing the present situation with that of five years ago, reveal that on the average half of the workers in modern sectors were new to the branch. What is more, on the whole, these new non-skilled workers were not industrial workers before and, more often than not, did not come from other jobs (women, the unemployed, young trainees, even immigrants who were unemployed in their own countries).

In 1973, 10 per cent of all women working in industry had not been working one year before. Of 1,800,000 women working in industry in 1970, only 900,000 were already working in the same branch in 1965. Of the 900,000 others, 564,000 (that is, about 32 per cent) were not working at all (442,000 of them younger than 35 in 1970), and 336,000 worked in another branch or outside industry (particularly in agriculture). Of 331,000 automobile workers in 1970 only 181,000 of them were already at work in this sector in 1965, 40 per cent of the others not working (three-quarters of them in training courses); 10 per cent worked in agriculture, 20 per cent in the tertiary sector, and 30 per cent in other branches. For the same year 1970 it was calculated that if 71 per cent of the workers' children became workers, 63 per cent of the sons of salaried agricultural workers did also, as well as 45 per cent of the sons of farmers.

Let us add that female industrial jobs are held mostly by young workers, particularly unskilled ones (in 1975, 31 per cent of unskil-led female workers were less than twenty-five years old, as opposed to a corresponding figure of only 20 per cent for males in the same category). Overall, female industrial jobs have widely expanded in ten years. The female labour force in industry, whose numbers had enor-mously fallen off (relatively speaking) since the turn of the century along with the decline in 'female' industries (textiles, clothing), has in thirteen years made up for a sixty-year slowdown. The proportion of the female labour force in industry was 34 per cent in 1906, 28 per cent in 1931, 23 per cent in 1962, and 30 per cent in 1975.

So, behind the spatial choices of firms is their wish to find a labour force likely to take on unskilled, poorly paid jobs. Indeed, from data of the Censuses of Population we can calculate that women accounted for 91 per cent of the new unskilled workers in 1975 while, in 1968, they represented only 26 per cent. As for women coming from rural backgrounds, they made up 88,000, that is, 28 per cent of the total number of new, unskilled, female workers. More detailed studies show that these women are also most often young (less than twenty-five years old), that old sectors seek out an old workforce while decentral-ised firms tend to employ young workers. Some typical situations may be cited: at the Moulinex plant of Alençon (Aydalot, 1981), women make up 48 per cent of the 2,750 salaried workers, but 72 per cent of the 1,430 unskilled workers (78 per cent of the female workers are un-skilled, while the corresponding figure for male workers is only 29 per cent). In Nogent le Rotrou's six largest decentralised establishments, out of 3,660 jobs, 1,840 are held by women, 1,600 of them unskilled workers, that is, 72 per cent of the entire unskilled labour force, but only 50 per cent of all workers. Numerous other examples can be readily cited, revealing that an increasing number of female workers goes hand in hand with the number of unskilled jobs in decentralised firms.

Generally, it can be seen that female employment in the provinces has replaced the employment of immigrant workers in the Paris region: at Renault, while immigrants make up two-thirds of the unskilled labour force in their establishments in the Paris region, quite often women have taken over their jobs in the establishments in the provinces. Renault is not the only example of that phenomenon. In recent years (since 1960), the number of jobs for workers has increased in the provinces, thanks to a policy of decentralisation; to a large extent, they have been filled by women.

Spatial patterns of movement

The trends and phenomena analysed above lead to contrasting spatial models for firms. Small firms, which have been shown to move less frequently than large ones (in other words, have a low relocation rate), and to grow primarily by adding on to their existing establishments, had better be disregarded. When such firms do change their location, except on rare occasions, they remain in the same urban area, where they try to set up installations near their old establishments, providing them with more space and enabling them to keep the firm running in much the same way as before (same staff, suppliers, and clients). Their infrequent moves are, by definition, unsystematic, prompted by the individual preferences of the head of the firm. High movement rates are only found among 'bonus hunters', firms that, experiencing difficulties themselves, are attracted by regional bonuses, which only serve to delay their eventual demise.

For large firms, on the contrary, the field is wide open. Every firm can be expected to decide on a strategy that, given its technical, economic, and financial limits, promises the best conditions for finding an adequate labour force.

A location is primarily determined by a firm's taking into account the kind of labour force it provides: urban or rural, with experience in agriculture or industry, or one that faces stiff competition on the labour market. Choosing a location is then choosing a certain access to a certain kind of labour. Once that decision is made, the firm will still have to have a labour reserve at its disposal. Let us see, for example, how a firm can secure the availability of a rural labour force (we have already examined its important role in recent spatial choices). Several alternative methods can be used:

1 *Commuting:* a method used, for example, by Michelin when recently installing its many establishments in France; it involves setting up a large factory (of more than 1,000 salaried workers) in a medium-sized city. In that case, a high proportion of its workers (around one in two) will not move out of their rural residences at 20, 40 or even 60 km from the factory. To make commuting easier for those who live more than 15 km away, the firm organises its own bus routes. In that way, many French cities have become gathering points, daily attracting a rural labour force; it has happened in La Roche sur Yon, Cholet, Bourg en Bresse, Blois, Chateauroux, and Auxerre (see Figure 3.1). A detailed study of the structure of commuting shows that always the labour arriving from outside the city is the least skilled, and to a large extent female.

2 The use of *rural sub-contracting:* sometimes a large firm decides to sub-contract varying portions of its production to small rural firms clustered within a radius of a few dozen kilometers of its factory. That is the case of the Thomsen's Laval factory, which, though it already employed a fair number of workers living in the country, resolutely went about developing the activities of half a dozen firms scattered over the Mayenne region.

3 *Direct clustering:* the end result of these practices is that the industrial firm scatters many workshops throughout villages. In that way it does not have the inconveniences of a concentrated labour force and takes advantage of its proximity to a rural labour force. The clustering can be of various kinds and may develop on a larger or smaller scale. Maps 3.13 to 3.15 provide three examples: from Michelin scattering factories 100 km away from one another (so as to combine clustering and bussing), to Moulinex with establishments at about 30 km away, and Legrand-Davaye, with establishments 15 km away. Many other examples can readily be found: in the Cholet region ERAM, a shoe manufacturer, owns seventeen factories of which the manpower is deliberately limited to 200. Maps 3.16 to 3.27 reveal that numerous firms make similar choices: Matra owns four factories in Sologne, Téléméchanique Electrique six factories in the Eure, etc. Thus, one combines the advantages of very short distances between establishments with those associated with a limited number of workers in each factory;

4 *Independence:* the new locations are independent from the old installations of the firm, the branch industry, markets, and com-

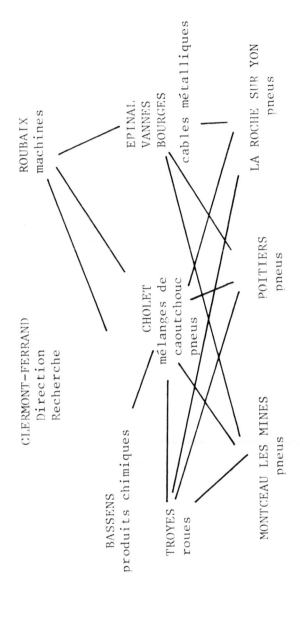

Figure 3.1   Functional linkages between different Michelin establishments in France

petition. Studying the locations of large automobile firms (see Maps 3.28 to 3.31) we find that each firm carries out its policies independently, showing itself completely indifferent to the choices of the others. In the same way a study of the location of six large establishments (more than 2,000 salaried workers) operating since 1965 in the same branch, clearly reveals a spatial explosion and their independence from the traditional locational choices of the branch: these new establishments are found in regions where, with few exceptions, they alone represent their branch: Basse Normandie, Poitou-Charente, Aquitaine, Lorraine; only the North region intensifies otherwise very recent specialisation in the automobile industry. Thus, moves farther away from the Paris region and, in general, from the north east of France, show that the proximity of markets and the dependence on these markets have become quite a secondary consideration.

The dispersion of establishments of large firms may coincide with various production structures. Let us contrast two types of characteristic situations by comparing the organisations of Michelin and Moulinex. Every establishment of Michelin is specialised in one stage of the production cycle (see Figure 3.1); the output of one factory is then an intermediary product used as an input in the production of other factories as the figure shows. That is not true of Moulinex, whose establishments are specialised in manufacturing a particular product: be it a coffee grinder, food chopper, oven, or pressure cooker. Sometimes firms specialise at their dispersed establishments in such a way that the same activity can be performed in at least two of them; they consider work stoppages due to strikes an important problem. Indeed, the way Michelin is organised risks the holding up of the entire firm's production, as a strike blocks the functioning of one link in the chain. Having alternative establishments to resort to restricts the momentum of that handicap: the production of a defective factory can be transferred to another one. Maps 3.14 to 3.25 express these alternative choices better than any further explanations. One can identify the unchanged concentration in Paris of the SNECMA (airplane engines), the spreading out towards the west of the Radiotechnique (television sets), the total dispersion of Carnaud or IBM, the multiple installations through France of Michelin, the regional development of Georges Perrin (textiles), the local preferences of Matra or Télémechanique—électrique, the double polarisation, a result of industrial concentrations, of Creusot-Loire, and the mastery of space of the Hutchinson group (rubber). These choices seem to be contradictory, and without a doubt sometimes reflect the indifferent spatial choices of footloose industries. But they also express the different conditions their firms evolve under,

Map 3.13 Michelin in France

depending on the sector they belong to, as well as their own, technical, commercial, and financial aspects. For instance, an industry in a declining sector that is hard hit by stiff international competition will seek out low salaries by using a system of rural clustering (Georges Perrin, Legrand-Davaye); technological advances, a highly skilled labour force, and the concentration of public markets explain the Paris concentration of the SNECMA; the international scale of its spatial calculations make the French IBM-model 'illegible'; the individualisation of the Moulinex firm explains its regional preferences; the large number of workers concerned calls for large-scale clustering in the case of Michelin.

More generally, the habits or technical limits of different branches may allow a scattering of small establishments (electric engineering) or disallow it (automobile). At this point, it is understandable that, for the time being, the automobile branch has decided to locate in big cities (often linked by company bus routes), while the electric industry prefers small cities.

Thus, locational choices have become 'commonplace', but that does not mean that every firm will follow the same model. On the contrary, the disappearance of technical obstacles has allowed an individualisation of spatial patterns that brings to the fore present-day behaviour trends.

Map 3.14 Moulinex in Normandy

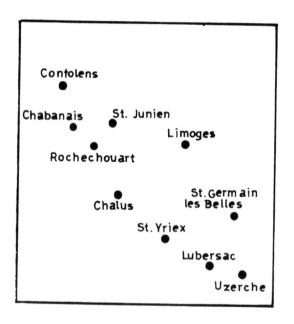

Map 3.15 Legrand-Davaye in Limousin

TELEMECANIQUE ELECTRIQUE

Map 3.16

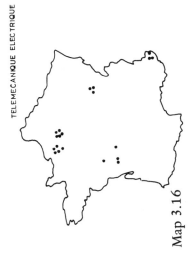

LE GROUPE HUTCHINSON

Map 3.18

EMBALLAGE METALLIQUE
DE CARNAUD

Map 3.17

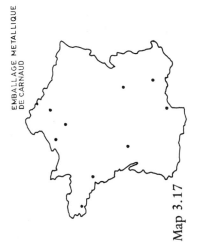

LE GROUPE MATRA

Map 3.19

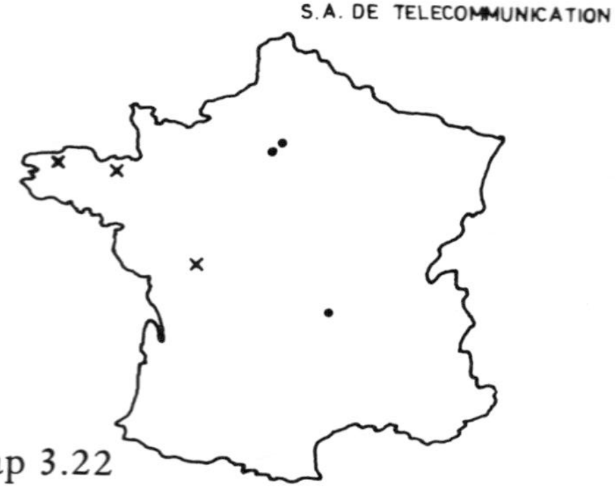

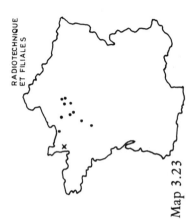

S.A. DE TELECOMMUNICATION

Map 3.22

RADIOTECHNIQUE
ET FILIALES

Map 3.23

PILES WONDER

Map 3.20

CLEMECY

Map 3.21

78

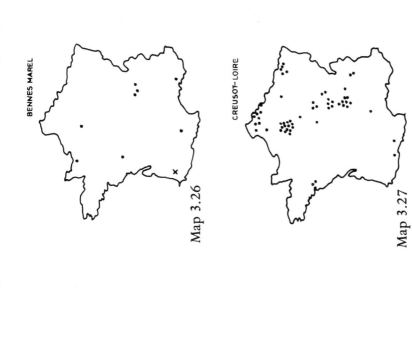

GEORGES PERRIN

Map 3.24

BENNES MAREL

Map 3.26

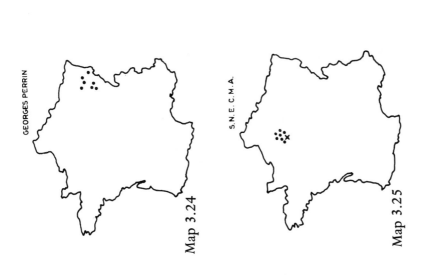

S.N.E.C.M.A.

Map 3.25

CREUSOT-LOIRE

Map 3.27

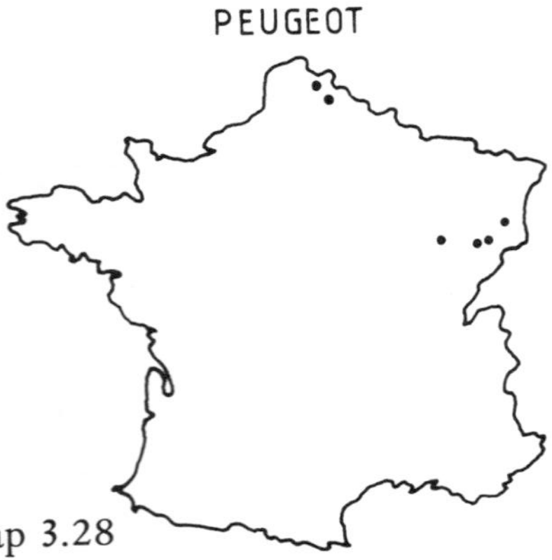

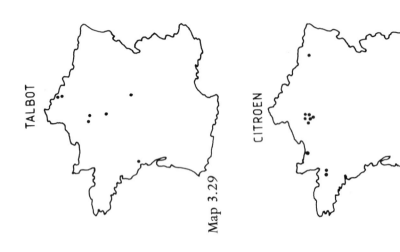

PEUGEOT

Map 3.28

TALBOT

Map 3.29

RENAULT

Map 3.30

CITROEN

Map 3.31

The impact of movement on the regional and urban structure of France

The trend towards dispersion and decentralisation

The various tendencies described in the previous sections have led to a wide dispersion of industry. This dispersion can be measured in various ways. Graph 3.1, using the only indicators available since 1850: the distribution of salaried employees in industry by sector and department, shows that industry, as a whole, is scattered more and more across the whole French space. One clearly sees that the progressive concentration of industry that had been going on through a long period, has been replaced with a dispersion trend since the Second World War. Over a long period one can measure that industry, scattered up to the 1850s, experienced a century of uninterrupted concentration, reaching its highest point between 1936 and 1950 (the dates vary with the studies), and that since then there has been a pronounced reverse trend, with every indication that industry is moving farther away from its initial place of concentration. Spatial concentration today seems comparable to what it was in 1850.

Of course, it is essential to point out that the dispersion of 1850 coincided with an enormous dispersion of capital, while today, spatial dispersion reflects the high concentration of capital.

Graph 3.2, measuring how the coefficients of geographical concentration in various branches developed between 1 January, 1968, and 1 January, 1978, confirms and enlarges upon the above findings: while still in 1968 the branches had very differentiated coefficients of geographical concentration (from 7 to 24), since then they have tended to group closer together: there has been a stepped-up decrease for the most concentrated branches (automobile, chemicals, electric engineering), stability or increase for mechanics and wood, both of which were formerly quite dispersed. From this and other indicators we can perceive the growing spatial indifference of branches: more and more, they are adapting to a common spatial pattern, while regions are losing their specialisations as the dispersion of industry goes hand in hand with the loss of regional specificities. We can conclude that today, branches are no longer valid indicators in deciphering locational patterns.

In the same way, calculations based on the study of Saint-Julien (1982) of large establishments in regions in west France, show that in all sectors the average distance between establishments is steadily increasing. It is important to realise that the dispersion takes place within the firms themselves at least as much as it differentiates their locations. If small firms (of one establishment) were initially dispersed throughout France, and for family and historical reasons, remained

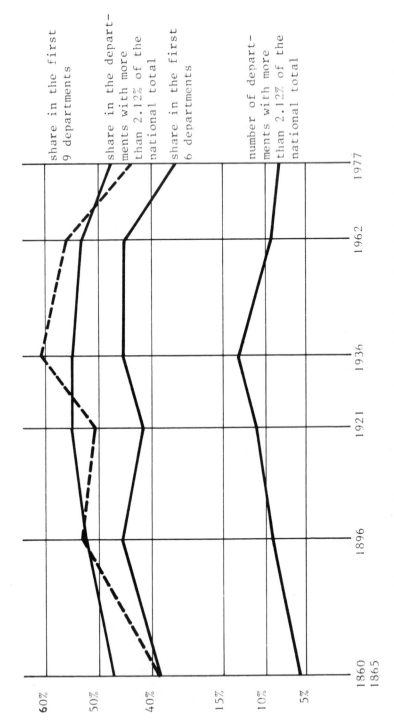

share in the first 9 departments

share in the departments with more than 2.12% of the national total

share in the first 6 departments

number of departments with more than 2.12% of the national total

Graph 3.1   Spatial concentration of French industry (salaried employees; all branches)

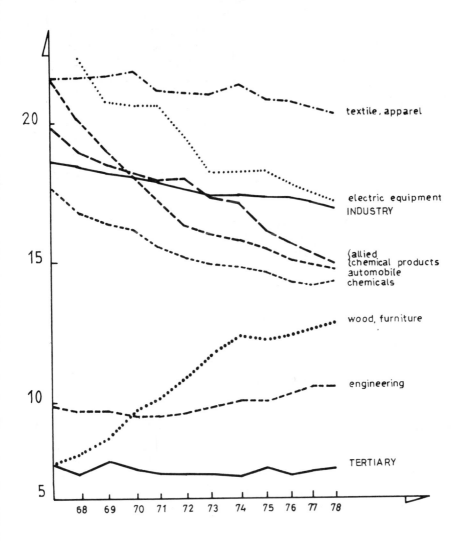

Graph 3.2 Co-efficients of geographical concentration of various
branches (1 January 1968 − 1 January 1978)

rooted to their original locations, they now rather tend to a gradual concentration. The phenomenon of dispersion is typical of large firms, independent of their environment and looking for a specific location for each of their specialised establishments. As a result of these movements, the structure of French space has been transformed. Sectoral specialisation has greatly decreased for a large number of cities and departments. On the other hand, social characteristics do still differ very much from one region to another and notably from one size class of towns to another. That is particularly true of the skill level of the labour force, the percentage of low skill being high in rural areas and small towns, while the proportion of high skills in total labour is large in the larger cities and conurbations.

The change in the relative position of Paris, the Paris Basin, and the other regions

More than half of the decentralising moves (and half of the jobs created by these decentralisations) go to the Paris Basin, for the simple reason that for a long time this zone's very proximity to Paris had constricted the growth of its cities, and so it now offers the double advantages of limited distances and an effortless recruitment of workers of rural origin. Why move far away when the Paris Basin offers small cities and pockets of rural workers? One may also wonder whether, in the last twenty years, the Paris Basin has been the only zone in France to increase its industrialisation. Graph 3.3 reveals that all over France, except in the Paris Basin, jobs in the manufacturing sector have become less important than those in service industries. Moreover, industrialisation at extensive distances has been halted. Only very large firms that care little about distance have headed towards more peripheral spaces.

Using the Aydalot survey for the period 1965–75, one can compare the skill level of jobs eliminated in the Paris region to that of jobs created in various French regions by large firms, (see Table 3.20).

If this sampling is perhaps not complete enough to allow us to draw any formal conclusions, we can see that movements which have taken place in the Paris agglomeration have led the way in the substitution of skilled jobs (often in the tertiary sector) for very unskilled jobs, while the jobs that were done away with in the Paris region were re-established in the Paris Basin. Thus, it is a question of firms spreading out their production establishments.

Let us now look at the entire country. Map 3.32 shows the distribution of large industrial establishments in 1961: the 1950 decentralisations had already laid the foundations of a massive industrialisation

84

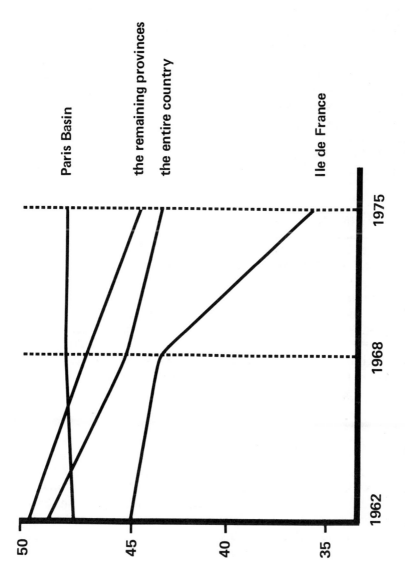

Graph 3.3 Proportion of secondary jobs in non-agricultural employment

Paris Basin

the remaining provinces

the entire country

Ile de France

1962   1968   1975

50   45   40   35

Table 3.20

Proportion of unskilled jobs among total jobs
(in per cent)

Category	
Eliminated in the Paris region	53
Created in the Paris region	17
Created in the Paris Basin	56
Created in the Nord region	27
Created in the Est region	26
Created in the Ouest region	24
Created in the Sud-Ouest region	33
Created in the Sud-Est region	44

towards the west, but, except for the Paris region, the three regions of the north, the Lorraine, and Lyon–Grenoble–St Etienne provided the highest concentrations of industry. Map 3.33, which reflects new movements between 1961 and 1977, is completely different: one can read here a decline or stagnation in the old, industrial regions and growth in the west is limited to a 300 km radius around Paris.

Where, then, are the new industrial locations concentrated?

Map 3.34 indicating the proportion of agriculture in regional employment in 1954 clearly emphasizes the importance of the potential reserve labour supply found in the western regions of France; it also shows that a very large number of agricultural workers were located at the very gates of Paris!

Regional policy impact

The effectiveness of regional-policy planning can be measured in several ways. Let us first see how closely the map of assisted zones corresponds to that of decentralisations: Map 3.35 shows that industrial decentralisations are almost completely outside the assisted zones. More precisely, when speaking of industrial movements, one finds that on half of the land that was accorded locational bonuses, there are only 17 per cent of the decentralised establishments of less than twenty-five workers and 42 per cent of the establishments of more than 1,000 salaried workers. If most of the 'assisted' jobs have actually gone to the predetermined zones, industrial growth, on the whole, has largely avoided these same zones.

86

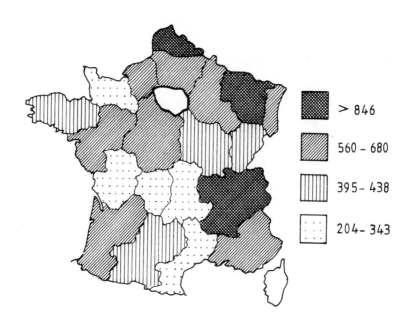

Map 3.32 Large industrial establishments 1961

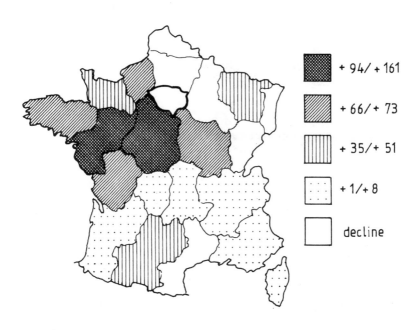

Map 3.33 Large industrial establishments 1961–77

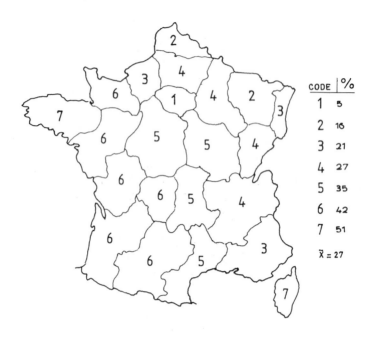

Map 3.34 Share of agriculture in employment (1954)

Map 3.35 Regional aid (dotted areas) and industrial decentralisation
(black area represents ± 70% of all decentralisations)

Likewise, one can see that regions where cities are granted the largest amounts of financial aid are often those that receive the fewest decentralised jobs.

Another way to study the effectiveness of regional planning is to ask firms to specify its degree of influence on their decision making. At this point, it should be added that public inducements are rarely given as decision factors by company directors. These inducements seem to come into play only when it is a question of a firm's choosing between two equally suitable locations. But, they are not important enough to turn the tide in favour of a city which, in other respects, presents a profile considered to be negative. This example shows the real, but highly restricted, degree of effectiveness of these policies.

Regional planning tends to favour large firms: only ten firms made up a quarter of the decentralised jobs; small firms, unable to get through the complicated forms which have to be filled out to obtain such aids, very rarely benefit from them. We have already seen that they are most often allotted regions very near to Paris, in an 'empty' (non-assisted) zone. This is illustrated even better by Map 3.35. This highly inefficient policy is being strongly criticised today by the representatives of the Paris region who have witnessed the even more dramatic decline in industrial jobs since 1974 and are amazed that sizeable reconversions should have to be the price to pay in order to provide the provinces with a few jobs. As the decentralisation policy was entirely based on the idea of Paris being a powerful 'motor' that, given its own growth, could push ahead the industrialisation of the provinces, it now seems to be in big trouble.

The current situation and outlook

How can the movement of activities be studied in 1982 and beyond if one is not informed about the developments since the rupture of 1974? That year marked the end of the post-war period of massive growth; until the general census of 1982, sources of information will be quite meagre: several annual surveys that cannot be studied until two or three years after they were held (notably, on a regional or local level); firms that are beset with numerous difficulties are less receptive to surveys and make only fragmentary information available.

Thanks to the study of the file of large establishments, there are some findings dealing with the period 1974—77; another study (Morniche, 1979) is available, but it is difficult to figure out new locational patterns from it. After eliciting some findings from these limited sources, present-day phenomena and their possible impact on industrial movement will be examined.

Since 1974 all the indicators of economic development have shifted downwards. We are not so interested in raising this curve as in the question whether it is homogeneous in every region. Are adaptations to the crisis 'spatially unbalanced'?

A first glance at the data leads one to suppose that the new trends are only a repetition of those that preceded them. If the industrial growth of decentralisation regions has been replaced with a period of stagnation, while the slow decline of old, industrial regions has been highly stepped up, regional hierarchy has hardly evolved. However, in terms of movement, it seems that industrial mobility has decreased. That can be seen in the compression of DATAR operations, which itself is struggling to be effective and is only able to act by participating in a growing number of industrial movements.

As adjustments from now on are associated with downward trends, the economy is adapting by closing the least profitable establishments (which does not necessarily mean the most poorly located). Moreover, the number of new locational decisions (creations and moves) is decreasing.

A study of the new spatial trends of new establishments in the electronics or textile industry also shows that the same zones are still refuge zones or reception zones, but, in this case, new causes have produced the same effects that were seen in the past.

If, for the time being, no major modifications in the movements of firms can be seen, a study of certain dynamisms today leads one to think that the future does hold some important changes. In terms of work, in the last twenty-five years France has become much more homogeneous than before; the widespread unemployment has restricted the role of reserve labour supplies; a limited but real reduction in the salary gap between cities and regions can be noticed; and the sharp division between old, industrial regions and agricultural ones has become less pronounced. This last reality might well reduce the decentralising push towards 'peripheral' zones, all the more so as decentralisations have already taken place and a stagnant growth economy can no longer assure a supply of jobs that could be decentralised. Besides, the mounting costs of energy have increased transport costs and favour locations which keep them at a low level. All this accounts for the halt in industrial decentralisation, and might even lead to a return to central zones.

Besides, the new economic activities which might boast of a positive growth rate tend to develop in central regions first, where there is a lot of research being carried out, a very experienced workforce on hand, and they are at a real proximity to decision-making centres; Furthermore, as firms more and more need to rely on a multitude of ancillary services — be they technical, legal, or supervisory — they would concentrate once again in the large metropolises which can only provide such facilities. Suppose that 80 per cent of the firms with data-processing services are located in the Paris region. Should not one then fear a new centralisation movement?

The concern with attracting high-level executives and engineers has led companies to propose pleasantly situated large cities as locations; their technical independence has tempered the concern with being a member of an established industrial complex; moreover, old industrial regions, as well as zones of recent decentralisation, are to be avoided. New projects, oriented toward the sun and universities, are on the horizon; they are completely different from the 1960s' model, character-ised by clustering, highly unskilled work, dispersion, and the use of a semi-rural labour force. Besides, today a new type of dualism is beginning to develop: that of a 'two-speed economy'. On the one hand, one finds reception zones for new industrial branches — those that export and give French industry its competitive character (aeronautics, nuclear, space, office data-processing, and biological industries), are the most technically advanced, and are located in central and dynamic zones, taking advantage of concentrated research activities, employing a highly skilled labour force, and distributing high incomes.

On the other hand one finds old activities, waiting to be trans-ferred to the Third World. They are located in areas designated as cast-offs with no specific function, and thus it is a question of adopting a wait-and-see policy, dealing with their unemployment, and improving living conditions, as they cannot promise a higher future standard of living. Marginal kinds of activities could develop here: cultural activities, 'moonlighting' jobs, new types of production methods (a return to working at home, a refusal of the traditional salaried jobs etc.). Grass-roots initiatives would multiply, replacing the quantitative with the qualitative! Not being able to include everyone in the modern sector, these marginal regions would at least be given the means to 'get by'. Now it is difficult to predict the field of action this parallel economy might engage in; but, as authorities are proving unable to fight against unemployment, it could be more and more wide-spread.

References

Association Bureaux-Province (1977), *Implantations tertiaires et centres de décision.*
Aydalot, Ph., Noël, M. and Pottier, Cl. (1972), *La Mobilité des Activités Economiques,* Gauthier-Villars, 1972.

Aydalot, Ph. (1978),'La Mobilité des Activités et de l'Emploi', *Revue d'Economie Régionale et Urbaine*, no. 4.

Aydalot, Ph. (1979), 'L'Entreprise dans l'Espace Urbain', *Economica.*

Aydalot, Ph. (1981), 'Politiques de Localisation des Entreprises et Marchés du Travail', *Revue d'Economie Régionale et Urbaine*, no. 1.

Aydalot, Ph. and Lorant, M. (1976), 'La Mobilité des Activités et de l'Emploi, Etudes Empiriques', *CETEM*, September.

Centre Economie—Espace—Environnement (under the direction of Ph. Aydalot) (1979), 'Décentralisations des Grandes Entreprises et Bassins d'Emploi', *Dossiers du CEE*, no. 9, November.

CETEC (1961), *L'influence sur la localisation industrielle des facteurs relatifs au transport*, Paris. (unpublished report for the Ministry of Construction).

Chesnais, M. (1975), 'La Localisation des Opérations de Décentralisation en France (1954—1974)', *Analyse de l'Espace*, no. 4, December.

Durand, P. (1975), *Industries et Régions*, La Documentation Française.

Falise, M. and Lepas, A. (1970), Les Motivations de Localisation des Investissements Internationaux dans l'Europe du Nord-Ouest', *Revue Economique*, January.

Gendarme, R. (1976), *L'Analyse Economique Régionale*, Cujas.

Hanoun, M. and Templé, Ph. (1975), 'Les Facteurs de Création et de Localisation des Nouvelles Unités de Production', *Economie et Statistique*, June.

Jaeger, J.P. (1975), 'Approche de la Localisation Industrielle en France à partir d'une Analyse Factorielle des Structures Régionales', *Revue Economique du Sud-Ouest.*

Jouffroy, P–Y., (1970), 'Réflexions sur les Facteurs de Localisation des Entreprises, Etudes et Enquêtes', *Economie Méridionale*, no. 71, September.

Lipietz, A. (1978), 'La Dimension Régionale du Développement du Tertiaire', *TRP*, no. 75, La Documentation Française.

Lojkine, J. (1976), *Stratégies des Grandes Entreprises et Politiques Urbaines, le Cas des Banques et des Assurances*, CEMS.

Morniche, P. (1979), *L'emploi et le Marché du Travail dans les Régions*, INSEE.

Planque, B. (1977), *La Diffusion Interrégionale du Développement*, CER, Aix-en-Provence.

Saint-Julien, Th. (1982), *Croissance industrielle et système urbain*, Economica, Paris.

SEMA, (1969), *La Localisation des Etablissements Industriels: Etude des Facteurs de Localisation en vue de l'Aménagement Régional*, Paris, May.

SOFDI, (1970), *La Localisation Industrielle, Leçons de l'Experience,*

Paris.

Valeyre, A. (1978), 'Emplois et Régions, la Polarisation de l'Emploi dans l'Espace Français, *TRP,* no. 75, La Documentation Française.

4 Federal Republic of Germany

F. J. BADE

Introduction

Preliminaries

In the Federal Republic of Germany, economic development as well
as spatial structure have had great influence on the volume and direction of industrial migration. Consequently, better to understand what
has happened in the FRG, the first section of this chapter presents
some of the main characteristics of the West German economy. Before
proceeding to the description and analysis of industrial migration in
the 1960s and 1970s, and of its effects on the regional structure of
the economy, the next section gives a synopsis of empirical investigations, informing about their methods and data base.

First of all, then, the relation of the subject in hand with some associated problems, will be clarified.

The analysis is restricted to the movement of industrial establishments;
investigations into the movement of establishments of other economic
sectors are, indeed, completely lacking.

Industrial movement represents a particularly obvious feature of
changing regional structures, and as such are an interesting object of
study in connection with theories of regional development. But, as
will be shown later on, the actual volume of industrial movements in
the FRG and their regional redistribution effects are not very large.
Therefore, when investigating changes in regional structure, one should

attach considerable importance to regional differences in the development of resident (non-migrating) plants.

In connection with location theories, migration is only one way of making a locational choice. Multi-plant enterprises, for example, have to meet locational decisions when relocating production between existing plants. Likewise, take-overs (or sales) of firms may be influenced by locational considerations and be interpreted as locational behaviour.

Economic conditions between 1960 and 1980

Between 1960 and 1980 the economy of the FRG experienced two periods of strong growth, both of which were ended by recessions: 1964−65 with the recession of 1966−67 and 1971−72 with the recession of 1975−76 (Graph 4.1). In contrast to the first cycle, however, the West German economy has not recovered since the slowdown of 1974. In terms of employment, economic equilibrium could not be reached again. Until 1973 the rate of unemployment remained under 2 per cent; even in 1967, the worst year of the first recession, the rate of unemployment only increased up to 2.7 per cent. By 1980 it had risen to over 5 per cent.

Graph 4.1 shows in which sectors the loss of employment was the strongest. In the 1960s only the primary sector had a negative effect on the general development of employment. Since 1970, however, the manufacturing industry has also suffered important decreases; during the recession of 1974−75 no less than one million industrial job opportunities disappeared. At the end of the 1970s the size of employment was 13 per cent smaller than at the beginning.

Why has the German economy not succeeded in reaching full employment after the recession, as it did in the 1960s? Among the various reasons, two processes above all seem to be responsible for the adverse development in the manufacturing sector. First, like most other industrialised countries, the number of employees directly or indirectly dependent on domestic private consumption, decreased. On the one hand this is caused by changes in consumption habits; on the other hand, productivity in the primary sector had considerably advanced so that much manpower could be economised. By 1972 this process could be compensated by the growth of employment in those sectors which produce goods for export and public consumption. Since 1972, however, the negative employment effects in the sectors of domestic private consumption have been so high that they could not be offset any longer by the employment increase in sectors of export and public consumption (Table 4.1).

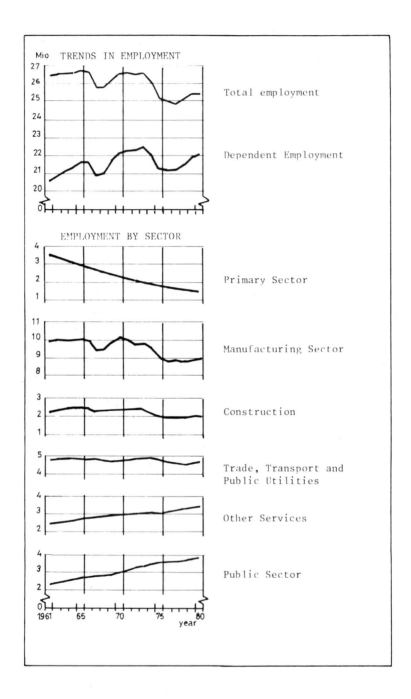

Graph 4.1   Trends in employment, 1960—1980
Source: Sachverständigenrat (1980) p. 54

Table 4.1

Employment effects by changes in the
structure of demand:
Annual average change (1,000 persons) in the amount of employment
directly or indirectly dependent on the sectors of final demand

	Manufactures, trade and transport[1]	
	1962—72	1972—76
Private consumption	−55	−156
State sector	− 5	− 36
Investment[2]	−19	−210
Domestic private demand in all	−79	−402
Export	+ 84	+ 72
Final demand in all	+ 5	−330

[1] Without mining and communications
[2] Including housing and business inventories change

Source: DIW (1980), Tables 2.5/7 and 2.5/9

Second, investment activities have considerably decreased in the
manufacturing industry. In 1974 alone, the volume of investment sank
by 10 per cent in real figures in comparison to the preceding year. The
previous level of investment of 1973 could not be regained before 1976.
The result was that between 1972 and 1976, year by year, 300,000
fewer people were employed in the production of investment goods.

Several factors were responsible for the sharp decline in private investment, which can only be sketched here. An important role is played
by the low utilisation of industry capacity, which had been considerably
expanded in the preceding upswing of the business cycle. First, the
demand for consumer goods has decreased as consumption preferences
changed and more services were demanded. Second, the import of consumer goods has increased, especially in the areas of non-durable goods.
Third, raised energy prices have caused substitution effects which ad-
versely affected the demand for consumption goods. Additionally, one
can mention the sharp increase of exchange rates, new burdens in salaries, and energy cost. In total, these factors have considerably increased the uncertainty about future economic prospects of West German
industry, which presumably led producers to an essentially more cau-
tious engagement of capital.

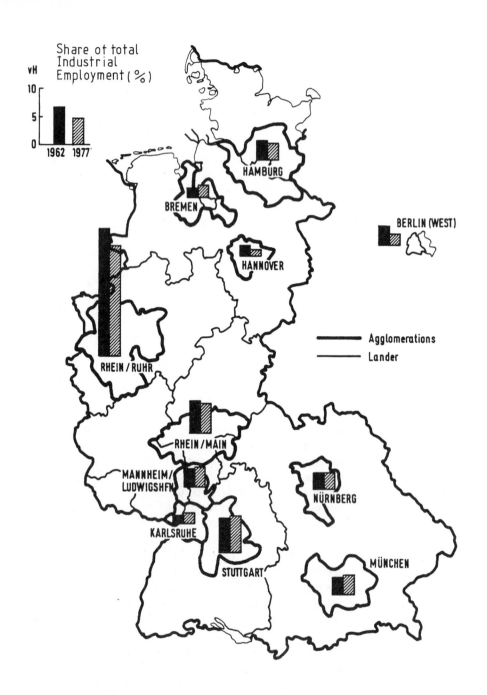

Map 4.1   Share of total industrial employment (in per cent)
in the main agglomerations in the FRG.

The spatial structure of the FRG

In relation to other countries like France, Denmark or the UK to be characterised in general as mononuclear, the FRG seems to have no essential regional problems. Its spatial structure is polycentral. Instead of one all-dominant centre, a series of large agglomerations exist, distributed over the whole area from the north (Hamburg) to the south (Munich) (see Map 4.1). Correspondingly, a well equipped net of traffic lines is available and the population density even in the more peripheral areas is relatively high by international standards.

In spite of the polycentral structure, economic conditions vary considerably between the fifty-eight regions of the FRG. Gross domestic product per head is twice as much in the leading region (Hamburg) as in the weakest region (Passau/Eastern Bavaria) as can be seen in Map 4.2

The migration of the labour force, which is primarily caused by the offer of stable employment and good promotion possibilities, is quite strong. The main agglomerations in particular achieve gains in labour force. If one leaves out the Rhine—Ruhr region as a special case because of its sectoral problems, then the border regions are the losers. Accordingly, this borderland constitutes the largest part of those areas whose economies are federally assisted. In 1962, nearly a quarter of all industrial employment was located in these assisted areas.

Surprisingly, assisted areas do better during the expansion and the following contraction of West German industry than the non-assisted areas. In contrast to the common view that assisted areas are the main losers in industrial contraction, these regions could increase their share of total industrial employment. Industrial employment in the assisted areas has in fact grown by 100,000 persons, (see Table 4.2). In comparison to the top year, 1970, they have experienced only a small loss. The explanation for this unexpected development is brought to light by an individual analysis. Those assisted areas which surround the main agglomerations, or are directly connected with them, experienced a particularly strong growth, for example, the northern region near Hamburg or the Middle—Rhine and the areas around Munich. By 1977, however, the classical assisted areas such as Nordhessen, West and Oberpfalz had lost what they had gained from 1962 to 1970.

Regional policy in the FRG

Quantitatively observed, the decentralisation of West German industry can surely be regarded as a political success. Whether the more favourable development in the assisted areas can be reduced to the influence

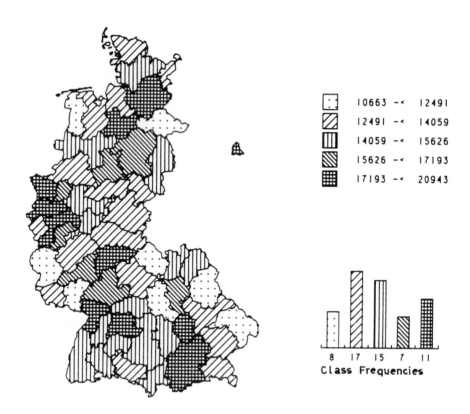

⋮	10663 -<	12491
▨	12491 -<	14059
▥	14059 -<	15626
▧	15626 -<	17193
▦	17193 -<	20943

8   17   15   7   11

Class Frequencies

Map 4.2   The regional structure of West German economy
          (GDP in DM per head (1974) by region)
Source: Bundesraumordnungsbericht 1980, p. 87

Table 4.2

The regional distribution of industrial employment
(in 1,000s)

	1962	1970	1977
All employment	8,348	8,672	7,632
of which:			
in assisted areas	2,123	2,670	2,235
	(25.4%)	(26.2%)	(29.3%)
in agglomerations	4,697	4,950	3,997
	(56.1%)	(57.1%)	(52.4%)

of the instruments of regional policy is a question which has not been definitely answered up to now.

In the FRG, the instruments of regional policy are essentially concentrated in two fields:

Direct assistance for establishments of industry and services in the form of investment aids as well as regional preferences for public supply contracts.
Indirect assistance by the improvement of the public infrastructure, for example the provision of industrial estates.

Since the end of the 1960s, the expenditure for these measures has amounted to nearly DM 2 thousand million for each year.

In spite of the volume of financial expenditure, some doubts persist as to the efficiency of these measures. One reason is that the measures consist only of incentives. Direct intervention in the entrepreneurial investment decision process is rejected for political reasons. On the other hand, it is argued that the incentives are not attractive enough to essentially influence the investment decision. First, the area in which investments are aided encompasses nearly 60 per cent of the whole area of the FRG (containing nearly one-third of the total population). Second, not all goods normall bought for investment are aided, so that the effective rate of subsidy is frequently much lower than the nominal value. Finally, the volume of regional subsidies is quite modest in comparison to other assistance, for example the assistance for new technology (DM 3.3 thousand million) or the subsidies for mining, housing, public transport and others whose benefits, above all, accrue to the agglomerations.

Methodological aspects of empirical investigations

Data basis

In the following survey the studies of industrial movement in the FRG will be classified according to the type of data used in the analysis. Three methods of recording form the basis for investigating industrial movement:

Annual recordings by the local labour agencies.
Recordings by the statistical offices (or other similar official institutions).
Special enquiries by research groups.

The records of the local labour agencies are the only ones which cover the whole area of the FRG. By the order of the federal labour agency (Bundesanstalt für Arbeit), each local agency collects information concerning the openings and closures of industrial plants in its own particular district and then transmits this information to the central agency.
The following plant features are registered:

The type of plant.
The sector of activity.
The year of opening or closure.
The 'Kreis' (district) where the (new) plant is located.
The 'Kreis' where − in the case of new branch plants − the parent plant is located or − in the case of relocation − the old location was vacated.
The number of employees: (a) for new plants, at the end of the year of opening; (b) for closed plants, the peak of employment in the last two years before closure.
The motives for opening or closure.

Besides closure, three types of new establishments are distinguished:

Relocation of a plant; that is the transfer of a plant to a new location while at the old location the premises are vacated.

Branch plant; that is the opening of a plant at a new location without closing down other existing plants of the company.

New creation; that is the opening of a plant associated with the creation of the company concerned.

Usually, only the first two types of opening are regarded and analysed as movements. However, one has to be aware that the distinction between the types of openings is not very clearly defined. In practice the classification of a move as a relocation, a branch plant or a new creation is left to the company concerned. Since in entrepreneurial language the term 'branch plant' has a rather narrow sense, one cannot ignore the fact that with large concerns when a new (subsidiary) company is simultaneously created, the opening of an additional plant is classified as a new creation. Likewise, with regard to international moves, most of the (first) plants of foreign companies are classified as new creations because in most cases a legally independent subsidiary was simultaneously created.

Up to 1963, only plants with more than 50 employees were registered. By 1964, the limit was lowered and plants with more than 10 employees were also recorded.

In 1977 and 1978 questionnaires were sent out to more than 8,000 plants to check the reliability of the annual record of labour agencies. The enquiry found out that the accuracy of the recording varied with the distance of move. More distant moves (crossing the border or district of a labour agency) were registered by more than 80 per cent, whereas moves of shorter distances were less completely recorded (BMA, 1981, p. 5). The reliability also depends on the density of a region. In centres of metropolitan areas the registration of openings seems to be less comprehensive than in the surrounding or peripheral areas.

More doubts concern the record of closure. In practice, a company cannot be compelled to announce the closure of its plant when the company is dissolved at the same time. Consequently, we must assume that the record contains only a small portion of all closures.

The records of statistical offices or other official institutions differ from those of labour agencies in several respects. First, they are not periodical, but usually done for special purposes only. Second, fewer features of the plants are asked — in general the recorded characteristics are restricted to the type of activity and the number of employees. Third, the registration of movement is usually based on an inventory of *resident* plants. While the records of labour agencies are based on the event of opening, the records of the statistical offices start from the resident plant which is asked for information about its opening, such as the year or the origin; consequently, plants which had been opened, but were closed down again before the enquiry, were not registered.

For the purpose of comprehensive studies of movement, the records of the statistical offices and of the other official institutions are of limited value. Since there is no common method for collecting this kind of data, the existing inventories of different parts of the country are seldom comparable.

Specific enquiries by research groups are even more disparate. In general, these enquiries do not aim at describing the number of migrations in a comprehensive way so much as at finding out either the causes or the consequences, or both, of industrial migration. Thus the recorded features as well as the temporal and regional scopes of the enquiries vary considerably from one study to another.

International investigations

In the last 20 years, the economy of the FRG has experienced a large increase in both exports and imports; thus, international flows of capital are of great importance on the national as well as regional level of the economy. For two groups of reasons, however, international migrations cannot be discussed in this chapter.

The first group concerns movement out of the FRG. There is a large number of studies analysing direct investment in foreign countries, but most of them discuss movement in pecuniary terms and not as moves of plants as is done here. As far as international locations of certain branches or of large concerns are investigated, no reference is made to the regional structure of home locations, nor are the regional consequences analysed which the foreign engagement has for the home locations.

Second, as far as industrial movement into the FRG is concerned, only information about new foreign branch plant is available in the form of the labour agencies' records. Foreign branch plants, however, are only a small part of the whole picture. Studies of foreign multinational companies suggest that in most cases the way to new production facilities in the FRG leads either via the take-over of a West German company or via the foundation of a subsidiary firm. However, neither case of foreign engagement can be detected in the labour agencies' records. The second case will be classified as 'new creation' while the take-over will not appear on the record, provided no new plant is opened. When in addition to the existing plants a new establishment is created, it will be classified as a (German) branch plant.

National investigations

All national investigations which cover the whole area of the FRG are

104

based on the records of the labour agencies. Because of confidentiality, only the Bundesforschunganstalt für Landeskunde und Raumordnung (Federal Research Institute for Regional Planning) has direct access to these data. Thus, it is not surprising that the first exploitation of movement data was done at this institute (BMA, 1961). Several publications followed, the last of which appeared early in 1981. All these reports are more or less confined to describing industrial moves in the FRG and to illustrating the number as well as the sectoral and regional structure of moves.

The first study to make use of the available data for a more elaborate analysis was that by Joachimsen and Treuner (1967). In their investigation, they concentrate on the motives for the location of plants as stated in the records for the years 1955 to 1965. By expanding the data base by an additional enquiry, they tried to work out the locational factors determining locational decisions, with a view to finding out what towns in peripheral regions need in the way of locational equipment if they are to be industrialised. Taking this study as a starting point, Treuner (1970) analysed the migrations in more detail, using regression methods to discover sectoral, regional and cyclical influences on the locational choice of industries.

Other studies followed this line of analysis prepared by Treuner; for example Fleck et al. (1977) and Wittenberg (1978). In both studies the period of analysis was expanded to 1971. While Wittenberg intended to prove the influence of spatial characteristics on locational choice, Fleck used the statistical results to develop a stochastic model of the regional distribution of industry.

Using the same data base, Bade (1977, 1979) pursued another line of analysis. Proceeding on the results of large sectoral and spatial differences in industrial mobility, the first aim of his studies was to explain and prognosticate the number of moves generated in various areas. Using these estimations, he then proceeded to the second step; to forecast the number and type of new establishments in the destination areas.

Regional investigations

Similar to the national investigations, the regional studies mentioned in this section are based on data which cover the whole area of analysis. However, in contrast to the national investigations, the lower level of region is chosen because it offers better data facilities. Additional information is generally provided either about the type of industry or about origin and destination.

According to the purpose of the study, three types of analyses can be distinguished. The first just sets out to obtain a more reliable inventory of both industrial openings and closures by using data other than those of the labour agencies (IfM 1977a, b and 1981). The second type of analysis directly refers to the national studies of Joachimsen and Treuner (1967) and others in which the amount and structure of industrial migration is explained by the attractiveness of new locations. Strunz (1974) and Spanger and Treuner (1975a and b), analyse the role of infrastructure in the choice of new location in detail. On the basis of this study, Gee et al. (1980) additionally includes labour-market characteristics for explaining the attractiveness of the new locations. The third type of investigation is concerned with the consequences industrial movement has exerted on destination regions. Most interest is focused on employment created in the new locations; only Strassert and Fleck (1975) explicitly discuss the effects on private and public income.

Some articles are solely confined to the quantity of newly created employment, for example Strunz (1974) and Schliebe (1976). Other authors inquire into the cyclical stability of the jobs (Gerlach and Liepmann, 19722), as well as the structural stability and other qualitative aspects of the new plants (Holdt, 1974; Kohler and Reyher, 1975; Georgi and Giersch, 1977).

Special enquiries

Unlike national and regional investigations, special enquiries are not intended to give a comprehensive survey of industrial migration and movement. Usually based on a smaller sample, they are conducted by researchers wishing to study industrial mobility and migration in more detail.

Nearly 20 of such enquiries in the FRG are known, the first study dating from 1953 (Müller). While the national and most of the regional investigations are confined to recording openings and closures only, most of the special enquiries use the register of resident establishments as a sampling frame for their survey. Exceptions are Fürst and Zimmermann (1973), von Ballestrem (1974) and Freund and Zabel (1978), who proceed from records of openings.

To identify those establishments which have migrated and examine the factors of locational choice, either a questionnaire is sent out or interviews are held, or even both. Both methods of asking are equally frequent. When a questionnaire is used, the sample tends to be larger. Ruppert (1979) received 4,000 answers from resident establishments and Kreuter (1974) received 2,208.

Apart from Brede (1971), Fürst and Zimmermann (1973) and Ruppert (1979), all enquiries are explicitly limited to special areas. Most of the earlier studies deal with urban regions and discuss intra-urban changes of location of industry, in particular — Goebel (1955), May (1968), Grotz (1971), von Rohr (1975) and Thürauf (1975). More recent enquiries are more concerned with the peripheral regions and their problems — Wolf (1974), Dohrmann (1976), and Freund and Zabel (1978).

With respect to the aim of study, the analysis of locational factors dominates. Either firms which had changed their location are asked the reasons why they had selected their new location, or firms — regardless of whether they have moved or not — are questioned about important locational conditions. In some cases — Fürst and Zimmermann (1973), Wolf (1974), Freund and Zabel (1978) and Kaiser (1979) — the analysis of locational factors is expanded by discussing how policy instruments may concur with the locational demands. Some studies, too, deal with characteristics of decision-making, in particular Förtsch (1973), Fürst and Zimmermann (1973) and Freund and Zabel (1978); here again, conclusions about efficiency of policy instruments are made. Rather more seldom analysed are the consequences caused by a particular locational choice. If it is the case, then the effects on regional economy are treated above all (Wolf 1974, Dohrmann 1976 and Freund and Zabel 1978). Only in one case are the effects of the new location on the fortune of the establishments examined (Dohrmann 1976).

Volume and patterns of industrial movement

Volume of industrial movement 1964–79

According to the labour agencies' records, the total number of industrial moves in the FRG amounted to 5,136 between 1964 and 1979 (BMA, 1981, 1979 and 1977; Bade, 1981 and 1979). New branch plants clearly prevail; nearly two thirds (63 per cent) of total moves belong to this type.

In the course of time, a strong decline in the volume of industrial movement (as well as of creations) is observable (see Graph 4.2). In the first eight years of the total period, 1964 to 1971, 3,809 moves took place. In contrast, their number sharply decreased by nearly two thirds to 1,327 in the following eight years. New branch plants were affected most by the economic contraction since the beginning of the 1970s; their share in total movement barely exceeds the relocations, while in the 1960s new branch plants were twice as frequent as relocations. Somewhat surprisingly, the type of opening diminishing the

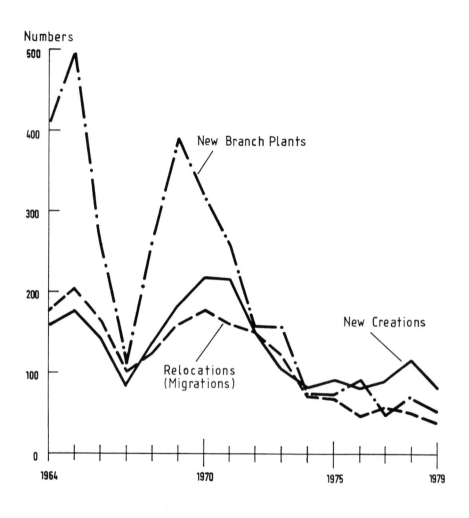

Graph 4.2   Temporal development of industrial movement

least is the new creation; its number decreased by only 42 per cent.

Table 4.3

New establishments in manufacturing industry
in the FRG 1964—79

| | 1964—79 | | 1964—71 | | 1972—79 | |
	No.	Per cent	No.	Per cent	No.	Per cent
Total new establishments	7,230	100.0	5,132	100.0	2,098	100.0
New creations	2,094	29.0	1,323	25.8	771	36.7
Total movement of which:	5,136	71.0	3,809	74.2	1,327	63.3
Relocations	1,888	26.1	1,282	25.0	606	28.9
Branch plants	3,248	44.9	2,527	49.2	721	71.5

Sectoral structure

Let us first turn our attention to the branch plants. Studying industrial movement by sector one finds that in the 1960s, a predominant proportion of new branch plants belonged to the clothing industry, namely, 26 per cent. The next largest groups, mechanical and electrical engineering, follow at some distance (11 per cent each). In the 1970s, the differences between industries diminished rapidly. In clothing alone, 545 fewer branch plants were set up, these being responsible for one-third of the total decrease in branch plants between the two periods. In particular those sectors which had an above average share in the 1960s were greatly reduced in the 1970s. As a result, the sectoral structure of new branch plants has become more uniform in the course of time (see Graph 4.3).

In respect to relocations, the temporal development of sectoral structure is similar. But, in contrast to branch plants, already in the earlier periods the differences between industries were not so large. The share of the leading industry (mechanical engineering) amounts to 17 per cent; the second (other metals) follows with 11 per cent.

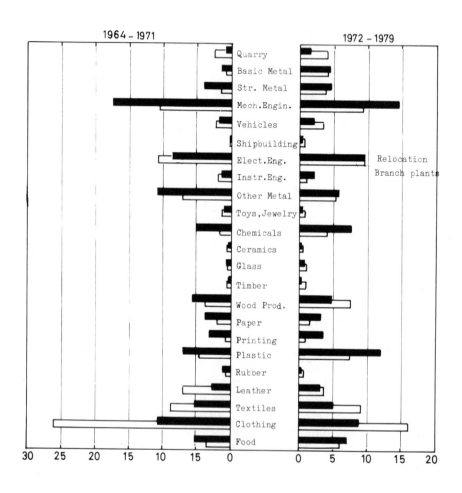

Quarry
Basic Metal
Str. Metal
Mech.Engin.
Vehicles
Shipbuilding
Elect.Eng.
Instr.Eng.
Other Metal
Toys,Jewelry
Chemicals
Ceramics
Glass
Timber
Wood Prod.
Paper
Printing
Plastic
Rubber
Leather
Textiles
Clothing
Food

Relocation
Branch plants

30 25 20 15 10 15 0   0 5 10 15 20

Graph 4.3   The sectoral structure of industrial movement in the FRG
            1964—79 (% of total)
Source: Bade (1981, p. 12)

110

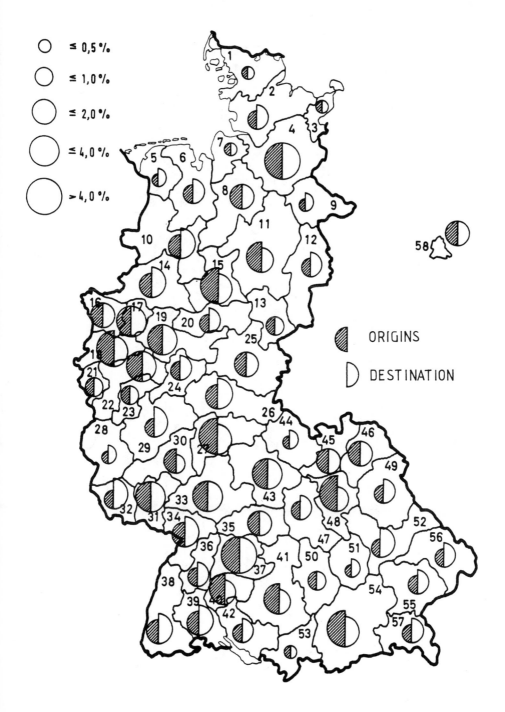

Map 4.3a Regional distribution of industrial movement 1964–71

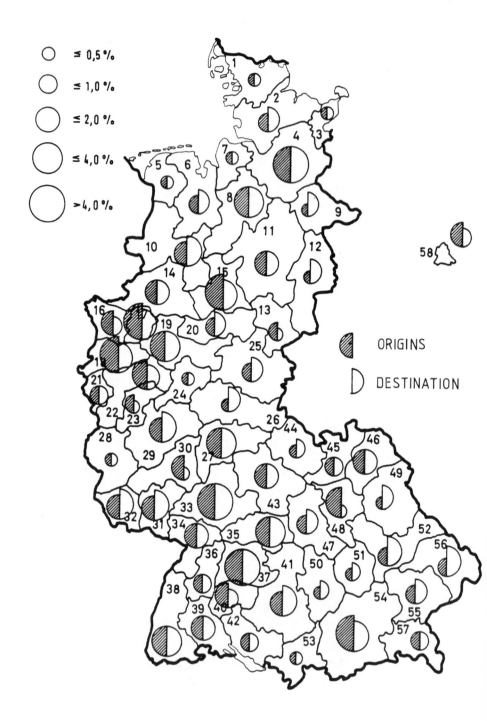

Map 4.3b Regional distribution of industrial movement 1972–79

Maps 4.3a and b show the regional distribution of movement in the two periods. Clearly, most moves have their origin in the central, industrialised regions, e.g. Hamburg (4), Essen (17), Düsseldorf (18), Dortmund (19), Frankfurt (27), Stuttgart (37) and München (54). On the other hand, the share of origins corresponds largely to the share of destinations in most regions, which is an indication that most moves are short-distance moves. In so far as both shares deviate, there is a tendency for central regions to have a somewhat lower share in total destinations than in total origins. Conversely, in the more peripheral regions, relatively more new plants were set up in relation to the volume of moves originating there.

Differentiated by type of region, this tendency can be observed more clearly. Between 1964 and 1971, more than half of all moves (52 per cent) have their origin in one of the eleven agglomerations shown in Map 4.1 (in the period 1972–79 the per centage even increased to 59), while only 32 per cent of all moving plants were located in these agglomerations. There are deviations with respect to type of new plant as well as to period of time. Migration (relocation) occurs more frequently in agglomerations than the creation of new branch plants; the share of relocations originating in agglomerations is higher (60 per cent) than the corresponding share of branch plants (48 per cent). That tendency is even stronger in respect to destination. Only a quarter of all new branch plants settled in agglomerations, while the share of relocations amounts to 47 per cent (see Table 4.4).

Confronted with a high proportion of moves originating in agglomerations, the proportion of moves into one of the agglomerations may be surprising at first glance. The reason, however, is rather simple; a large portion of the moves remain within the border of their agglomerations (43 per cent), since, in general, the new plants are sited near their original location. That tendency is shown in Graph 4.4. Half of total relocations were transferred within a distance of 15 km (nearly 10 miles), three-quarters covered a distance of less than 34 km (21 miles); only 10 per cent went further than 100 km (62 miles). The distances covered by branch plants are a little larger: half of them remained within 35 km (22 miles), three-quarters within 100 km (62 miles) and 10 per cent of total branch plants were established more than 230 km (143 miles) away.

In the 1970s the preference for both the agglomerations and the shorter distances increased. 59 per cent of all migrations had their origin in one of the eleven agglomerations. Since half of them (50 per cent) remained in their agglomeration, the share of destinations increased to 39 per cent. Relocations in particular are responsible for

113

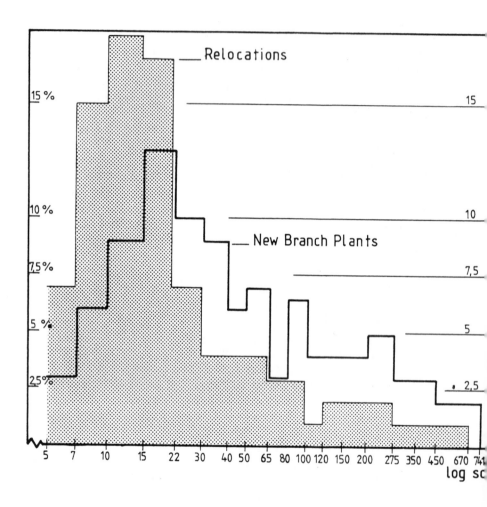

Graph 4.4 The distance between old and new location 1964—71
Source: Bade, 1979, p. 123.

114

Table 4.4

Origin and destination of industrial migration (1964–79)

	Origin				Destination			
	1964–71		1972–79[a]		1964–71		1972–79[a]	
	abs.	rel. (%)	abs.	rel. (%)	abs.	rel. (%)	abs.	rel. (%)
All moves								
agglomerations	1,979	52	557	59	1,206	32	373	39
remainder	1,830	48	393	41	2,603	68	577	61
Relocations								
agglomerations	768	60	315	69	607	47	243	53
remainder	514	40	140	31	675	53	212	47
New branch plants								
agglomerations	1,211	48	242	49	599	24	130	26
remainder	1,316	52	253	51	1,928	76	365	74

[a]only plants with more than 20 employees

Source: Bade, 1981, p. 13.

that change, agglomerations increasing their share in them as origins as well as destinations. In addition, the total volume of new branch plants (with their lower preference for agglomerations) decreased to a larger degree than relocations as is mentioned above. Consequently the overall share of migrations having their origin as well as their destination within the agglomerations increased in the second period.

To illustrate the change through time, the outflows of the five main agglomerations are shown by the following Maps 4.4 to 4.8. It is clearly seen that the preference for shorter moves has risen in the course of time. In particular, long distance moves are now rather rare.

Determinants of industrial movement

Motives

The kind of analysis mostly used in the studies mentioned in 'Methodological aspects of empirical investigations', is characterised by two features which have large consequences for the results of the investigations. First, the analysis of determinants is restricted to the essential

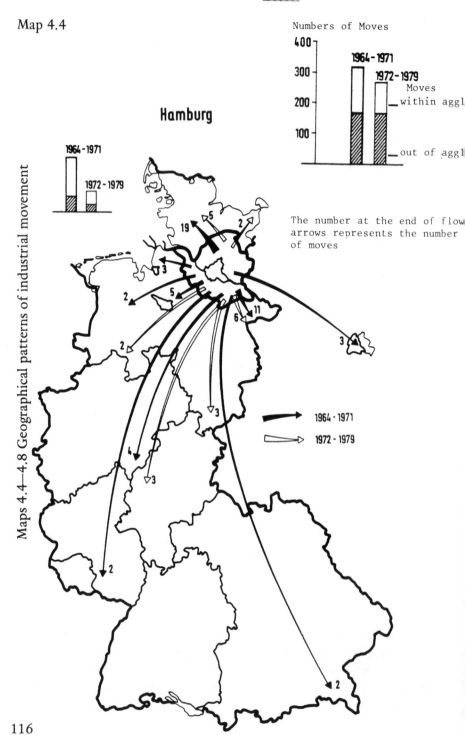

Legend

Map 4.4

Numbers of Moves

1964-1971

1972-1979

Moves
within aggl

out of aggl

The number at the end of flow
arrows represents the number
of moves

Hamburg

1964-1971

1972-1979

1964 - 1971

1972 - 1979

Maps 4.4—4.8 Geographical patterns of industrial movement

116

Map 4.5

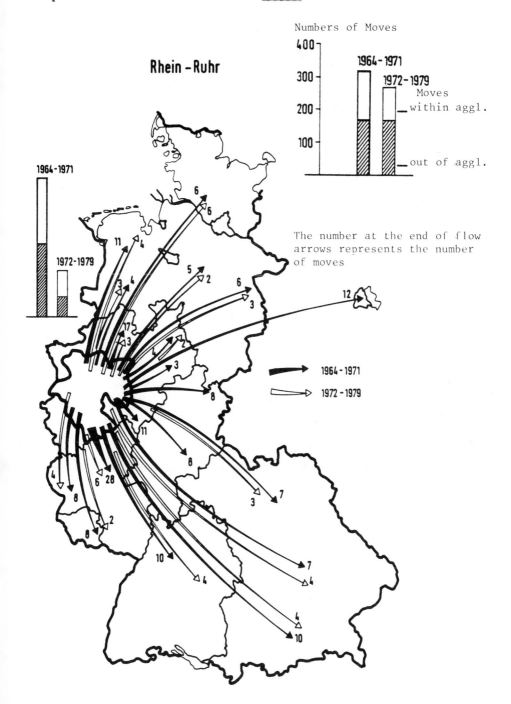

Legend

Rhein – Ruhr

Numbers of Moves

The number at the end of flow arrows represents the number of moves

1964 - 1971

1972 - 1979

Map 4.6

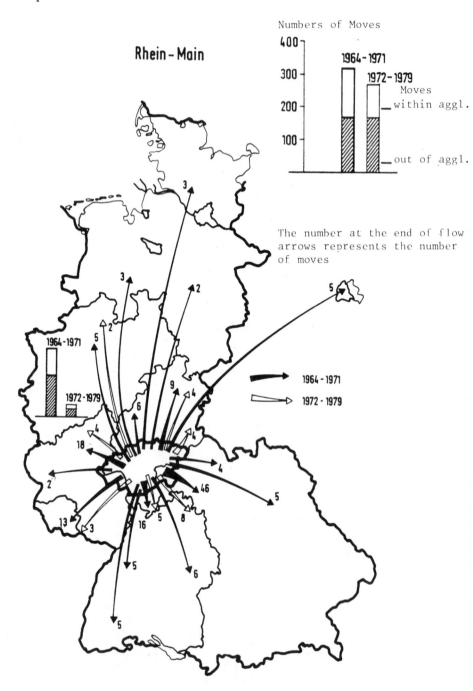

Rhein - Main

Numbers of Moves

1964-1971

1972-1979

Moves
within aggl.

out of aggl.

The number at the end of flow
arrows represents the number
of moves

1964 - 1971

1972 - 1979

1964-1971

1972-1979

Map 4.7

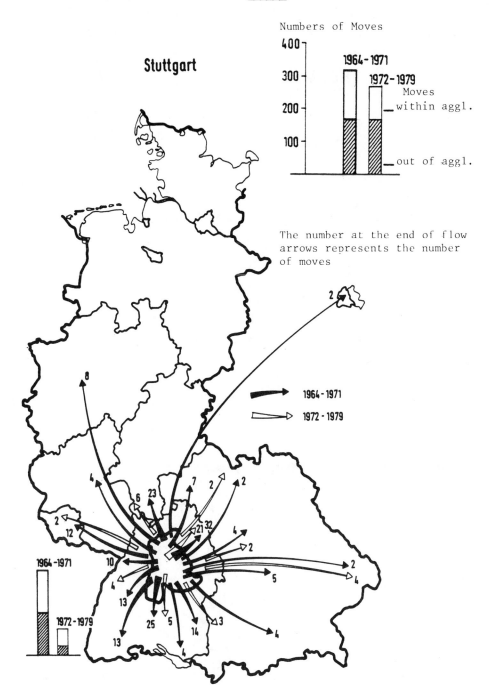

Legend

Numbers of Moves

Stuttgart

The number at the end of flow
arrows represents the number
of moves

Map 4.8

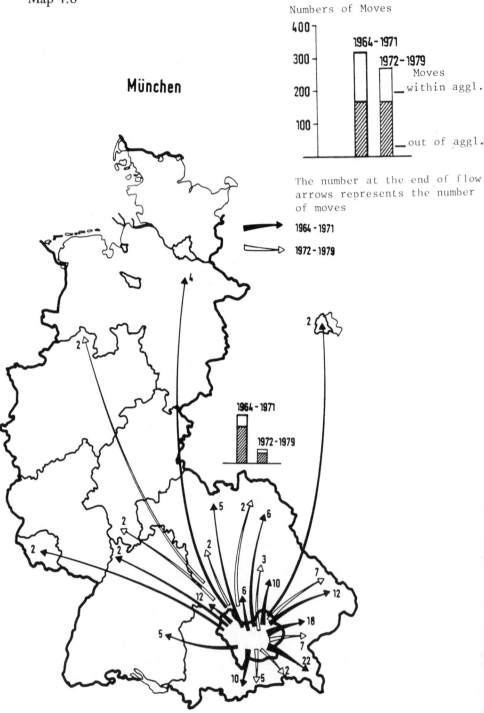

Legend

Numbers of Moves

München

The number at the end of flow
arrows represents the number
of moves

1964 - 1971
1972 - 1979

Table 4.5

The importance of locational factors: results of selected studies

	1968–69	BMA 1970–71	1972–79	Brede	Dohrmann	Freund and Zabel	Furst and Zimmermann	Gaebe
Number of respondents	?	?	?	912	53	36	346	32
First rank	space	labour	space	space	labour	space	transport	labour
Second rank	labour	space	labour	labour	space	transport	space	space
Third rank	transport and sales	transport and sales	transport and sales	sales	agglomerate economies	financial aids	labour	public infra-structure
Fourth rank	public aids	personal preferences	personal preferences	public aids	transport	labour	financial aids	transport
Fifth rank	personal preferences	public aids	public aids	transport	personal preferences	sales	industrial ambience	—

Table 4.5 (cont.)

	Grotz	Kaiser and Hoerner	Kreuter	Ruppert	Wolf	von Ballestrem and Förtsch	von Rohr
Number of respondents	?	125	2208	4000	164	283	165/220
First rank	labour	labour	labour	labour	space	space	space
Second rank	personal contacts	transport	space	space	labour	transport	labour
Third rank	space	space	transport	transport	other	labour	transport
Fourth rank	—	public infra-structure	take-over of premises	financial aids	financial aids	local contacts	financial aids
Fifth rank	—	sales and purchases	sales	pollution restrictions	sales	personal preferences	—

Note: For reasons of compatibility, the terms of factor used here assume physical as well as pecuniary aspects, e.g. 'labour' includes the availability of workforce and the level of wages, while 'transport' summarises accessibility and costs of transport; in addition, 'sales' comprehends facilities and proximity to sales markets.

reasons for selecting just that new location. Second, to explain the choice of location and to find out important factors of location, written or oral forms of enquiry are used. Firms are asked either for their highest locational preferences or — in the case of a move — for the factors determining the final choice. Table 4.5 gives a synopsis of results. Considering the number of those studies, the synopsis had to be somewhat arbitrary and selective and includes only the more recent studies.

As most of the studies accentuate different aspects of the factors of location and use particular definitions, it was necessary for the comparison to summarise them in more general terms. The table shows that in most of the studies, the factors 'labour', 'space' and 'transport' are most frequently cited, their ranking varying with each study.

Since the classical investigation of Katona and Morgan in 1952, it is conventional to distinguish between 'push' and 'pull' factors. Above all, the studies mentioned focus on 'pull' factors. As far as 'push' factors have been explicitly discussed, the emphasis is laid on the lack of space reserves impeding a necessary expansion of plant or preventing a necessary change of production (cf. for example Fürst and Zimmermann 1973, Kaiser and Hoerner 1980, p. 128). Only at first glance, however, does the distinction between 'push' and 'pull' factors seem highly important for the choice of location. Following Förtsch (1973, p. 112), Fürst and Zimmermann (1973, pp. 141f) or Kaiser (1979, p. 34), in reality the assessment of pull factors is strongly influenced by the push factors given at the old location insofar as a new location is sought in order to bypass the bottlenecks of the old one.

Another convention in analysing factors of locational choice is to differentiate between types of plants (or of firms). The assumption is that different types of plants show different locational preferences. Generally, the kind of opening (relocation, branch plant or new creation), the sector of activity and the size of plant, are considered to have an essential influence on the ranking of locational factors. According to Joachimsen and Treuner (1967, pp. 34ff), Brede (1971, pp. 63ff) or Fürst and Zimmermann (1973, p. 77) the availability of space has more importance for relocations, while for a large part of branch plants the cost and availability of labour dominate.

The influence of the industrial sector is not very marked; in addition, the results of different studies are not in full agreement. There is consensus about the fact that the three complexes of factors 'space', 'labour' and 'transport' are most important for each industry, but the ranking differs with the sector. According to Kaiser (1979, p. 81) there seem to be three relevant groups of sectors, the first consists of metal and structural metals manufacturing, mechanical engineering, vehicles and chemicals, which have a high preference for space and (somewhat lower) for labour, while transport is regarded as not so important.

The second group subsumes electrical and instrumental engineering as well as textiles and clothing. In these groups of industries, labour market characteristics clearly dominate. The last group comprehends timber and lumber, wood products, paper, printing and food, which highly estimate transport factors, including the proximity to sales markets, but consider labour aspects of minor value.

The size of plant only affects locational preferences to a small extent. If at all, then the importance of labour factors seem to be positively related to size of plant, while a negative relation exists to sales, smaller plants prefering proximity to sales markets to a higher degree than larger plants (Brede, 1971; Kreuter, 1974, pp. 326 ff).

Some points should be kept in mind when evaluating the results of these studies:

1 Methods of ranking differ greatly, as do definitions of locational factors. Moreover, the questions do not agree. In addition, the enquiries are always based on different samples of respondents, and the effects caused by different structures of respondents are rarely taken up in an explicit manner. For example, consider the above mentioned influences of types of plants on locational factors; none of the studies take all three effects — industry, type of opening, and size — simultaneously into account. Thus, it is not possible to judge if in reality the size effect is an effect of industry, and so forth. Moreover, the general conditions under which the choice is made seem to be important; for example, the year and the area of enquiry should be taken into account when results are compared (cf. the findings of Kreuter 1974 or Ruppert 1979, who get different results for a different period of time).

2 There is inconsistency between given opinions and revealed behaviour. One main reason for such inconsistency is that nearly half of all enquiries are not restricted to firms having just made a locational choice; other resident firms are also included in the question for locational preferences. Even in those studies where only firms having made a locational choice are interviewed, there may be interference if the choice was made some years ago and the reasons for decision had to be reconstructed (e.g. Kreuter, 1974 covers the whole period up to 1971 and Brede, 1971 asks for locational decisions between 1955 and 1967; most studies go back five years).

3 Another reason for inconsistency is caused by the inter-dependence of locational factors. The importance of one factor may depend upon the availability and existence of other locational factors, so that the overall weight of a group of factors is not the sum of individual weights. Often in these situations bottlenecks are particularly stressed

124

while obvious necessary locational conditions are not mentioned.

4 The inconsistency between questioned opinions and revealed behaviour can also be caused by neglecting the influence of the decision-making process on the importance of locational factors. Some factors may play an essential role in the early stage of locational search, e.g. when the new area is selected, but are of minor importance for the choice of site.

5 One last reason for inconsistency to be mentioned here lies in the two facts that opinions are necessarily subjective and that locational decisions, above all in larger firms, involve several people. If they have different opinions about the relevance of different factors, it is not clear which of these opinions is decisive. This personal influence is also important with respect to the above mentioned reconstruction of a locational choice analysed some years later.

Statistical analysis of new locations

In view of the problems associated with enquiries, some authors choose another way of investigating the reasons that determine the choice of new locations. With one exception (Dohrmann, 1976, who confronts the locational preferences expressed by the firms in his sample with the actual conditions of their locations) these investigations use nationally or regionally comprehensive data of industrial moves. Locational conditions of the area in question are examined in order to detect statistical relationships between the amount of new establishments and the locational characteristics of destination area and site.

A first step on this way is the analysis of destination areas according to type of area, as is shown in the section 'Volume and patterns of industrial movement'. Whatever delineation was chosen, all national studies came to the conclusion that nearly two-thirds of new plants were located in rural areas while the share of agglomerations was not more than one-fifth (Treuner, 1970; Bade, 1977, 1981; Wittenberg, 1978). That clear tendency to decentralise, however, oscillates in the course of time. Apparently the strength of decentralisation is dependent upon economic cycles. In the period 1955 to 1958, new plants favoured agglomerated areas to a higher degree than in the following years till 1965, when new branch plants above all were established in peripheral areas. In the period of recession of 1966 to 1967, the direction changed again, the share of new plants located in agglomerated areas increasing. By contrast, in the following period of growth 1968 to 1971, peripheral locations, especially those near the border of agglomerated areas, are preferred again (Wittenberg, 1978, p. 140).

Differentiated by type of plant, new branch plants show the highest preference for peripheral areas. In the case of new creations, no particular choice emerges, while relocations relatively favour agglomerated areas and their borders. Labour-intensive branches tend to open new plants in assisted areas (although financial aids consist of capital subsidies!), whereas capital intensive branches choose new locations in agglomerated areas (Treuner, 1970, pp. 50ff; Wittenberg, 1978, p.140). Similar relationships exist for the size of plant; the larger new plants with more than 500 employees are located, above average, in agglomerated areas, (Treuner, 1970, pp. 50ff; Wittenberg, 1978, p. 140).

The next step to analysing new locations is to explore the locational conditions of new locations in more depth. Wittenberg (1978, p. 141) finds out that the degree of centrality forms a minimum threshold for new locations, for the greater part of new plants were located in centres of middle or higher order. The role of infrastructure, especially the influence of transport facilities, has been examined by Spanger and Treuner (1975 a and b). Differentiating by sector and type of new plant, they detect strong statistical relationships between the availability of transport facilities in the local units analysed and the frequency of new plants. Four rather active industries in particular showed high correlation between their location choices and the index characterising the infrastructure of the locations. For the textile, clothing and wood-processing industries on the contrary, no strong relationship can be found, which may indicate the minor role infrastructure plays for these industries.

In addition, the influence of the size of the local unit (measured by the number of inhabitants) and of its economic structure is tested, but the results show no better correlation than produced by infrastructure alone. From this the authors conclude: '. . . that it is not the population size of a place, but its general equipment . . . which must be regarded as key factors (of location)', and they continue, '. . . that neither the common hypothesis that growth poles attract growth . . . nor the hypothesis that new industries have a tendency to settle down where declining industries prevail . . . could be confirmed' (Spanger and Treuner, 1975b, p. 151).

The same type of analysis is applied by Gee et al. (1980). They make use of the same data base (new plants in Nordrhein-Westphalia, 1955 to 1971) but include additional information about labour-market characteristics of the spatial units in question. They come to the conclusion that as a rule industries prefer units whose employment structure is in agreement with their demand for qualified employees. That means that industries with highly qualified employees localise their new plants in areas of highly qualified employment, whereas industries with low demands for qualified labour prefer new locations in areas of low quality employment. Thus, in perspective of regional policy and in contrast to the above citation, taken from the earlier study, the authors come to the conclusion that industrial movement favours spatial segregation between low and highly qualified employment (Gee et al., 1980, p. 153).

Deciding about the choice of location

Only few studies are known which explicitly examine entrepreneurial decision-making on their own empirical data base (Förtsch, 1973; von Ballestrem, 1974; Fürst and Zimmermann, 1973; Freund and Zabel, 1978). Their common starting point is the conviction that in view of the neoclassical idea of homo oeconomicus, traditional location theories are not soundly based on reality, and that in reality another kind of behaviour is observed.

To sum up in advance, one can state that in general the empirical findings do not differ very much from results gained in studies abroad. The more actual decision-making is taken into account, the more complex and intricate the results become; greater realism has resulted in loss of clarity and simplicity. No general comprehensive theory of location decision is discerned by which the old ideas of entrepreneurial behaviour can be replaced without having to abandon their clearness and easy handling. (Considering the state of sociological and psychological theories, one may even question that such a general theory is actually possible.)

Following Simon (1952) and others, the decision process is frequently divided into sequential phases, with the delineation of phases varying with the scope of investigation. Usually at least three separate phases are recognised: identification of the problem, search for alternative solutions, and final choice of solution. Most researchers, however, are aware that the separation of phases is only for the purpose of theoretical analysis. Once a problem has arisen there is no general obligatory sequence. The search for alternatives often has feed-backs to the identification of the problem as well as the choice of solution, which may influence the search of alternatives. Frequently, several phases occur simultaneously.

Two areas of investigation can be distinguished. These can be described by the following questions: (a) under what conditions is the existing location called into question and how has it become a decision problem? (b) given the decision problem, in what manner do companies react to the problem and how do they manage the problem and achieve a solution to it?

127

Most research efforts concentrate on the second problem area. Concerning the reasons why a new location is searched for (problem area one), the analysis is mostly restricted to locational conditions. Thus, in agreement with the importance of locational factors mentioned above, lack of labour and space are the decisive reasons for looking for an alternative location (Fürst and Zimmermann, 1973). The question is not asked how strong the lack of these factors has to be to induce the search for alternative locations. Nor are the determinants (e.g. organisational structure, personal preferences, characteristics of decision process) analysed which may influence the intensity necessary for calling the location into question. The only difference made is that with respect to type of new plant. Most empirical studies of locational choice indicate that lack of labour often results in establishing new branch plants, while lack of space tends to lead to relocation (Fürst and Zimmermann, 1973). More intuitively formed than empirically tested is the (plausible) assumption that in the case of most branch plants, the lacking (or very expensive) possibilities of expansion were decisive. The same holds for relocations, but in addition there are reasons which are not necessarily connected with the demand for expansion, such as the necessity of rationalisation and spatial concentration, strong increases in land prices, pollution controls, and so forth.

The second problem area has been explored more often. The central point of interest is the question of how the information about alternative locations is provided and how this information is processed. All authors agree that normal decision-making is 'suboptimal' (in the neoclassical sense) and that only those alternatives are chosen which are first to meet certain (minimum) demands of locational conditions.

The oft mentioned steps of location search — first area and then site — are not as common as assumed. If at all, the step-by-step method is only used in the case of branch plants. For relocations as well as for new creations, the choice of the new location is made directly from a list of alternative locations. This is because in most cases the macrolocation is self-evident, namely the home area (Fürst and Zimmermann, 1973).

The number of alternatives involved in the process of choice is not large; in half the decisions only one alternative was considered (Fürst and Zimmermann, 1973; von Ballestrem, 1974). The share of firms with only one alternative location even increases to 85 per cent when only the number of final alternatives is counted, i.e. those alternatives which form the base for the final decision (von Ballestrem, 1974). Differentiated by size of firms and by type of plant, more alternatives are considered by larger firms and in the case of new branch plants (Fürst and Zimmermann, 1973, p. 64).

This picture of companies which seem rather averse to information does not change very much in respect of the number of locational factors considered. Of all firms, 90 per cent had no more than five criteria upon which alternative locations are compared and the final choice is made (von Ballestrem, 1974). Deeper analysis shows, however, that behind this picture of apparently irrational behaviour lies quite a reasonable method to cope with the problem of locational choice. As a rule, it consists of a two-stage comparison: on the basis of a few dominant criteria (presumably strongly influenced by the push factors) a search is conducted for those locations which potentially come into consideration for the new plant. In general, the prime criteria are selected in such a way that only a few locations are left over for the next stage. Here, the prime criteria are replaced with generally more special and refined demands which determine the final choice.

The essential advantage of this two-stage procedure is that it allows short work to be made of the locational choice. More than half of all decisions are taken in less than half a year (Fürst and Zimmermann, 1973). Likewise, it helps to concentrate the efforts required for more sophisticated methods of comparison to a few locations. More than three-quarters of all respondents using calculation methods limited their calculations to three alternatives (von Ballestrem, 1974).

It must be borne in mind, however, that in the inquiries of Fürst and Zimmermann and von Ballestrem one-third of all respondents did *not* use calculation methods (cf. Bade, 1979, for the values of Fürst and Zimmermann). This — from a theoretical viewpoint — poor result does not improve when only large firms are considered. In the enquiry of Fürst and Zimmermann, for example, not more than 4 out of 68 large firms that were questioned, answered that they had compared the cost of investments for the different locations considered (cf. Bade, 1979, p. 169). More influence on the quality of method seems to be exerted by the type of move. For selecting the location of a new branch plant, calculation methods are more usual (Bade, 1979, p. 169).

A two-level model for explaining and forecasting industrial movement

Coming back to the determinants of industrial movement in the FRG, we will end this section with a report on an approach that differs considerably from the investigations discussed in the introduction. Their main characteristic was — to repeat it briefly — that they limit the exploration of the determinants of migration to the analysis of the choice of location, either by analysing the location of destination or indirectly by questioning the importance of locational factors. Apart from the remarks made in the section on 'Methodological aspects of empirical investigations' (concerning the possible interferences of enquiries of motives) this kind of analysis has the disadvantage that at best its results determine the necessary conditions a location must have in order to be attractive. Since necessary conditions need not be sufficient ones, the exclusive analysis of new locations cannot conclusively explain how many new plants will be established nor from where the new plants originate.

This consideration may be illustrated by an example of the study by Spanger and Treuner (1975a, b). They explain the number of new plants in a spatial unit by its degree of infrastructure: $A = f (I)$, and find a strong positive relationship. We know that since 1971, the end of their period of analysis, the level of infrastructure has largely increased, particularly with respect to the important transport facilities and to more peripheral areas. Consequently, we have to conclude from their results that the number of new plants must have risen in the last few years. In the section on 'Volume and patterns of industrial movement', however, we learned that in reality, the volume of industrial movement sharply decreased.

To bypass that deficiency, in Bade (1977 and 1979) an analysis approach is chosen which consists of two parts. In the first, the volume and origin of industrial movement is investigated, while in the second, the destination of moves is examined with respect to their origin. Since the second step does not differ too much from the statistical analysis by Treuner (1970) or Wittenberg (1978) and, necessarily, gets nearly the same results, emphasis in this section is given to the first step of the investigation.

The starting point for the first step is given by studies of entrepreneurial decision making (such as the enquiries mentioned above). They suggest that as a rule firms have a strong tendency to remain *in situ,* mobility, i.e. the willingness to change the location, being present only in situations of high pressure inspired e.g. by location-connected (but not necessarily location-caused) deficiencies which endanger the essential objectives of a firm. As long as the firm is more or less satisfied with conditions at the old locations, the habit of investing in the existing location(s) is not broken. With respect to the advantages of alternative locations, that means that in the 'normal' course of investment decisions, they will be left out of consideration.

Two components of influence constitute the primary reasons for firms to consider leaving their old location (see also Chapter 1). First, the intensity of locational deficiencies at the present site has a positive effect on the propensity to move. Second, certain plant- and firm-specific characteristics (determining the firm's mobility as defined in Chapter 1) may lower or increase the degree of stimuli necessary to make the decision to move. In principle, there is a third component of influence. The stimuli to move may, of course, have their origin in

130

the (differential) attraction of a new location (even if the old location has no major deficiencies); given the rather uniform spatial structure of the FRG, however, such differences in attraction are not very likely. Moreover, there is no change of location known where a strong push factor did not come into the picture.

In accordance with the importance attached to the above aspects in the studies of entrepreneurial behaviour, the aggregate analysis of industrial movement in the FRG is based on the assumption that the mobility of firms and the strength of the external influencing factors are decisive for the explanation of industrial movement. To find out what factors have a strong influence on the movement of industrial firms, the rate of movement, measured by the number of moves out of an area divided by the total number of plants resident in that area, has been calculated. The rate of movement is very different for different types of regions, as is shown in Table 4.6, which gives a division of the total set of moves into three categories according to the regions from which they originate: urban, sub-divided into core and ring, and rural.

Table 4.6

Rate of movement by type of area
1964—71 (0/00)

| | Urban regions | | | Rural areas |
	FRG[a]	Core	Ring	
All moves	66.3	114.7	33.5	46.7
Relocations	22.9	45.8	11.0	12.8
New branch plants	43.4	68.9	22.5	33.9

[a]without West Berlin

Source: Bade (1979, p. 11)

The division is relevant in as much as it shows the strength of push factors. Cores of urban areas show a rate of movement almost three times as high as the two other areas. The spatial difference increases to four to one if only relocations are considered.

The above picture is valid for all sectors of activity. As far as there are differences among industries, they seem associated with the corresponding share of all establishments resident in the core of an urban region. Establishments of industries with above average location in core areas have a relatively low rate of movement. If the industrial share of establishments located in core areas is interpreted as the result of locational affinities, then establishments preferring agglomeration locations – for example the printing industry – show a higher resistance to location change. That seems to be confirmed by the fact that these industries have an above average share of moving firms which coming from a core area settle again in the same core area.

Location deficiencies that have arisen in congested areas, however, are only one of the primary determinants of movement referred to above. Another main influence on the rate of movement emerges when the differences between industries (see Graph 4.5) are confronted with other sectoral characteristics. Such mobility-influencing variables as capital intensity, investment in fixed capital, and production capacity (in absolute terms or as growth rates, cf. Bade 1979, p. 140), do have some effect, but growth of industry, measured by employment changes, showed the strongest correlation with differences in rate of movement.

On the micro level, the influence of economic growth is easy to explain. On the one hand, growth of production aggravates locational bottlenecks; reversely, if production capacity is under-utilised, location deficiencies are felt less. On the other hand, the willingness to move is influenced by the risk involved in a move and by the strength of the firm to cope with that risk; both the risk and the strength depend strongly on economic growth (Bade, 1979).

As far as branch plants are concerned, in the period 1964–71 the relation between the growth of industries and their rate of movement was disturbed by some industries which show a relatively high rate of branch plant creation in comparison to their relocation rate, in particular clothing, textiles, leather, and electrical engineering. From the analysis of additional data concerning these sectors the impression is gained that special organisational and technical conditions obtaining for these sectors considerably diminish the complexity and uncertainty usually associated with the establishment of a new branch plant. In the 1960s, these industries – in response to demand pushes – founded additional production facilities with relative speed and without great cost commitments. The production of these branch plants was relatively routine, so that only unskilled and semi-skilled labour was needed. Accordingly, the new production units had no strong affiliation with their location; when the boom was over, most of them were closed down again.

In the period since 1972 things have changed, however. First, with the economy declining, the time for these extremely mobile branch plants, so-called 'extended work benches', was past. Second, the strong

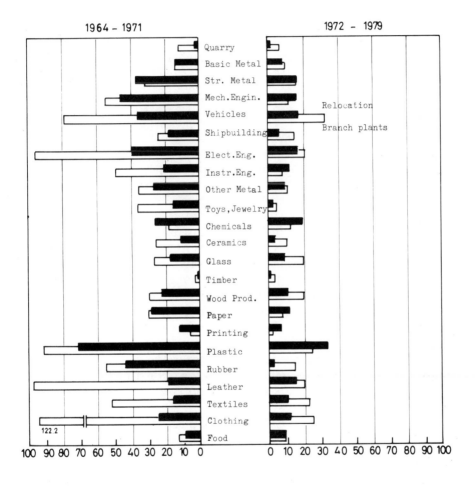

Graph 4.5   Sectoral differences in relative frequency of moves (moves for 1,000 resident plants) in the FRG, 1964—79

Source: Bade (1981, p. 3)

relation between growth and movement ceased to exist. Growth rates have become negative in most industries; the overall number of moves has sharply decreased, and the inter-industrial differences in rate of movement have become quite small and have ceased to vary according to growth rates. The cause of that development is obvious. In a period when all industries contract, it does not make much difference whether a particular industry declines by 10 or by 20 per cent, for in either case a move is unlikely. The process of decline has indeed strengthened the tendency to remain at the old location, as is shown by the decreased influence of locational deficiencies. In the 1970s, deficiencies have had to be much worse to produce the same number of moves as in the 1960s (Bade, 1981, pp. 34ff).

Regional effects of industrial movement

To what extent has industrial movement in the past helped to reduce regional disparities in the FRG? A first indication of the volume of industrial migration was given earlier. Table 4.7 shows, in addition, that even in the peak years 1964 and 1969 less than a half per cent of all existing jobs were redistributed by industrial movement.

While in 1964 more than 8 million persons were employed in manufacturing industry, the number of jobs created by the end of the year of establishment at the new location, did not go much beyond 36,000; in 1969 the number was 34,000. Since the middle of the 1970s the share of movement has even sunk below one per 1,000, reaching an absolute low of 5,761 redistributed jobs at the end of the decade.

But volume alone does not say very much about the extent to which industrial movement has produced a change in the regional structure of the West German economy. For the actual reduction in regional disparities the following facts are also important:

The direction of redistribution, i.e. the place from where the redistributed jobs moved and where they were moved.
How the new established plants developed at their new location.
The quality of the new jobs.

An answer to the first question is given by Maps 4.9a and b which, taking 58 regions, illustrate how important migrations are for the regional supply of jobs (Bade, 1978).

Only those establishments are taken into account whose origin or parent plant was in another region. The regions which achieved the highest gain in relation to total employment in all resident plants

Table 4.7

Employment in new industrial establishments[1] 1964–79

Year	All industrial establishments X 1,000	Relocations and new branch plants		Including new firm foundations	
	(1)	(2)	(3)	(4)	(5)
1964	8,301	36,263	0.44	42,819	0.52
1965	8,460	30,885	0.37	35,972	0.43
1966	8,385	21,851	0.26	25,945	0.31
1967	7,843	11,856	0.15	15,799	0.20
1968	7,899	25,175	0.32	33,902	0.43
1969	8,308	34,341	0.41	41,696	0.50
1970	8,603	33,250	0.39	42,548	0.49
1971	8,538	23,839	0.28	35,808	0.42
1972	8,340	17,517	0.21	22,062	0.26
1973	8,368	15,332	0.18	20,837	0.25
1974	8,144	9,652	0.12	13,179	0.16
1975	7,789	7,080	0.09	11,029	0.14
1976	7,698	6,979	0.09	9,043	0.12
1977	7,632	5,407	0.07	7,660	0.10
1978	7,584	5,956	0.08	10,357	0.14
1979	7,608	5,761	0.08	9,001	0.12

[1]measured at the end of the year of location

Source: Bade, 1981, p. 39

are, from the north to the south, Emden, Bremerhaven, Trier, Regensburg and Ansbach. There, the number of persons employed in new establishments between 1964 and 1971 (measured at the end of the year of location) is more than 7 per cent of total regional employment in manufacturing in 1970. The lowest values with less than a quarter of one per cent are those for Bielefeld, Düsseldorf, Stuttgart and Kempten. The maps show that a large part of the peripheral regions were favoured by the industrial movement. Conversely, most of the central agglomerations are below average. The reasons are obvious: first, most of the moves had their origin in one of the central regions, while the choice of a new location from outside into the central regions was seldom made. Second, the denominator of the ratio — employment in all resident plants — is much lower in the peripheral regions.

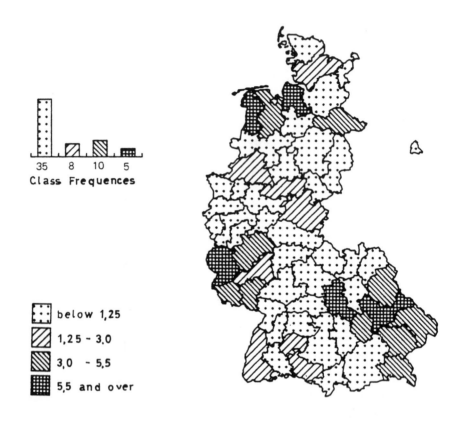

35 8 10 5
Class Frequences

below 1,25

1,25 - 3,0

3,0 - 5,5

5,5 and over

Map 4.9a Regional employment effects of industrial movement
(Share of industrial employment (%) due to movement 1964–71)
Source: Bade, 1978.

136

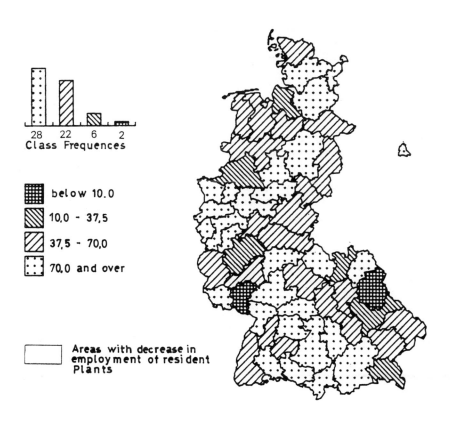

Map 4.9b Regional employment effects of industrial movement
(Share of increase in industrial employment (%) due to movement 1964–71)
Source: Bade, 1978.

If regional employment created by industrial movement is related to the total change in regional employment (cf. Map 4.9b), the importance of moves for the peripheral regions is further accentuated. With a few exceptions, its share amounts to more than one-third in the peripheral regions; i.e. one-third of the absolute increase in employment between 1964 and 1971 is due to inward movement.

Thus, the two maps give a relatively favourable picture of the inflow of employment produced in the peripheral regions by industrial moves between 1964 and 1971. However, as the numbers of employees in the new establishments are recorded only at the end of the year of establishment, these maps can only give a relatively crude idea.

More exact results, especially concerning employment growth in new establishments and the quality of the jobs provided in comparison to the resident plants require additional investigations, which are, however, available only for some regions, e.g. Oberpfalz, Lower Bavaria, parts of Hessen (assisted areas) and of Northrhine-Westphalia as well as for Saarland (Strunz, 1974; Gerlach and Liepmann, 1972; Kohler and Reyher, 1975; Wolf, 1974; Holdt, 1974; Giersch and Georgi, 1977). A detailed discussion of these studies is given in Bade (1978).

For all these regions it is shown that the regional supply of jobs would have been considerably lower without the employment in incoming plants. In fact, employment in resident plants suffered a considerable decline in the period of analysis. This decline was almost compensated by employment growth in new plants.

This quantitative evaluation requires some modification when quality of employment is taken into account. In this respect the new establishments in the different regions of analysis show different results. In Oberpfalz, Lower Bavaria and the assisted areas of Hessen, a large part of the new plants were of relatively low quality. Neither in respect of industrial structure nor in that of cyclical stability of the quality of jobs generated did the new establishments improve economic conditions in these regions. Non-durable goods industries (like textiles and clothing) were dominant. As a rule the new establishments were branch plants, which seemed to be a kind of cyclical buffer for the parent plants. Thus, the employment of the new establishments showed greater variations than that of the corresponding parent plant (Gerlach and Liepmann, 1972). A large part of the employment consisted of un- or semi-skilled female workers, and the shares of skilled salaried employees were below the sectoral average, which is anyhow relatively low compared to other industrial branches.

In Saarland, on the other hand, the new establishments did improve the industrial structure and regional income, despite a high share of branch plants. More than two-thirds of all new plants produced investment goods and showed themselves surprisingly stable in the recession of 1974—75. The shares of skilled and salaried employees were partly above the industrial average.

The differences between Saarland, on the one hand, and Oberpfalz, Lower Bavaria and Hessen, on the other hand, can presumably be explained to a large extent by the different periods of analysis. In Oberpfalz, Lower Bavaria and Hessen, establishments were only observed in the 1960s, while the analysis for Saarland included establishments up to 1975 as well. As was mentioned above, in the 1960s especially the non-durable goods industries showed extremely high mobility. By the contraction of the 1970s, however, the larger part of these branch plants were closed down and thus were omitted from the analysis for Saarland.

This explanation for the differences between the regional studies may also help to estimate how the industrial moves of the 1970s might be classified with regard to their effects on the regional structure of the economy. If the information available for industrial movement in the the 1970s is compared with the results of the regional studies and with the analysis of the 1960s given above, two great differences between the 1960s and 1970s can be observed. In quantitative terms, the moves of the 1970s have had considerably less influence on the regional structure of the economy. This is partly due to the fact that the total volume has decreased. In addition, the regional distribution has changed to the disadvantage of the peripheral regions as is shown on Map 4.4 to 4.8 above.

In qualitative terms, however, industrial movement seems to have changed positively. The industrial structure of moving plants has shifted in favour of industries with better chances of meeting international competition. Additionally, the time of 'extended work benches' seems to be over, as was mentioned earlier (cf. Freund and Zabel, 1978, pp. 59ff).

In the 1960s as well as in the 1970s, the larger part of new plants in the peripheral regions consisted of branch plants. The difficulty of evaluating this type of plant is caused by two aspects. On the one hand, the share of higher skilled employees in branch plants is, as a rule, lower than in parent plants. Thus, in most cases those activities estimated as critical for the development of the plant, for example the more important administration and decision functions of a firm, are concentrated at the parent plant. On the other hand, however, branch plants help to reinforce the industrial base of a regional economy by importing new capital and know-how. Moreover, it is suggested by some authors such as Pred, (1977), that the impulses of economic development have their origin in the central agglomerations. In that vision, branch plants have a specific importance for peripheral regions: they build up a stable organisational connection with the centres of growth and thus facilitate the regional diffusion of economic development.

Outlook

What can we expect from industrial movement in the future? The preceding analysis shows that there is a strong connection between general economic growth and volume of industrial movement. Therefore, given the mediocre prospects of the West German economy in the coming years it can be concluded that industrial movement will not return to the volume it had in the 1960s and early 1970s. In addition, the last section reveals that the effects industrial movement has had on the regional structure of the economy must be regarded as rather small. Consequently, there are no reasons to assume that industrial movement will play a major role in changing the location of the West German industry in the 1980s.

In what manner should regional policy react to the expected development? At present, in many political institutions, a departure from traditional political goals can be observed. The focus of political interest is no longer on the peripheral traditionally underdeveloped areas of the FRG but on some of the central agglomerations suffering from economic contraction, for example, the Rhine region. Because, internationally compared, the regional structure of the FRG seems to be quite favourable, the assistance of peripheral regions is now interpreted as a social goal which can not be afforded in times of economic pressure.

If one disregards this political development and holds to the traditional goal of taking work to the workers, then two conclusions can be drawn from the observation that industrial movement has decreased regional disparities only to a minor extent. First, the small influence of industrial movement on changes in regional structure stresses the importance of indigenous firms for the development of regional economy. Consequently, at least as much attention should be paid to the assistance and promotion of the indigenous potential of a region as to the attraction of new firms.

Second, given the distinction between these two kinds of addressees of political instruments, the preceding analysis has shown that the traditional instrument of capital subsidies does not seem very appropriate for inducing industrial movement and attracting new firms to the peripheral regions. Given the strong preference of firms to remain *in situ*, one can assume that only high subsidies which are concentrated on a few strategic locations are able to attract new firms. At present, incentives are also offered in areas touching the main agglomerations of the FRG.

Likewise, capital subsidies alone do not seem to be very helpful for increasing the effectiveness of indigenous firms and their capabilities to adopt economic changes. Actually, subsidies were given to all investment in manufacturing sectors without any hard restrictions. Thus, the allocation of subsidies tends to retain old production structures rather than promote the modernisation of the regional economy.

To discuss the appropriateness of regional policy in detail is another topic which can not be dealt with here. However, to sum up the conclusions which can be drawn from the analysis of industrial movement, it is obvious that regional policy has to change its instruments if it is to make the most of its possibilities of influence.

Above all, a differentiation of instruments for the group of addressees is urgent. Attracting new firms needs other measures than promoting the economic adaptability of indigenous firms; neither kind of measure is comparable to a general subsidy of investment.

References

Bade, Franz-Josef (1977), *Die Mobilität industrieller Betriebe,* Berlin, (International Institute of Management, Science Centre Berlin, IIM/dp 77—14).

Bade, Franz-Josef (1978), 'Der Beitrag von Standortveränderungen zum Abbau regionaler Unterschiede' in *Informationen zur Raumentwicklung,* pp. 555—568.

Bade, Franz-Josef (1979), *Die Mobilität von Industriebetrieben,* Meisenheim/Glan.

Bade, Franz-Josef (1981), *Industrial Migration in the Federal Republic of Germany between 1960 and 1980,* Berlin (International Institute of Management, Science Centre Berlin, IIM/dp 81—10).

Ballestrem, Ferdinand Graf von (1974), *Standortwahl von Unternehmen und Industriepolitik,* Berlin (Finanzwissenschaftliche Forschungsarbeiten, N.F., H.44).

Ballestrem, Ferdinand Graf von, and Niessen, Hans-Joachim (1975), 'Standortentscheidungen und Ansiedlungswerbung' in *Standort-Marketing,* (ed.) by Nieland, Manfred, Essen pp. 93—141 (Siedlungsverband Ruhrkohlenbezirk).

BMA (Bundesminister für Arbeit und Sozialordnung) (1961, 1964, 1967, 1968, 1971, 1973, 1975, 1977, 1979 and 1981), (ed.) *Die Standortwahl der Industriebetriebe in der Bundesrepublik Deutschland und Berlin (West), bearbeitet in der Bundesforschungsanstalt für Landeskunde und Raumordnung,* Bonn.

Brede, Helmut (1971), *Bestimmungsfaktoren industrieller Standorte,*

Berlin (Schriftenreihe des Ifo-Institutes für Wirtschaftsforschung, Nr. 75).

Bundesminister für Raumordnung, Bauwesen und Städtebau, Sachverständigenrates (1980), in Zusammenarbeit mit der Bundesforschungsanstalt für Landeskunde und Raumordnung (ed.), *Raumordnungsbericht 1980 und Materalien*, Schriftenreihe "Raumordnung" Bd. 06.040, Bonn.

DIW (1980) Abschwächung der Wachstumsimpulse, Strukturberichterstattung 1980, Gutachten im Auftrage des Bundesministers für Wirtschaft, Berlin.

Dohrmann, Jörg (1976), *Empirische Ermittlung der Standortfaktoren im Unternehmerkalkül,* Bremen (thesis).

Fleck, Werner, Strassert, Günter and Treuner, Peter (1977), *Analyse und Prognose von Neuerrichtungen (Verlagerungen, Neu- und Zweigbetriebsgründungen in der Industrie),* Berlin (Internationales Institut für Management und Verwaltung, dp/75—82).

Förtsch, Hans-Jürgen (1973), *Industriestandorttheorie als Verhaltenstheorie,* Köln (thesis).

Freund, Ulrich and Zabel, Gerhard (1978), *Regionale Wirkungen der Wirtschaftsstrukturförderung,* Bonn (Schriftenreihe "Raumordnung" des Bundesministers für Raumordnung, Bauwesen und Städtebau, 06.023).

Freund, Ulrich and Zabel, Gerhard (1978), 'Zur Effizienz der regionalpolitischen Industrieförderung in der Bundesrepublik Deutschland' in *Raumforschung und Raumordnung,* 36. Jg., pp. 99—106.

Fürst, Dietrich and Zimmermann, Klaus (1973), *Standortwahl industrieller Unternehmen,* Bonn (Schriftenreihe der Gesellschaft für Regionale Strukturentwicklung Bd. 1).

Gaebe, Wolf (1978), 'Erklärungsversuche industrieller Standortenscheidungen' in *Seminarberichte 1977 der Gesellschaft für Regionalforschung* 13, pp. 161—184.

Gee, Colin, Keller, Ulrike and Treuner, Peter (1980), *Infrastrukturelle und Wirtschaftsstrukturelle Bestimmungsgründe der industriellen Standortwahl,* Stuttgart (IREUS-Schriftenreihe des Instituts für Raumordnung und Entwicklungsplanung, Bd. 4).

Georgi, Hanspeter and Giersch, Volker (1977), *Neue Betriebe an der Saar,* Saarbrücken (Staatskanzlei der Regierung des Saarlandes und Industrie- und Handelskammer Saarbrücken).

Gerlach, Knut and Liepmann, Peter (1972), 'Konjunkturelle Aspekte der Industrialisierung peripherer Regionen — dargestellt am Beispiel des ostbayerischen Regierungsbezirks Oberpfalz' in *Jahrbuch für Nationalökonomie und Statistik* 187, pp. 1—21.

Goebel, R. (1955), 'Die Standorterfordernisse von Klein- und Mittelbetrieben in der Großstadt Kiel', Kiel (Ms.).

Grotz, Reinhold (1971), *Entwicklung, Struktur und Dynamik der Industrie im Wirtschaftsraum Stuttgart,* Stuttgart (Stuttgarter Geographische Studien Bd. 82).

Hengstenberg, R. (1956), 'Industriebetriebe im ländlichen Raum' in *Der ländliche Raum als Standort industrieller Fertigung,* Köln pp. 93ff (Forschungsberichte des Landes Nordrhein-Westfalen, Nr. 677).

Holat, Wolfram (1974), 'Industrieansiedlungs förderung als Instrument der Regionalpolitik', Münster.

IfM (Institut für Mittelstandsforschung, Forschungsgruppe Bonn) (1977), *Analyse der An- und Abmeldungen gewerblicher Arbeitsstätten in Bayern 1963–1975,* H. 27, Bonn.

IfM (Institut für Mittelstandsforschung, Forschungsgruppe Bonn)(1977), *Analyse der Gewerbean- und abmeldungen im Saarland 1963–1975,* H. 28, Bonn.

IfM (Institut für Mittelstandsforschung, Forschungsgruppe Bonn) (1981), *Analyse der Zu- und Abgänge der Betriebe und Beschäftigten in Rheinland-Pfalz 1962–1980,* Bd. 58, Bonn.

Joachimsen, Reimut and Treuner, Peter, (1967), *Zentrale Orte in ländlichen Räumen,* Bad Godesberg (Bundesforschungsanstalt für Landeskunde und Raumordnung).

Kaiser, Karl-Heinz (1979), *Industrielle Standortfaktoren und Betriebstypenbildung,* Berlin.

Kaiser, Karl-Heinz and Hoerner, Ludwig (1980), 'Zum Standort der Industriebetriebe' in *Wirtschaft und kommunale Wirtschaftspolitik in der Stadtregion,* ed. by Szyperski, Norbert et al., Stuttgart, pp. 115–35.

Katona, George and Morgan, James N. (1952) 'The Quantitative Study of Factors Determining Business Decision' in *Quarterly Journal of Economics,* vol. 62, pp. 67–90.

Kohler, Hans and Reyher, Lutz (1975), *Zu den Auswirkungen von Förderungsmaßnahmen auf dem Arbeitsmarkt des Regierungsbezirks Niederbayern nach kreisfreien Städten, Landkreisen und Arbeitsamtsbezirken,* Nürnberg (Institut für Arbeitsmarkt- und Berufsforschung der Bundesanstalt für Arbeit, Beitrag 6).

Kreuter, Hansheinz, (1974), *Industrielle Standortaffinität und regionalpolitische Standortlenkung,* Berlin, (Schriftenreihe zur Industrie- und Entwicklungspolitik, Bd. 13).

May, H.-D. (1968), *Junge Industrialisierungstendenzen im Untermaingebiet unter besonderer Berücksichtigung der Betriebsverlagerungen aus Frankfurt am Main,* Frankfurt (Rhein-Mainisch Forschungen H. 65).

Müller, W. (1953), 'Untersuchung über Struktur und Standort von Industriegründungen in Niedersachsen in der Zeit von 1939 bis 1951, in *Neues Archiv für Niedersachsen,* pp. 11ff.

Olbert, Gerd, (1976), 'Der Standortentscheidungsprozess in der industriellen Unternehmung', Würzburg (Diss.).

Pred, Allan (1977), *City Systems in Advanced Economies*, London.

Rohr, G. von (1975), 'Der Prozeß der Industriesuburbanisierung' in *Beiträge zum Problem der Suburbanisierung*, Hannover, pp. 95—121 (Forschungs- und Sitzungsberichte der Akademie für Raumforschung und Landesplanung, Bd. 108).

Ruppert, Wolfgang (1979), 'Produktionsstandorte der Industrie im Urteil der Unternehmen' in *IFO-Schnelldienst*, pp. 7—15.

Sachverständigenrates (1980), Jahresgutachten 1980/81, Stuttgart.

Schliebe, Klaus (1976), 'Wirtschaftsentwicklung und Industrieansiedlungen in Baden-Württemberg von 1961 bis 1970' in *Geographische Rundschau*, H. 1, pp. 5—13.

Schliebe, Klaus (1979), 'Zum Standortwahlverhalten der Industriebetriebe' in *Informationen zur Raumentwicklung*, H. 6, pp. 351—62.

Schliebe, Klaus and Hillesheim, Dieter (1980), 'Das Standortwahlverhalten neuerrichteter und verlagerter Industriebetriebe im Zeitraum 1972 bis 1979' in *Informationen zur Raumentwicklung*, H. 11, pp. 611—33.

Simon, H.A. (1952), 'A behavioral model of rational choice' *Quarterly Journal of Economics*, vol. 69, pp. 99—108.

Spanger, Uwe and Treuner, Peter (1975), *Standortwahl der Industriebetriebe in Nordrhein-Westfalen 1955—1971*, Dortmund (Schriftenreihe Landes- und Stadtentwicklungsforschung des Landes Nordhein-Westfalen, Bd. 1.003).

Spanger, Uwe and Treuner, Peter (1975), 'Statistical Analysis of Location Determinants' in *Papers of the Regional Science Association* 35, pp. 143—56.

Spehl, Harald, Töpfer, Klaus and Töpfer, Peter (1975), *Folgewirkungen von Industrieansiedlungen*, Bonn (Schriftenreihe der Gesellschaft für Regionale Strukturentwicklung, Bd. 3).

Strassert, Günter and Fleck, Werner (1975), 'Fallstudie Saarlouis/Saar zu den regionalen Auswirkungen neuerrichteter Industriebetriebe' in *Beiträge zur Raumplanung in Hessen/Rheinland-Pfalz/Saarland* 2. Teil, Hannover (Forschungs- und Sitzungsberichte der Akademie für Raumforschung und Landesplanung, Bd. 100).

Strunz, Joachim (1974), *Die Industrieansiedlungen in der Oberpfalz in den Jahren 1957—1966*, Regensburg (Regensburger Geographische Schriften, Heft 4).

Treuner, Peter (1970), 'Untersuchungen zur Standortwahl der Industriebetriebe in der BRD 1955—67', Kiel, mimeo.

Thürauf, Gerhard (1975), *Industriestandorte in der Region München*, München (Münchner Studien sur Sozial- und Wirtschaftsgeographic, bd. 16).

Wittenberg, Wilfried (1978), *Neuerrichtete Industriebetriebe in der Bundesrepublik Deutschland 1955—1971*, Giessen (Giessener Geographische Schriften, H. 44).

Wolf, Folkwin (1974), *Effizienz und Erfolgskontrolle der regionalen Wirtschaftsförderung*, Wiesbaden (Hessische Landesentwicklungs- und Treuhandgesellschaft).

5 Italy
R. P. CAMAGNI

The spatial dimension of national growth (1951–80)

In a space-time dimension, economic growth takes place in long historical waves. Underneath the long-run cycles of concentration and dispersion, different and contrasting forces are at work; aggregate indicators cannot capture more than the algebraic balance of these forces.
The main phenomena determining their relative strength are the long
waves of innovation and imitation, the characteristics of technical and
organisational progress, the features and the relative power of the social
classes on the labour market.

Forces pushing towards the spatial concentration of economic growth
are scale and agglomeration economies, the centripetal propensity of
primary innovations, the spatially conservative character of the learning-
by-doing process. On the other hand, the spreading forces are based on
the physiological processes of imitation and diffusion of technological
and organisational models, the hierarchical distribution of the various
productive functions, the system of cities and the differentiated locational needs of the individual products in their life cycle, and the competitive search for cheaper production factors (Camagni and Cappellin,
1981). In each historical phase either tendency may prevail, though in
the long run we can identify a general trend towards increasing spatial
homogeneity due to the spread of cultural, educational, and organisational factors.

Spontaneous diffusion or concentration trends can be strengthened
by macro-economic or structural government policies: industrial re-

Map 5.1   Administrative division of Italy by region

structuring allowances, credit facilities to exports, a permanent under-valuation of the national currency are examples of measures likely to enhance the growth capacity of already industrialised regions.

After the Second World War centripetal and polarisation tendencies prevailed in Italy until the mid-1960s. Regions in the north-west above all profited from an extremely rapid economic growth which proceeded in the circularly cumulative way described by Myrdal (1957), and left other regions behind. The 'economic boom' was based on the import-ation of foreign technology and on the fact that wage rates were rising slower than productivity. The only really mobile production factor in those years was labour. Between 1951 and 1961, the towns of Milan and Turin grew about 31 per cent in population and 39 per cent in jobs.

As we can see from Tables 5.1 and 5.2, north-western regions suc-ceeded between 1954 and 1964 in maintaining their leading and domin-ating role in the national industry, in spite of the general development 'climate' of the country and the strong investment programme of state-owned enterprise in the south after 1960; in fact, they even managed to widen the gap between them and the central and southern regions, only some north-eastern regions being able to keep up with them, thanks to a strong autonomous industrialisation process in light sectors such as mechanical products (Emilia-Romagna) and textiles—clothing (Veneto).

The excessive speed rather than the absolute dimensions of the first post-war economic crisis (1964—65) brought the unbalanced evolution in Italy to a sudden stop. Rents and salaries, pushed up by chaotic urban growth combined with full employment in the congested areas of the north-west, for the first time engendered inflation (1963) and consequently a large deficit in the balance of payments (1964); the social cost of the 'anthropological revolution' caused by massive country-to-town migration began to give rise to social conflicts in most conges-ted areas. Since then, the north-western regions have never regained their status of the most dynamic regions. By contrast, the north-eastern regions, some central regions on the Adriatic coast, and Puglia showed the highest industrial-growth rates in the second half of the 1960s (Table 5.3). As a consequence, the overall disparity indexes began to show a downward tendency (Secchi, 1974) (Table 5.4).

The Mezzogiorno as a whole, however, did not benefit much from the trend reversal. A much undervalued fact is that, especially in the crisis of the mid-1960s, the local economic structure of the Mezzo-giorno faced rising competition from northern production: the new 'autostrada del sole' enabled northern firms to capture markets in the south, even in the light industrial sectors in which the Mezzogiorno was specialised and therefore, theoretically at any rate, was at an advan-tage: food, clothing, shoes and leather, textiles, wood and furniture.

Table 5.1

Gross regional product of Italian macro-regions
(per cent of national figures)

	Macro	1951	1954	1959	1964	1969	1974	1978
Total	NW	38.63	37.86	38.34	38.41	37.88	36.93	35.81
	NE	19.77	19.77	20.08	20.18	19.81	20.37	21.23
	C	18.78	19.36	19.31	19.07	19.44	19.03	19.67
	S	22.82	23.01	22.27	22.34	22.87	23.67	23.49
	Italy	100.00	100.00	100.00	100.00	100.00	100.00	100.00
Industry	NW	50.74	48.26	49.18	48.98	46.78	45.62	43.50
	NE	17.07	18.04	18.64	19.44	20.32	20.95	21.71
	C	16.57	16.69	16.36	15.32	15.74	15.91	16.71
	S	15.62	17.01	15.82	16.26	17.16	17.52	18.08
	Italy	100.00	100.00	100.00	100.00	100.00	100.00	100.00

Source: ISTAT, *Annuario di Contabilità Nazionale,* vol. 2 1974 and 1981

Table 5.2

Gross fixed investments in industry; Italian macro-regions
(per cent of national figures)

	51/54	55/59	60/64	65/69	70/74	75/79
NW	47.96	50.22	47.78	42.48	36.42	38.07
NE	20.07	18.79	16.50	17.50	18.68	20.42
C	16.69	14.77	12.56	14.37	12.81	14.30
S	15.28	16.22	23.16	25.65	32.09	27.21
Italy	100.00	100.00	100.00	100.00	100.00	100.00

Source: See Table 5.1

The Mezzogiorno trade balance in these sectors turned from a small surplus to a large deficit in the 1970s (Camagni, 1976), preventing any employment increase in these industrial sectors[1] (Giannola, 1977; Graziani, 1979). Another retarding mechanism hampering growth in the Mezzogiorno was the growth-pole experiment led by state-owned companies and an incentive policy favouring large capital-intensive investments. In the absence of more variant instruments of public intervention and of 'real' rather than just 'financial' incentives, self-sustained growth based on the local entrepreneurship proved impossible or extremely weak; on the other hand, the experiment with industrial poles did not generate the hoped-for linked activities. The southward migration of big plants inspired many scholars to such expressions as 'industrialisation without development' and 'cathedrals in the desert', but

Table 5.3

Gross regional product in industry 1963—74
(per cent of national figures)

	1963	1970	1978
Piemonte	14.87	13.74	13.17
Val d'Aosta	0.40	0.20	0.20
Liguria	4.67	3.85	3.13
Lombardia	29.76	28.22	26.93
Trentino A.A.	1.51	1.43	1.72
Veneto	7.27	8.05	8.29
Friuli—V.G.	2.13	2.21	2.31
Emilia—Romagna	8.07	8.30	9.31
Toscana	7.06	7.01	7.37
Lazio	5.43	5.84	5.69
Umbria	1.23	1.34	1.38
Marche	1.54	1.91	2.25
Campagnia	5.15	4.94	4.77
Abruzzi	1.06	0.90	1.51
Molise	0.20	0.20	0.30
Basilicata	0.40	0.60	0.80
Puglia	2.99	3.48	3.83
Calabria	1.14	1.47	1.13
Sicilia	3.69	3.93	3.76
Sardegna	1.29	1.70	1.88
Total	100.00	100.00	100.00

Source: ISTAT, 1974, 1981.   Unioncamere, 1973

reality in the short- and medium-run was often worse: the 'cathedrals', upsetting the local price structure of labour, land, and all commodities, actually *created* the desert. Small firms and traditional handicrafts were expelled from the town centres, the only places where they could find favourable locations, and, failing a public policy addressed to their specific problems, they often just disappeared (Camagni and Mazzocchi, 1976).

Table 5.4

Gross industrial product by person employed (GiP/P)
and private consumption per capita (PCP);
Italian macro-regions (Italy = 100)

		1951	1961	1971	1978
GiP/P	NW	119	123	115	112
	NE	93	97	101	107
	C	96	92	95	95
	S	68	66	75	76
	Italy	100	100	100	100
PC/P	NW	131	125	119	118
	NE	101	104	106	113
	C	109	112	112	107
	S	73	73	74	74
	Italy	100	100	100	100

Source: See Table 5.1

In the 1970s the situation changed once again (Map 5.2). The grave crisis of large firms after the 'hot autumn' of 1969, and the following five years of social conflict, after the oil crisis aggravated by the even worse financial and productive crisis of the system of state-owned enterprise, substantially reduced the southward migration of large plants. At the same time, however, small- and medium-sized firms profited increasingly from the depression among large plants and the favourable exchange-rate policy. Such firms, still present in the north-eastern region, were now spreading towards rural areas of advanced regions (such as Lombardia) and towards all central and southern regions of the Adriatic coast (Marche, Abruzzi, Molise, Puglia, and Basilicata). It was these last regions that, together with the two north-eastern regions Trentino Alto Adige and Emilia—Romagna, showed the highest industrial and total growth rates in the 1970s (Camagni and Cappellin, 1980).

Old industrial regions, in particular Liguria, showed weaker results. Their strategy is one of slow tertiarisation and of restructuring existing productions by raising the factors quality and productivity. No selective decentralisation or intersectoral reconversion is visible in this

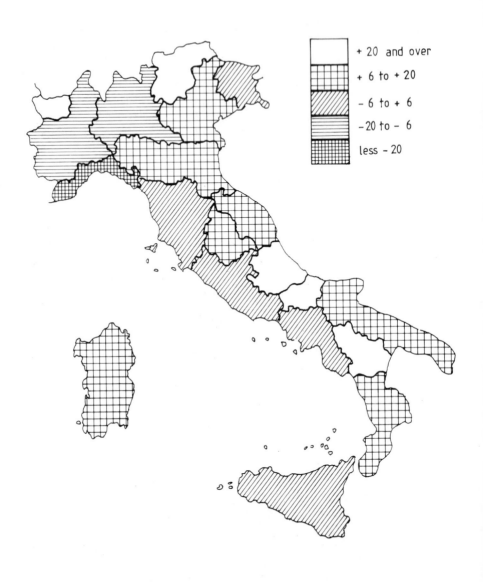

Map 5.2   Regional differential growth rates (1970–77) (current prices)
Source: Camagni and Cappellin, 1981

strategy, as almost *all* sectors, whether mature or modern, even some tertiary ones, are decentralised, and almost all of them, in particular the traditional ones, have been carried to very high productivity gains. Such trends bring to mind the 'equilibrated' or 'sectorally balanced' character of both growth and decline processes (Camagni and Cappellin, 1981), due to the intersectoral and horizontal impact of space variables on economic activity; in addition, they show the possibility of defensive answers to industrial change, as opposed to the 'pure' *filtering-down* of *product-cycle* hypothesis, expressed in the strategies followed — not only in Italy — in the last decade by 'strong' regions, strategies labelled 'industrial conservatism' (Camagni, 1980b).

An important role in these processes is played by the accumulation rate. The rapidly growing share of southern regions in national investments, and the parallel fast decrease in the share of north-western regions (Table 5.2) can be interpreted by means of a 'shift-share analysis' of the investment-to-product ratio of Italian regions in 1977[2]. The following elements emerge (Table 5.5).

1 In four southern regions (Puglia, Basilicata, Sicilia and Sardinia) the relatively high accumulation rate is explained partly by the sectoral composition of investments (Mix effect), but that effect accounts for only half the difference between the regional and the national accumulation rate (57 per cent on the average in the four regions), the other half being explained by a stronger investment process[3].

2 In all other regions, the sectoral composition of investments appears biased towards light productions, showing a clear-cut interregional 'division of labour'.

3 All the above mentioned fast growing regions of the so-called 'third Italy' show a positive differential in sectoral accumulation rates (DIF effect), or a low negative differential: Trentino, Friuli, Emilia, Marche, Abruzzi, Molise, together with, fortunately, two such problem regions as Calabria and Campania.

4 The deeply negative differential of sectoral accumulation rates in the three old industrial north-western regions is a sign of the locational disadvantage and the decentralisation process that characterises these regions nowadays, but can, in part at least, be interpreted as a tendency towards a more efficient use of the capital stock[4], thanks to faster technical and organisational progress, 'soft' investments in R and D and human capital, and selective attraction of the skilled labour-intensive functions within each sectoral production.

Thirty years of 'special intervention' have changed the Mezzogiorno

Table 5.5

Static shift-share analysis on the accumulation rate:
Italian regions (1977)*

	DIF	MIX	TOT
Piemonte- Val d'Aosta	-100	-164	-264
Liguria	-110	- 20	-130
Lombardia	-115	-169	-284
Trentino Alto Adige	32	-107	- 74
Veneto	- 88	-149	-237
Friuli-Venezia Giulia	98	-137	- 38
Emilia—Romagna	- 13	-110	-123
Marche	173	-253	- 80
Toscana	- 32	- 52	- 84
Umbria	-155	- 11	-166
Lazio	- 25	-140	-165
Campania	57	- 50	7
Abruzzi e Molise	45	-181	-136
Puglia	124	159	283
Basilicata	166	65	231
Calabria	40	- 38	2
Sicilia	31	106	137
Sardegna	120	272	393

* See notes 2 and 3 — thousands lire

considerably: some polarising processes begin to have effect around the
'cathedrals', and some local entrepreneurship is rising in many regions,
not just in 'traditional' sectors, but in virtually all branches of industry.
No longer does the Mezzogiorno appear as a solid block of underdeveloped areas, and even in regions like Calabria, Campania, and Sicilia,
where no real take-off has occurred, there are small but dynamic growth
areas. This new reality has been confirmed by many inquiries (Lizzeri,
1979; Cao-Pinna, 1979; Census, 1979; Camagni and Cappellin, 1980;
Saraceno, 1980), but is still not accepted by all scholars of the Italian
Mezzogiorno.

The industrial development of many southern areas in the late 1970s
appears completely different from the preceding one: it is based mainly
on local, autonomous companies, oriented to the domestic market. In
a period in which northern industry has almost completely stopped its
southward movement, and addresses itself mainly to foreign demand

(helped in that strategy by the progressive real devaluation of the national currency), southern industry is slowly strengthening its position on the local market, widely lost in the previous decade, for both final and intermediate productions; what remains lacking is local productive capacity of capital goods.

Three characteristics of regional growth emerge from the analysis of Italian as well as European regions: (a) the long-term character of economic growth, not allowing short cuts to faster growth (La Francesca, 1979); (b) the sectorally balanced character of both growth and decline, and the selective impact on different productive functions (direction, administration, manual operations, research); (c) the gradual spatial spread, touching neighbouring areas in succession along the main communication and transportation networks (Camagni and Cappellin, 1981).

To sum up: in the 1950s there was mainly labour migration; in the 1960s and early 1970s some movements of large plants and a southward movement of commodities occurred, while in the late 1970s, autonomous and dispersed growth prevailed.

Inventory of empirical investigations

Italy has no tradition of empirical studies of industrial migration and movement. That seems strange and even funny if one considers the historical nature of regional imbalances in this country and the great political efforts that have been made to equalise employment conditions among regions and make capital flow towards labour. Only recently have the public research institutes of certain northern regions promoted direct investigations into short-distance industrial relocation from the core of large metropolitan areas, but long-distance movement has not been studied at all.

Trying to figure out how such almost complete indifference to such an important problem could exist, I have found five main reasons:

1 The Mezzogiorno problem is a development rather than a simple location problem; therefore, it has been tackled in the past mostly with the tools supplied by the theory of economic development, and rarely with those used by regional scientists or economic geographers.
2 Because of the dramatic employment situation in the Mezzogiorno, the greatest concern has always been with the situation of acceptor regions rather than that in donor regions, while in studies of industrial movement political and scientific interest has been focused on the decentralising regions, or at best equally distributed between

155

them and the acceptor regions.

3 The debate of the 1960s about the effectiveness of alternative systems of public intervention and financial incentives was mainly carried on in highly abstract, institutional and micro-accounting terms (see the articles by Ackley and Dini, Coppola d'Anna, and Momigliano, now collected in Marzano, 1979); no macro-regional or micro-behavioural empirical test was made, partly because the information was lacking and the phenomenon itself was very weak, partly because the use of econometric methods for testing location factors is not quite convincing, and partly because Italians tend to deal with real and objective problems in a theoretical and abstract fashion.

4 Perhaps scholars have unconsciously shunned the problems of movement and migration for yet another, secret, ideological reason: everybody's main political concern was supposed to be how to help local entrepreneurship to spread and become stronger, the non-autonomous branch plants dependent on head offices in the north often being looked at as a sort of second best solution by decision-makers in the south. That might explain the scanty answers given to the question 'who are the owners of southern industry?'

5 The part of industrial movement known as 'relocation' has long remained an unimportant phenomenon; indeed, large plants still tend to remain in central cities, and Italy has not experienced really severe urban crises. In the past, cases of relocation mostly concerned small firms and small distances, and were resolved mainly within the same city borders.

Especially as far as point 5 is concerned, the situation is now rapidly changing, as firms find it more and more difficult to find suitable alternative locations, and local authorities are trying to encompass the phenomenon of relocation in their planning efforts.

As long-distance and short-distance movements have different economic and planning dimensions, we will devote a separate section to each. Because within each class of problems different kinds of analysis have to be applied with respect to objectives, dimensions, and statistical complexity, we will make a general presentation by homogeneous groups.

The most detailed information on the location of large plants in the Mezzogiorno is provided by the list of all southern establishments with more than 1,000 employees recently composed by Saraceno, the father of the 'special intervention' in the Mezzogiorno and one of the leading personalities of the 'new meridionalism' (Saraceno, 1980). For the express purpose of this investigation, an attempt has been made to map north—south industrial movement of the thirty-nine major industrial firms in different time periods, and to compare the results with such movements to other regions. Failing deeper and more specific information on industrial north—south movements, some other indication of the relative magnitude of our phenomenon can be found in reports on efforts to quantify external control of southern industry, both foreign and coming from other regions (Cassa per il Mezzogiorno, 1957 and 1972; Ferrara and Quirini, 1975; Cesan, 1978). More accurate information on the motivations of in-movers to choose a southern location is supplied by two interesting studies on foreign investment, the first made by Confindustria, 1971, and the second by Business International, 1974. Other analyses of local entrepreneurship in such specific areas as Sardegna, Latina, and Siracusa, may give some further insight into location factors, but their statistical methodology needs to be tested in detail (Sassu, 1980; Cafiero and Pizzorno, 1962).

A brief analysis will be devoted to the dynamics of investments by state-owned companies, which, thanks to precise legislation, have accounted for the greater part of southward industrial movement.

With respect to short-distance movements some very direct inquiries have been made in north-eastern regions: in Piemonte, Regione Piemonte, 1980; IRES, 1980b; Ortona, Parodi and Santagata, 1981; in Liguria, Federindustria Liguria, 1980, and a first inquiry in the Lombardy region, Regione Lombardia, 1981. Other studies (such as IRES, 1980a), based on the census and concerning large companies (with more than 50 employees) do not give much insight into the nature of the phenomenon, but allow a precise quantification of its dimensions. One study, in addition to a direct inquiry, tries a deeper analysis with the aid of more sophisticated statistical methods (Ortona and Santagata, 1980).

Long-distance industrial movement: the case of the Mezzogiorno

As previously stated, the overall panorama of empirical research into long-distance industrial movement is very poor. Let us divide the existing information according to its reference to foreign enterprise, national non-southern enterprise, and state enterprise.

The aggregate share in total regional industry of national non-southern companies has been investigated in different periods of time, unfortunately in different, not easily comparable, ways. According to the Cassa del Mezzogiorno (1957), of the *new* initiatives in terms of number of plants of the 1950—56 period 24 per cent could be ascribed to entrepreneurs coming from central and northern regions, 70 per cent to local entrepreneurs, 2 per cent to public companies, 0.7 per cent to foreign enterprise. In terms of total investments the shares are quite different: 44 per cent central and northern enterprise, 35 per cent local, and 18 per cent public enterprise. The last percentage drops to 11.5 per cent in terms of total output, owing to the capital intensity of state enterprise, while the share of local companies in total output rises to 41 per cent. From a second report of the Cassa (1972) we know that the share of *local* entrepreneurship had grown substantially in the late 1960s not perhaps so much in the number of new plants as in terms of total investment and new employment. In the 1966–70 period, the share of private national companies in total investment rises from 43 to 60 per cent; the share is even greater if we consider only the new plants built in the last year of the period, 1970 (81 per cent) or the investments planned for the subsequent 1971–75 period (72.5 per cent).

Another inquiry (Ferrara and Quirino, 1975) informs us about the 1970 employment in all plants located in industrial nuclei (50 per cent of total industrial employment in the Mezzogiorno). In terms of employment, the shares are divided 50–50 between local plants and extra-regionally owned plants (state-owned companies have their legal seats outside Mezzogiorno); in terms of plant units, however, the figure is different, local firms attaining 81 per cent of the total.

With regard to *ownership* the situation of firms with more than 20 employees in 1977 (CESAN, 1978) can be seen in Table 5.6.

Table 5.6

Number of firms and employment by ownership type 1977

	Local	Private national non-local	Public	Foreign	Total
Number of:					
plants	4,647	478	266	197	5,588
per cent	83.2	8.5	4.8	3.5	100.0
employment	267,272	127,598	152,445	61,239	608,554
per cent	43.9	21.0	25.0	10.1	100.0

Foreign companies often having their legal and administrative seats in the Mezzogiorno, we observe that the results of the studies by Ferrara and Quirino (1975) and CESAN (1978) are consistent, and that the positive trend of local entrepreneurship continued in the 1970s.

With respect to large plants only, the complete situation in the Mezzogiorno is represented in Table 5.7, which lists plants with over 1,000 employees by their first year of construction (Saraceno, 1980). Only one plant belongs to a local group (Acciaierie Pugliesi), while 23 plants accounting for 62 per cent of total employment depend on public groups; private national non-southern groups control 21 plants (out of 52) with 29.5 per cent of total employment, and foreign groups control seven plants with 7.2 per cent of total employment.

The *time* aspect of industrial movement towards the south is interesting as well. If the plant, regardless of its size, is taken as a unit, the situation is as represented in Table 5.8.

Table 5.8

Number of plants according to type of ownership

Time period	Public	Private non-local	Private local	Foreign	Total
Before 1950	7	2	1	1	11
1951—59	2	4	—	—	6
1960—64	9	4	—	5	18
1965—69	5	2	—	—	8
1970—74	—	8	—	—	8
after 1974	—	1	—	—	1
Total	23	21	1	6	52

The southward movement was most intense in the period from 1960 to 1964, thanks mainly to state-owned enterprise, but also thanks to the good image and confidence the country was enjoying abroad. To judge from new large initiatives, the intervention of state-owned enterprise had stopped by 1969; afterwards we had just some joint ventures with private capital, such as the Ottana plant (Anic—Montedison). Private initiatives, on the contrary, were flourishing especially in the 1970—75 period, which gives some support to the hypothesis of a precise decentralisation strategy of private capital, inspired by the search for a less unionised and less concentrated labour force in peripheral areas,

Table 5.7

Establishments in the Mezzogiorno with more than 1,000 employees by starting year of construction

Year	Location	Region	Company	Activity	Employment 1978	ownership
1783	Castellamare	Campania	Italcantieri	Shipbuilding	2,440	public
1850	Palermo	Sicilia	Cantieri Nav. Riuniti	Shipbuilding	3,610	public
1910	Napoli (Bagnoli)	Campania	Italsider	Iron and steel	7,800	public
1923	Giovinazzo	Puglia	Acciaierie Pugliesi	Iron and steel	1,200	private, local
1923	Napoli	Campania	Snia Viscosa	Rayon and polyesters	1,500	private, national
1928	Crotone	Calabria	Montedison	Phosphate fertilisers	1,000	private, national
1930	Napoli	Campania	Mecfond FMI	Presses, machinery	1,270	public
1934	Brindisi	Puglia	IAM (SACA)	Aerospatial	1,000	public
1937	Napoli	Campania	Mobil Oil	Refinery	1,050	foreign
1938	Napoli	Campania	Italtrafo	High-power transformers	1,190	public
1939	Napoli	Campania	Alfa Romeo	Industrial motor vehicles	2,990	public
1952	Bacoli	Campania	Selenia	Telecommunications appl.	2,150	public
1954	Napoli	Campania	Sebn	Shipbuilding	1,350	public
1955	Pozzuoli	Campania	Olivetti	Electronic appliances	2,000	private, national
1957	Priolo	Sicilia	Montedison	Petrochemical	6,500	private, national
1958	Salerno	Campania	Marzotto Sud	Apparel	1,490	private, national
1959	Brindisi	Puglia	Montedison	Petrochemical	4,400	private, national
1960	Marcianise	Campania	G.T.E.	Telecommunications appl.	1,650	foreign
1960	Sulmona	Abruzzi	ACE Adriat. Comp. Elet.	Electrical appliances	1,500	foreign
1961	Maddaloni	Campania	Face Standard	Telecommunications appl.	1,200	foreign
1961	Taranto	Puglia	Italsider	Iron and steel	20,780	public
1961	Catania	Sicilia	S.G.S.–ATES	Electronic appliances	2,100	public
1962	S.M. Capua Vetere	Campania	SIT–Siemens	Telecommunications appl.	4,670	public
1962	Gela	Sicilia	Anic	Chemicals	4,250	public
1962	Chieti	Abruzzo	Adriatica Confezioni	Apparel, linen	1,600	public
1962	Villafranca Tierrena	Sicilia	Pirelli	Tyres	1,450	private, national

Year	City	Company	Region	Product		Ownership
1962	Bari	Brema	Puglia	Tyres, rubber	1,350	foreign
1962	Assemini	Rumianca Sud	Sardegna	Petrochemical	1,100	private, national
1963	Palermo	SIT–Siemens	Sicilia	Telecommunications appl.	2,170	public
1963	Porto Torres	SIR–Alchisarda	Sardegna	Petrochemical	3,250	private, national
1963	Pisticci	Anic	Basilicata	Synthetic fibres	3,000	public
1963	Villacidro	Filati Industrial	Sardegna	Synthetic threads	1,200	private, national
1963	San Salvo	Soc. Ital. Vetro	Abruzzo	Plain glass	2,900	public
1964	Napoli	IRE	Campania	Electrical appliances	1,950	foreign
1964	L'Aquila	SIT–Siemens	Abruzzo	Telecommunications appl.	4,940	public
1965	Aversa	Texas Instruments	Campania	Electrical machinery	2,200	foreign
1965	Napoli	Aeritalia	Campania	Aerospatial	4,490	public
1966	Villacidro	Snia Viscosa	Sardegna	Nylon and acrylic fibres	1,400	private, national
1966	Taranto	Icrot	Puglia	Steel plants repairing	2,000	public
1968	Monte Silvano	Monti Tescon	Abruzzo	Apparel	1,500	public
1968	Pomigliano d'Arco	Alfa Sud	Campania	Motor vehicles	15,330	public
1969	Portoscuso	Alsar	Sardegna	Aluminium	1,300	public
1969	Modugno	Fiat	Puglia	Motor vehicles components	2,700	private, national
1970	Lecce	Fiat Allis	Puglia	Ground-moving machinery	2,000	private, national
1970	Termini Imerese	Fiat	Sicilia	Motor vehicles	2,200	private, national
1970	Marcianise	Olivetti	Campania	Robotics and machine tools	1,100	private, national
1972	Sulmona	Fiat	Abruzzi	Parts for motor vehicles	1,000	private, national
1972	Termoli	Fiat	Molise	Motor vehicles	2,900	private, national
1974	San Salvo	Magneti Marelli	Abruzzi	Elect. appliances for auto	2,400	private, national
1974	Ottana	Fibre del Tirso	Sardegna	Synthetic fibres	2,300	public/priv. nat.
1974	Foggia	SOFIM	Puglia	Diesel motors	1,000	private, national
1975	Acerra	Montedison	Campania	Artificial and synthetic fibres	1,800	private, national

Source: Saraceno, 1980

and the attempt to separate the entire production cycle into small multi-localised plants (Brunetta, 1981). After the oil crisis, however, this movement stopped.

From a *sectoral* point of view the following picture can be drawn. In the 1950s and 1960s most movements of private capital towards southern regions took place in chemical and petrochemical production; in the 1970s the production of motor vehicles and related industries took the lead. In the 1950s, two integrated chemical complexes were built by Montecatini (now Montedison) in Sicilia and Puglia (the latter in an unfortunate joint venture with Shell), while in the 1960s SIR, Rumianca and Snia Viscosa took the initiative to create in Sardegna some large centres for the production of petrochemical fibres, an initiative that, as a general strategy, was heavily supported by public funds. In 1969 a southward movement started of Fiat branch plants and related productions (Magneti Marelli, Fiat group, which produces batteries and electric appliances for motor vehicles); the new locations were mostly on the Adriatic coast (Abruzzi, Molise, Puglia) and in Sicilia (see Maps 5.3 to 5.6).

Initiatives involving foreign capital, on the contrary, are concentrated mainly in the sectors telecommunication and electric appliances; they too show temporal and spatial concentration, being directed towards the provinces of Caserta and Napoli and happening prevalently in the early 1960s. Foreign capital was also involved in new smaller initiatives in the Mezzogiorno during the 1960s, especially in the pharmaceutical sector, and in the metropolitan area of Naples.

It is worth noting that, out of the 25 new branch plants built in the Mezzogiorno since 1950, both foreign and private national, 19 are located in small municipalities, four in the principal towns of provinces, and only two in the principal cities of regions.

A direct inquiry into the *location factors* and connected problems for private national companies, carried out by Confindustria, the entrepreneurs' association, among 472 firms (Confindustria, 1971) shows that financial incentives had had but little influence on location decisions (11.5 per cent of the firms indicating them as a possible location factor), especially among non-local firms (8.5 per cent). A very important factor proved to be the forward and backward linkages with the market (mentioned by 31 and 44 per cent, respectively, of local and non-local firms), and with suppliers of raw materials (33 and 17 per cent, respectively). The latter two location factors are also pre-eminent in other inquiries, centred on the specific acceptor areas Sardinia, Latina, and Siracusa (Sassu, 1980; Cafiero and Pizzorno, 1962) or the donor area Emilia—Romagna (Federindustria Emilia—Romagna, 1979). Especially in the last mentioned investigation, carried out among 63 firms which had built new plants in the Mezzogiorno,

162

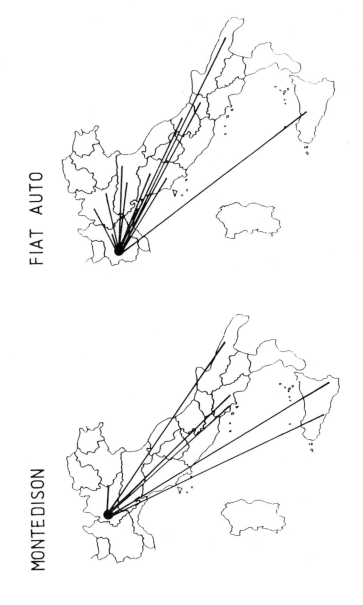

Maps 5.3 and 5.4 New branch plants of two private enterprises (1954–74)

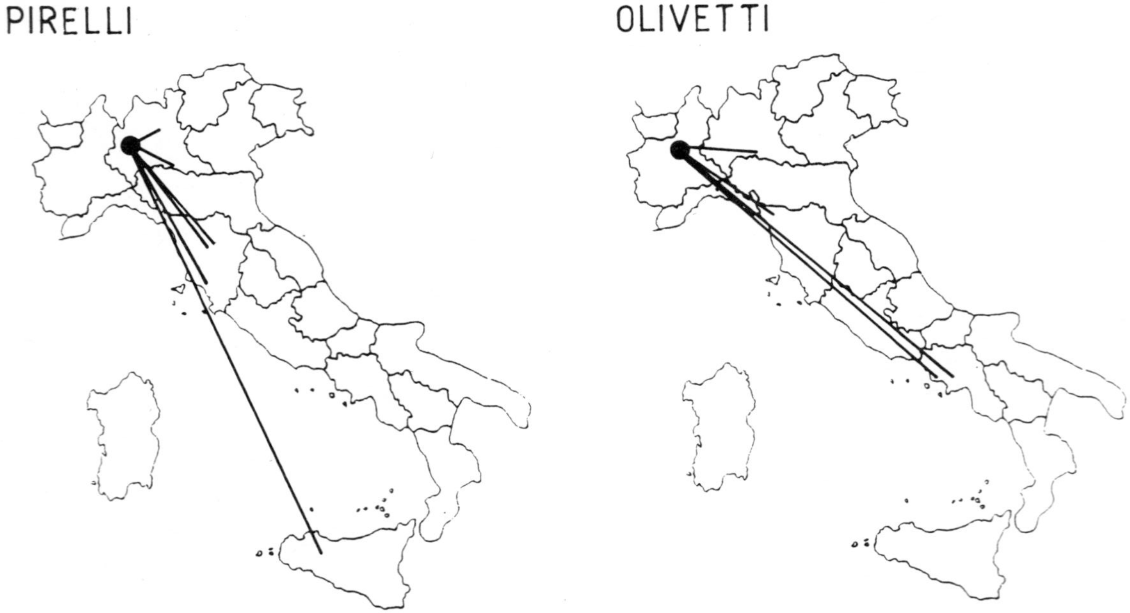

OLIVETTI

PIRELLI

Maps 5.5 and 5.6 New branch plants of two private enterprises (1954–74)

the wish to enlarge the firm's share in the southern market and the presence of specific customers or market areas were given as the main reasons for a southern location and the choice of a specific site (Feder-industria Emilia—Romagna, 1979; Asta, 1980). Of the total investments made by Emilia firms in the Mezzogiorno, 80 per cent were realised between 1971 and 1978; rising congestion costs and scarcity of local labour and building space were indicated as important push factors; the acceptor regions most in favour were those lying on the Adriatic coast. From the Confindustria figures, other important location factors appear to be associated with the infrastructure conditions, e.g. availability of buildings and land (especially for local firms, 41 per cent), water for industrial uses, energy, general infrastructure (25.7, 24.3 and 21.4 per cent, respectively, for non-local firms).

As far as the importance of financial incentives is concerned the results are somewhat ambiguous. For one thing, the results previously quoted are contradicted by the answers to other questions in the Confindustria inquiry, which complain of the delays and bureaucratic obstacles besetting the attribution of incentives and public funds in the phase of project realisation and plant construction. For another, in the interpretation of financial incentives as location factors a distinction should be made between the macro-regional locational choice and the micro-spatial choice of the specific site. In the Emilia survey, incentives were not included in the list of location factors, but rightly considered as a pre-condition for southward movement: 55 per cent of the firms answered that it was a 'determinant' factor in the investment decision. Finally, an entrepreneur looks upon a financial incentive as a counter-balancing factor to the higher costs implicit in a southern location; therefore, making a sort of sum of costs and benefits, he might underestimate the direct importance of the incentive to his locational choice.

The importance of financial incentives, then, cannot be disregarded (as the author of the Confindustria study himself rightly asserts in spite of some quantitative evidence from his inquiry), although many other location factors are progressively gaining in importance. From both the Confindustria and the Emilia study new factors, widely underestimated by entrepreneurs in previous stages, become crucial in the third phase of plant operation and management, namely, general education and skill of the labour force, general spatial infrastructures, transport and communication networks, availability of public facilities. The need for 'real' incentives emerges very strongly from these results.

Let us now turn our attention to foreign companies located in the Mezzogiorno. We have already seen that quantitatively they are not very important. According to Business International (1974) they sell on the north Italian market (65 per cent) rather than on the local one (12 per cent). The location factors explaining the presence of the foreign firms that have been interviewed (44) are: incentives (64 per cent), the opportunities offered by the Italian market (52 per cent), the low wage rates at the time of their arrival (50 per cent). By the authors' interpretation, firms first decide whether or not to produce in Italy, comparing costs and market opportunities with those of other countries; next, incentives widely determine the choice of a southern region (Franco, 1975). Within the Mezzogiorno, other location factors become relevant when a specific site is chosen: general infrastructure and overhead capital, efficiency of the transport and communication networks. Though 64 per cent of the firms are satisfied with their location decision, many negative opinions are expressed about the general 'social climate': rising labour costs, absenteeism, low professional skill and poor adaptability to a factory job. Very interesting are the conclusions from the research: the outlook for the future is judged to be generally positive, thanks to good accessibility, the growing local market, and the rising level of general education and productivity.

Are there any differences in the *employment structure* between local, national, and multinational companies? According to recent research into the electronics industry in Campania (Del Monte, 1980), multinational firms employ the greatest proportion of white collar workers, national firms the greatest proportion of blue collar workers in respect of total employment.

As we have seen before, some 25 per cent of industrial employment in the Mezzogiorno is accounted for by *state-owned companies.* In fact, they have been one of the most powerful agents of industrial development in southern regions, thanks to an explicit wish of Parliament: by Act no. 634/1957, art. 2, state-owned companies have to invest at least 40 per cent of their total fixed capital, and at least 60 per cent of their new capital, in new plants in southern regions; by Act no. 853/1971, art. 7, the percentages have been raised to 60 and 80, respectively.

At the end of the Second World War, state-owned enterprise, in comparison with the general weakness of local industrial structure, was relatively important in the south, especially in Campania (with the IRI-controlled plants of Bagnoli, iron and steel, Castellamare, shipbuilding, Pozzuoli, mechanical products), and in Sardegna (with the Azienda Carbonifera Italiana, operating in the coal mining sector). By 1950 the two regions of Campania and Sardegna had come to encompass about 16 per cent of total employment in state-owned companies, while north-western regions accounted for about 55 per cent. The strong industrialisation effort that started in the late 1950s, and the birth of other state-controlled groups (ENI, EGAM, EFIM) raised the employment share of southern regions to 24 per cent in 1974 (30 per cent if only manufacturing employment is considered), a share that has been maintained since (Giannola, 1977).

We can observe two periods in which the state-owned system was particularly involved in the process of southern industrialisation: the 1960–65 period and the 1970–73 period. During the first period, the intervention strategy was directed towards basic sectors, such as iron and steel (the Italsider plant in Taranto, IRI-group), hydrocarbon and petrochemical products (the Anic plants of Gela in Sicilia and Pisticci in Basilicata, ENI-group); during the second period a more diversified strategy was followed, and we find new initiatives in the mechanical sector (the Alfa-sud plant in Pomigliano d'Arco, near Napoli, IRI-group, started in 1968 but completed four years later); the chemical sector (the Anic plant in Ottana, Sardegna, ENI-group), the electronics, apparel and food sectors along with the doubling of the steel plant at Taranto. In these two periods, the target of allocating 40 per cent of total investments (60 per cent after 1971) to southern regions was largely attained; in the years following 1973, dropping the project of a fifth iron and steel complex in Gioia Tauro (Calabria) due to adverse demand forecasts, and the financial and productive crisis of the main public holdings, helped to slow down the southern involvement of the state-owned industrial system.

To compare north–south movements with industrial movements towards other regions, the new branch-plants created by the first 39 industrial firms (both private and state-owned) in different time periods have been mapped[5]. Map 5.7 shows the location of all establishments in 1953, regardless of their size, and the subsequent maps 5.8–5.10 give the new establishments created in 1953–58, 1958–67, and 1967–73, according to their production sectors[6]. The emerging aggregate situation can be synthesised as shown in Table 5.9.

Table 5.9

Number of new branch plants by macro-regions

Macro-regions	1953–58	1958–67	1967–73
N–W	11	13	24
N–E	11	7	7
C	7	7	9
S	11	16	19
Italy	40	43	59

Sectors:
a = mechanical and electrical appliances
c = food
e = chemical productions
g = rubber
o = petrochemicals

Sectors:
s = iron and steel
t = motor vehicles and shipbuilding
f = synthetic fibres
u = cement

Map 5.7   Situation in 1953

168

Sectors: a = mechanical and electrical appliances
          c = food
          e = chemical productions
          g = rubber
          o = petrochemicals
Sectors: s = iron and steel
          t = motor vehicles and shipbuilding
          f = synthetic fibres
          u = cement

Map 5.8   New establishments in 1953—58

Sectors: a = mechanical and electrical appliances
         c = food
         e = chemical productions
         g = rubber
         o = petrochemicals
Sectors: s = iron and steel
         t = motor vehicles and shipbuilding
         f = synthetic fibres
         u = cement

Map 5.9   New establishments in 1958—67
Source: see note 5

Sectors: a = mechanical and electrical appliances
         c = food
         e = chemical productions
         g = rubber
         o = petrochemicals
Sectors: s = iron and steel
         t = motor vehicles and shipbuilding
         f = synthetic fibres
         u = cement

Map 5.10   New establishments in 1967–73

The figures in Table 5.9 confirm the two large waves of expanding industrial presence in the south: the first in the expansion period of the early 1960s and the second in the rationalisation period from 1969 to 1973. In addition they support the hypothesis of 'decentralisation' and 'multi-localisation' relating to the behaviour of private firms after 1969, the greater part of new initiatives in the last period being accounted for by private enterprise (in our sample, 29 out of 39). But the new information to be taken from these maps is associated with the strong and rising attractiveness of north-western locations well after the 'economic boom'. Evidently, decentralisation is also possible over short distances, in which case it is very similar to what in the Anglo-Saxon literature is referred to as 'rural' or 'non-metropolitan' industrialisation.

Short-distance industrial movement: the case of north-western Italy

The production factor we call land is deeply interwoven with the entire productive life of the firm. In economic textbooks it is referred to as the typical 'fixed factor' in short- and medium-run analysis. But real life proceeds in a dynamic setting, where economic decisions are taken all the time with respect to both short-run and long-run perspectives. It is no surprise, therefore, to find in almost all direct inquiries that through the years firms have used this production factor in many different ways. Industrial movement, especially the migration, creation, or closure of plants, has contributed much to the modifications in land use, which also includes the extension of present locations, the restructuring of existing buildings and private infrastructure, and the change of products and processes which implies a different relation to land.

Recognising that the entire process constitutes more and more a challenge to local public authorities and calls for new and more efficient land-use planning, the regional governments of some north-western regions have recently sponsored research into the phenomenon of industrial movement and relocation. The main results obtained in each of the regions Piemonte, Liguria and Lombardia are worth a separate analysis.

Piemonte

The main results of the survey of industrial movement in Piemonte are the following:

1 With reference to the Turin Metropolitan Area, the absolute magnitude of industrial movement in the years 1970–77 is shown in Table 5.10. Migrations to outside the Turin Metropolitan Area are few and far between (1 per cent of total employment); on the other hand, migrations originating in the core involve 10 per cent of establishments and 3.7 per cent of employment, and are mainly directed towards the first ring (58 per cent), where they account for about 25 per cent of total employment growth. New plants, on the contrary, are mainly attracted by the second ring, where we also find the highest growth rates of pre-existing firms (Ires, 1980a).

2 We observe a great variety of land-use patterns: about one half of the firms (employing more than 10 persons) located outside the Turin Metropolitan Area that filled in the questionnaire had applied to planning authorities for a new building licence in the previous five years (1974–78); 55 per cent were planning some change in their land-use pattern, and specifically 12 per cent for restructuration of buildings, 27 per cent for extension of plants or buildings, 8.5 per cent for opening a new plant, 8.3 per cent for migration (Regione Piemonte, 1980, page 90–5; Ires, 1980b). For the Turin Metropolitan Area, the figures for the same planned initiatives are: 2.4 per cent for building restructuration, 27 per cent for expansion, 6.8 per cent for new plants, and 9.4 per cent for relocation (Table 5.11; Ortona, Parodi, Santagata, 1981).

3 Small firms show in general a lower propensity to expansion, restructuration, and opening new plants; they show on the other hand a higher propensity to migration (12.9 per cent and 13.7 per cent for firms located respectively outside and inside the Turin Metropolitan Area in the class with 10–19 employees, versus respective averages of 8.3 per cent and 9.4 per cent for all classes, as seen before). These facts, together with the higher tendency to open new plants shown by relatively young firms, are interpreted as reflecting the new way to expand production by a 'modular' repetition of identical, multi-localised, small plants (Ires, 1980b).

4 Eighty per cent of the migrations concern small plants with less than 100 employees.

5 New locations tend to be planned at limited distances from the old ones. Among firms located outside the Turin Metropolitan Area, 66 per cent will migrate or open a new plant within the same municipality, 26 per cent within the same county ('comprensorio'), 4.7 per cent within the region and 3.3 per cent outside the region. Among the firms located in the Turin Metropolitan Area, 69 per cent are planning to move no more than 20 km, and no

Table 5.10

Industrial employment in the Turin Metropolitan Area 1970—77
(establishments with >50 empl.)

	Total Area		Core		I Ring		II Ring	
	establish-ments	employ-ment	establish-ments	employ-ment	establish-ments	employ-ment	establish-ments	employ-ment
Employment 1971	812	346,520	358	207,430	360	107,230	94	31,860
Variations (+)								
growth of existing plants	333	35,370	122	16,270	161	9,820	50	9,280
new plants	37	6,140	5	550	22	2,770	10	2,820
internal migrations	41	7,480	10	670	3	80	—	—
migrations from inside MA	—	—	1	60	18	5,020	9	1,200
incomers from lower empl. class (<50 empl.)	99	6,970	39	2,940	48	3,340	12	690
Variations (−)								
reductions in existing plants	301	45,480	132	30,230	139	13,110	30	2,140
outgoings to lower class (<50 empl.)	71	5,670	36	2,790	27	2,350	8	530
closures	59	12,930	29	3,440	24	8,840	6	650
internal migrations	29	5,690	—	—	—	—	—	—
migrations to outside areas	19	3,100	45	7,700	7	640	—	—
of which:								
to first ring	—	—	15	4,450	—	—	—	—
to second ring	—	—	15	550	3	240	—	—
to outside MA	—	—	15	2,700	4	400	—	—
Employment 1977	811	329,610	309	183,760	391	103,320	111	42,530

174

Table 5.11

Planned initiatives of industrial movement and land use in the Turin Metropolitan Area
(by employment classes)

	10–19	20–49	50–99	100–199	200–499	500–999	Total
No initiative	178 32.5 50.7	210 38.3 53.4	78 14.2 48.8	55 10.0 56.1	20 3.6 43.5	7 1.3 50.0	548 100.0 51.6
Extension	80 27.9 22.8	103 35.9 26.2	56 19.5 35.0	29 10.1 29.6	17 5.9 36.9	2 0.7 14.3	287 100.0 27.0
New plant	28 28.9 8.0	23 31.9 5.9	9 12.5 5.6	6 8.3 6.1	3 4.2 6.5	3 4.2 21.4	72 100.0 6.8
Migration	48 48.0 13.7	33 33.0 8.4	10 10.0 6.3	5 5.0 5.1	3 3.0 6.5	1 1.0 7.1	100 100.0 9.4
Building restructuring	3 11.5 0.9	10 38.5 2.5	4 15.4 2.5	3 11.5 3.1	3 11.5 6.5	3 11.5 21.4	26 100.0 2.4
Mixed	21 37.5 6.0	25 44.6 6.4	6 10.7 3.8	3 5.4 3.1	1 1.8 2.2	0 0.0 0.0	56 100.0 5.2
Total	358 23.9 102.0	484 37.1 102.8	163 15.9 101.9	101 9.3 193.1	47 4.3 102.2	16 1.5 114.3	1089 100.0 102.5

Source: Ortona, Parodi, Santagata, 1981
Note: The first percentage refers to the row, the second to the column. The column totals do not sum up to 100 as some firms are planning to take more than one initiative.

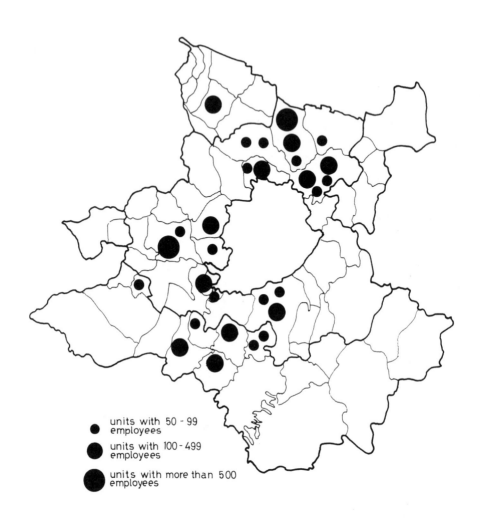

Map 5.11 Turin Metropolitan Area: new establishments (1971–77)
Source: IRES, 1980a

units with 50 - 99
employees

units with 100 - 499
employees

units with more than 500
employees

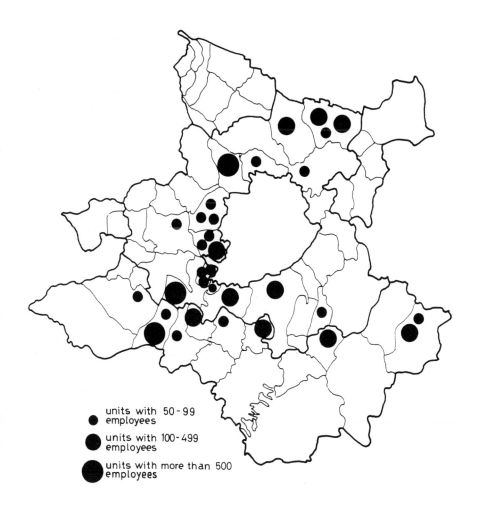

units with 50-99 employees

units with 100-499 employees

units with more than 500 employees

Map 5.12 Turin Metropolitan Area: in-migrated establishments (1971–77)
Source: IRES, 1980a

one is going to leave the region (Maps 5.11 and 5.12).

6 The effects of the project (migration of new plant) are expected to be very important: they will imply changes in products (39 per cent), processes (66 per cent) and skill requirements of the labour force (43 per cent) (Regione Piemonte, 1980, p. 128). That and other facts[7] show that the location decision is not an autonomous one, but one that is firmly tied to other decisions about the firm's life; actually, firms do not move until forced by the need to expand their production (Ortona and Santagata, 1980).

7 In time, migrations appear positively related to the entrepreneurs' general expectations as to the business cycle, and negatively to the presence of official land-use master plans (Ortona and Santagata, 1980).

Liguria

A direct survey among all medium-sized and large firms (over 50 employees) and among a sample of small firms in Liguria (Federindustria Liguria, 1980) shows that 20 per cent of local firms are dissatisfied with their present location, especially so the medium-size firms, located mainly in the area of the principal town. The reasons for their dissatisfaction are purely spatial: no possibility of extending the existing buildings on land already in their possession, nor of expanding into neighbouring areas. A plant migration is planned in 8.8 per cent of cases (a percentage very similar to that found in Piemonte), in particular by the firms already quoted as 'dissatisfied', and a new plant in 5.5 per cent of cases, all referring to main-town firms. Alternative locations are mostly foreseen in the same area, and appear in sharp contrast with the re-equilibrium suggestions of the Regional Development Plan (Soro, 1980).

Lombardia

The main concern of regional authorities with respect to industrial location in this region has always been the establishing of a new economic equilibrium between the central area and the periphery. Almost all regional efforts with respect to industry have been addressed to that goal. The main instruments of that policy are the 'industrial zoning' in depressed areas and the 'eligibility appreciation' the regional government has to pronounce of firms and areas applying for credit allowances on the basis of a national-incentive scheme (DPR 902/1976). From two official documents on these matters it is learnt that not just local entrepreneurs have used these two facilities. In the 35 per cent of total new

178

employees, 6 per cent came from other regions or abroad (Regione Lombardia, 1980a). On the other hand, 4.2 per cent of the firms benefiting from the 902 DPR allowances were not only restructuring but also migrating (Regione Lombardia, 1980b).

Two separate inquiries have been carried out recently, the first into the new industrial location licences issued by municipalities in the period 1978—80, and the second into the movements planned by industrial firms for the near future. As far as the first inquiry is concerned, the new locations for both migrations and new plants represent 1.5 per cent of industrial employment, a percentage that moves up to 4.4 and 4.2, respectively, for small firms employing 10—19 and 20—49 persons, firms that account for the greater part of the movements surveyed (71 per cent in terms of establishments and 59 per cent in terms of employment). Employment-wise, the relative importance of migrations and new plants is almost equal, though migrating plants are on an average larger than new ones. Over 25 per cent of total migrations were realised within the borders of one municipality, and almost all kept within the borders of the province (Regione Lombardia, 1981). The share of small firms in plant migration is overwhelming, but it is exceeded by their share in the creation of new plants. The conclusions are quite similar to those reached in the Piemonte case: 'small is dynamic', 'small is mobile', but it moves very short distances.

Planned movements involve 3.7 per cent of total industrial employment in the region, and refer mainly to medium-size firms, located mostly in the Milano province (65 per cent in terms of present employment). Once again, the majority of the migration or new-plan projects are planned to remain within the same province. In Table 5.12 these projects are shown, arranged by the nature of the changes involved and the spatial constraints met, with reference to migrations only. In over 80 per cent of cases, a spatial constraint or a spatial discrepancy between present and projected land uses emerges as a 'prima causa' of migration, but in over 75 per cent of cases an 'ultima causa' (see Molle and Klaassen, chapter 12 of this book) lies in some projected major change in the productive structure of the firm or its projected growth; that holds even in those cases where the municipal land-use plan has changed the land use prescribed for the present site, thus imposing an exogenous constraint.

Government policy on industrial movement

There is no need to analyse here the national incentive policy for less developed areas, as that task has already been accomplished (Ronzani,

Table 5.12

Migration projects in the Lombardia industry (1981)

Productive changes	Spatial constraints: Discrepancies in land-use attribution by Plan to actual site		Impossibility of spatial widening *in situ*		Other constraints		No spatial constraint		Total	
	P	E	P	E	P	E	P	E	P	E
No relevant change	29	1941	3	100	35	2580	2	55	60	4676
Physical merger with other production units	7	335	1	180	6	1003	16	1705	30	3243
Growth of existing productions	30	1552	31	1799	16	588	14	624	91	4563
New products or processes	14	790	10	788	9	319	6	303	39	2200
General change in the production structure	14	528	5	298	6	362	11	1021	36	2209
Total	94	5166	50	3165	114	4852	49	3708	265	16891

Source: Regione Lombardia, 1981.

P = number of projects; E = number of employees involved.

1978; Marzano, 1979); a few remarks about the most recent developments may suffice here.

After 1975, all incentive legislation was organised into three Acts, due to expire in 1981: n.183/1976 on the Mezzogiorno, DPR 902/1976 on small firms, n.675/1977 on industrial reconversion and restructuring. With respect to the Mezzogiorno the main concern of this legislation, and also of the recent new proposal of the Minister for the Mezzogiorno (December 1980), is: to allow small firms to touch a substantial part of total allowances, to raise the importance of labour subsidies in respect of capital subsidies, to enlarge the field of subsidised activities to tertiary functions, both internal and external to industrial firms, to supply 'real' incentives and know-how aid through the regional governments and some public ad hoc financial institutions (FIME, INSUD, SPI, SFIRS, ESPI).

Act n.675 introduced a strange industrial incentive case with reference to north—south migration, the so-called 'reconversion by relocation'; this case was invented to make peace between the northern and southern regions' political sponsors by enlarging the southern regions' potential share in the public funds of the reconversion Act. The measure was completely ineffective, as this case already received extra financial support by the Mezzogiorno Act.

Very common regional tools that had never been used in Italy are location control and the use of disincentives. In January 1971, a project of law was presented to parliament by Mr Antonio Giolitti, at the time Minister for the Budget and Economic Planning, with a view to controlling the location in congested areas with the help of a location tax and location authorisation; however, the final draft of the law, which widened the licence mechanism to the entire national territory for large establishments (without any fine to transgressors) and abolished the location tax, made this attempt at gaining control completely ineffective (Ciciotti, 1980).

For the purpose of keeping short-distance industrial movements under public control, an important legal instrument of regional intervention has been created by the Piemonte Regional Government, and is now under study in other northern regions, namely, the 'industrial-relocation contract', to be signed by the firm and the regional government, and implemented by a new semi-public financial and real-estate institution. The contract is intended to guarantee a fair division of the rent of central land between the private and the public interest, a better use of urban space, an easier, planned way for the firm to find a new suitable location, with no financial burden on the metropolitan government.[8]

Conclusions and general outlook

Italy has no tradition of empirical studies of industrial movement such as is found in other countries (Molle, 1977; Townroe, 1979; Camagni, 1980a); there are only some very recent empirical surveys of some northern metropolitan areas. Picking up all the information on our subject from other studies not directly concerned with it, we can conclude that:

1 For the firm, the decision to relocate or open new plants is hardly a purely locational one, autonomous and separated from other strategic decisions on products, processes, and markets; on the contrary, as Aydalot points out (Aydalot, 1976, p. 157), all these decisions are closely tied and the firm selects simultaneously its technology and its location. That fact, which is naturally true of new plants, proves very important for relocation also.

2 Consequently, relocation and creation occur mainly in periods of economic expansion and high investment rates, and slowed down substantially during the late 1970s.

3 North—south industrial migration is mainly associated with the opening of new plants, particularly by large firms, it has been realised mainly by a 'planned bargaining' procedure between firms and the central government, a procedure that has proved effective and might be continued in the future on a European Community level.

4 Financial incentives in the Mezzogiorno appear relevant, but deeper and more accurate analyses would be required to confirm the relevancy. Other location factors have proved important: the presence of a large market of 20 million people, inter-industry linkages, and, for the choice of specific sites, infrastructure and communication facilities.

5 Industrial migration has been, in the Italian experience, mainly a short-distance phenomenon, being confined in most cases within a municipality or a metropolitan area, on a radial pattern. It is tied in particular to land-use problems, but the final decision to relocate is made only when other development decisions make the existing location economically and physically obsolete. The quantitative importance of relocations for total new employment is relatively great in the first ring of metropolitan areas, but drops rapidly with increasing distance from the core; the strong regional re-equilibrium and 'non-metropolitan' industrialisation process of the 1970s was due more to autonomous local initiatives than to industrial moves from the centre.

What can we expect from future trends? The slow-down and even

182

reversal of the growth of industrial employment, not visible in the last few years, will probably reduce the impetus of north—south industrial mobility. Residential housing shortage and the conservative attitude of trade unions towards existing jobs will also keep down possible medium-distance relocations among industrial areas in the north. The territorial dynamics of industrial structure, a crucial process in terms of both efficiency and social welfare, will rely mainly on regional differentials of industrial birth-and-death rates, as it did in the 1970s. The main concern of government authorities in that respect should be the strengthening of the productive structure in peripheral regions, to avoid truncation of the recently started 'balanced' growth by the shortage of high-skilled manual and intellectual workers and the dearth of urban tertiary activities.

In large metropolitan areas, careful land-use planning could greatly speed up short-distance industrial movement, and thus create the conditions for improving the quality of urban life in large industrialised areas.

Notes

1 The total growth rate of employment in these sectors in the Mezzogiorno in the years 1951—80 was 17.5 per cent (2.4 per cent in the north-west and 14.7 per cent in the north-east); in the years 1958—70 it it turned into a negative rate of -12.8 per cent (-11.2 per cent in the north-west and +11.3 per cent in the north-east). Total employment in the Mezzogiorno fell from 1955 to 1972.

2 Taking into account the accumulation rate (or, better, its reciprocal, Y/I) instead of the growth rate of the traditional shift-share analysis, we can split the difference between the regional and national accumulation rates in one year (= Total Shift = $Y_r/I_r - Y_n/I_n$) into two parts: a mix effect, showing whether a higher aggregate accumulation rate is due to an investment composition biased towards capital-intensive sectors, and a differential effect, showing whether in the observed region the accumulation rate in each sector is on the average higher than the national sectoral performance.

$$\text{MIX effect} = -\sum_i \frac{I_{ir}}{I_{*r}} \left(\frac{Y_{in}}{I_{in}} - \frac{Y_{*n}}{I_{*n}} \right)$$

$$\text{DIF effect} = -\sum_i \frac{I_{ir}}{I_{*r}} \left(\frac{Y_{ir}}{I_{ir}} - \frac{Y_{in}}{I_{in}} \right)$$

Where Y, I, i, r, and n mean, respectively, value added, investment, sectors, region and nation; a * means sum over sectors. A minus sign is put before each formula to keep the interpretation of the results close to an accumulation rate context. The absolute value of the results has to be interpreted as a differential in value added by unit of investment, and it could be presented as a percentage of the national aggregate value of the same ratio (see: Camagni, 1980b).

3 In Table 5.5, the preceding static shift-share analysis of regional accumulation rates is applied to 55 industrial sectors in 1977; the data refer to establishments with more than 20 employees.

4 The (inverse of the) ratio considered can be split into two terms: $I/Y - I/K$. K/Y, the 'pure' accumulation rate and the capital/product ratio. In the Lombardia region a lower K/Y ratio with respect to the nation was discovered in the majority of industrial sectors, suggesting a better use of capital stock. In the absence of such a mechanism, the severe fall of the accumulation rate through fifteen years would have implied a more dramatic fall of regional product and employment (Camagni, 1980b).

5 The source of our information is the Assonime *Repertorio delle Società per azioni,* published at irregular intervals, and the observation unit is the firm, not the financial group (consequently, when a new firm is created, it is not considered among the new establishments of the controlling company). The firms encompassed are the following:

mechanical and electrical appliances (a): Olivetti, IBM, Sit Siemens, Zanussi, Philips, RIV—SKF;
food (c): Galbani, Eridania;
chemical products (e): Montedison, Anic, Liquigas, Rumianca, Saffa, Lepetit, Snia Viscosa;
rubber (g): Pirelli, Michelin, CEAT;
petrochemicals (o): Agip, Esso Italiana, Mobil Oil, Shell Italiana;
iron and steel (s): Italsider, Dalmine, Acciaierie Falk, Nuovo Pignone, Acciaierie di Piombino;
motor vehicles and shipbuilding (t): Fiat Auto, Alfa Romeo, AlfaSud, Cantieri Navali Riuniti;
synthetic fibres (f): Montefibre;
cement (u): Cementir, Unicem, Italcementi, Cementerie della Puglia, Cementerie della Lucania, Cementerie della Sicilia, Cementerie della Sardegna.

6 The list of branch plants was published no more after 1973. The figures are probably non-exhaustive, as some plants of minor importance have been ignored in the firms' statements.

7 The firms that are planning to migrate or to open new plants far outnumber those which have declared to be 'dissatisfied' with their

present location.

8 Regione Piemonte, legge 56/2977, and *Convenzione Quadro,*
1/2/1979. See: Finpiemonte, 1980.

References

Allen, K. (1978), *Balanced National Growth,* Lexington, Lexington
Books.

Asta, L. (1980), 'La politica meridionalista delle aree attrezzate', *Nord
e Sud,* no. 10.

Aydalot, P. (1976), *Dynamique spatiale et développement inégal,* Paris,
Economica.

Brunetta, R. (1981), *La multilocalizzazione produttiva come strategia
d'impresa,* Venezia, mimeo.

Business International, (1974), *Survey of Foreign Investments in the
Mezzogiorno (1950—73),* Geneva.

Camagni, R. (1976), 'La struttura settoriale della bilancia commerciale
del Mezzogiorno: una indagine quantitativa', *Giornale degli Economisti.*

Camagni, R. (1980a), 'Teorie e modelli di localizzazione delle attività
industriali', *Giornale degli Economisti.*

Camagni, R. (1980b) 'Il mutamento strutturale nell'industria di una
regione europea', *Economia e Politica Industriale,* no. 26.

Camagni, R. and Cappellin, R. (1980), 'Regional Economic Structures
and European Economic Integration', paper presented to the First
World Congress of the Regional Science Association, Boston.

Camagni, R. and Cappellin, R. (1981), 'Policies for Full Employment
and Efficient Utilization of Resources and New Trends in European
Regional Development', paper presented at the XXI European Congress of the Regional Science Association, Barcelona; also in
Economia e Politica Industriale, no. 30.

Camagni, R. and Mazzocchi, G. (1976), 'Contrasti nello sviluppo urbano:
Milano — Torino — Taranto', *Rivista Internazionale di Scienze Sociali,*
no. 4—5.

Cafiero, S. and Pizzorno, A. (1962), *Sviluppo industriale e imprenditori
locali,* Svimez, Milano, Giuffre.

Cao-Pinna, V. (1979), (ed.), *Le regioni del Mezzogiorno,* Bologna, II
Mulino.

Cassa Per II Mezzogiorno, (1957), *Primi rilievi sulle modificazioni della
struttura industriale del mezzogiorno,* Relazione al Bilancio, 1956—7,
Roma.

Cassa Per II Mezzogiorno, (1972), *Tipologia industriale e infrastruttura-*

zione del territorio per una politica di sviluppo del Mezzogiorno, vol. 6, Roma.

Censis, (1979), *XII Rapporto sulla situazione sociale del paese,* Roma.

Cesan, (1978), *Di chi è l'industria meridionale,* Napoli.

Ciciotti, E. (1980), *Le politiche regionali per il controllo degli investimenti,* Milano, Giuffrè.

Confederazione Generale Dell'Industria Italiana, (1971), *Per un rilancio della politica di industrializzazione del Mezzogiorno,* Studi e documentazione no. 26, Roma.

Del Monte, A. (1980), 'Dipendenza, proprietà e struttura organizzativa delle imprese: il caso dell'industria elettronica campana', *Rivista di Economia e Politica industriale,* April.

Federindustria Emilia-Romagna, (1979), *L'industria dell'Emilia-Romagna e il Mezzogiorno,* Bologna.

Federindustria Liguria, (1980), *Indagine sulle localizzazioni industriali in Liguria,* Genova.

Ferrara, G. and Quirino, G. (1975), 'Tendenze della partecipazione esterna allo sviluppo economico del Mezzogiorno nel periodo 1956–77', in B. Barberi (ed.), *Il meccanismo dello sviluppo economico regionale,* Roma.

Finpiemonte, (1980), *Rilocalizzazione industriale e aree industriali attrezzate,* Torino.

Franco, C. (1975), 'Investimenti stranieri nel Sud', *Nord e Sud,* no. 3.

Giannola, A. (1977), 'Imprese pubbliche e industrializzazione nel Mezzogiorno', in S. Cassese et al., *L'impresa pubblica,* Milano, Franco Angeli.

Graziani, A. (1979), 'Il Mezzogiorno nel quadro dell'economia italiana', in A. Graziani and E. Pugliese (eds), *Investimenti e disoccupazione nel Mezzogiorno,* Bologna, Il Mulino.

Ires, (1980a), 'Dinamica occupazionale e movimenti delle imprese manifatturiere nell'area metropolitana torinese', *Quaderni di ricerca,* no. 1.

Ires, (1980b), 'Struttura e localizzazione delle imprese manifatturiere in Piemonte', *Quaderni di ricerca,* no. 2.

ISTAT, (1974, 1981), *Annuario di Contabilità Nazionale,* Roma.

La Francesca, S. (1979) (ed.), *Iniziativa privata e sviluppo industriale nel Mezzogiorno,* Svimez, Giuffrè, Milano.

Lizzeri, G. (1979), 'Consumi di energia e sviluppo industriale nel Mezzogiorno', *Quaderni Isveimer,* no. 17–18.

Marzano, F. (1979) (ed.), *Incentivi e sviluppo del Mezzogiorno,* Milano, Giuffrè.

Molle, W.T. (1977), 'Industrial Mobility: a Review of Empirical Studies and an Analysis of the Migration of Industry from the City of Amsterdam', *Regional Studies,* vol. 11, pp. 323–35.

Myrdal, G. (1957), *Economic Theory and underdeveloped regions*, London.

Ortona, G. Parodi, L. and Santagata, W. (1981), 'Problemi della localizzazione dell'industria nel comprensorio di Torino', Ires, Torino.

Ortona, G. and Santagata, W. (1980), 'Mobilità industriale nell'area metropolitana torinese', paper presented to the First Italian Congress of the Regional Science Association, Roma.

Regione Lombardia, (1980a), *Interventi regionali per la realizzazione di Aree Industriali Attrezzate: Stato di attuazione al 30/9/80*, Assessorato Industria e Artigianato, Servizio Industria, no. 2.

Regione Lombardia, (1980b), *Adempimenti regionali relativi al DPR 902/1976: Stato di attuazione al 30/9/1980*, Assessorato Industria e Artigianato, Servizio Industria, no. 3.

Regione Lombardia, (1981), *Aspetti e prospettive di mobilità territoriale delle imprese*, Assessorato Industria e Artigianato, Servizio Industria, no. 7.

Regione Piemonte, (1980), *L'industria manifatturiera in Piemonte*, Torino, EDA.

Ronzani, S. (1978) 'Background notes to Regional Incentives in Italy', in K. Allen (ed.) op. cit.

Saraceno, P. (1980), 'Cattedrali nel deserto?', *Informazioni Svimez*, no. 1, January.

Sassu, A. (1980), *Strategia d'impresa e sviluppo economico: l'esperienza della Sardegna*, Milano, Giuffrè.

Secchi, B. (1974), *Squilibri regionali e sviluppo economico*, Padova, Marsilio.

Soro, B. (1980), 'Interventi regionali sulle localizzazioni industriali; le esperienze della Lombardia, del Piemonte e della Liguria', *Piemonte Economia*, no. 1, September.

Townroe, P.M. (1979), *Industrial Movement: Experience in the U.S. and the U.K.*, Farnborough, Saxon House.

Unioncamere, (1973), *'I conti economico regionale'*, Roma.

6 Denmark
U. CHRISTIANSEN

Introduction

In this chapter results of Danish studies concerned with locational behaviour are presented. Most studies look at the 1960s and the 1970s, a few refer to earlier times; none are future-oriented. Manufacturing industry is the focus of interest, though some of the studies give information about different aspects of the service sector.

In the next section the general background for spatial developments in Denmark is sketched together with the policy context.

Subsequently an inventory of relevant studies is made. In the following sections the migration pattern and the decision process as seen by the studies are described. Finally the employment impact of movement on the Danish regions is considered.

The spatial and policy settings

Changes in the structure of the Danish economy

After the Second World War, the Danish economy returned to pre-war conditions by about 1948. The economic situation was far from brilliant: restrictions on trade prevailed, rationing still existed and unemployment was fairly high, although the situation was not so bad as in the 1930s.

The period 1948—80 is best divided into three sub-periods: 1948—58, 1958—73 and 1973—80. In the first period the economy took off with an average annual growth in GNP of 3.2 per cent. There were, however, structural problems, as the agricultural sector was too large and the industrial sector too small. Whenever the level of industrial investments went up, there followed a set-back for the balance of payments, and restrictive policies were pursued by the government, whether social-democratic or liberal. Growth was thus slower than in other countries in Western and Northern Europe with the possible exception of Britain. Around 1958 a jump upwards took place. In that year industrial employment for the first time was larger than employment in agriculture, and investments in industry moved to a new and higher level. The growth rate rose to an average of 4.7 per cent per annum between 1958 and 1973. An important contribution to that result was made by the creation of EFTA (the European Free Trade Association), which are good opportunities for Danish industrial exports and incidentally entailed much higher exchanges between the nordic countries than before. Swedish industry's demand for subcontracting work also acted as a powerful stimulant.

At the same time a sectoral redistribution took place. The public services grew and agriculture's part of the GNP fell, while industry's relative position improved slightly (see Table 6.1).

Table 6.1

Composition of GDP 1948—76 (%)

	1948	1958	1968	1976
Industry, construction	34.9	36.7	39.6	36.4
Agriculture	20.9	16.2	8.9	6.9
Commerce	19.0	18.7	17.9	18.2
Transport	8.9	10.1	9.9	9.5
Public services	7.9	9.8	14.9	21.1
Other	8.4	8.5	8.8	7.9
Total	100.0	100.0	100.0	100.0
GDP (mill. kr.)	17662	33981	89318	230071

Employment in industry grew considerably. In 1972 about 650,000 persons were employed in industry, 420,000 in establishments with more than five employees. This was out of a total work force of about 2.5 million.

The total population of Denmark has grown from 4.6 million in 1960 to 5.1 million in 1980. The metropolitan region contains about one-third of the population and there is also a relatively high concentration in eastern Jylland. The changing distribution of employment among sectors and regions is shown in Table 6.2. A spatial division of the country into four large regions has been made for this table. Each of these regions has a different economic structure and has developed differently during the 1960—75 period.

The subdivision is a modified[1] version of the urban core/periphery division made by Hall and Hay (1970), who divide the country into urban and non-urban regions in the context of a European comparative study.

The following regions are defined:

1 Metropolitan influence area (Sjaelland).
2 Southern island periphery (the island in Storstrom county).
3 Central economic area (Fyn and eastern Jylland).
4 Peripheral Jylland (rest of Jylland).

These macro-regions are all further divided into an 'urban' part and a 'rural or semi-urban' part. The metropolitan region is divided into 'urban core' and 'urban ring' (see Map 6.1).

Table 6.2 gives the distribution of employment in 1960 and 1976, respectively. Agriculture and industry experienced a fall in employment (both in percentage terms and absolutely), construction and transport stagnated relatively with a small absolute increase, whereas private services, trade, banking and administration and public services experienced considerable growth. Administration and public service more than doubled their employment in the period.

When looking at total employment we see that the metropolitan influence area saw its employment decrease, especially in the core, whilst employment in the urban ring doubled. The central economic areas saw growth in the 'rural or semi-urban' areas, whereas the urban areas experienced a slight decrease. The Jylland periphery had growth both in urban and rural or semi-urban areas.

Analysis of manufacturing industry only makes the decentralisation tendencies even clearer. The metropolitan influence area had been reduced by more than 10 per cent and all other areas had grown in percentage terms. In the metropolitan core, manufacturing employment was reduced by half (from 231,700 in 1960 to 119,250 in 1976), whilst in the urban ring it has grown. In the central economic area, manufacturing regressed in the urban areas and grew very considerably

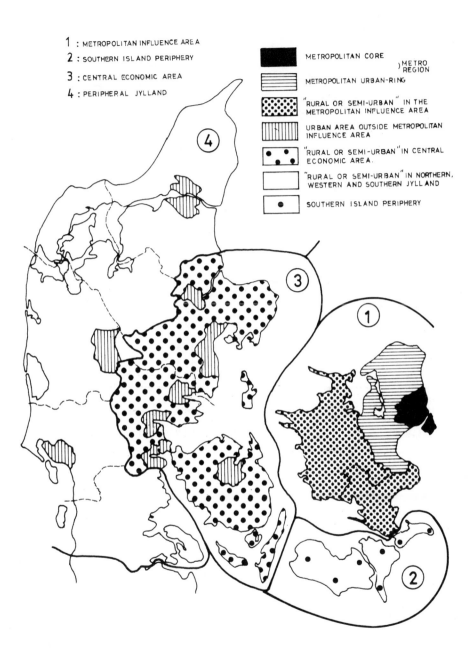

Map 6.1 Functional vs. regional division of Denmark

Table 6.2

Distribution of employment by type of district and zone 1960—76

Zone[1]	Area	Agriculture etc.		Manufacturing		Construction and building	
		1960	1976	1960	1976	1960	1976
1	Core	1.9	1.6	39.4	24.5	25.9	18.6
	Urban ring	5.0	4.5	6.2	9.6	7.7	11.3
	Rest	12.6	10.0	6.1	7.3	9.1	9.5
	Sub-total	19.5	16.1	51.7	41.4	42.7	39.4
2	Rest	0.0	0.0	0.0	0.0	0.0	0.0
	Urban	5.3	4.5	2.5	2.7	2.8	2.6
	Sub-total	5.3	4.5	2.5	2.7	2.8	2.6
3	Urban	5.0	4.7	16.6	15.1	13.3	12.7
	Rest	23.5	23.4	8.9	13.1	12.7	14.6
	Sub-total	28.5	28.1	25.5	28.2	26.0	27.3
4	Urban	3.0	3.5	5.7	6.3	6.2	5.9
	Rest	43.7	47.8	14.5	21.3	22.3	24.9
	Sub-total	46.7	51.3	19.2	27.6	38.5	30.8
Total	Urban + core	14.9	14.3	67.9	55.5	53.1	48.5
	Rest	85.1	85.7	32.0	44.4	46.9	51.6
	Total	100.0	100.0	99.9	99.9	100.0	100.1
Total employment (x 1000)		361	203	587	486	148	192
Per cent		18.9	8.6	30.7	20.7	7.8	8.2

[1] See Map 6.1

192

Trade, banking private services		Transportation		Administration public services		Total employment		Total (x1000) employment	
1960	1976	1960	1976	1960	1976	1960	1976	1960	1976
41.1	32.3	38.6	34.7	41.5	31.3	31.9	26.8	611	629
5.7	11.5	5.7	10.3	7.4	11.9	6.1	10.5	117	247
6.3	6.6	7.2	7.1	7.2	7.5	7.8	7.5	150	177
53.1	50.4	51.5	52.1	56.1	50.7	45.8	44.8	878	1053
0.0	0.0	0.0	0.0	0.0	0.0	0.0	0.0	—	—
2.7	2.1	2.9	2.7	2.3	2.3	3.1	2.5	59	60
2.7	2.1	2.9	2.7	2.3	2.3	3.1	2.5	59	60
15.3	14.3	13.9	13.0	13.7	13.5	13.3	13.2	254	309
8.0	10.3	9.6	10.4	7.8	10.3	11.6	12.4	223	291
23.3	24.6	23.5	23.4	21.5	23.8	24.9	25.6	477	600
5.8	5.7	5.9	5.9	4.8	5.5	5.1	5.6	98	132
15.1	17.1	16.2	16.0	15.2	17.8	21.0	21.4	402	501
20.9	22.8	22.1	21.9	20.0	23.3	26.1	27.0	500	633
67.9	65.8	64.1	63.9	67.4	62.2	56.4	56.1	1081	1317
32.1	36.1	35.9	36.2	32.5	37.9	43.6	43.8	834	1029
100.0	99.9	100.0	100.1	99.9	100.1	100.0	99.9	1915	2346
408	691	146	165	265	609	1915	2346		
21.3	29.5	7.6	7.0	13.8	26.0	100.1	99.9		

in the 'rural or semi-urban' areas. Peripheral Jylland saw a growth of more than 20,000 employed in this sector. It can be said then, that manufacturing had not only spread out from the metropolitan area but also decentralised very considerably in the rest of the country.

The policy context

Industrial policies in Denmark have always been fairly liberal. The goal has been to smooth the way for industrial development without being too interventionist. In the 1950s the gradual abolition of import restrictions created a new climate of competition and it was felt that some support for both large and small industry was needed. Funds from Marshall Aid were used for that purpose, especially to increase productivity of small- and medium-sized industries.

During the 1960s the focus shifted away from small industry to more general support for which the funds were raised by loans or taxation. The education of technicians was improved and expanded, and so was industrial research. The taxation of limited companies was lightened together with price controls and an institute for financing industry and small-scale enterprise was created. Finally new and favourable depreciation rules were enacted in 1958.

As far as regional and location policies are concerned governments have supported the creation of manufacturing employment in lagging regions since 1958, when the first law[2] on subsidies to industry was passed in the Danish parliament. Officially the legislation led to the creation of 15,000 industrial workplaces in the lagging regions during the period 1958–73. (This figure does not include any multiplier effects.) In the same period the net increase in employment in industry in these regions was 30,000. How much of the workplace creation by the development aid would have come about without a policy is of course not known.

Sizeable growth in industrial production had been observed nationally since about 1955–6, after the recession created by the deterioration in the terms of trade at the beginning of the 1950s had spent itself. Something like full employment was reached in 1958 with some structural unemployment remaining in the peripheral regions of the country.

In the central government it was felt that stronger measures of a more integrated nature were needed in the form of a national policy for urban growth and spatial planning together with a regional economic and social policy. The National Physical Planning Agency elaborated the so-called 'Zoning Plan 1962', which in conjunction with the designation of growth centres in northern and western Jylland, adequate financing of infrastructure and possibly locational controls of the Industrial-Development-Certificate type known in Britain was to lead to a more vigorous regional policy. This, however, was not to be. The then social-democratic government tried to enact a comprehensive reform of land, zoning and planning laws, which would have curtailed traditional property rights still further. The complex of laws was enacted in parliament but fell at a referendum in 1963 demanded by the conservative parties within the framework of the constitution.

The first renewed attempt to explicitly start a debate on the location of the private sector was made in the spring of 1972. At that time the second largest party (Venstre), which traditionally represents farmers' interest and also has a considerable following in provincial towns, proposed more direct measures to restore the economic and demographic balance between eastern and western Denmark. Initially the instrument for promoting this should be the installation of an advisory board for the location of industry and nation-wide services.

The proposal was not accepted by parliament and therefore not included in the new law about regional and national planning in 1973. The idea was not dead, however, and the possibility of creating such a locational advisory board backed by the necessary staff was mentioned in the annual report on national planning in 1975. That policy has now been given up. The main policy problem now (apart from regional unemployment) is the co-ordination on the national level of the regional plants which are now in the process of getting approval from central government.

Inventory of empirical investigations

Introduction

In this section we distinguish between studies made on different spatial levels: national, regional and urban. Practically within each spatial level studies are either of a statistical nature, describing the migration pattern over time, or concerned with locational motives and decisions.

International movements

There are no studies available that are specifically related to international movements and the location of transnational firms. International ownership without regional differentiation has been studied in 'Perspektiv planlaegning II' (1974) and by Danmarks Statistical (DS 1979). Both are used in this chapter.

National investigation

Today, only one comprehensive national investigation on moves of firms and plants in Denmark is known (Christiansen, 1979). The study covered the period 1961–76 and contains information about the location and number of openings and closures of establishments as well as their geographical movements. It was conducted as a sampling experiment and the sampling unit was the firm. One thousand nine hundred and twenty-six firms which were active in May, 1976 were drawn in a stratified random sample from the Register of Business Firms kept by the Danish Central Bureau of Statistics. The population of firms from which the sample was drawn, distributed by sector, is shown in Table 6.3, together with the final sample and the number of firms which answered the questionnaire. The 790 firms in manufacturing represent approximately 182,000 employees, the 316 firms in wholesaling approximately 32,000, and the 143 in civil engineering approximately 15,000. The 139 firms in 'service' had approximately 8,000 employees, and finally the 152 transportation firms had approximately 5,000 employees. Thus a total of approximately 240,000 employees were covered by the survey.

For the size groups with more than 500 employees all firms in the population were selected. In all other groups the selection was made at random with the sampling fractions varying from two-thirds to one-fifteenth. The firms were asked to answer a mailed questionnaire. The information sought was data about the locations at which the firms operated on 1 May, 1976 (including addresses identification and employment in all branches), data about addresses which they had used during 1961–76 but now abandoned, and the locational moves made. The information was directly inferred from data on closed and existing addresses.

The investigation uses five categories to characterise the birth and death processes of addresses belonging to the firms:

1 *Transfer,* i.e. a simultaneous opening of a new address and closure of an old one where activities are moved from the old to the new (since 1 January, 1961).

Table 6.3

Number of firms in population, final sample and respondents
of industrial movement survey

Sector	Population	Sample	Responding
Manufacturing industry	6,591	970	790
Civil engineering	612	190	147
Wholesale trade	3,413	403	316
Transportation (part)	816	192	152
Selected services (part)	629	171	139
Total	12,061	1,926	1,540

2 *Branch establishment,* i.e. an opening of a new address in a firm already possessing other addresses without closure elsewhere (since 1 January, 1961).

3 *New opening,* i.e. opening of an address after 1 January, 1961 without formerly owning other addresses.

4 *Take-over,* i.e. acquisition of an address owned by another firm (since 1 January, 1961).

5 *Opening of address* before 1 January, 1961 regardless of 'cause'.

It is clear that all moves are taken into account, i.e. also those within the same municipality.

An investigation concerned with the results of the locational changes on the national level and leading up to the period treated by the SBI study ought to be mentioned. It is the 'Placering af Danmarks industri 1938 til 1960' (Location of Denmark's manufacturing industries 1938 to 1960) by K. Antonsen, (1964). This pioneering work, which is based upon data from the National Statistical Bureau, studies the industrial locational dynamics in the period, using such indicators as number of industrial workers, degree of industrialisation and growth in the number of industrial workers. One result is a new division of the country in industrial regions. Four types of regions are characterised:

1 The industrial region of north-east Sjaelland comprising 50 per cent of the industrial workforce (1960). It has a dominant position due to the national functions of the Copenhagen agglomeration.

2 Three medium-sized industrial areas: east Jylland and the cities
  of Odense and Alborg. They all have a rather large industrial workforce and some national service functions.
3 Two smaller industrial areas: the town of Herning and the island
  of Als. In the period covered these areas had a significant industrial growth. They have no national service functions.
4 Five industrial towns: Naestved, Silkeborg, Randers, Frederikshavn
  and Nakskov, which are seen as industrialised towns with a limited
  range of services; the manufacturing industries in these towns have
  not the same importance for the country as the other three.

Studies on the regional level

An investigation into the movement of industrial establishments employing five or more in the period 1961—76 has been made for Arhus County
(Arhus County, 1977). The method used was a mailed questionnaire
survey. In the questionnaire information about establishment age, moves,
employment, areal size of plants, locational factors and locational plans
was asked for; 542 industrial units (out of a total of 734, i.e. 74 per
cent) answered the questionnaire. 212 moves were registered, mostly
local. Only a few had plans or the wish to move (see also the section
'Motives and decision processes').

The other purely regional studies all relate to locational factors, motives and behaviour for a limited number of firms. Northern Jylland has
been favoured with several investigations of which two will be mentioned here. The so-called 'Nordjyllandsundersogelse' (Jensen, 1966) was a
mailed survey answered by 108 industrial firms, which were asked about
factors considered important for the opening of plants, locational changes and existing location. The managers were asked to mark seven out
of 31 possible location factors.

In the same region 75 industrial firms located in small towns were
interviewed at the beginning of the 1970s as to locational motivation,
growth, contact pattern and sensitivity to external change (Jensen
Pederson et al., 1974). For the Oresund region a survey of locational
motives among 85 departing firms was published in 1967, covering the
period 1950—66 (Henriksen, 1967).

Studies on the level of urban regions

The only study concerning an urban region has been made for the urban
core of Odense and three surrounding municipalities (ICP, 1970). It
forms part of a larger investigation into the regional distribution of

population, employment and economic activities (except the public sector) on the island of Fyn (part of the central economic area). Both manufacturing (including firms with one to four employees), construction, wholesale trade, banking, transportation, and private services were covered in a sample of 787 establishments (26 per cent of the population of firms in the Odense region). A distinction was made between the inner city, an inner and an outer ring. Three hundred and seventy-eight establishments answered the question about origin, i.e. whether it was a new opening, a change of owner (or name) or a move. The largest number of new openings were found in the outer ring; moves were consistently high in all areas (41 per cent of total).

The study's main purpose was to identify the most important locational factors as a function, among others, of production branch and size.

Patterns of movement

Introduction

The mobility of firms depends on several factors both internal and external to the firm, such as type of product (whether goods or services), size of firm and industrial branch. The number of moves per firm (shown in Graph 6.1) is highest for 'selected services to industry etc.', followed by 'wholesaling' and, somewhat behind, 'manufacturing industry'. The figure also shows that the rate of movement increases with size of firm. The increase is at a minimum for manufacturing. The number of branch moves per firm is seen to be consistently smaller than the number of transfers.

The different branches of manufacturing industry show quite different rates of movement. The firms in the SBI sample may be divided into 'stationary' and 'moving' firms. The 'firm-rate of movement' of an industrial sub-sector is defined as the number of firms in the sub-sector which have either newly established themselves, taken over plants belonging to other firms, migrated or opened a new branch plant between 1961 and 1976 divided by the total number of firms in that sector represented in the sample. The firms which on the contrary have done no such thing are considered 'stationary'.

A firm may (and will very often) own more than one plant (address). Locations opened before 1961 are named 'stationary' and after 1960 'mobile'. A firm established before 1961 may thus own both 'mobile' and 'stationary' addresses. If it was established after 1960 all its addres-

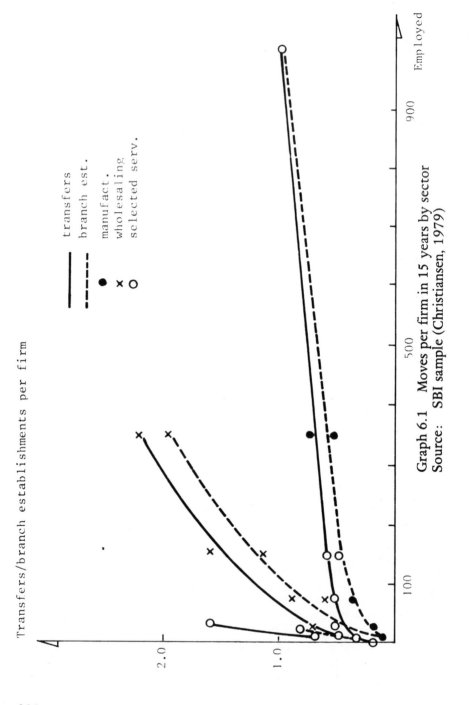

Graph 6.1   Moves per firm in 15 years by sector
Source: SBI sample (Christiansen, 1979)

ses are by definition 'mobile'.

Analogously to the definition used before, we define the rate of 'employment' movement for a given sub-sector of industry as the employment at 'mobile' addresses divided by total employment in the subsector. This figure may be divided according to 'cause' i.e. according to whether it originated in new creations, branch establishments, takeovers or transfers.

Employment is measured as of 1 May 1976. The figures on employment thus contain all developments after the setting up of a given address, i.e. also *in situ* expansion at the mobile addresses.

With two indicators one cannot hope to capture the whole locational dynamics experienced by the sub-sectors of industry. They are not intended, for instance, to capture the distance element. They are closely related to similar concepts developed by Dahmén (1950). The two indicators vary from 0 to 1.

In Graph 6.2 the two indicators based on the sample data are shown for the twenty two-digit industrial branches that manufacturing is divided into following the old ISIC classification. If both indicators are high, it is interpreted as a high rate of movement for the industrial sector in question.

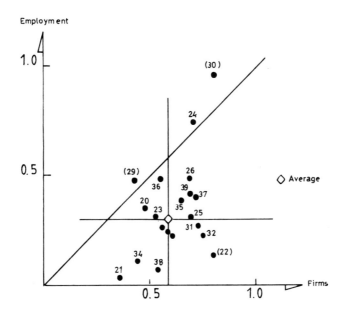

Graph 6.2   Rate of movement (firms and employment) by branch of manufacturing activity (1961—76)

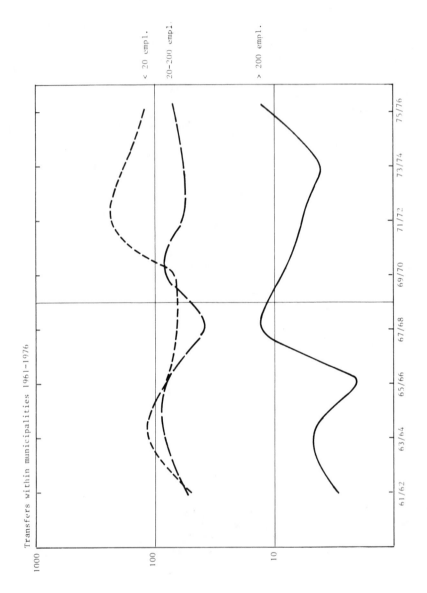

Figure 6.1   Transfers within municipalities 1961—76

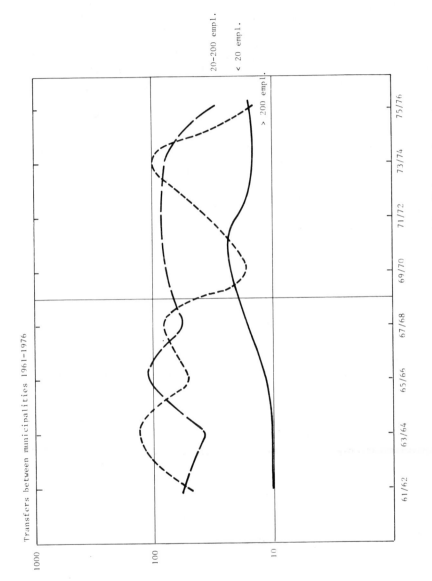

Figure 6.2   Transfers between municipalities 1961—76

The 'firm indicator' varies between 0.36 and 0.80 (average 0.59) and the 'employment indicator' between 0.04 and 0.96 (average 0.30). If only branches having more than 30 firms in the sample or employing more than 9,000 are taken into account, the 'employment indicator' varies between 0.04 and 0.74.

The clothing and shoe industry (24) records the highest rate of movement followed by the furniture industry (26), 'other' industry (39)[3], the electrical and electronics industries (37), metals goods (35), and wood (25). At the other end of the scale one finds the following industries: 'breweries' (21), 'iron and metal works' (34) and 'shipbuilding' (38); not a surprising result.

As to the 'causes' the clothing industry (24) has the highest number of newly created establishments and take-overs followed by the food industry. In the food industry which, among other things, encompasses meat packing and slaughtering, large combines have been created since the mid 1960s and this clearly reflects in the value of the indicator for the foods industry. 'Transfers' is the most important cause for the metals goods and machinery industry. Branch establishments are relatively most important in the electrical industry (37) and in 'other' industry (39) (see appendix, Table 6A.3).

The *time-pattern* of moves has also been studied — so far only for transfer. Figure 6.1 relates to transfers within municipalities and Figure 6.2 to transfers between municipalities (whole country). There seem to be high levels of movement from 1963 to 1966 and from 1971 to 1974 for firms with less than 200 employees. For transfers between municipalities the smallest firms experience a set-back in the years 1965–66 possibly corresponding to the recession at that time. The decline is quite steep for these firms (< 20) around 1968–70. 'Large' firms (> 200) behave differently, especially for moves between municipalities. Their movement is quite steady with a peak in 1969–70. If we look at Figure 6.1 a simple hypothesis offers itself: that after a set-back the transfer-intensity picks up first in the largest firms and last in the small firms, which have to be more prudent.

The *distance* bridged by transfers is illustrated in Table 6.4. Plants belonging to larger firms clearly move the largest distance (represented by the category 'moves between municipalities').

International movements

The part of Danish industry directly owned by foreign firms is quite small if we omit the oil refineries. In the wholesaling sector it is considerably larger at least in terms of total turnover. In manufacturing industry about 12 per cent of the turnover (oil refineries included)

Table 6.4

Transfers within and between municipalities related to size of firm (sample), per cent

Firm size	within	between	Total
	municipalities		
<20	67	33	100
20–50	52	48	100
50–100	50	50	100
100–200	36	64	100
200–500	24	76	100
>500	42	58	100

originated in plants owned by foreign firms; for wholesaling the figure was 23 per cent (1979). About half of the wholesaling turnover in foreign-owned firms originates in automobile, gasoline and oil sales. Of industrial firms with more than 12 employees 5.3 per cent were foreign owned[4] in 1979. Seen in an international perspective the proportion of foreign-controlled production is small, but in certain branches foreign firms are important. Outside oil this is the case in the chemical industry and to some extent in the electronics industry, where most telecommunications firms are foreign owned.

Foreign firms almost never start plants from scratch (again except oil refineries of which there are a total of three). There are 'cheap labour' areas to be tapped which would justify the construction of large-scale plants. In most cases foreign ownership comes about through take-overs. These take-overs mainly touch firms with a steady local demand and mature know-how (e.g. in foods) or R and D-intensive firms producing mainly for export. At the same time the take-overs should be seen in the perspective of the increasing concentration of industry. Even though most take-overs have taken place in the Copenhagen region, locational preferences have probably not been decisive in any one case. The foreign investors buy the market position and the know-how irrespective of location. A few 'new starters' may have been attracted, though, by regions where industrial investment grants can be obtained and others by the frontier region with the FRG. The USA and Sweden are the main investors if the oil sector is excluded[5]. The FRG and the Netherlands are also important. Plants owned by foreign firms tend to be larger than average (DS, 1979; Froslev, 1978).

Industrial movement is an important cause of change in the number of plants in a region although not the most important. The creation of new establishments (firms) comes way before. Thus the SBI study (Christiansen, 1979) estimates the number of new industrial establishments created in the study period for the whole country at 964, while the net regional influx of plants was only 540 (200 net transfers, 340 branch establishments, regional subdivision as given on Map 6A.1 in the appendix). Of the 964 new establishments, only 3 per cent had reached a size of 100 employees or more in 1976, however. For transfers and branch establishments the corresponding figures were 18 and 6 per cent, respectively.

In manufacturing industry as a whole, 13 per cent of the firms had more than 100 employees (DS, 1976).

Turning to migration, we find that the flows from the metropolitan region to the other parts of the country (east—west) were the most important feature of the movement pattern. All regions except the metropolitan region experienced net in-movement. There is still a significant flow between the central economic area and peripheral Jylland (see Tables 6A.1 and 6A.2 in appendix).

For the movement of plants from the metropolitan region we use the division of the country shown in Map 6.1 (Table 6.5[6]) with a further division of the metropolitan region into metropolitan core and the rest of that region.

Table 6.5 shows that transfers from the metropolitan region move in equal proportion to the other economic regions. Branch plants prefer the rest of the metropolitan influence area and the southern island (on these islands regional industrial aids may be obtained) to the rest of the country. In fact the creation of branch plants there decreases with distance from the Great Belt. That becomes even clearer in Table 6.6, but here the sending area is narrowed down to the metropolitan core proper.

More than half the establishments created through in-movement originate in the metropolitan region (Table 6.5, row 5); that goes in particular for the eastern metropolitan influence area (75 per cent). For the areas to the west of the Great Belt, only about 50 per cent originate in the metropolitan region. There is indeed no doubt that the Belt acts as a significant barrier to movement. In the Netherlands for instance, a much higher percentage of intermediate or peripheral in-migration originates in the Randstad (see Chapter 8).

Industrial movement from the metropolis is a fairly important 'cause' of the creation of new plants in the rest of the metropolitan influence area; 31 per cent of the 1976 stock. (Plants > 20, row 7 in Table 6.5). This is in marked contrast with the rest of the country: 8 per cent on average of origins in other regions are taken into account, interrregional

Table 6.5

Decentralisation of manufacturing plants or offices etc. from the metropolitan region (Hovedstadsregionen), plants with 20 employees or more 1961–76

Type of move etc.	To rest of metropolitan influence area and southern islands		To southern island periphery		To central economic area		To peripheral Jylland		Total	
	abs	%	abs	%	abs	%	abs	%	abs	%
1 Transfers	50	(.35)	–	(–)	44	(.31)	47	(.33)	141	(1.00)
2 Branch establishments	58	(.45)	–	(–)	46	(.36)	25	(.19)	129	(1.00)
3 Total moves from Metropolitan regions	108	(.40)	–	(–)	90	(.33)	72	(.27)	270	(1.00)
4 Total moving into region	144		–		181		132		457	
5 Share of Metro. in total (3 : 4)	.75		–		.50		.55		.59	
6 Stock in 1976 (>20 empl.)	353		–		1015		1045		2413	
7 Share of total moves in stock (3 : 6)	.31		–		.09		.07		.11	

Table 6.6

Decentralisation of manufacturing plants from the
metropolitan core 1961—76, all sizes of plants

Type of move etc.	To metropolitan influence area outside core		To rest of country		Total	
	abs	%	abs	%	abs	%
1 Transfers	90	(.45)	112	(.55)	202	(1.00)
2 Branch establishment	99	(.76)	32	(.24)	131	(1.00)
3 Total moves from metro core	189	(.57)	144	(.43)	333	(1.00)
6 Stock 1976 (> 5 empl.)	1161		3700		4861	
7 Share of total moves in stock (%)	.16		.04		.07	

movement as a cause of plant creation in the central economic area will
at most double (to 16 per cent). Intra-regional movement will add to
this figure but, as mentioned above, new firm creation and take-overs
are responsible for most of the new plants established in the 1960s and
1970s.

The region of the country where the proportion of new establishment is highest is peripheral Jylland, more particularly the western
part (region 6 in appendix Map 6A.1).

The overall result of movement, new creations and take-overs has
been a steady decline of industrial employment in the metropolitan
region. If we compare the years 1967 and 1976 (for which we have regionally distributed employment data from 'Danmarks Statistik'), where
total industrial employment was about equal for the whole country

(385,000 and 375,000, respectively) we find that the industrial employment part for the metro-region was 43 per cent in the former year and 33 per cent in the latter. With respect to specific industrial sectors, the figures tell us that the sectors producing consumer goods had the greater relative decline and the metals, mechanical, electronics and chemical industries the smallest. Chemicals thus still have 55 per cent of national employment located in the metro-region. For the electronics sector the figure is even higher.

To find out whether plants go to urban, or rather to semi-urban, or rural areas a separate investigation has been made of moves from the metropolitan core (Folgenotat 1. SBI, 1980). Only results from the sample are given, but these allow in addition a breakdown on industrial branch. We find that the metals and machinery branch has the largest amount of transfers, while the largest amount of incomplete moves occur in the electrical goods industry (including electronics). It is clear that most moves are interregional, i.e. the firms leave the metropolitan region altogether. Transfers go all the way to the central economic region or to peripheral Jylland, whereas branch establishments have a propensity to stay in the metropolitan influence area or on the southern peripheral islands (equal to the propensity to cross the Great Belt).

Transfers in the metals industry mostly locate in smaller local authority areas. Only one is located in an urban core as defined on Map 6.1. For branch plants, contrary behaviour is seen for Jylland and Fyn. There only one locates outside a core. For the electrical goods industry all but one branch plant location in Jylland and Fyn refer to sales branches, while the opposite is the case on Sjaelland. Sales offices are located in large- or medium-sized towns. Among interregional moves in the other sectors (chemical and 'declining') most moves in 'declining' branches go to peripheral areas, chemicals also to the central economic area. Two urban cores are represented; the rest (7) go to semi-urban or rural places.

Intraregional moves: metropolitan region

There has been a steady movement of industrial plants away from the metropolitan core to the surrounding municipalities and farther to the rest of the metro-influence area and to other parts of the country (see Table 6.7).

Suburban moves in the metropolitan region i.e. moves from the city to the periphery within the region, are defined as moves from the municipalities of Copenhagen and Frederiksberg (approximately 600,000 inhabitants) to other municipalities within the region. In the sample, most moves go to the western suburbs (35 transfers, 12 branch estab-

209

Table 6.7

Industrial establishments, both transfers and branch establishments, moving from the metropolitan core to other local authority areas, by destination area (sample) 1961–76

Establishments	Absolute numbers	Per cent
Area of destination:		
Metropolitan region	128	55
(of which metropolitan core)	(108)	(46)
Rest of metropolitan influence area plus southern island periphery	43	18
Central economic area	30	13
Periphery of Jylland	32	14
Total	233	100

lishments), the rest to the north (16 and 3, respectively). Only one plant moves to the airport area (Tarnby). The ring cities (Helsingor, Frederikssund, Roskilde and Koge) are also attractive with their good transportation connections to Copenhagen (four transfers, one branch plant).

The development has followed the intentions of the regional planning and municipal authorities, which in the 1960s allocated industrial areas to the west and the south-west (Roskilde and Koge — 'fingers' of the old 'finger-plan').

The industrial sectors involved are chemicals, metals, mechanical engineering, and the electrical and electronics industries (about 75 per cent of the moves).

Moves between urban areas 1961—76 (Hall and Hay, 1970): intra-regional moves

We shall look at establishments with more than 500 employees and with 100—199 employees in order to get a grip also on intraregional moves in other parts of the country.

In the sample which covers 80 per cent of all industrial firms with more than 500 employees, we observed 20 births of establishments with 500 + employees during the fifteen year period: 12 as a result of transfers, 4 as branch establishments from a parent firm and 4 as new creations. 10 were located in urban cores, 8 in urban peripheral areas and 2 in non-urban regions. The moves are shown in Tables 6.8a and b.

Table 6.8a

Transfers: plants of 500 + employees

	To urban regions		To non-urban regions	Total
	Cores	Periph.		
From:				
Urban regions				
Cores	6	1	0	7
Peripheries	1	4	0	5
Non-urban regions	0	0	0	0
Total	7	5	0	12

Only one of the transfers crossed the Great Belt from eastern to western Denmark; none went in the opposite direction. Non-urban regions seem to have very little appeal for plants of this size.

Establishments of the size 100—199 employees (sampling fraction: ½) naturally have a larger absolute propensity to move: of 93 openings, 30 occurred in core areas, 46 in peripheral areas of urban regions, and 17 in non-urban regions. Tables 6.9a and b illustrate the moves.

Urban cores have next to no attraction for plants located outside cores (only one in eighteen of the plants which settled in cores came from outside, all others originated in cores and three-quarters of these in their own cores). There is further a net movement away from cores,

Table 6.8b

Branch establishments: plants of 500 + employees

	To urban regions		To non-urban regions	Total
	Cores	Periph.		
From:				
Urban regions				
Cores	2	0	1	3
Peripheries	0	1	0	1
Non-urban regions	0	0	0	0
Total	2	1	1	4

Table 6.9a

Transfers: plants of 100—199 employees

	East DK			West DK			
	To urban core	To periph.	To non-urban	To urban core	To periph.	To non urban	Total
From:							
East DK							
Cores	5	5	0	1	0	0	11
Peripheries	0	4	0	0	3	1	8
Non-urban							
regions	0	0	2	0	0	0	2
From:							
West DK							
Cores	0	0	0	11	1	0	12
Peripheries	0	0	0	1	5	0	6
Non-urban							
regions	0	0	0	0	0	2	2
Total	5	9	2	13	9	3	41

but not to non-urban regions. There is no movement from west to east in the sample. Not unnaturally, branch plants have a predilection for peripheral and non-urban areas.

Table 6.9b

Branch establishments of 100—199 employees

	To urban regions		To non-urban regions	Total
	Cores	Periph.		
From:				
Urban regions				
Cores	3	4	2	9
Peripheries	0	5	1	6
Non-urban regions	0	1	3	4
Total	3	10	6	19

Table 6.10

Moves of establishments and employees to the county of Arhus and within the county 1960—76

Moves	No. of establishments	Per cent	No. of employees	Per cent
From other counties	14	7	1,247	11
Within labour markets	194	91	9,981	87
Between labour markets	4	2	203	2
Total	212	100	11,431	100

In the Arhus regional study 212 establishments (or 39 per cent) moved at least once during 1960—76 (about 10 per cent moved more than once). They have 34 per cent of the total number of employees. A characteristic feature is that more than 90 per cent of the moves take place within the local labour-market area (see Table 6.10 and Map 6.2). Only 14 establishments came from other counties.

There are very clear tendencies of suburbanisation (see Table 6.11).

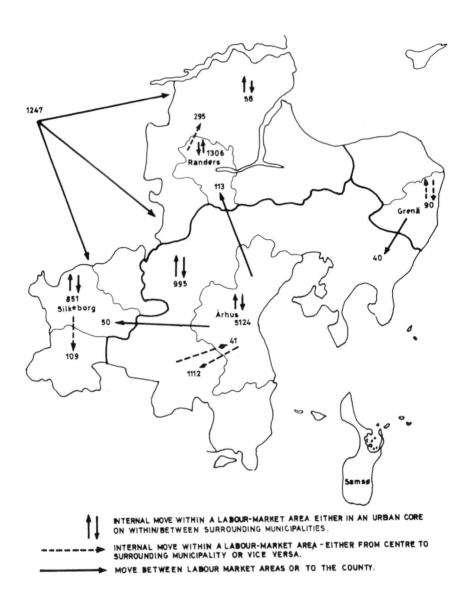

Map 6.2   Patterns of movement in Arhus county

Table 6.11

Moves within labour-market area 1961–76 (Arhus county)

	Employees in moving firms	Percentages
Inside cores	7,371	74
From cores to surrounding municipalities	1,516	15
From surrounding municipalities to cores	41	—
Within surrounding municipalities	970	10
Between surrounding municipalities	83	1
Total	9,981	100
Moving firms	194	

Motives and decision processes

Introduction

Until the mid-1970s most industrial location studies centred on the topic of motives. This has now changed and at the same time the more recent motivational studies tend to become more precise.

The location decision

Location decisions are few and far between in the life of a firm (see e.g. Figure 6.1) and it is not surprising that the use of formal procedures such as investment and programming models in the preparation of a relocation is quite rare. The available Danish evidence (Kolind and Mathiesen, 1978, Christiansen, 1979) indicates that policies for relocating the firm's plants, sales premises or offices do not form part of the firm's long-term strategy. A move in an industrial firm[7] is in most cases triggered by events which might be considered as random or at least acutely important in a way which was not foreseen. This does not mean, of course, that a long period with site or labour or other problems cannot have preceded. Once it is recognised that the solution to the problem might be locational, the decision to move is taken very early in the total process of readaptation, so that a systematic evaluation of locational alternatives is not undertaken (see the ALAS study; Kolind and Mathiesen).

Even though data from the 1970s show that methods used by firms when selecting a location are fairly blunt or non-existent (except for normal search behaviour), there are signs that rationality is increasing in that area. The ALAS study itself is an indication of this. The cases described in it are all selected from management consultants who had followed the firms for some time and who later identified with them and helped them in their locational planning quite apart from the day-to-day consultation.

The ALAS study of 22 firms in the Copenhagen region was initiated in order to investigate possibilities for relocation of metropolitan firms in industrial development areas of Denmark. What barriers to relocation exist and how can improved policy instruments induce firms to move if they are potentially mobile? Locational behaviour and decision making were an integral part of the study. Factors which retain firms in a metropolitan area were found to be either barriers such as fixed investments, a labour force already trained, and key employees, or long-term advantages such as a large and varied labour market, easy communications, etc. Factors which attract firms to non-metropolitan regions were found to be lower wage costs, lower rents, and better availability of stable workers. Nature's amenities and cultural factors seem to gain in importance as well.

Christiansen (1979b) has looked in detail into the locational problems of four firms in order to illustrate the effects of the economic down-turn after 1973.

The firms belong to the following branches of manufacturing industry: food processing, printing, engineering and metals, porcelain and pottery.

They were characterised by sales volume, export share, market type, and number of employees. The data are summarised in Table 6.12.

The table also indicates the organisation of decision making after 1973. The firms have their main offices in Copenhagen or Odense. Three of them produce consumer goods (1, 3 and 4), and one small investment goods (2).

The proportion of wages and salaries in the total costs is relatively high for (1), (2) and (3) and very low for (4). It seems that at least potential profitability is very high for (4).

Firm (1) produces quality porcelain entailing the use of high craftmanship labour in processes where cost-saving technological innovation is virtually impossible. Prices are high. In general, intensive sales promotion

Table 6.12

Main data for four Danish firms

Location of firm	(1) Copenhagen	(2) Odense	(3) Odense	(4) Copenhagen
Branch of industry	Porcelain	Engineering	Printing	Foods
Year	1977	1977	1976	1977
Total sales	200 mio. kr.	33 mio. kr.	18 mio. kr.	614 mio. kr.
Export share (%)	65	75	0	95
No. of employees (approx.)	1400	160	105	750 in 5 locations
Location decisions taken by:	managers + board	small group of owners; are also heads of divisions	managers, board, consultation with staff	managers + board
Location decision after 1973	+	+	(+)	÷ (+ expansion on site)
Market type	monopolistic competition	light investment goods, competition by innovation	strongly competitive	market regulated by FEOGA

is necessary in foreign markets, as competition from other European producers is strong. Industrially produced 'simple' pottery is not in line with the company's policy (and image), but it may want to increase production of this.

For firm (3) competition, which is entirely domestic, is also very strong. The industry is going through a process of technological change, which makes it less labour-intensive. It is a high-wage sector with a strong union. The economic recession has undoubtedly increased its difficulties, but the structural changes are more important, the more so as printing of Danish texts can now be done in low- and medium-wage countries (Eastern Europe, UK, etc.).

Firm (2) is in a branch of manufacturing that is extremely diverse and which has shown much growth and mobility in Denmark during the last 15 years. The firm in question has a very tight organisation structure: it has the directors of the technical divisions as its only shareholders. It produces timers, electrical measurement instruments and valves for use in the beer industry. It also does some sub-contracting. The firm is highly innovative and efficient and does not feel any specific effects of the recession.

Finally (4) is part of a large international concern. Its production of milk powder is steadily expanding, and since 1973 it has profited from the common market for agricultural products in the European Community. It imports and distributes several brand-named products.

None of the firms have solved any of their problems, whether structural or caused by lagging demand in the short term or high costs through relocation. The porcelain firm (1) has seriously thought of moving some of its routine activities, i.e. a few production lines for low-priced porcelain, either to an area some 90 kms from Copenhagen or to an assisted area in northern Jylland. In both cases investment costs were found to be too high. The move might have eased some of the strain that labour relations have in the Copenhagen factory. It could also have made it possible to regain a larger share of the low-price market in Denmark from foreign firms. (Expansion is impossible on the Copenhagen site, which is now fully utilised.) A Portuguese firm has sub-contracted the work, however. The creation of a branch plant in Ireland has also been considered.

The engineering firm (2) has so far been able to expand through its own inventiveness and has had no problems. It acquired a small instruments' firm in Copenhagen in 1975 and decided in 1977 to move the plant from Copenhagen to a locality not too far from the main office (20–30 kms). The move was caused by the end of the Copenhagen lease.

The printing firm (3) moved to its present location in the suburbs of Odense (from the centre of that town) before the recession. It tries to solve its problems by the introduction of new printing technology.

Firm (4) is expanding its production in Jylland. It owns three plants in different locations there and expands where the forecasts of regional milk production are highest (eastern mid-Jylland). The market is expanding very considerably, especially in the Middle East.

Two of the firms examined have had (and still have) structural problems. For one of them this has had an impact on locational decisions. The other two are still expanding and are not much affected by the recession, but naturally have had to solve some of their expansion problems by investment in plant, offices and distribution facilities. Among the less problem-ridden firms the machinery-producing firm (2) reacts very quickly to change and is in general innovative. Its take-over and relocation of a small Copenhagen firm was effected smoothly thanks to high organisational efficiency. The food-products firm (4) has had a relatively simpler task as its product gets FEOGA price support (if needed). Its plant-expansion policies are rational and effective.

Of the firms experiencing structural change, the pottery firm (1) had plans for the opening of branch establishments in regions (states) where labour costs were lower. It seems that such moves either do not work or look inconclusive *ex ante*, as qualified or at least very specialised labour is necessary for the operation's success.

The printing firm (3) experiences technological change and strong union pressure. Within the country no low-wage regions for this trade exist and a move to a foreign country is impossible as the product has to be closely co-ordinated at short notice with customers' demands.

'National studies'

No studies covering the whole country have been carried out. The closest we come to a national study is the recent investigation on 'Manufacturing in rural areas and small towns' (Andersen, 1980), but this study only pertains to the parts of the country defined in the title. Further only a minor part is related to motives for locational behaviour.

Otherwise moves having their origin or destination in the *metropolitan region* and in *northern Jylland* as well as new starts made in those regions are the only ones which have been investigated as to motives and decision processes with the exception of the Odense study.

In Jensen (1966) 108 establishments in northern Jylland answered questions about location factors considered at the opening of an establishment as well as for the existing location (1964). Forty per cent marked raw material sources and the founder's home address as the most important locational factors for the birth of an establishment. Good accessibility and factors related to site and building followed. Labour force problems proved to be much less important. As the region had high structural unemployment in the 1950s, this is perhaps not so surprising. Small establishments weighted 'site and buildings' high together with 'urban amenities', 'central position in the market', whereas large establishments weighted 'water provision', 'direct rail connection to site' and 'own wharf in harbour' highest. When it comes to the actual locational situation in 1964, 'lack of qualified labour' was found to be a drawback.

In Jensen, Pedersen et al (1974) 75 establishments in 6 small towns were interviewed. Fifty per cent of the firms had been started locally, two-thirds after 1969. Most in-migrants (whether by transfer or branch establishment) came in that period with the highest intensity between 1970 and 1974.

The transferred establishments had 'lack of space' as the main motive; branch plants indicated 'lack of labour'.

The first motivational study for the *metropolitan region* was published in 1967 (Henriksen, 1967). It is a transnational investigation as it also considers the coastal counties in southern Sweden (Oresundsregionen). On the Danish side of the Sound the region is delimited by the western limits of Copenhagen, Copenhagen county and Frederiksborg county and the coastline, which means that Roskilde county is omitted if we compare with the definition used in the SBI study. Industrial firms started in the region or having moved to the region or out of it were interviewed.

The investigation of the out-migration firms covered 85 establishments with 20 or more employed. Eighty per cent of the establishments mention lack of labour as the main reason for moving out of the region. Lack of space for expansion on site comes next. Higher costs are also mentioned among the reasons for moving. In the final locational choice, availability of labour, cheap premises and sites as well as activities of local authority are prominent among the incentives. Larger firms take markets into account together with regional aids. Competition and market factors play a larger role for moves going to Jylland than for moves to other regions.

Suburban and urban studies

It seems clear from the ICP (1970) study of establishments in Odense that both manufacturing and wholesaling firms move to the suburban areas in fairly large numbers. If they had not moved at the time of the survey, many of them expressed a wish to do so if the possibility arose. Thirty-seven per cent (217) of all firms interviewed, covering all private sectors except retailing, expressed preference for alternative locations, while 34 per cent (199) were satisfied with their present location. The remainder (170) did not express an opinion. Firms were classified according to existing location in 'centre', 'rest of urban area' and 'periphery'. They expressed their weighting of preselected factors of importance for a future location. For manufacturing firms in all urban areas physical factors and cost factors related to buildings and sites were by far the most important. Such factors as 'possibilities for expansion on site', 'easy accessibility for cars and lorries', 'good parking lots' scored high together with the factors 'low rent' and 'possibility of concentrating dispersed production plants on one site'.

'Stability of the labour force' also scored high, most however for small firms in the periphery. (It must be remembered that at the time the economy was booming.) For these firms 'supply of qualified labour' also had high scores.

Effects on donor and acceptor regions

International moves

As mentioned above there are very few studies about international moves of establishments into Denmark. On the basis of DS (1979) it is possible to say that in 1976 31,100 persons were employed in foreign-owned manufacturing firms with 20 or more employees; this corresponds to 9.2 per cent of manufacturing employment (> 20).

Interregional moves

The volume of employment is inferred from the SBI study and published figures from the statistical bureau (DS, 1976 and others from the same series). Table 6.13 shows the result. In this table the employment caused by net-immigration to the regions concerned, local new creation, take-overs etc., and the net effect of *in situ* expansion and closure (taken together) are indicated.

It seems quite clear that 'local new creations etc.' has the largest employment effect in the regions outside the metropolis, greater effects being located in southern and western Jylland (63 and 65 per cent of the 1961 stock, respectively) and the smallest in the metropolis and eastern Jylland (between 10 and 20 per cent), i.e. in the 'old' industrial areas. Net immigration always lies somewhere between 10 and 20 per cent. The net effect of *in situ* expansion (contraction) and closures is very great in the metropolitan region (36 per cent of the 1961 stock). The rank ordering of these percentages corresponds to results found in other studies (notably the Netherlands), but the order of magnitude is much higher, about double or more. One explanation may be that the SBI-study covers the period of industrial expansion in the 1960s and the first half of the 1970s only, whereas the Netherlands study also covers the 1950s, when economic growth was smaller and business failures possibly more prevalent than in the 1960s. Another explanation could be that Danish manufacturing industry is much younger than the Dutch one and thus prone to larger initial growth. There is also a simple statistical explanation, however. On the SBI-study the employment was measured at the very end of the time period and this means that the 'net immigration' and 'local' figures will contain the *in situ* expansion of the locationally dynamic firms from the time of the move until the end of the period. This *in situ* effect should be subtracted from columns (2) and (3) and added to column (4), which is of course impossible to do.

Table 6.13*

Employment in manufacturing at the beginning and end of the
period 1961−74 and employment effects of net immigration,
local creation and *in situ* expansion and closures (x 1000)

Area code (from appendix Map 1)	Stock 1961	Net immigration	Local new creations take-overs, branch establishments	Net effect of *in situ* expansion and closures	Stock 1974
	(1)	(2)	(3)	(4)	(5)
1 Metro-region	204.9	−13.4	27.9	−73.2	146.2
2 Vestsjælland + Storstrøm	30.1	6.8	15.7	−12.5	40.1
3 Fyn	39.6	3.9	12.2	−12.1	43.6
4 Vejle + Arhus	62.1	8.1	12.6	−10.5	72.3
5 Sønderjylland	13.9	1.8	8.7	− 3.5	20.9
6 Ribe + Ringkjøbing	23.4	− 3.0	15.2	2.4	38.0
7 Viborg + Nordjylland	33.7	6.4	12.5	− 6.2	46.4

*Considerable uncertainty is attached to the distribution between effects.

In spite of this qualification there is no doubt that the employment
effects in the peripheral regions mostly originate in new creations and
that the very considerable losses in the metropolitan region are mainly
due to closures and employment contraction, although net out-
migration also plays a role.

Outlook

At the moment of writing the immediate future for the European economy seems pretty bleak. Interest rates are higher than ever, and investment opportunities become severely curtailed. The situation is exacerbated in countries where the government is obliged to borrow heavily
to cover its current-account deficit and to maintain even higher interest rates than elsewhere lest heavy losses of the country's currency reserves are suffered. Passive investment is at a premium against active
investment in production. The Danish economy is in just this quandary

and has more difficulty than most other members of the European Community in reaching equilibrium. A lack of political will to curb private consumption and imports at the end of the 1960s and during the first half of the 1970s is in part responsible but the three oil-price revolutions have, of course, added to the problem. They have hit the country severely. In spite of heavy unemployment, industry has not suffered more in its current activity than industries in the best performing member states. Its international competitiveness is still quite good, and it should be able to regain its position on foreign markets if and when international demand picks up again. But investment in new capacity and new plant is now much lower than what was 'normal' in the 1970s. Moreover there is a structural problem. The distribution of the GNP will have to be changed so as to reflect a higher proportion in the sectors producing goods and export services, if the fundamental weakness of the Danish economy is to be corrected within a system of open economies. This has been clearly recognised by the government and the Federation of Danish Industry. Employment in manufacturing industry will have to increase from about 400,000 to 500,000 together with an increase in productivity.

The Federation has published a proposal, suggesting its implementation by government in 1981 and the next five years. The proposal contains a mixture of interest, tax, monetary and budget policies, which as one consequence entails on average a constant real wage for the labour force over the next six to seven years. But — more importantly — it is estimated by the Federation that 165,000 new jobs will be created at the same time — 90,000 in industry. There is no indication in the proposal as to where in the country this net increase in the number of industrial jobs is expected to be located — the topic which is of immediate interest to us. In fact no specific quantitative studies have been made by anyone concerning the future location of Danish manufacturing. This does not mean that nobody is taking the problem seriously. On the contrary. The future location of industry has to be stipulated in all regional plans. In all countries ideas have been sketched as to urban growth and location of industry, and the National Planning Agency in its report on the future pattern of the urban network (Planstyrelsen, 1979) reasoned about the geographical pattern of industrial jobs. The report's assumptions contrast with the Federation's plan: it does not see any increase in industrial employment nationally; perhaps even a further decrease in the period up to 1990.

The report divides the country into two regions: the metro-region and the rest of the country. Within 'rest of country' an urban distinction is made between municipalities with cities above 100,000 inhabitants and municipalities containing only villages and rural areas. A set of population-distribution models is simulated; one in which no urban population distribution policy is assumed, and three 'policy' models:

— concentration to regional centre and metropolitan region;
— concentration to sub-regional centre;
— decentralisation to small towns and rural areas.

It is said that towns below 20,000 inhabitants will receive most industrial development if present trends continue (up to 1977) while manufacturing can be made to follow the urban pattern of the models if corresponding location policies are pursued. The statements about industry are deliberately held vague, as the uncertainty is considerable.

The location of the new jobs will of course depend upon the type of industry to be developed. In my view it is to be expected that the research-intensive electronics and chemical industries together with the production of machinery (where research is less pronounced) will grow further in the medium and long term. To these industries must be added firms that produce equipment for the energy-producing industries. From 1985 natural gas will be brought in from the Danish part of the North Sea and fed into a pipeline from Esbjerg to Copenhagen. My bid for the future location of additional jobs in industry will therefore produce more changes to the metro-region as regards research and contact intensive industries and in general to the southern part of the country due to the installation of the pipeline. But serious future-oriented studies are needed before scenarios can be written.

Notes

1 Especially for Sjaelland; note also that Bornholm has been omitted.
2 The law has since been revised several times. Latest revision 1972, when for the first time a grants system was introduced to supplement loans and guarantees of loans.
3 Includes *inter alia* instruments and parts of the plastics industry.
4 Ownership defined as owning more than 50 per cent of the shares in joint stock companies.
5 If included, UK moves to second place (1971).
6 Nearly all moves relate to production plants.
7 In other sectors 'rational' location decisions are more common. Both large-scale retailing chains and banks e.g. use statistics, and models when expanding the number of outlets.

224

References

Andersen L. (1980), et al., *Fremstillingsvirksombeder i landkommuner og mindre byer*, Landsbykommissionen.

Antonsen, K. (1964), *Placeringen af Danmarks Industri 1938 til 1960*, LPUS.

Arhus county (1977), *Undersøgelse af industriens arealforbrug, flytninger og lokalisering i Arhus amt 1960–76*, Arhus.

Christiansen, U. (1978),'Moves of firms 1961–1976 between Danish functional urban regions', IIASA, Laxenburg, (seminar paper).

Christiansen, U. (1979), 'Storbyerhvervenes mobilitet 1961–76', *SBI-Byplanlægning* 35, SBI.

Christiansen, U. (1979b), *Changes in locational behaviour in the sixties and seventies*, Siegen.

Dahmén, E. (1950), *Svensk industrieel företagarverksamhet*, Lund.

DS (1979), *Statistiske Efterretninger*, A46, pg 1362ff.

DS (1976), *Statistiske Meddelelser*, Industristatistik 1974.

Engelstoft, S. (1977), *Forskning om erhvervslokalisering og regional udvikling*, BYREF, København.

Frøslev Christensen, J. (1978), *Industrikapitalen og Krisen*, RUC.

Hall, P. and Hay, D. (1970), *Urban regionalization of Denmark*, Reading.

Henriksen, T. (1967), *Øresundsregionen og industriens lokalisering*.

ICP, (1968 and 1970), *Virksombedsundersøgelse for Fynsregionen*, Bind I og II, Odense.

Jensen, S. (1966), *Industriens beliggenhedsvalg i Nordjylland*, LPUS.

Jensen, S. and Pedersen, P.O. (1974), et al., *Erhvervsudvikling i Nordjylland*, Institut for vejbygning m.v. DTH.

Kolind, L. and Matthiesen, P.M. (1978), *Alternativ lokalisering af storbyerhverv*, København, (ALAS).

Pedersen, P.O. (1981), *Regionale strukturforandringer, rapport nr. 4*, Sydjysk Universitetscenter.

Planstyrelsen, (1979), *Rapport om det fremtidige bymønster*, Copenhagen.

SBI (1980), Folgenstats.

Map A.1 Alternative functional regional division of Denmark

Table A.1

Manufacturing industry, population, number of firms, transfers between regions 1961–76

		Area code (Map A.1)				
Size (employees)	To From	1	2	3+4	5+6+7	Total
1 – 19	1	–	21	75	11	107
	2	11	–	0	0	11
	3+4	0	0	–	11	11
	5+6+7	0	0	11	–	11
	Total	11	21	86	22	140
20 – 49	1	–	30	17	15	62
	2	22	–	0	0	22
	3+4	0	0	–	8	8
	5+6+7	0	0	8	–	8
	Total	22	30	25	23	100
50 – 99	1	–	8	11	14	33
	2	1	–	3	0	4
	3+4	0	0	–	7	7
	5+6+7	0	0	1	–	1
	Total	1	8	15	21	45
100 – 199	1	–	6	11	8	25
	2	1	–	0	0	1
	3+4	2	0	–	3	5
	5+6+7	0	0	3	–	3
	Total	3	6	14	11	34
200 – 499	1	–	5	4	7	16
	2	0	–	0	0	0
	3+4	2	0	–	3	5
	5+6+7	0	0	0	–	0
	Total	2	5	4	10	21

Table A.1 (cont.):

Size (employees)	To / From	1	2	3+4	5+6+7	Total
500 +	1	—	1	1	3	5
	2	0	—	0	0	0
	3+4	1	0	—	1	2
	5+6+7	0	0	6	—	6
	Total	1	1	7	4	13

Table A.2

Manufacturing industry, population, number of firms,
branch 'moves' between regions 1961—76

		Area code (Map A.1)				
Size (employees)	To / From	1	2	3+4	5+6+7	Total
1 — 19	1	—	17	26	9	52
	2	11	—	3	3	17
	3+4	11	3	—	6	20
	5+6+7	3	6	11	—	20
	Total	25	26	40	18	109
20 — 49	1	—	18	16	8	42
	2	6	—	4	4	14
	3+4	4	1	—	4	9
	5+6+7	4	2	6	—	12
	Total	14	21	26	16	77
50 — 99	1	—	13	10	6	29
	2	5	—	3	2	10
	3+4	3	1	—	2	6
	5+6+7	1	1	5	—	7
	Total	9	15	18	10	52

Table A.2 (cont.)

Size (employees)	To From	1	2	3+4	5+6+7	Total
100 – 199	1	—	11	8	5	24
	2	3	—	2	2	7
	3+4	2	1	—	2	5
	5+6+7	1	1	3	—	5
	Total	6	13	13	9	41
200 – 499	1	—	8	5	3	16
	2	2	—	1	1	4
	3+4	1	0	—	1	2
	5+6+7	1	1	2	—	4
	Total	4	9	8	5	26
500 +	1	—	8	7	3	18
	2	2	—	1	1	4
	3+4	2	0	—	1	3
	5+6+7	0	0	3	—	3
	Total	4	8	11	5	28

Table A.3

Indication of the rate of movement (employment)
by branch of industry 1961–76

Industrial branch	Total	Branch establishments	Transfers	Other
(1)	(2)	(3)	(4)	(5)
20	0.35	0.02	0.10	0.22
21	0.04	0.02	0.01	0.01
22	0.14	0.12	0.01	0.01
23	0.31	0.07	0.18	0.06
24	0.74	0.11	0.24	0.40
25	0.30	0.06	0.06	0.19
26	0.48	0.01	0.28	0.19

Table A.3 (cont.):

Industrial branch	Total	Branch establishments	Transfers	Other
(1)	(2)	(3)	(4)	(5)
27	0.23	0.08	0.11	0.05
28	0.24	0.03	0.18	0.03
29	0.47	0.01	0.38	0.08
30	0.96	0.04	0.90	0.01
31	0.27	0.05	0.20	0.02
32	0.22	0.20	0.02	0.00
33	0.26	0.07	0.03	0.15
34	0.11	0.01	0.07	0.03
35	0.38	0.06	0.30	0.02
36	0.48	0.10	0.29	0.09
37	0.39	0.12	0.19	0.09
38	0.07	0.02	0.04	0.01
39	0.41	0.13	0.22	0.06

(1)   ISIC code 1948;
(2)   defined as employment in plants that moved or were newly created, divided by the total employment in plants in the sample.
(3), (4) and (5)   identical to (2) but originating from transfers etc.

7 Greece
G. A. GIANNOPOULOS and M. GIAOUTZIS-FLYTZANIS

The great majority of manufacturing plants were established in the country in the last two decades; most of the incentives for relocation have been introduced in the last ten years. Therefore, no substantial relocations of manufacturing can be expected to have happened in Greece. That is perhaps why data on industrial movements are so scarce, and research on the subject is so frustrating.

Available statistics come from the ten-yearly censuses and the special census of manufacturing industry conducted by the National Statistical Service. Three ten-year censuses (1961, 1971 and 1981) and three censuses of manufacturing (1963, 1973 and 1978) have already been held; from these we can obtain most of the existing information on industrial location and employment, but no data on industrial movement. From experience we know that most of the new manufacturing plants in a given region will be totally new plants, while the remaining ones are new branches of plants operating in other regions, which need not necessarily have closed down.

Thus as far as the data are concerned, we can only try to picture the present industrial location in the country, and identify the factors most likely to affect that location with the help of the results of a special survey carried out by the Institute of Economic and Industrial Studies.

Before describing these factors, however, let us first depict the general setting in which the problem has to be regarded, namely the development of the Greek economy and the spatial structure of Greece. Some attention will also be given to measures of regional policy.

The structure of the Greek economy

The Greek economy at the end of the Second World War was characterised by approximately 10 per cent of the Greek population depending almost entirely on government support, an inefficient domestic
production of basic consumption goods, a completely disorganised
public finance and monetary system, and a very high rate of inflation
(Ellis et al., 1965).

In the early 1950s the Greek economy was showing severe structural
inefficiencies, originating mainly in the country's pre-war structure,
and having as a prominent feature a trend towards very high imports,
especially of basic consumption goods. Greek exports consisted mainly
of five agricultural products, with strongly fluctuating prices reflecting
basically the economic situation of the importing countries, while the
only resources worth mentioning were the transfers from emigrated
Greeks. Manufacturing and agriculture were characterised by very low
productivity (KEPE, 1965).

In 1953 a new policy was started by the depreciation of the currency,
followed by the elimination of import duties and the inflow of foreign
capital, to boost the development of the Greek economy. Indeed, by
1960 the pre-war structure of Greek manufacturing had been recovered,
which gave an impulse to the government to go on encouraging the inflow of foreign capital for the next decade (Argyris, 1981). GNP increased at an average yearly rate of 5.8 per cent in the period 1950—60, 7.2
per cent during 1960—70, and 5.6 per cent during 1970—75. The average annual rate of increase in the whole period 1950—75 was 6.3 per
cent, and in the years 1976 and 1977 it was 5.8 and 3.8 per cent, respectively (National Accounts, 1976; Current Accounts, 1978).

The industrial product increased at an average rate of 8.4 per cent
in the period 1950—60, 9.3 per cent in 1960—70, 5.6 per cent in 1970—
75, the average rate for the period 1950—75 being 8.2 per cent (the
rate of increase in the years 1976 and 1977 was 8.8 and 4.3 per cent,
respectively). The contribution of the industrial product to GNP increased from 20.1 per cent in 1950 to 31.8 per cent in 1975; in 1977
it was 30.8 per cent (Argyris, 1981).

Despite the above positive changes, the industrial sector has not contributed sufficiently to the growth of employment in the country; indeed, the share of industrial employment changed from 19.2 per cent
in 1951 to only 28.9 per cent in 1976 (NSSG, 1971). The structure of
employment, which remained basically unchanged during the last three
decades, can be characterised as follows. Of the persons employed in
the agricultural sector, amounting to about a quarter of total employment, many are active only in certain seasons; thus this sector is responsible for a high rate of hidden unemployment. In the manufacturing

sector the rate of increase of employment is low, as we have seen; it is not possible for a large portion of the economically active population to find employ in sectors of high productivity. As a result the unemployed or underemployed have turned towards the service sector, the excessive growth of which is characteristic of Greek employment, and hides a high degree of underemployment.

The spatial structure of Greece

Contemporary Greece took its shape after the First World War, when the northern part of the country was recovered from foreign occupation. The period between the two wars was one of internal political instability with frequent changes of government, civil wars, etc. The resulting insecurity and lack of opportunity made agriculture the only safe occupation of natural survival. The development of the regions took place against that background, and the early 1950s — the beginning of a period of considerable political stability — found more than 55 per cent of the economically active population engaged in agriculture.

After the Second World War, in the mid 1950s, the infant industry and other enterprises were left with very little choice as to their location. The system of centralised government, by which even decisions of secondary importance had to be made in the capital, the inequality of natural resources among regions, and the poor transportation facilities in most areas outside Athens and Thessaloniki, had severely restricted the flexibility of location decisions. As a result Athens first, and Thessaloniki later, were the focal points of industrial development and experienced a fast increase in their population at the expense of other regions. In spite of measures introduced from time to time, those trends have continued until today; characteristically, in 1978 48 per cent of manufacturing plants, 60 per cent of manufacturing employment, and 59 per cent of the horsepower established in industry were concentrated in the Greater Athens area.

Administratively, the country consists of 52 departments (Nomos) as shown in Map 7.1. For planning, another division into 10 planning regions has been introduced by KEPE; it is shown in Map 7.2.

As to the distribution of *population*, there is a very dense concentration along the main transportation axes of the country (Giannopoulos, 1979). In 1951, 36.8 per cent of the total population was concentrated in urban areas; by 1971 the proportion had gone up to 53.2 per cent, the proportion of people living in rural areas being 47.6 per cent in 1951 and 35.1 per cent in 1971.

Map 7.1   The administrative regions of Greece

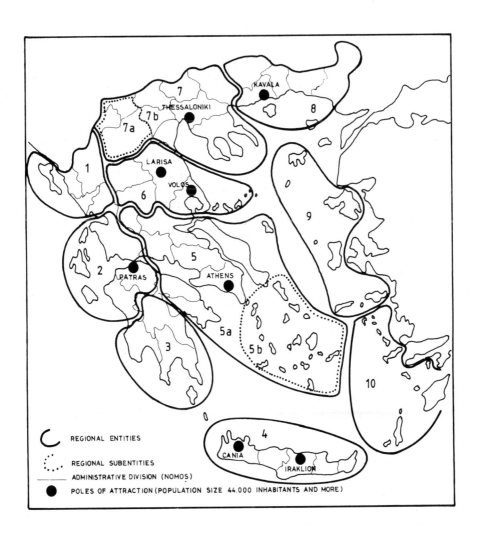

Map 7.2   The 10 regional entities (after KEPE)

In 1951, 40.1 per cent of *employment* was concentrated in urban areas, 44.4 per cent being spread among rural areas and the remainder in semi-urban areas. Two decades later, in 1971, the percentage of employment in urban areas had gone up to 48.0, that in rural areas was down to 40.8 (Table 7.1).

Table 7.1

Distribution of manufacturing and total employment
by type of area, 1951—61—71

	Manufacturing			Total employment		
Area	1951	1961	1971	1951	1961	1971
Urban	71.8	75.4	78.9	40.1	34.6	48.0
Semi-urban	13.2	9.9	9.0	15.5	12.9	11.2
Rural	15.0	14.7	12.0	34.4	52.5	40.8

Source: NSSG, *Census of population,* 1951, 1961 and 1971.

Investigations on regional development and industrial movement

Information on the movement of firms and industries on a national or regional scale in Greece is very scarce. During the three decades since the war and more particularly during the last two, the growth differentials between the regions in the country and the effect they have on the economic development of the nation have become the most controversial and dominant issues in the field of regional planning in Greece. Most of the work done on the problem has been confined, however, to the migration of people among the regions and between Greece and other countries, for that movement was seen as the major problem of regional development in the 1960s and 1970s (see Papageorgiou, 1973, Dimitras 1971 and 1972, Dimitras and Vlachos, 1973, Lianos, 1975, 1977, 1979, 1980, Sandis, 1973, Matsouka, 1963, Andrikopoulos, 1978, Zolotas, 1966, Fakiolas, 1967, 1975, 1980, Siampos, 1976, Sandis, 1973, Burgel, 1972). Other major concerns were industrial location and employment opportunities, but little effort was made to investigate systematically the movement of firms and industries from one region to another. One important reason could be that after the mistakes of the 1950s and 1960s, when the greater part of industry settled near Athens and Thessaloniki, very few firms have

236

relocated in spite of the various incentives offered to them.

Traditionally, therefore, the location and relocation of industry has been treated in connection with efforts for regional development. In the mid-1950s the first criticisms of the regional imbalance in the country were uttered and the first articles published, forecasting that if the forces responsible for those imbalances were left alone, the situation was bound to become worse. At that juncture, the first government policies were applied aiming at an increase in the income per capita, either with the help of income transfers or by the use of favourable incentives for the location of plants in the most backward regions. In the absence of reliable data and analyses no coherent and effective regional policy materialised. As one member of the Greek delegation to an OECD concerence (OECD, 1965) pointed out: 'In 1958 we had started doing something in the poor regions of Greece, without knowing exactly what we were looking for. We just felt we had to do something in that poor region — Epirus — from which people were emigrating to Germany, where incomes were low and everything was disappointing . . .'.

Apart from the contributions of a small number of individual academics and scholars, a major step towards the investigation of industrial location and its motives as well as population migration and employment opportunities in Greece was the creation of the Centre of Planning and Economic Research (KEPE) in 1963, of the National Centre of Social Research (EKKE) a few years later, and of the Institute of Economic and Industrial Research (IOBE) in the early 1970s. As regards information on industrial movement: whatever meagre data do exist are being collected by the new service created within the Ministry of Co-ordination to monitor the effects as well as to supervise the application of the very recent law (1116 of 1980), which provides incentives for the relocation of industries.

The main body of work done up to date in the field of industrial location and employment opportunities is summarised below. Industrial migration as such will not be mentioned separately, as there are no major investigations to be reported.

A major investigation into the location of industries, employment opportunities, and the incentives needed to realise a desired regional distribution of industrial plants and employment, was undertaken in 1973 by Doxiadis Associates, namely, the study of the National Regional Plan and Programme of Greece. This study went through several stages over a number of years, and the most recent report (Doxiadis, 1980) gives a good insight into the whole problem. Its main data sources are the three surveys of manufacturing in Greece conducted by the National Statistical Service of Greece (NSSG) in 1963, 1973, and 1978; it also draws data from the recent study by Cottis to be referred to later.

The Doxiadis report, after a thorough presentation of the current situation of employment, number of plants, and horsepower in each of the 52 administrative units (Nomos) of the country, discusses the existing problems in their relation to regional development and a set of goals and objectives laid down for the Regional Plan of the country. The administrative, financial, and economic incentives and the legislative measures introduced up to 1979 are reviewed and evaluated, although it is pointed out that for lack of data a proper evaluation, especially of the cost of the measures introduced, cannot be made. The report also compares the situation in Greece with that in other countries of the EEC, reviews the effects on the manufacturing sector expected from Greece's adhesion to the EEC, and goes on to propose a set of policies as well as a plan for the manufacturing sector in the country until the year 2000.

The study by Cottis and the Institute of Economic and Industrial Research (Cottis, 1980) is perhaps the only one to collect original data on the motives and factors influencing industrial location and movement. A special questionnaire survey was conducted in 1979 among manufacturing plants throughout the country, and its results were analysed by the author to give an insight into the locational criteria and motives of Greek firms. The study by Cottis examines first the spatial characteristics of Greek industrial development and the various incentives that have at times been employed to effect a better regional distribution. It then goes on to analyse and present the results of the survey, which touch on all aspects of industrial location, from transport modes for and costs of the transportation of raw materials to the availability of labour and the effects of the incentives.

Another study of particular importance, concerning the manufacturing sector, was carried out in the context of the latest regional plan prepared by KEPE (Centre of Planning and Economic Research). A separate research volume (KEPE, 1980) contains the most detailed analysis so far of the results of the National Statistical Service industrial surveys for the years 1963, 1973, and 1978. The location of industries is traced in space and time across the 52 administrative units (Nomos) of the country. The standard two-digit classification of commodities is used to classify the industries according to their type of product, but some results are also given by a three-digit classification. This KEPE study is mainly an exercise in data analysis and presentation, and comprises the most thorough presentation so far of the pattern of industrial location in Greece. It does not investigate the motives for this location or the effects of the incentives given at various times on the spatial distribution of industries.

The spatial distribution of manufacturing

The statistics available on industrial development by area in Greece enable one to follow developments in all 52 administrative units (Nomos) into which the country is divided. Note that the censuses consider all establishments, even very small ones, as manufacturing plants, which may explain the fairly large number of plants included in Table 7.2.

A general idea of the development on that areal level is given by Map 7.3, which once again shows the clear preponderance of first Athens and at some distance Thessaloniki. However, for the present discussion we have regrouped the figures referring to the Nomos to represent the nine planning regions into which the country has been divided by KEPE in its regional plans and which have been referred to in the previous section (Map 7.2); the same regions are also used in the Doxiadis regional plan. Table 7.2 shows the distribution of manufacturing plants in these nine regions for 1978, the rate of change between 1963 and 1978 and between 1973 and 1978, as well as some average figures for 1963, 1973 and 1978 concerning the average horsepower established by plant and by employed person. From this table and the more detailed data available from the NSSG census mentioned earlier, the following picture can be drawn.

The region of the capital has always been and still is today the region with by far the highest concentration of industry. Indeed it accounts for 48 per cent of the total number of plants in the country, 60 per cent of manufacturing employment, and 59 per cent of the horsepower. While in the period 1963–73 there was a distinct trend towards higher concentration in this region, in the period 1973–78 a slight trend towards relative decline can be observed (Doxiadis, 1980).

The regions of Thessaloniki and Kozani, together making up the region of northern central Greece, show the other major concentration of industrial plants, coming second after that of the capital. It has shown the highest rate of increase in the number of plants located and the horsepower established there through the period 1963–78.

The region of north-eastern Greece, which until 1973 showed a relatively small increase in horsepower and even a decline in the number of plants, after 1973 exhibits an impressive recovery, and has the country's highest rates of increase in the number of plants and the amount of horsepower established, namely 2.96 and 20.39 per cent respectively. This is probably the result of the various incentives given for the development of depressed border areas in the country, which apply to three of the five Nomos in that region.

The most 'modern' manufacturing plants as expressed by the horsepower/plant ratio in 1978 are to be found in the region of the capital, and more specifically in the Nomos of Beotia just north of Attica. The

Table 7.2

Basic statistics on the spatial distribution of manufacturing plants in Greece

Regions (a)		1978 Figures			Rates of
No. in Map 2	Name	No. of plants	Horsepower (000 HP)	No. of plants 1963–78	1973–78
5	Capital	55,072	3,223	0.79	0.09
9, 10	East Aegean	4,290	55	−2.70	−2.50
2, 3	West and southern Greece	10,596	319	−1.89	−0.49
1	Epirus	4,832	94	1.38	−0.30
6	Central Greece	9,905	603	−0.47	−0.25
7β	Thessaloniki area	21,426	775	1.24	2.42
7α	Kozani area	5,362	148	2.15	2.97
8	North-eastern Greece	6,344	260	−0.53	2.96
4	Crete	6,757	118	−1.20	−0.02
	Total	124,584	5,596	0.12	0.53

Source: Doxiadis, 1980 Table 4

(a) The Nomos in each region are given in Map 7.2

| change | | Averages | | | | | |
Horsepower 1963–78	1973–78	Horsepower/plant 1963	1973	1978	Horsepower/employee 1963	1973	1978
11.40	7.59	12.92	40.36	57.93	2.43	6.29	7.77
4.38	2.66	4.51	9.99	12.93	2.07	3.97	5.12
6.47	6.00	9.01	22.41	30.74	3.04	6.17	7.23
9.01	10.83	4.35	11.52	19.56	2.24	4.15	6.66
14.32	16.35	7.62	28.20	60.89	2.76	7.37	13.00
11.22	5.53	8.83	31.18	36.20	2.35	6.16	6.57
12.85	1.92	6.19	29.06	27.61	2.39	8.57	8.52
13.44	20.39	5.69	18.70	40.89	2.08	6.15	10.21
7.12	8.23	5.19	11.73	17.43	2.43	4.56	6.58
11.08	8.22	9.46	31.07	44.92	2.46	6.24	7.90

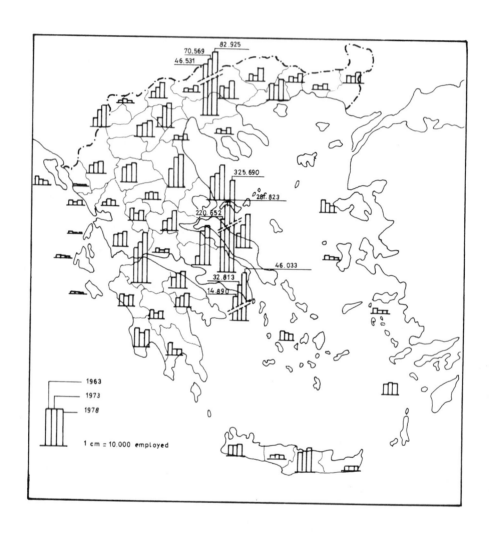

Map 7.3 Employment in manufacturing per nomos 1963, 1973, 1978

same Nomos has the largest manufacturing plants of the region and the highest rate of increase of employment and established horsepower in the period 1963—78. That is probably the result of the incentives given before 1973 to decentralise Attica, which treated Beotia as a peripheral Nomos instead of including it in the Greater capital area, as was the case in later legislation.

The third highest concentration of manufacturing is observed in the Nomos of Larisa and Magnisia in the region of Central Greece. These two Nomos also show a relatively high 'modernisation' of machinery as well as of working methods, as can be deduced from the change in the horsepower-by-plant and horsepower-by-employee figures, respectively.

To summarise: concentration of manufacture is most marked along the country's main transportation axis, that is, the axis between Athens and Thessaloniki, along which, apart from Attica and Thessaloniki, lie the Nomos of Beotia, Fthiotis, Magnesia, and Larisa. All the other regions of the country, and especially the islands of the Aegean, are rather problematic both in absolute figures and trends.

In general, the concentration of manufacture tends to increase in areas where:

1 there is already adequate industrial infrastructure as well as population and services;
2 favourable incentives have been introduced to foster industrial development; and
3 there are adequate transportation connections either by sea or by land. Perhaps these connections are even more important than the incentives themselves.

Regional policy and industrial location

The regional policies that were applied up to the mid-1950s could hardly be called appropriate at that stage. Along the lines of programmes for regional development, a considerable amount of capital was invested in irrigation works, land levelling, road construction, and experimental cultivations in some of the most backward regions. Parallel to such actions, differential-treatment legislation was introduced in the same period, to induce industry to locate outside Greater Athens. An improved road network was built at the same time to lower distance costs, hydro-electric power stations were built in a number of places scattered about the country to meet future industrial and household demands for electricity, and reduced rates were introduced for electricity used by industrial plants.

In the five-year Development Plan of Greece 1960—64, the decisions were taken with only a shade of regional consideration; no regional information being available at the time, there was no way to evaluate properly the existing regional problems and policies. In the early 1960s, migration within the country began to increase startlingly. The flow of the semi-urban and rural population into the major towns and particularly into Athens, already strong in the whole 1950—60 decade, continued in the 1960s to reach a peak in 1965; then a decline set in, while agricultural and other wages began to rise rapidly. In the period 1959—61 measures were initiated by three different Acts to counteract the prevailing trends by decentralising industry. The main objective was to entice industry away from Athens by financial allowances. However, as no provisions had been made in the regions of destination in terms of infrastructure, networks, decentralisation of administrative and banking facilities, etc., the effect of the measures was limited.

As late as the early 1960s the first notion of growth poles was conceived in the five-year Development Plan 1960—64, and various measures establishing industrial zones were proposed for Greater Athens, Thessaloniki, Patras, Volos, Kavala, and Heraklion. A more systematic approach to regional development was made in the second Development Plan 1966—70, which laid the foundations for a long-term approach to the regional problem. However, the political upheavals of the next year made it impossible for this Development Plan to be carried through. A new plan was made for the period 1968—72, in which some of the objectives of the previous plan were kept, but which again fell short of proposing effective measures on the regional level. As a result, regional differences increased, industry concentrating even more, mostly in the Greater Athens region, but also to a considerable extent in Thessaloniki. A limited number of plants located in western Macedonia, Thrace, Kavala, and Heraklion, but the bulk of 'out of Athens' industrial concentration was located along the transportation axes of Athens—Volos—Thessaloniki and Athens—Patras.

During the period 1968—72 the efficiency of the existing economic measures for the decentralisation of industry was reconsidered. Four new Acts were introduced in the years 1971 and 1972, which divided the country into four regions and established various incentives for industrial location in the outer regions. Among these incentives were an increase of the non-taxable profit, subsidisation of interest rates, and various other allowances. Their application depended on a rating of the regions according to their location along a national scale, and the state of their development.

The Development Plan for 1973—77 laid more emphasis on the problems of regional development. Instead of the relatively unplanned industrial development of the previous periods, this plan prescribed 'regional centres' and aimed at developing these into real growth poles and centres. According to this plan, Greece was divided into:

1 'regions of dynamic development':
    (a)   the Greater Athens and Aegean Islands regions;
    (b)   the central and western Macedonia regions;
2 'developing regions':
    (a)   the Peloponnese and western central Greece;
    (b)   Thessaly;
3 'depressed regions':
    (a)   Crete;
    (b)   eastern Macedonia and Thrace;
    (c)   Epirus.

In all regions industrial zones were developed, while in the depressed areas some development of agriculture and tourism was foreseen as well.

In October 1977 a new Act was issued, which gave more importance to the development of some industrial zones, characterising them as 'industrial centres', while also establishing new industrial zones in other areas.

After 1977 the importance attached to industrial decentralisation for the development of certain regions was reflected in the issue of a number of Acts of parliament and administrative decrees. Act no. 1116 of 1980 refers generally to regional development, giving incentives for the development of industries, tourism, trade, etc. in the more depressed regions of the country. The incentives given are of four types:

1 direct subsidisation by the government of so-called 'productive investments' (buildings, machinery, transport means, etc.);
2 coverage by the government of part of debt-repayment taxes and duties if the debts concerned loans under public guarantee;
3 untaxed income equal to the amount of total investment that is deducted from the taxable net profits;
4 acceptance of 'additional' amortisation above that normally calculated for the kind of investment made.

For the application of these incentives the country is divided into the following three regions:

Region A: Attica, the part of the Nomos of Corinth next to Attica down to the Corinth canal, and part of the Thessaloniki eparchy;

Region B: in which are included a number of Nomos at an intermediary stage of development; and

Region C: the rest of the country consisting mainly of Nomos near
the borders which in the past experienced a serious outflow of population.

It is still early to judge the results of this new Act. Its application in
practice is monitored by a special new service created at the Ministry
of Co-ordination. This new service is also hoped to collect the statistics
required for the proper evaluation of industrial migration in Greece, especially in the light of the above incentives.

Motives and factors affecting industrial location and movement in Greece

The only effort to investigate the motives behind the choice of industrial location and the factors affecting the movement of industries in
Greece, is the questionnaire survey undertaken in the study by the Institute of Economic and Industrial Research (Cottis, 1980). This survey
was divided into two parts. One questionnaire was addressed to industries and manufacturing plants in the Greater Athens Area (GAA), and
another to those in the rest of Greece. The number of establishments
that answered the questionnaire was a relatively small percentage of the
total, and therefore the results cannot really be used for any detailed
statistical analysis; nevertheless they are indicative of the prevailing
motives for industrial location in Greece. Note that the establishments
that answered the questionnaire were mostly of medium to large sizes.

Table 7.3 summarises the reasons why establishments in the *Greater
Athens Area* chose this area for their location, and why they are still
remaining there. In both cases the availability of manpower and the
closeness to the market were the reasons given most frequently.

Lack of space for expansion was given as the most urgent problem
facing the establishments involved, followed by such factors as high
wages, high cost of land, strict measures for the protection of the environment, etc. They are shown in Table 7.4.

Another set of drawbacks for the firms wanting to stay in the Greater Athens Area has been created by the various disincentives imposed
by the government in its efforts to deal with the problems of over-
concentration, namely, high rates of taxes, absence of investment incentives, measures for environmental protection, absence of tax allowances, problems of competition created by the priorities given to peripheral firms for the supply of goods to meet governmental needs, difficulties in expanding existing installations, etc.

246

Table 7.3

Reasons for choosing Greater Athens Area for industrial location and
for remaining there

Reasons	Percentage stating this reason	
	For original location[a]	For staying in the area[b]
1 Availability of working personnel	68	72
2 Proximity to market	61	55
3 Good general infrastructure	49	41
4 Owned land	48	53
5 Proximity to public and banking services	40	30
6 Availability of managerial personnel	39	39
7 Availability of other personnel	38	41
8 Residence of owner	37	27
9 Proximity to ports of Pireaus and Elefsis	35	34
10 Proximity to raw materials	27	26
11 Proximity to the airport of Athens	10	10
12 Other reasons	10	10

[a] Based on 196 answers
[b] Based on 176 answers
Source: Cottis, 1980.

Table 7.4

Problems facing manufacturing establishments in the Greater
Athens Area[a]

Problem	Percentage of establishments
1 Shortage of space	51
2 High cost of land for expansion	49
3 High cost of labour	45
4 Shortage of labour	36
5 Strict environmental control	22
6 Transport problems (mainly street congestion)	20
7 Other	12

[a] Based on 152 answers
Source: Cottis, 1980.

Table 7.5

Reasons for location outside the Greater Athens Area (rest of the country)

Reasons	Percentage of establishments
1 Government incentives	56
2 Low cost of land	40
3 Availability of manpower	30
4 Availability of good transportation	28
5 Raw materials	25
6 Place of origin of the owner	24
7 Proximity to market	21
8 Existence of satisfactory urban infrastructure	19
9 Others	17

Source: Cottis, 1980.

Table 7.6

Evaluation of location incentives, by establishments outside Greater Athens Area[a]

	Incentive	Percentage considering incentive as:		
		Fundamental	Important	Non-important
1	Increase of the non-taxable income	55	36	8
2	Increased factors of amortisation	32	57	11
3	Reduction of VAT	24	59	17
4	Coverage of debt re-payment duties	14	43	43
5	Deductions of tax in property transfers	1	29	70
6	Increased loans	27	42	31
7	Subsidies on building infrastructure costs	15	27	58
8	Preference on company products	22	42	36
9	Others	13	50	37

[a]Based on 942 answers
Source: Cottis, 1980.

Despite these problems, most of the firms (73 per cent of the sample) appear unwilling to move from GAA to the periphery. Most unwilling are the branches of food preparation except beverages, the manufacture of textiles, the manufacture of footwear and the sewing of fabrics, rubber and plastic products, chemical industries, manufactured metal products except machinery, electrical machinery, appliances and spare parts, and transport equipment. There is another group which looks hesitant — but not absolutely unwilling — to move out of Athens; it consists of tobacco manufacture, wood and cork, manufacture of paper, leather and fur products, non-metallic mineral products, machinery and appliances except electrical ones. A third group is eager to move; it includes firms in the beverage industry, furniture and fixtures, printing and publishing, petroleum and coal refining, basic metal industries, and 'miscellaneous manufacturing industries'.

The study examines a number of incentives which have been demonstrated to be most effective for industrial movement in Greece:

1 tax allowances on net profit;
2 increased rates of amortisation;
3 allowances on gross-receipts tax;
4 subsidised interest rates;
5 increased long-term loans;
6 subsidised expenses for building installations;
7 reduced rates of real-estate transfer taxes;
8 priority for peripheral firms as suppliers of products needed by public services.

The attitudes of manufacturing establishments in *the rest of the country* differ slightly from those in Greater Athens; the relevant results are summarised in Tables 7.5 and 7.6. Table 7.5 gives the answers to the question 'Why have you located in the area?'; note that the government incentives given at times score highest, with the price of land as a good second. Table 7.6, finally, quotes the results of the evaluation of the various incentives given to these establishments from time to time. In accordance with expectation, the appraisal of these incentives does not differ much from that given by establishments in the Greater Athens Area. Highest among them ranks the increase of non-taxable income, that is the reduction in the taxation of profits.

Meanwhile some motives have been expressed that seem to enhance the effectiveness of the aforementioned incentives, namely:

1 Better conditions in the existing network of industrial zones along with further expansion of it.
2 Rational development of the peripheral urban centres, and further development of the quantitative and qualitative level of the urban infrastructure.
3 More reasonable terms on the housing market.
4 Better public transport facilities.
5 Decentralisation of public services along with a number of attached centres of decision making.

The principal problems facing establishments outside the Greater Athens Area seem to relate to insufficient urban infrastructure, i.e. telecommunications, sewage, water networks, etc. Another major problem stated related to transportation facilities for both raw materials and finished products. Of these, the high transportation costs were referred to as the most important, closely followed by the delays and unreliable delivery times. Environmental protection did not seem to cause any serious concern, perhaps owing to generally relaxed government control and regulation outside the Greater Athens Area.

Complaints frequently voiced by companies established outside the Greater Athens Area concern the inefficiency and centralisation of government and banking services. Deliveries that ought to be taken locally require clearance from the centre and thus take a long time. Finally, several companies stated that they find it difficult to find specialised manpower outside Athens and Thessaloniki.

A large proportion of the entrepreneurs seem to fear that a movement towards the periphery would create major problems, such as:

1 shortage of skilled labour;
2 increase in transportation costs;
3 difficulty in communication with their customers;
4 loss of customers;
5 problems with the supply of raw materials;
6 bad condition of the urban infrastructure;
7 deterioration of access to custom authorities.

Moreover, the following minor problems were also mentioned:

8 there will probably be difficulties in finding activities complementary to the firm's main ones;
9 mainland transportation difficulties may cause damage to products, notably heavy installations;
10 changing the owner's family residence may create problems related to the comparative disadvantages of the urban infrastructure between core and periphery.

On the other hand there is a group of owners originating from the periphery who take a different attitude towards the inefficiencies of the urban infrastructure and transport networks, expressing the opinion that efforts should first and foremost be made to improve the infrastructure of industrial zones, the condition of housing for workers, public transport for the home-to-work trip, to create possibilities for better training of skilled and unskilled workers, and better management along with decentralisation of public and banking services. As problems of some importance are also mentioned the difficulty of finding skilled workers, the lack of complementary activities especially for plants specialised in semi-processed products, the lack of social infrastructure and leisure provisions, etc.

Outlook

The preceding sections have indicated that industrial development in Greece has largely tended towards concentration. The question arises whether that tendency will be continued in the future. There are strong reasons to believe that it will not. The obstacles to increased concentration have already become apparent in the study by Cottis. Moreover, Greece may well pass through the same development that has characterised other European countries in the past decades, and which has predominantly been one of deconcentration. On the other hand, Greece might skip that stage and proceed at once to a new type of spatial organisation, for which there is as yet no precedent in Europe. Indications are too fragmentary, however, for a firm opinion to be based on them with respect to the future.

References

Andrikopoulos, A. (1978), 'Industrial Structure and Regional Change: the case of Greek Economy 1963–69', *The Greek Review of Social Research,* no. 32.

Argyris, A. (1981), 'A Policy for Dependent Developments' Regional Development', paper for the Conference of Regional Development, Technical Chamber of Greece, Thessaloniki.

Burgel, G. (1972), *La Condition Industrielle à Athènes,* Centre Nationale de Recherches Sociales, Athens.

Cottis, G.C. (1980), *Industrial decentralisation and regional development,* Institute of Economic and Industrial Research, Athens.

Dimitras, E. (1971, 1972), *Enquêtes Sociologiques sur les Emigrants Grecs,* Centre Nationale de Recherches Sociales, Enquêtes nos 1 et 2.

Dimitras, E. and Vlachos, E. (1973), same as above – Enquête no. 3.

Doxiadis Associates, (1980), 'National Regional Plan and Programme of Greece: Secondary Sector', Report no. 19, vol. III.

Ellis, H.S. et al. (1965), *The industrial capital in the development of Greek economy,* Centre of Planning and Economic Research, Athens.

Fakiolas, R. (1967), *Prospects of return of Greek emigrants to Western Europe and possibilities for their assimilation in the Greek economy,* KEPE, Athens.

Fakiolas, R. (1975), *Surplus labour in countries at the intermediate stage of development,* KEPE, Athens.

Fakiolas, R. (1980), *Problems and opportunities of the Greek migrants returning from Western Europe,* KEPE, Athens.

Giannopoulos, G. (1979), 'Transport and Regional Development: the case of lesser developed economies', ECMT 8th International Symposium, Istanbul.

KEPE, (1965), National Development Plan 1966—70, Athens.

KEPE, (1980), *Programme for Regional Development: Spatial distribution of Industry 1963, 1973, 1978,* Athens.

Lianos, T.P. (1975), 'Flows of Greek Out-Migration and Return Migration', *International Migration,* vol. 13, no. 3.

Lianos, T.P. (1977), 'Employment Growth and Spatial Allocation of Labor in Greece', *Metroeconomica,* vol. XXIX.

Lianos, T.P. (1979) Paper concerning Greece in *The Politics of migration policy,* edited by D. Kubat, Centre for Migration Studies, New York.

Lianos, T.P. (1980), 'Movement of Greek Labor to Germany and Return', *Greek Economic Review,* vol. 2, no. 1.

Matsouka, K. (1963), *The internal migrant,* National Centre of Social Research, Athens.

Ministry of Co-ordination, (1976), National Accounts of Greece 1958—75, Athens.

NSSG (1951), (1961), (1971), Census of Population, Athens.

NSSG (1969), Census of Manufacturing, Athens.

OECD (1965), *Regional Development and Accelerated Growth,* Paris, p. 13.

Papageorgiou, C.L. (1973), *Regional Employment in Greece,* National Centre of Social Research.

Sandis, E.E. (1973), *Refugees and Economic Migrants in Greater Athens,* National Centre of Social Research, Athens.

Siampos, G.S. (1976), 'Emigration from Greece to industrialised Europe', in *Emigration from Mediteranean Basin to Industrialised Europe,* edited by Institute of Demography, University of Rome, editor Franco Angeli.

Ward, B. (1963), *Greek Regional Development,* KEPE, Athens.

Zolotas, X. (1966), *International Labor Migration and Economic Development with special reference to Greece,* Bank of Greece.

8 The Netherlands

W. T. M. MOLLE

In the Netherlands, a good deal of attention has been given to the movement of industry. Two phenomena in particular have been objects of interest, phenomena that have largely determined the spatial situation now prevailing and governed regional policy in this country. The first is the tendency for industry to decentralise from the central areas in the west to the rest of the country, a tendency that was corroborated by the government's policy to improve the balance among the various parts of the country; the second is the movement towards the suburbs, much encouraged by urban policy. Together with the country's general economic development, these two phenomena set the scene for the study of industrial movement in the Netherlands. To describe that scene, we shall draw on a variety of studies previously published, the variety lying in their nature, objectives, and statistical backgrounds.

After sketching the two phenomena referred to above, we shall continue our presentation of the Dutch case by describing the patterns of movement, giving an account of how many and what kinds of industries have moved these last years, and in what directions.

Next, we shall go into the reasons why companies leave one site and choose another.

Finally, we shall present some quantitative evidence of the impact industrial movement makes on economic developments in the regions of origin and destination, in terms of establishments and employees.

The spatial and policy settings

Introduction

The movement of industry cannot be well understood unless placed in the context of a country's spatial economic development and policy. To provide this context for Dutch industrial movement, we shall give in this section first an analytical description of the general socio-economic and demographic development of the Netherlands since the war, next an outline of the spatial configuration of growth in that period, and finally a sketch of regional, economic, and spatial planning in the last 30 years.

Changes in the structure of the Dutch economy

By the early 1950s, industrialisation in the Netherlands, in spite of its ancient roots, had not advanced very far. Indeed, in 1950 the share of industry in GDP was lower in the Netherlands than in most other European countries. The industrial sector consisted mainly of transformation of agricultural products, metal industries, and some traditional industries such as textiles and shoemaking.

Between 1950 and 1965, employment in nearly all manufacturing branches was growing, growth figures in some being quite high; only three branches, i.e. textiles, clothing and leather, could not keep up their employment levels in that period. From 1965 onward, employment in total manufacturing as well as in most constituent branches was declining, a tendency that increased in the 1970s, when quite a few branches showed heavy employment losses; indeed, by 1980 employment in the manufacturing sector had dropped back to the 1950 level.

In most branches of the service sector, on the contrary, employment increased steadily. For total services this increase amounted to 70 per cent in the 1950–80 period; many individual service branches have grown even faster.

In the 1950–80 period, the overall labour force steadily became better educated (in 1950, 70 per cent of them had only primary education, compared to some 35 per cent in 1980). Investment levels being generally high, too, labour productivity in manufacturing industry went up by an average of 4 to 5 per cent per annum in the 1950s and 1960s. In the 1970s, contraction of some low-productivity sectors and stimulation of some high-productivity ones helped to sustain the rise in productivity; as in this period production growth was relatively slow a fast

255

drop in employment ensued.

In the 1950s and 1960s there was a marked tendency towards large-scale production. Data from various sources reveal that up to 1974 the proportion of smallish establishments (employing 10—50 people) gradually decreased (Vijverberg, 1980). Since then some indications suggest a slight reversal of the trend.

The policy of the Netherlands government has purposefully contributed to a favourable employment situation on the one hand, but on the other to the structural labour shortage prevailing by the end of the 1950s, in spite of productivity gains and a high 'natural growth' of the working population.

In an attempt to overcome this shortage, labour was imported, especially from Mediterranean countries, and average wages were raised fast. After 1971 the situation changed radically into one of structural over-supply of labour and return migration.

Spatial dynamics of employment growth

Far from being spread evenly across the country, employment, like the population, has historically been concentrated in the western part of the country, where the three major cities Amsterdam, Rotterdam and The Hague are located. For an earlier study (Boeckhout and Molle, 1981) we divided the country functionally (on the basis of labour-market districts) first into three large zones: the Randstad (encompassing broadly the three western provinces, North Holland, South Holland, and Utrecht), the periphery (mainly the North and South Limburg), and the intermediate zone, defined in line with Dutch spatial-planning practice. Next a distinction was made within each zone between 'urban' and 'rural and semi-urban' districts; from the urban districts the three large metropolises were separated out. The division, which is reproduced on Map 8.1, follows only partly the administrative division into 11 provinces, which is not particularly suitable for spatial analysis.

How have total employment and manufacturing employment (our main concern) developed through the past decades? (Table 8.1.) On manufacturing employment we possess data for the period 1950—75; data on total employment are available only for the years from 1960 to 1975. For easy comparison, all figures of total and manufacturing employment will be presented as percentage shares of the country totals.

Turning our attention first to *total employment* we find that the strong position of the western area (Randstad) was consolidated through the years, and that the intermediate zone increased its share considerably

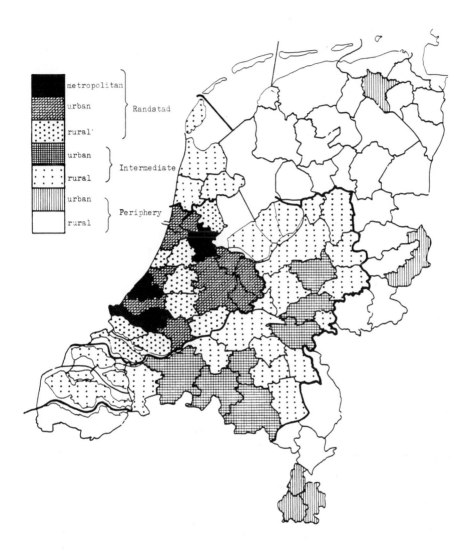

Map 8.1   Regional division of the Netherlands into 80 districts and
7 non-contiguous areas.

257

Table 8.1

Distribution of manufacturing and total employment by type of district and zone 1950–75

Zone	Area	Manufacturing						Total			
		1950	1955	1960	1965	1970	1975	1960	1965	1970	1975
Randstad	metropolitan	22.7	n.a.	20.0	18.7	17.3	15.7	25.0	24.9	24.4	23.2
	urban (ex metro)	17.3	n.a.	17.3	16.7	16.3	17.1	15.8	15.9	16.5	17.1
	semi-urban + rural	3.7	n.a.	4.3	4.6	4.8	4.9	4.8	5.1	5.2	5.5
	sub-total	(43.7)	n.a.	(41.6)	(40.0)	(38.4)	(37.7)	(45.6)	(45.9)	(46.1)	(45.8)
Intermediate	urban	16.4	n.a.	17.6	17.8	17.6	17.2	13.4	13.7	14.1	14.4
	semi-urban + rural	15.2	n.a.	15.1	15.7	16.7	17.1	15.0	14.9	15.3	15.7
	sub-total	(31.6)	n.a.	(32.7)	(33.5)	(34.3)	(34.3)	(28.4)	(28.6)	(29.4)	(30.1)
Periphery	urban	9.0	n.a.	8.5	8.2	8.2	8.3	8.5	8.2	7.6	7.3
	semi-urban + rural	15.7	n.a.	17.2	18.3	19.1	19.7	17.5	17.3	16.9	16.8
	sub-total	(24.7)	n.a.	(25.7)	(26.5)	(27.3)	(28.0)	(26.0)	(25.5)	(24.5)	(24.1)
Total	urban + metro	65.4	n.a.	63.4	61.4	59.4	58.3	62.7	62.7	62.6	62.0
	semi-urban + rural	34.6	n.a.	36.6	38.6	40.6	41.7	37.3	37.3	37.4	38.0
	total	100.0	n.a.	100.0	100.0	100.0	100.0	100.0	100.0	100.0	100.0
	Absolute (x 1000)	1,139	n.a.	1,247	1,341	1,286	1,183	4,225	4,579	4,633	4,521

Source: Total; Boeckhout and Molle, 1981;
Manufacturing: own calculations on the basis of various statistical sources.

at the expense of the periphery. Within the Randstad, the metropolitan areas lost some employment to urban and other areas, the former benefiting the most. In the intermediate zone, both urban and other areas increased their shares, while in the periphery both types of areas were losers.

The picture of the development of employment in *manufacturing* industry is slightly different. The Randstad appears to have lost quite a large proportion, mainly owing to the very strong decrease of the metropolitan areas; the urban areas stayed approximately on the same level, while the other areas increased their shares slightly. The decrease in the Randstad's share in industrial employment was matched by increases in the shares of the intermediate and peripheral zones. In both zones it was the 'other' (rural and semi-urban) areas that gained the most; indeed their shares steadily increased all through the period 1950–75. Urban areas in the intermediate zone increased their shares up to 1965, when a decrease set in; in the periphery, on the contrary, urban areas lost industrial employment up to 1965 and stabilised afterwards.

From the figures, then, a decentralising trend in employment can be observed in the Netherlands as a whole, and a suburbanising trend in the western part of the country, notably from the larger metropolises. The suburbanisation tendencies are still rather vague however, perhaps because the areal division used was too crude. For that reason we present in Table 8.2 total employment data for the period 1950–1975 for a sample of 24 urban agglomerations of more than 100,000 inhabitants in Holland, each divided into a core (the central municipality) and a ring (municipalities which have a certain minimum proportion of inhabitants commuting to the central city). For ready comparison, all data have again been expressed as percentage shares in the country's total.

Employment in the total sample of 24 agglomerations accounted for about 60 per cent of total Dutch employment during the whole period, leaving ± 40 per cent to cities not considered here and to rural areas. Recently, the Randstad share has been decreasing slightly and that of the intermediate zone increasing significantly, while the periphery is falling farther behind. All this is quite in line with the conclusion drawn from the previous table. On the intra-urban level, as can be observed from the row total, core cities have on the whole lost some employment to the rings; the loss amounted to some 2 per cent in the Randstad. In the intermediate zone both cores and rings increased their share in total Dutch employment, while in the periphery employment decreased in the rings as well as in the cores. Evidently, suburbanisation of employment is still only a Randstad phenomenon.

In the earlier study (Boeckhout and Molle, 1981) we compared the

Table 8.2

Distribution % of total employment in agglomerations, cores and rings by zone 1960–75

		1960	1965	1970	1975
Randstad	core	30.5	30.2	29.7	28.7
	ring	5.6	6.1	6.5	7.1
	agglomeration	(36.1)	(36.3)	(36.3)	(35.8)
Intermediate	core	8.2	8.4	8.8	8.9
	ring	2.9	3.0	3.1	3.1
	agglomeration	(11.1)	(11.4)	(11.8)	(12.0)
Periphery	core	8.6	8.6	8.0	8.0
	ring	3.2	2.9	2.6	2.5
	agglomeration	(11.7)	(11.5)	(10.8)	(10.7)
Total	core	47.3	47.2	46.7	45.7
	ring	11.7	12.0	12.2	12.8
	agglomeration	(58.9)	(59.1)	(58.9)	(58.5)
Total	Netherlands	100.0	100.0	100.0	100.0

Source: Boeckhout and Molle, 1981.

development of total employment, both on the level of seven types of districts and on the level of cores and rings, with the development of total population, the conclusion being that on both levels of analysis, population is spreading fast, with employment following somewhat reluctantly. Thus, in relation to population, employment is increasingly concentrated in core cities with respect to rings, in urban areas with respect to semi-urban and rural areas, and in the west with respect to the rest of the country.

The policy context

Neither the national economic development nor the regional developments depicted earlier have come about spontaneously. To achieve certain social objectives, the government has intervened in the process by active policies on the macro- and regional levels. For example, the government set in motion, when the war was over, a large drive for rapid industrialisation, giving quite a bit of attention to the regional aspect. The government directed its policy to the development of seaport-oriented activities in the western part of the country, and designated some 30 growth poles in the intermediate and peripheral zones to stimulate ('light') industrialisation there. The general policy objective of both physical planning and regional economic planning was to deconcentrate people and economic activity from the west — considered overcrowded — to the other parts of the country, by means of investment incentives and all types of infrastructure policy; regions faced with unemployment and low income were the government's first concern. This policy, which was backed up by physical-planning measures, was adhered to until about 1970.

In the beginning of the 1970s, comprehensive plans were drawn up for the various development regions, integrating physical and socio-economic planning. Moreover, to the measures stimulating development areas and growth poles were added measures to dissuade firms from settling in the west, such as financial levies on investment and special permits from the Ministry of Economic Affairs required for investment projects.

The policy intentions have not been backed up, as in other countries, with a purposeful policy of industrial migration from the centre to the periphery. All instruments apply to investments whether or not these are made in connection with industrial moves.

In the recent White Book on Urbanisation (RPD, 1977), a new policy has been introduced. The government recognises indeed that, with people suburbanising faster than employment, commuting distances tend to grow longer, a development the government, for various reasons,

261

considers undesirable. The proper spatial integration of the various functions in a city region is much emphasised, the assumption being that population growth is fixed and employment must follow the population. Unfortunately, the government has no instruments to make its new policy operational, and it is hardly surprising that the Memorandum has been heavily criticised for its failure to take the essential dynamics of employment growth into account; too little is known as yet of the reasons why plants are moved.

Some conclusions

The Netherlands have seen quite dramatic changes in their industrial structure since the war. Efforts in the first part of the post-war period were devoted to the construction of a strong manufacturing industry; in the second decade the accent was on an increase in quality. In the last decade of the study period, the whole manufacturing sector was contracting; new opportunities for this vital sector are now being looked for. During the whole period service activities continued to grow.

The spatial development of the Netherlands is largely dominated by two aspects: the equilibrium between the various parts of the country; and the distribution of economic activity among the various parts of urban agglomerations. The latter aspect is especially important for the larger towns in the west, but, as shown earlier, attention should also be given to smaller cities both in the west and in the other parts of the country.

Government policy has tended to promote decentralisation — for reasons of regional policy — and suburbanisation — for reasons of physical planning. Recently these policies have been under revision.

Inventory of empirical investigations

Introduction

The previous section will have made it clear that there is a need in the Netherlands to understand better certain spatial phenomena related to the dynamics of economic activity. The present section will serve to establish what knowledge has already been acquired on that score from empirical studies in the Netherlands. Apart from studies of international moves, two kinds of studies will be distinguished: those dealing primarily with inter-regional industry movement — to be split further into national and provincial investigations — and those primarily concerned with moves within urban regions. While enquiries into the nature and size of the phenomena will be the staple fare, research into motives will also be included. The section will be concluded with a survey showing up what gaps are still to be filled. The inventory to be presented here is taken from a report of the Netherlands Economic Institute (Beumer, Van Holst and Molle, 1979).

International movements

International movements of industry have received relatively little attention in the Netherlands. They were taken up in the 1960s by de Smidt (1966), who analysed the location of foreign establishments in the Netherlands; his study has recently been updated (Kemper and de Smidt, 1980). Finding no suitable statistics in the Netherlands on the number of foreign establishments or the employment they create, the authors had recourse to the listings regularly published by the Ministry of Economic Affairs, selecting establishments that (a) had been founded as new plants since 1945, (b) were involved in manufacturing, and (c) were fully foreign-owned. They surveyed these establishments three times, in 1964, 1972 and 1978, to obtain the information required to study certain aspects of location. Most of the industries surveyed must be regarded as branch plants.

The scarce and scattered pieces of information to be gathered from other studies are too poor for any conclusions to be drawn, with the exception perhaps of the inventory provided by the SISWO study (1967) (to be discussed in the next sub-section) of 131 manufacturing establishments which, by the definition of the study, had moved in from abroad; these, too were mostly branch plants.

National investigations

Only one large-scale investigation has so far been reported on in the Netherlands, an investigation moreover that dated back quite some time (SISWO, 1967). It consisted of two parts: an inventory and analysis of 1,251 manufacturing establishments that in the study period 1950—62 had moved from one municipality to another; and a socio-psychological motive survey among 151 plants in the metal industries that had migrated in the last part of the study period, the years 1959—62. The inventory part, based on the company records of the provincial Economic-Technological Institutes, gives a picture of the geographical, sectoral, and temporal migration patterns, and indicates some explanatory variables (labour market, for instance). Some more explanation of movement phenomena can be derived from the motive study. The investigation made it clear that two types of movement can be identified: decentralisation, often partial moves over relatively long distances, mostly due to labour-market or marketing problems; and suburbanisation, often integral moves, generally due to spatial constraints of expansion on the existing site.

A move is called integral when all parts of the company involved are moved; it is partial when only part of the company is moved, or when a new, secondary establishment is founded away from the mother company. Moves in the sense of the SISWO definition cross municipal borders but remain within the national territory, involve a staff of ten or more at the new location, and refer to manufacturing industry only.

A more recent national survey on a far more modest scale deals mainly with the motives behind moves in the years 1974 and 1975 (Pellenbarg, 1977). It is based on interviews with the managements of 64 companies (both in services and in manufacturing) which had moved in the period 1974–75; 50 had been selected from the Databank of Chambers of Commerce, and 14 — migrants from Amsterdam — from the material of the Amsterdam Municipal Statistical Bureau. Most of the moves involved were of the suburbanising kind. In the interviews, questions were asked about the company's reasons for moving and for choosing their new locations; efforts were made to verify the motives offered against the known quantified location factors in both the chosen and alternative locations.

Provincial investigations

Investigations into the movement of industrial establishments employing ten or more in the period 1950–75, using, like SISWO, the material available at the Economic-Technological Institutes have been made for the provinces of Overijssel and Noord-Brabant (Wever, 1978; Grit, de Weert, Wever, 1977), Limburg (de Weert, 1980), Friesland (van Lierop, 1978), Gelderland (Grit, 1980). All reports discuss such aspects as number of moves, distance, and some characteristics of the establishments involved, for instance industrial class, size class, shares of men and women in the staff. Moreover they go into the relation between moving industries and the production environment offered by rural, urbanised rural, and urban municipalities. The reports all use the following definition of industrial moves: 'The closing-down of (part of) an establishment in a municipality with the object of at once taking up the same activities outside that municipality', a definition that leaves intra-municipal moves out of account. In total, the reports published so far record a rather limited number of moves: 195 in Overijssel, 395 in Gelderland, 346 in Noord-Brabant, 105 in Friesland and 101 in Limburg; the Noord-Brabant study makes explicit mention of the inclusion of moves to Belgium, the Friesland report to moves from abroad. The Gelderland and Limburg surveys refer not only to moves but also to closures and newly created establishments. The study period was variable: 1955—75 for Limburg and Gelderland, 1960—75 for Friesland, and 1950—75 for the others. For Noord-Brabant a study for the motives of movement has also been made with the help of an oral enquiry among 74 manufacturing firms that has moved to or within the province in the period 1960—70 (Poolman, Potters and Wever, 1978).

A study of the motives for movement of industries and services has also been made for the province of Utrecht (Schalk, 1971); written enquiry among companies that since 1964 had arrived in the province or moved within its borders.

Studies on the level of urban regions

Studies of the phenomenon of industrial movement on a relatively small regional scale have been confined to the large Randstad agglomerations Amsterdam, The Hague and Utrecht; for the second largest urban agglomeration of the country, Rotterdam, only one study is known.

For *Amsterdam* the Municipal Statistical Bureau has registered since 1966 closures, new settlements, and moves; a move occurs in the Bureau's definition when a whole establishment is closed down to continue the same activities elsewhere (migration in our definition). An analysis of the motives given by 106 establishments migrating out of the city in the period 1964—69 has been made by the Statistical Office of Amsterdam (BSGA, 1970). Molle (1977) has analysed patterns of migration from the city of Amsterdam for the period 1967—73, using for the first time a simple model to try to explain these patterns. Part of this analysis has recently been updated by Molle and Vianen (1982). The University of Amsterdam (SEOUA 1978) analysed size and composition of intra-city moves and out-migration, and also went into the motives for these moves. For the southern rim of Amsterdam Kemper et al. (1975) have analysed the motives for the migration of plants to that area.

Amsterdam is also the object of the only — descriptive — study made so far to have placed movement in the total framework of creations, closures and *in situ* development (Kruyt, 1979). Zaanstad, one of Amsterdam's satellite towns, has been the object of an investigation (Klok, 1975) which is interesting in that it identifies certain settlements in Zaanstad as corresponding to suburbanising moves from Amsterdam, and points out that some of the original industries of the Zaan area have suburbanised farther afield.

The Hague: the Municipal Department of Town Development (van de Linden, 1977) has analysed the sectoral classifications, size classes, town quarters of origin, and new locations of industries and services that, from the companies' register, left the municipality in the period 1969–74.

In The Hague as in Amsterdam, the companies' register records only migrations, or integral moves, the establishment being the statistical unit. Moreover, the study reports the results of a written enquiry with 432 plants that left the city in the period 1969–74.

Utrecht: the ETI study of movement in the province of Utrecht (Schalk, 1971) has yielded as well some results on the level of the ur-ban region, they refer to motives only.

Finally, for *Rotterdam,* a descriptive analysis of movement patterns has been made by Buunk and Elderman (1982) covering the period 1977 up to 1981. Some information could be produced on creations and closures.

Two other studies deserve mention, particularly because they form a good complement to the urban-region studies referred to above, namely, studies of the so-called *'Green Core of the Randstad'* (Ottens, 1976; Buit, 1981). The parts interesting for the present research of the Ottens study are those concerned with closures, new settlements, and immigration of manufacturing industries in the 'Green Core' during the years 1960–72, the motives behind the moves, and some sectoral and other characteristics. The Buit study deals only with 25 movements of manufacturing industries selected from the total of all plants that migrated to the area up to 1979.

Evaluation

As appears from the previous inventory, present knowledge of indus-trial movement in the Netherlands is rather fragmentary.

The analysis of size, character, and geographical *patterns of move-ment* carried out so far can be evaluated as follows:

1 Empirical studies do not cover the whole territory of the Nether-lands, as is evident from Map 8.2. No complete picture of the phenomenon involved is available or can be constructed from local and regional studies. Coverage varies greatly among the three large zones of the Netherlands. In the Randstad some 'agglomeration' studies have been made, but no regional ones. The intermediate zone has been fairly well covered by regional

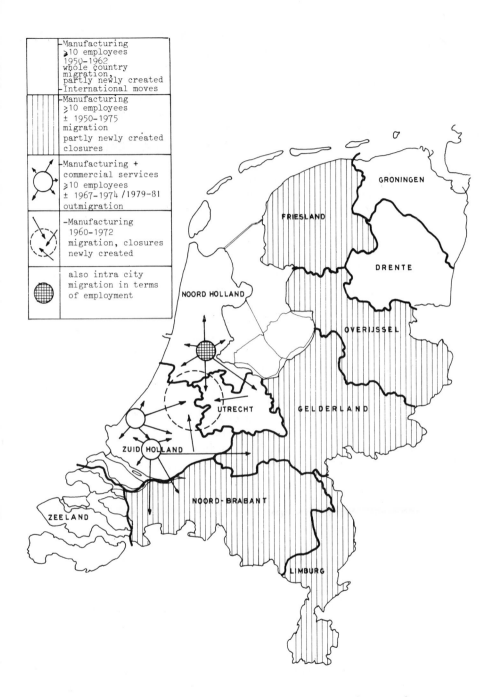

Map 8.2 Areal coverage of studies on the volume and type of movement.

studies (with only the province of Zeeland left out), while in the periphery two out of four provinces have been studied.

2 Not much is known either about the types of activity involved in movement. Inter-regional studies are confined to manufacturing plants employing ten or more persons; the movements of plants in the service industries are known for a few agglomerations only, a staff of ten being again the lower limit in most investigations.

3 As to the temporal aspect, all studies cover parts of the period 1950—80; the national study refers to the first part only (1950—62), most regional studies to quite a long period (1955—75), with the exception of the Friesland study which spans a shorter length of time (1960—75). Most agglomeration studies treat the period 1967—74; that of the Randstad Green Core adds the year 1960 to this study period. The Buit study is somewhat more recent, as is the Molle—Vianen study.

4 Most studies deal only with complete and partial moves, neglecting new settlements and closures; only two of the regional studies also account for 'births and deaths'. The agglomeration studies, on the other hand, do not even cover all movement; indeed, those of Amsterdam and The Hague are virtually confined to out-migration. The Green Core study, on the contrary, takes creations and deaths into account. Practically all studies consider only moves across municipal boundaries, data about moves within municipalities being exclusively available for Amsterdam.

5 The majority of studies are also lacking in statistical coverage. True, the five regional studies make a valiant effort to present an exhaustive enumeration of moves, but given the shortcomings of the basic data set they are unlikely to have succeeded or even to have come close to the ideal; the same applies to the Green Core study. The two agglomeration studies are more likely to have achieved a full enumeration because they rely on fairly good statistical sources.

The so-called *motive studies* may be evaluated as follows.

1 Total coverage of the national territory is provided by two studies, while five regional ones, and the three agglomeration studies of Amsterdam, The Hague, and the Randstad Green Core refer to specific areas only.

2 Most studies are not restricted to manufacturing industries, but also take services (commercial services mainly) into account (that is indeed true of agglomeration studies, a recent national study, and one regional study).

3 The studies vary a great deal in the time periods they cover:

1959—62 and 1974—75 for the national studies, 1965—70 (Utrecht) and 1960—76 (Noord-Brabant) for regional studies, and the years since 1967 for agglomeration studies.

4 Most studies cover only migrated and some newly created establishments, analysing them mostly at the point of arrival or creation; because of their very disappearance, closed-down establishments not associated with migration have not been analysed.

All studies inventoried, whether concerned with numbers or with motives, are of a descriptive nature. One attempt has been made at a different approach, namely at explaining the pattern of migration by *econometric methods,* combining the results of statistical and motive studies concerned with Amsterdam.

The general conclusion must be, then, that much information needed for a complete picture of the dynamics of economic activity in the Netherlands is still lacking. Our knowledge of the movements of services, intra-city developments, and the factors determining mobility should improve, and consistency in the coverage of creations, closures, and migrations would be welcome. To improve the present unsatisfactory data situation, new avenues of analysis need to be explored, notably the use of as yet untapped data sources and the coupling of existing data (Beumer, van Holst and Molle, 1979). On the other hand we do have valuable, albeit scattered, information, and from what we have we will try to draw the most complete possible picture.

Patterns of movement

Introduction

Several kinds of plant moves can be distinguished, characterised by distance and the type of origin and destination. We shall deal with international moves first. Next we shall go into the moves within the Netherlands. For that group the SISWO study (1967) distinguished inter-regional and intra-regional moves. The former, accounting for some 40 per cent of the total number, are discussed first. The discussion of the latter category of intra-regional moves has been divided into two; the SISWO study had revealed that intra-regional moves were more frequent in the western part of the country than elsewhere, and moreover of a different type. Internal moves in the west were largely suburbanising moves: firms migrating from urban centres to municipalities in the rings of the agglomerations, or to rural places (80 per cent of total moves in the west originated in agglomerations). In the other parts of the country only 40 per cent of the industrial moves sprang from agglomerations. This discussion of movement patterns will be rounded off with some conclusions.

International movements

Plants have been created by foreign capital in the Netherlands at quite a high rate. Between 1950 and 1962, 131 plants moved in from abroad (SISWO, 1967). The annual number of new manufacturing establishments coming from abroad averaged 4 up to 1953, rose to 12 between 1953 and 1958, reached 22 between 1959 and 1965, to fall back to 12 between 1966 and 1970; in total some 300 settlements from abroad were inventoried (Kemper and de Smidt, 1980). No direct information is available for the period since 1970, but the impression is that the rate has fallen further. In the early 1950s the USA was the main investor, the UK and France following at quite a distance. From 1959, the year the European Community came into being, establishments from European countries outside the EC began to settle here; indeed, the entailing tariff barrier induced UK, Swiss, and Scandinavian firms to invest. In that period the dominant position of the USA was not fundamentally undermined, however. Some French and German investment has occurred since, in particular from large corporations anxious to join their UK and USA competitors in taking advantage of the so-called Delta location for basic industrial investments.

The plants created by foreign investment tended to be large. Particularly in the petroleum and chemical sectors, and to a lesser extent in the transport-equipment sector, multinationals were responsible for a group of very large plants. In the sectors of metal working, electrotechnics and instruments specialist foreign companies set up another group of, mostly smaller, production units in the Netherlands.

The geographical orientation of foreign investment in the Netherlands showed a very clear pattern. Up to the 1960s, the largest group of plants — 40 to 50 per cent — had opted for a location in one of the three Randstad provinces; almost all of them went to an agglomeration in the west (SISWO, 1967), notably to Rotterdam and Amsterdam (Kemper and De Smidt, 1980). In the course of the 1960s, however, the south-east of the Netherlands (central to the EC market) came to be more and more preferred. Locational patterns differed somewhat by nation of origin; USA firms showed a strong tendency to move production units to the Randstad (49 per cent of their establishments), in sharp contrast to other foreign establishments created in the period 1945—78: indeed, of these, only 34 per cent were located in the west in 1978 (Kemper and De Smidt, 1980).

Inter-regional moves

A systematic investigation into inter-regional moves is possible for manufacturing establishments of ten or more employees that were moved completely or created a branch plant.

Flows from the western part of the country to the other parts were the most striking feature of the total spatial patterns. All regions indeed showed a positive balance (net movement) except the west, which recorded a net outflow of 400 plants (SISWO, 1967). Moreover, the flows among the parts of the country making up the intermediate and peripheral zones, and the moves from these zones to the west, were relatively insignificant compared to the flow west to rest (SISWO, 1967). From the six provincial studies (all outside the west), there seem to have been very few emigrations. Most were between neighbouring districts along both sides of the provincial boundary; evidently, these moves do not really differ from intra-regional moves, their recording as inter-regional being purely accidental.

Given that conclusion, we will leave aside movements from regions outside the west, to concentrate on the mainstream of inter-regional movement: the exodus from the west to the other parts of the country. To that end, we have brought together a number of indicators in the following rather synoptic table (Table 8.3). As in the following tables this one is based on the SISWO study, the country has been split up into four large geographical areas, namely, the west (provinces of North and South Holland and Utrecht), the north (provinces of Groningen, Friesland and Drente), the east (provinces of Gelderland and Overijssel), and the south (provinces of Zeeland, Noord-Brabant and Limburg). As the data cannot be regrouped to our functional division of Map 8.1, they will be reproduced here for the division of the country into these four geographical areas.

The first thing to note in Table 8.3 is that the spatial patterns of complete and partial moves are largely identical. The next interesting point is the relation between the total number of moves from the west to a particular region and the total number of moves from all other regions into that region, expressed in percentages in row 4 of the table. The figures confirm that by far the larger portion of firms settling in the regions outside the Randstad, that is, in the intermediate and peripheral zones, emanate from the western zone.

That observation is largely corroborated by the findings of four studies giving relevant information concerning Noord-Brabant, Limburg, Gelderland and Overijssel. Although these studies are in principle

Table 8.3

Decentralisation of manufacturing plants ($\geq$ 10 employees) from the western to the three other parts of the country, 1950—62

	North	East	South	Total
1 Complete moves from west	45	58	35	138
2 Partial moves from west	72	101	79	252
3 Total moves from west (1 + 2)	117	159	114	390
4 Total number of plants moving into the region	152	195	130	477
5 Share (%) of west in total (3 : 4)	77	82	88	82
6 Stock in 1950, number of plants	2,228	3,728	4,276	10,232
7 Share of total moves in stock	5.3	4.3	2.7	3.8
8 Closures after move	10	10	15	24
9 Share of total net moves in 1950 stock (3 - 8) : 6	4.8	4.0	2.3	3.5

Source: SISWO, 1967.

Table 8.4

Moves of manufacturing establishments $\geq$ 10 employees into four provinces (total and originating in the west)

	Overijssel	Gelderland	N. Brabant	Limburg	Total
Total number of moves into the province	115	174	137	15	441
of which: originating in west	66	141	121	11	339
%	57	81	88	73	77

Source: Grit, de Weert and Wever, 1977; Grit, 1980; and de Weert, 1980.

based on the same data as the national one, the figures they present may differ. For one thing, the provincial studies do not always explicitly take all branch moves into account; for another, they consider a longer time period (up to 1975). We have assembled the relevant data in Table 8.4.

From the point of view of the receptor provinces, Table 8.4 shows broadly the same picture as Table 8.3. Once more the west emerges as the major source of inmoving industry, accounting for as much as 80 per cent of the total in the provinces adjacent to the west, and still more than 50 per cent in Overijssel and even 70 per cent in Limburg, both provinces at considerable distance from the Randstad; these figures compare well with the percentages in the previous table, which range from 70 to 80.

The 'trek' of plants from the west to other parts of the country may further be broken down by type of origin and destination area. Out of the 390 plants that had made 'decentralising' moves (SISWO, 1967), 320 originated in one of the 21 agglomerations in the west; out of these 320, 280 had chosen to settle down in non-agglomeration municipalities in the other parts of the country. A distinct pattern thus emerges: plants tend to move from urban agglomerations in the west to semi-urban and rural municipalities in the destination areas. That finding is corroborated by some of the provincial studies. Indeed, de Graaf (1978) and Poolman, Potters and Wever (1978) have shown in their studies that most of the 'immigrant' firms in Noord-Brabant had come from the Rotterdam area; according to Grit (1980) most of the moves into the province of Gelderland also originated in the 'largest cities of the Randstad'.

The Noord-Brabant and Gelderland studies both reveal a clear influence of distance on inter-provincial moves, reporting that most moving firms relocated in the zone adjacent to the west.

The direction of the flows from the west having been dealt with, we now proceed to the consideration of its volumes. The total number of 390 plants recorded by SISWO (1967) may not be correct; we do not know whether the inventory made for this study was an exhaustive one. The apparently rather small figure of 390 is given some relief if compared to the total stock of plants in the donor and receptor regions. In 1950, there were in the west some 10,320 manufacturing industrial establishments of ten and more workers; 390 movers represent a loss of 3.8 per cent in a period of 12 years, or only 0.3 per cent per annum. The gain of the acceptor regions is in the same order of magnitude, as the last column of rows 6 and 7 of Table 8.3 show. It is true that subsequent closures undo some of the gains, but not to the extent of affecting the relative position of the various regions.

Another point that needs to be considered is the sectoral composition of the industries that move inter-regionally. Table 8.5 breaks down the total number of plants that were moved from the west to the three other regions by branch of activity.

Table 8.5

Sectoral composition of decentralising plants, 1950–62

Branch	North	East	South	Total	Stock 1950 west	Total stock (%)
Food	3	17	10	30	1323	2.3
Textiles	1	7	4	12	174	6.9
Clothing	10	28	24	62	1518	4.1
Leather	5	4	5	14	159	8.9
Wood	13	11	8	32	553	5.8
Paper	4	2	5	11	134	8.2
Printing	–	2	1	3	538	0.6
Chemicals	9	11	10	30	467	6.4
Stone/ glass	9	7	9	25	223	11.2
Metals	63	70	38	171	2568	6.7
Total	117	159	114	390	7657	5.1

Source: SISWO, 1967; Census of Manufacturing, 1950.

One observes at once that in absolute terms the metal industry is by far the largest single group, accounting for almost half the total moves in the period 1950–62. The next largest group is clothing, accounting for some 15 per cent of total moves. The same ranking applies to the three destination regions.

It would be attractive to extend the period somewhat by analysing the results of provincial studies that take the period 1950–75 into account. Three of them (Friesland, Overijssel, and Noord-Brabant) give information on the sectoral composition of 'immigrant' plants. The results of that limited sample largely confirm the picture of Table 8.5; not only the rankings, but also to a very large extent the percentage distributions across the sectors, are identical. Would the picture change if we took relative data instead of absolute ones? To find that out, all absolute figures were divided by the stock of plants in the western part of the country in 1950. The relative figures indeed talk a different language: the sector metals, though showing a slightly above-average figure, is far surpassed by the groups stone/clay/glass, leather and paper. Printing companies seem hardly to be moving at all.

Intra-regional moves in the west

The spatial pattern of inter-communal moves in the west is dominated by the emigration of plants of the major cities to various destination areas; immigration into these cities is insignificant. From the studies for Amsterdam and The Hague we have taken the data on out-migration to compose Table 8.6. The figures from these studies refer to manufacturing industries as well as to commercial services. Firms move out from Amsterdam and The Hague to settle to an overwhelming extent (80 per cent) elsewhere in the same region. The intermediate zone is the next important receiving region, while the periphery gets only a minor portion of all the plants that leave the two cities.

Table 8.6

Establishments migrating from the cities of Amsterdam and The Hague to other municipalities, by destination area

| Area of destination | Establishments | | | |
| | Den Haag[a] | | Amsterdam[b] | |
	Total	%	Total	%
West	825	79	375	84
(of which own province)	(653)	(63)	(268)	(60)
Intermediate zone	161	16	57	13
Periphery	53	5	14	3
Total	1039	100	446	100

[a] All establishments (1969–74). Source: van der Linden (1977), pp. 28–9.
[b] Establishments $\geq$ 10 employees (1967–73). Source: Molle (1977), p. 328.

Within the western region we observe a very distinct influence of distance; indeed, about two-thirds of all the emigrating plants relocate within the same province (row 2). The picture stays quite the same for the more recent period of 1977—80, which could be analysed for Amsterdam (Molle and Vianen, 1982). Information not included in the table reveals that 50 per cent of all plants leaving the city relocate in a municipality belonging to the same urban agglomeration. This shows that in the west of Holland economic activity is suburbanising; moreover the information of Table 8.6 suggests that the suburbanisation tendency smoothly passes into a tendency to decentralise over somewhat longer distances.

For a more detailed insight into the spatial pattern of suburbanisation, Maps 8.3 and 8.4 reproduce the number of relocations from Amsterdam to all municipalities of the three western provinces (Molle). Clearly, most relocations are oriented to the direct surroundings of Amsterdam, with a preference for the southern rim. The North Sea Canal may well have presented a formidable psychological barrier to firms oriented towards the Amsterdam and Randstad markets: more than 85 per cent of firms moving in the period 1967—73 resettled in the municipalities of the southern rim, and only 15 per cent opted for the north. In the period since 1973 these patterns have stayed largely the same (Molle and Vianen, 1982), as a comparison of Maps 8.3 and 8.4 the situation in each sub-period (1967—73 and 1974—79) shows. Once the barrier is crossed, however, migration continues northward: according to Klok (1979), a large majority of the plants that moved out of Zaanstad (a town immediately to the north of the North Sea Canal) went indeed to other communities in that part of North Holland. On the other hand the immigration figures of Zaanstad show up the preponderance of Amsterdam as a source; this city accounted for two-thirds of total immigration into Zaanstad.

Another study (Ottens, 1976) enables us to go somewhat deeper into the dynamics of industrial growth in the so-called Green Core of the Randstad, the primary destination of most Amsterdam firms leaving the city. Map 8.5 taken from this study gives the total number of industrial plants that moved to the Randstad Core between 1960 and 1972, this time registered at their place of arrival, revealing that the pattern observed for Amsterdam in the latter part of the period generally applies to the other cities as well. Most moves are effected close to the city of origin; indeed, very few plants move more than 20 km, which entails overlapping of the expulsion zones of Rotterdam, The Hague, and Leyden in the south-western wing of the Randstad, and of Amsterdam and Utrecht in the north-eastern wing. This pattern of movement was also found by Buit (1981) in his more recent but also more restricted survey. Map 8.5 also shows the preponderance of the migration from Amsterdam. The differences in importance of the three cities of origin are, according to Ottens, due to differences in the indus-

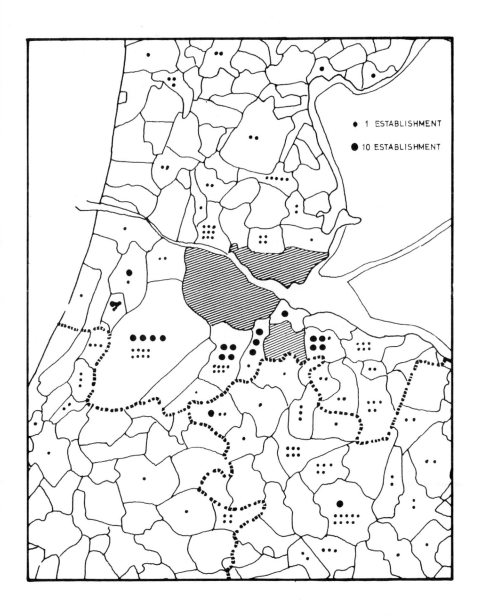

Map 8.3 Number of plants that migrated from the city of Amsterdam
to the surrounding municipalities 1967–73.

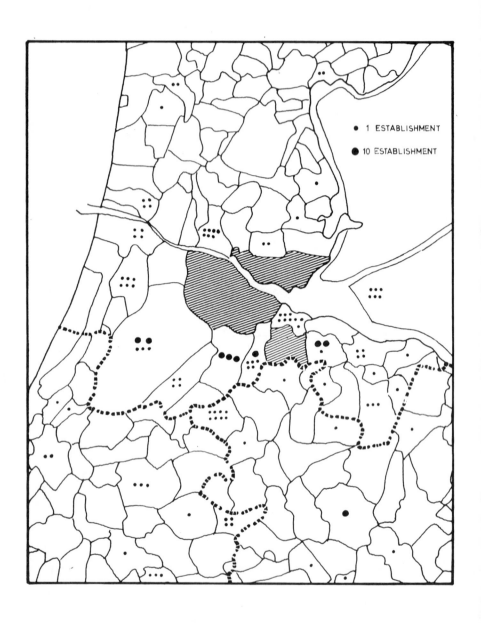

Map 8.4 Number of plants that migrated from the city of Amsterdam to the surrounding municipalities 1974–78.

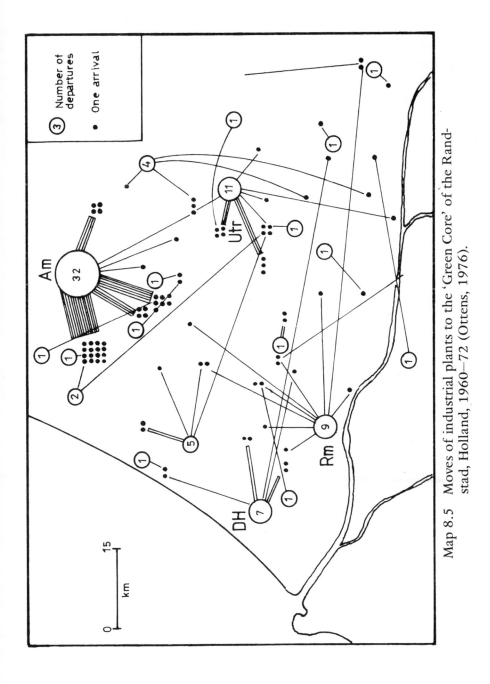

Map 8.5 Moves of industrial plants to the 'Green Core' of the Randstad, Holland, 1960—72 (Ottens, 1976).

trial structure of the various cities (The Hague, for instance, has very few industrial activities), their urban structure (the ancient town of Amsterdam expels more plants than the reconstructed towns of Rotterdam). To these arguments may be added that Rotterdam firms have alternative destinations apparently not open to Amsterdam; they can go to the outer ring of the Randstad instead of the inner zone of the Green Core, and even to the intermediate zone, for instance to the nearer parts of Noord-Brabant, as we have seen in the previous section.

Both Amsterdam and The Hague are large cities, but their boroughs are entirely different. If differences among cities lead to different volumes of moves, as we have just seen, then the same assumption may hold for different parts of the same city. There is some information available about the *geographical pattern of origin within cities* which enables us to go somewhat deeper into this point. For Amsterdam, the total number of emigrations to municipalities outside the city, e.g. can be broken down by town quarter. The figures have been compared to the stock of establishments found in each quarter in 1966 (the beginning of the period) (Molle, 1977), in order to calculate spatial-movement ratios. The variance found is small: the percentage shares range from 4.2 to 9.1 in the seven year period investigated. An analysis of the differences suggests two major reasons: type of activity (for instance a number of wholesale traders, concentrated in one quarter, all had to move for lack of space), and urban-renewal schemes (Molle, 1977). A similar comparison had been made for The Hague by Van der Linden (1977), who used stock figures of 1972. The ratio for total movement as well as the variance are almost the same in both cities; in The Hague, it ranged from 3.0 per cent in residential areas built before the war to 6.5 per cent in pre-war quarters with a mixed type of building, over a five year period. This last analysis does not, like the previous one, clearly point out particular areas as the main purveyors of plants; it seems that the spatial industrial structure of central cities is too complex to grasp in simple concepts, and that to obtain satisfactory results a much more refined analysis would be required.

Having analysed the geographical pattern, we will now turn our attention to the *sectoral composition* of the migrated plants. The sectoral pattern of plants that emigrated out of the three large cities is given in Table 8.7. The numbers given, though not strictly confined to suburbanisers, may be considered representative of them in view of their large share in the total number of movers (see Table 8.6).

In all three major cities, manufacturing represents only a minor portion — between 10 and 20 per cent — of total emigrating establishments. Commercial establishments account for one in three to one in two of all moves in all three towns; banks and insurance form another important group. The group 'other establishments' not being completely

Table 8.7

Sectoral composition of establishments migrated from the three major cities

| | Amsterdam* | | | | Rotterdam | | | | The Hague | | | |
| | 1967–73 | | 1974–78 | | 1969–76 | | 1977–80 | | 1969–74 | | 1975–80 | |
Sector	EP	MR	EP	MR	EP	MR	EP	MR	EP	MR	EP	MR
2/3 Manufacturing	97	1.2	48	1.3	n.a.	n.a.	48	1.0	118	1.4	n.a.	n.a.
4 Construction	48	1.6	22	1.2	n.a.	n.a.	35	1.2	80	0.9	n.a.	n.a.
6 Commerce	212	2.2	123	2.0	n.a.	n.a.	238	0.7	328	0.6	n.a.	n.a.
7 Transport	25	1.0	13	0.9	n.a.	n.a.	25	0.6	18	0.6	n.a.	n.a.
8 Banks, insurance	18	0.8	52	1.4	n.a.	n.a.	52	1.0	234	2.0	n.a.	n.a.
9 Other	46	0.8	10	0.7	n.a.	n.a.	45	0.4	290	1.0	n.a.	n.a.
Total	446	1.4	268	1.5	n.a.	n.a.	443	0.7	1068	0.9	n.a.	n.a.
All establishments	2114	0.8	1386	0.9	n.a.	n.a.	443	0.7	1068	0.9	n.a.	n.a.

EP = number of emigrated plants.
MR = movement ratio (EP divided by stock of establishments in the beginning of the period, the result once more divided by the number of years).
* plants with over 10 employees.

Sources: van der Linden, 1977; Molle, 1977; Molle and Vianen, 1982; Buunk and Elderman, 1982.

registered in Amsterdam, a comparison of the three towns on that score calls for some caution.

While in general terms the three cities show a resemblance, on detailed inspection the sectoral movement ratios vary quite a bit among towns and through periods. The causes may be quite specific, and we do not believe that a further analysis would reveal many interesting general facts.

The bottom row of Table 8.7 tells us how the comparison works out in relative terms for *all establishments*. Taking the total number of establishments, for Amsterdam too, we find that the movement ratios in all three cities are about equal: every year, between 0.7 and 0.9 per cent of all plants leave the large cities of Holland. Strikingly, the movement ratios of the periods since the crisis are about equal to the ones in the periods before the crisis, which would imply that the factors inducing movement from the large cities are as strong as ever.

Intra-regional moves in the other parts of the country

Industrial movement outside the west (apart from the immigration of firms from the west) is mainly characterised by short-distance internal moves. That point is highlighted by all studies, for Overijssel, Noord-Brabant, Gelderland, Limburg, and Friesland. As these studies show, a large majority of the moved plants located in the immediate vicinity (less than 20 km away), or in the district bordering on the one they had left (20—50 km). Once more we may conclude to the general rule that the number of moves clearly decreases as distance increases.

Outside the west, short-distance moves seemed to coincide far less with moves from agglomerations (SISWO, 1967). The question arises whether the phenomena of suburbanisation are at all present in these regions. Recently, Wever (1981) published a new analysis of the data gathered with respect to the five provinces in which short-distance moves had been studied. The analysis could only be approximate, though, for the basic data had not been organised to fit the functionally defined areas of urban cores, urban rings, and others, as used in Table 8.2; instead, they were grouped by U—urban, UR—urbanising rural, and R—rural areas as defined by the Central Statistical Office. The data are reproduced in Table 8.8.

Because the data refer to all moves and do not distinguish moves within one agglomeration from others, we cannot draw from them any definite conclusion with respect to suburbanising tendencies outside the Randstad. However, let us assume for the moment that each move took place within an agglomeration, an assumption that seems justified given the short distances involved, as observed earlier. According to

Table 8.8

Number of manufacturing plants ≥ 10 employees that moved within the provinces of Friesland, Overijssel, Noord-Brabant, Gelderland, and Limburg between two municipalities, by type of municipality of origin and destination

Origin \ Destination	R	UR	U	Total
Rural	22	21	26	69
Urbanising	41	56	65	162
Urban	67	129	44	240
Total	130	206	135	471

Source: Wever, 1981.

Table 8.8, some 50 per cent of all moving industries leave an urban municipality, and of these, 82 per cent settle in a rural or urbanising rural municipality, which suggests suburbanisation. On the other hand, one quarter of all moves (the cases on the diagonal) remain in the same type of place, and nearly an equal number move against the suburbanising direction, from rural to semi-urban and from semi-urban to urban municipalities (above right of the diagonal). The figures of the separate columns give no conclusive evidence of suburbanisation either. If we drop the assumption that short-distance movers remain in their own agglomerations, there is even less support left for the idea of suburbanisation outside the Randstad.

Another approach for finding the patterns of intra-regional moves, was to analyse the number of plants that left the cities in the provinces of study. We have seen in the preceding section that such departures were quite numerous in the two major cities of the Randstad. The same is not true of the cities in the other regions of the country: in the whole post-war period 1950–75, only 7 plants left the city of Den Bosch, 10 that of Zwolle, 16 that of Tilburg, 15 that of Breda, and 31 that of Eindhoven. For the somewhat shorter period from 1955 to 1975 the corresponding figures were 24 for Arnhem, 23 for Nijmegen, and 4 for Maastricht (Wever, 1981). It is true that these cities, with their population of 100,000 to 200,000 inhabitants, have far fewer plants than the great cities of the west, counting about 700,000 inhabitants, but if the total stocks of plants are taken into account, relative figures come out much lower than in the west, too.

The conclusion of this section may be, then, that intra-provincial movements outside the west are largely a matter of local moves, and that no clear suburbanisation pattern reveals itself.

Conclusions

In this section, a synthesis has been given of what has been discovered so far about the numbers, locational orientation, sectoral composition, and size of manufacturing industries that since the war have moved to new locations. A few distinct patterns have been found to dominate the scene. Apart from international moves largely directed towards the west, these patterns reveal a decentralising tendency of plants from the west of the country to other parts, and a suburbanising tendency of plants from the major cities in the west. These patterns correspond to those of total decentralisation of manufacturing (Table 8.1); moreover, the pattern of short-distance moves is in line with the findings about total employment in urban agglomerations represented in Table 8.2, in spite of the fact that the data for regions outside the Randstad apply to manufacturing only. Recall that this table showed total employment in the cores of the Randstad agglomerations as rapidly decreasing to the benefit of the rings, while the share of agglomeration cores outside the Randstad did not systematically decrease, but even increased in some instances.

If some topics have been thoroughly treated in this section, much information had to be left out of the text, in particular many cross tables of movement characteristics such as size and destination patterns, sectoral composition and type of move. However, any additional information to be extracted on those points from the various studies could only have added some more details but never changed the basic patterns. It seems we have managed, notwithstanding the relative paucity of the information, to show the main characteristics of the process of industrial movement in the Netherlands as far as migration (complete moves) and the creation of branch plants (or so-called partial moves) is concerned. For lack of data the other elements, new creations and closures, regrettably had to be left aside.

Motives and decision process

Introduction

The motives behind the movement of industry have been investigated
in several studies (see section on inventory). We will now take a close
look at the results of these studies.

Motives for moving or not moving are not just isolated facts; rather
they are elements of a major decision-making process before passing on
to the actual motive studies. Those on international moves will be dealt
with first, as the motives inducing firms to move from one country to
another indeed form a special category. Next we propose to review
'national' investigations followed by studies of suburbanisation moves
in the western part of the country.

Making the decision to move

Motives for movement cannot be well understood unless they are looked
upon as part of a firm's total operation. Most scholars make a distinction between motives for leaving the present location (so-called push
factors) and motives for choosing a certain new location (so-called pull
factors). Several studies have treated with varying thoroughness such
questions as: how decisions had been taken, what information had been
available, how many alternative locations had been studied and in what
depth, and whether the location finally chosen had been evaluated after
the move. From the material contained in these studies a quite clear-
cut and consistent pattern emerges, a picture that hardly varies with the
distance of the move.

A first major element of this picture is that very few managers consider alternatives for a new location; rather they tend to adapt their
views to the condition of a new site they happened to come across. Even
those that do go about the preparations for a move in a slightly more
systematic way, seldom consider more than three alternatives, and that
only superficially; in most cases only one criterion, e.g. the price of
land, was considered before the decision was made. Nor is it only small
independent firms that are guilty of such poor decision making — that
would be understandable, because they have neither the equipment nor
the know-how that larger concerns or their branches have at their disposal. On the contrary, even large companies seem to make such important decisions, anchoring their establishments for quite some time on
the poorest of foundations. That is remarkable, for while a plant director may be credited with sufficient awareness of the problems of the

present location — which he feels every day and all day long — he cannot know sufficiently what he is letting himself in for at the new location.

The quality of the information is indeed of paramount importance for the quality of the decision. Once more the believer in rationally acting economic man is disappointed by the outcome of the studies that have gone into the problem: much information appeared to have reached the decision makers by accident, from personal contact, from publicity, while public and semi-public bodies (ministries and municipalities on the one hand, regional industrialisation offices, labour exchanges on the other) seem to play only a minor role. If they are involved at all, seldom are they contacted by a firm looking systematically for relevant information.

International moves

The motives that induce firms to move abroad are quite different in nature from those that determine intra-national moves. They are in general related to the comparative advantages of a country over another country, advantages which may be due to factors that are practically constant within the area of our country. Indeed we may assume that firms settling in the Netherlands from abroad have been motivated by the advantages the Netherlands offer to foreign investors over other countries. According to Kemper and De Smidt (1980) a comparative cost analysis of various locations in Europe indicates that locating a branch plant in Europe became very attractive to American firms in the course of the 1950s, because lower labour cost compensated for higher raw-material cost. In the first post-war decades wages were very low in Holland even by European standards, owing to deliberate industrialisation and wage and price policies of the government. There was also an ample supply of labour, for the population was growing fairly fast. Moreover, the Netherlands were attractive because they were socio-economically stable and had remarkably good industrial relations. In the course of the 1960s and notably in the 1970s, most of these advantages were lost. Others remained, however, factors that had attracted quite a few heavy industries, notably the unique location in the so-called Golden Delta that had made Rotterdam the 'port of Europe'. This geographic position, skilfully organised and equipped with adequate infrastructure, is indeed the principal reason for the location of many (petro) chemical and other industries in the Netherlands.

The first national study to be discussed is the enquiry among some 150 plants in the metal sector into their motives for the moves they had made between 1959 and 1962 (SISWO, 1967). About half of these plants could be said to have decentralised (from the west to the rest), the other half having made internal moves within the region; of the latter moves, one-third could be labelled suburbanisation moves in the west. Unfortunately, the detailed table presented in the study listing motives for leaving the present and choosing the new location does not make the same distinction.

The results for all moves show that in 35 per cent of the cases 'lack of space' was the main reason for leaving, in 25 per cent 'labour market problems', and in 11 per cent 'local regulations'; finally, for leaving 'transportation difficulties' also figured quite often among the reasons mentioned.

With respect to the reasons for choosing a particular new location the study indicates that all entrepreneurs considered the availability of space a *conditio sine qua non*, 67 per cent mentioned the labour market as a major reason to locate at a given site, and one half of the respondents favoured pleasant living environments. A wide variety of other factors were also found of some importance, such as 'co-operation of local authorities', 'location close to other plants of the corporation', but they were not seen as decisive.

Interpretation of some very succinct tables from the study permits us to study a bit more closely the differences between motives for decentralisation and suburbanisation. Many of the decentralisers mentioned 'insufficient availability of both qualified and unqualified workers, the poor productivity and the high turnover of the labour force' as major motives for moving, some of them adding 'distance to the market'. For the suburbanisers the main reasons were lack of space, bad adaptation of premises to specific needs, too strict local regulations, poor traffic conditions and insufficient accessibility. The positive counterparts of these motives for both types of moves are found back as major pull factors for choosing the new location.

We may conclude, then, that industrial movement breaks down into two distinct categories: short-distance moves for reasons associated with the premises and their accessibility, and long-distance moves associated with labour-market factors.

In a more recent study, Pellenbarg (1977) reports on an analysis of 64 interviews with managers of plants that had recently moved. Lack of space and poor accessibility were mentioned most frequently. Often a move is made as a result of specialisation and rationalisation after a merger, or on starting new activities. Pellenbarg mentioned other motives as rather insignificant. The author remarks that the motives he reports coincide mostly with those that in the SISWO study had been found for short-distance moves; indeed, long-distance moves had almost completely run out by 1975, most moves now being of the suburbanis-ation variety. The author supposes this is due to the changed general ec-onomic environment: labour is no longer scarce; Third World countries cater for many plants that used to locate in the peripheral regions of the country.

The difference in motives between the two types of moves distingu-ished here has also been observed in a study of Noord-Brabant (Pool-man, Potters and Wever, 1978) albeit that some short-distance moves within the province also seem to have been motivated by labour-market considerations. Indeed, such considerations are not completely absent from the decisions on short-distance moves; according to some of the above-mentioned studies they tend to keep a plant tied to its old loca-tion, the critical element being the fear of losing key staff and qualified workers.

Suburbanisation

The studies of the motives inducing firms to move from Amsterdam and The Hague largely confirm the findings of the previous sub-section on suburbanising moves.

The analysis of the reasons why 106 firms had left the city of Am-sterdam for a location in the agglomeration (BSGA, 1970), exposed lack of space for expansion as the most important reason (60 per cent); traffic problems came next (14 per cent), followed by organisational reasons (mergers, etc.) (10 per cent). It was in particular the manufac-turing and warehousing companies that wanted space for expansion; office-oriented activities apparently had no problems on that score. Traffic problems were encountered mainly in the centre of the city; other areas scored less on that variable. The most frequently cited fac-tors were space for loading and unloading, and parking problems.

Earlier, AIV (1969) had carried out a survey among 113 firms in Amsterdam into the problems they encountered at their present loca-tion; the reasons they gave for wanting to leave Amsterdam were the same as found in BSGA, 1970 for plants that had actually left the city. However, poor access to the premises for staff and goods was given as an additional motive for leaving. Kemper, Kroeske and Steynenbosch (1975) found that 54 of the firms they surveyed had decided to leave the agglomeration and relocate in the southern rim of Amsterdam for the same set of reasons; finally, a fairly recent report (SEOUA, 1978) came to the same conclusions and even to about the same ranking of the various motives by their importance, after an enquiry among a sample of 112 firms that had left Amsterdam in the period 1970–74.

For The Hague, the analysis made by van der Linden (1977) of a sample of 432 plants that had left the city shades the picture a bit differently, although the basic factors were the same: again lack of space, inadequate premises, expiring contract, etc. came on top. Perhaps because the centre of The Hague is more accessible than that of Amsterdam, traffic problems carry much less weight in The Hague than in the capital, though still ranking high. Next came quite a list of miscellaneous factors, such as organisational reasons, poor residential conditions all of much less importance. Labour-market problems were found to be of a rather minor importance.

Given these findings, it does not come as a surprise that firms reported to Ottens (1976) and Buit (1981) how they had been pushed to leave town and settle in the Green Core of the Randstad by the same set of causes.

The study for Utrecht (Schalk, 1971) is a variation of the same song; astonishingly, with different definitions, another sample (here 140 plants), and a different surveying method, the author concludes to virtually the identical frequency and weight of the motives given, in order of magnitude, as the previously reviewed studies.

Now let us turn our attention to the *pull factors* of the municipalities in which the migrating plants have relocated.

From an early study (BSGA 1970) we know that about 50 per cent of all the plants that left the city of Amsterdam had relocated in a municipality of the agglomeration to preserve contact with their existing output markets, while some 40 per cent felt tied to the agglomeration by their present labour force. Now that may explain why these firms moved only a short distance away, but it does not explain why they had chosen their particular new location. The study revealed that the push factors were almost exactly matched by the pull factors: availability of space (price and quantity of industrial sites), better traffic conditions, good accessibility, and quite often the facilities offered by local authorities: housing for staff, speedy permits for construction, etc. were all mentioned as important reasons for having selected the new location.

Other studies invariably put forward the same motives (Kemper et al., 1975; SEOUA, 1978; Ottens 1976) of the Amsterdam area; they reappear in the studies of Utrecht and The Hague. In the latter case some more accent is placed on such factors as housing environment than in the other studies. That may be due to the fairly large number of one-person firms included in The Hague sample in contrast to that of Amsterdam and Utrecht; perhaps the environment is more relevant to such small firms than to others. This suggests different weights of motives for different sub-sets of the total samples studied.

The authors of some of the studies analysed have tried to find out whether the motive patterns changed significantly if the samples were divided into classes by some major characteristic, such as branch plants, size, sector of activity, etc. Some differences could indeed be identified between sub-samples; such large traffic-creating activities as wholesale trade, for instance, are inclined to highlight traffic conditions, while large-space consumers like some manufacturing firms tend to mention industrial sites more often; on the whole, however, the general picture sketched above was found valid for specific classes as well, so overwhelmingly so, indeed, that no further attention will be paid to the sub-samples.

Conclusions

From the study of the motives for industrial movement in the Netherlands, most moves nowadays appear to be short-distance moves, induced mostly by a wish to readapt the direct infrastructural environment of the firm to its changing needs.

Inter-regional moves for labour-market reasons have become much less frequent lately; the Netherlands continue to attract a limited amount of large-scale foreign investment, thanks to its favourable geographical position.

Effects on donor and acceptor regions

Introduction

Almost by definition, the movement of industry makes an impact on the spatial distribution of economic activity as well as the economic structure of both donor and acceptor regions.

However, as has been said on several occasions, moving is not the only, and probably not even the principal response of industrial activity to changing conditions. For a proper evaluation of the effects of total movement, we thus have to consider them alongside the quantitative effects of closures, the creation of new establishments, and the growth and decline of existing establishments. Unfortunately the information on those phenomena is very scarce. From the bits and pieces available we have nevertheless tried to compose a total consistent picture, notably in terms of employment effects. As in the previous sections, we will treat the effects of international moves first, inter-regional ones next, and intra-regional ones last. After that we will consider briefly the question whether the movement of plants induces movement of employees. Finally we will draw some policy conclusions.

International moves

The lack of a complete picture of international moves into the Netherlands makes it impossible to determine how much they have contributed to the creation of employment. From the data of Kemper and De Smidt (1980) it appears, however, that by 1964, 27,000 people were employed with foreign firms, a figure that had gone up to 56,000 in 1971 and 59,000 in 1978. Viewing these figures in the light of the total number of employees in manufacturing (Table 8.1) we may calculate that in 1964 some 2 per cent of the total were completely foreign-employed; in the 1970s their proportion had gone up to about 5 per cent. As not all foreign establishments have been inventoried, however, their total contribution to employment creation in Holland has probably been greater than these figures indicate.

Inter-regional moves

The volume of employment involved in inter-regional moves can be inferred from four provincial studies. Table 8.9 summarises, for each of the provinces involved, the effects of immigration, emigration, creation of new establishments and closure of old ones, and *in situ* developments.

Although the delineation of categories used is not above reproach, the picture evoked by the table shows clearly enough that the effect of emigration and immigration on provincial employment is of limited importance. Immigration into the four provinces accounted for only about 3.9 per cent of total employment, emigration for about 1.4 per cent, a net effect of some 2.5 per cent in terms of the average number of employees in a period of 20—25 years. The (incomplete) data for the province of Friesland corroborate these findings. Indeed, total growth is influenced far more by the difference in the rates of creations and closures and by the net growth of existing establishments than by the emigration—immigration patterns.

We can estimate the total effect on the donor region on the assumption that the total number of jobs moved to the four provinces included in Table 8.9 all originated in the Randstad. Comparing the 17,200 employees reported there to the total number of persons employed in Randstad manufacturing establishments of 10 or more employees

Table 8.9

Employment in manufacturing at the beginning and end of the period 1950 (1955)–1975, and employment effects of immigration, outmigration, creations, closures, and *in situ* growth during the study period (x 1000)

	Stock 1950–5	Immigration	Emigration	Creations	Closures	*In situ* growth	Stock 1975–7
			Period 1950–55 to 1976–77				
Gelderland	110.4	+ 4.8	−2.5	+16.8	−20.3	− 2.0	107.2
Noord-Brabant	159.9	+ 7.4	−2.6	+42.9	−43.7	+ 55.4	219.3
Overijssel	91.0	+ 3.1	−0.6	?	?	?	83.4
Limburg	48.5	+ 1.9	−0.6	+14.4	−11.7	+20.2	72.7
Total	409.8	17.2	6.3	*	*	*	482.6

Source: Grit, 1980; Grit, de Weert and Wever, 1977; de Weert, 1980.

(averaging approximately 400,000 in the period 1950—75) we observe that the Randstad lost some 4.5 per cent of its employment in manufacturing to the four provinces, which as we have seen, received the bulk of total moves from the Randstad. Estimation of the emigration from the Randstad to the other provinces of the country at some 1.5 per cent implies that the total loss of jobs due to emigration experienced by the Randstad was less than 6 per cent of its stock. The total loss of employment in manufacturing in the total period may be estimated at some 18 per cent, so that once more the conclusion is that the loss of manufacturing employment in the Randstad has been due more to an excess of closures over creations and a net *in situ* decrease than to emigration to the rest of the country.

Suburbanisation

Industrial movements may have a far greater effect on small areas than on larger ones. That is *a fortiori* true of metropolitan centres, as is confirmed by the data brought together in Table 8.10 with respect to the total movement of manufacturing industry and services in the cities of Amsterdam, The Hague and Rotterdam and for the core of the Randstad.

In *Amsterdam*, total employment fell by 12 per cent in the period 1966—74, the loss in manufacturing being 30 per cent and that in services 2 per cent. As the table shows, *in situ* developments accounted for the greater part of this loss (approximately 55 per cent) as far as manufacturing is concerned, the migration balance and to a lesser extent the creation—closure balance contributing the rest (respectively, 26 and 20 per cent). The service sector has only marginally contributed to the loss of jobs in Amsterdam in the study period; in this sector the losses due to net migration are largely compensated by positive closure—creation and *in situ*-growth balances. Relating outmigration (almost equal to net migration in Amsterdam) to the average number of people employed during the period of study, we find that about 1 per cent a year tend to leave the city, in manufacturing as well as in services.

The picture for *The Hague* is largely identical with that for Amsterdam. Total employment fell by some 10 per cent, which means an annual loss not much different from the one measured in Amsterdam. Again, both the secondary and the tertiary sector saw their employment figures drop, the decrease of the secondary sector, in spite of its small size, exceeding in absolute figures the loss sustained in the service sector. The loss of total employment is completely due to net migration, but detailing further by sector we find the service sector to be largely responsible. Indeed, net migration in this sector is very negative, the figure for services even slightly exceeding the total net decrease of

Table 8.10

Components of change of employment: Amsterdam, The Hague, Rotterdam, and Central Randstad (x 1000)

	Stock t	Creations minus closures	Net migration	In situ	Total	Stock $t+1$
Amsterdam 1966–74						
Manufacturing	120.0	−7.6[1]	− 9.2	−19.1	−35.9	34.1
Services	228.5	+8.0	−19.0	+ 6.1	− 4.9	223.6
The Hague 1969–74						
Manufacturing	50.1	−2.7[1]	− 2.8[2]	− 5.0	−10.5	39.6
Services	175.8	−1.3[1]	−10.4[2]	+ 1.5	−10.2	165.6
Rotterdam 1977–81						
Manufacturing	122.8	−4.4	− 2.8	− 6.1	−13.3	109.5
Services	269.2	+1.5	− 3.4	+ 1.0	− 0.9	268.3
Central Randstad 1960–72						
Total	55.7	−8.9[3]	+ 8.8[4]	+10.4	+10.3	66.0

Source: Kruyt, 1979; van der Linden, 1977; Ottens, 1976; Molle and Vianen, 1982, Buunk and Elderman 1982.
[1] Creation + immigration − closures; immigration very low. [2] Only outmigration: immigration very low.
[3] Closures inclusive outmigration (very low). [4] Only immigration.

employment. In the secondary sector, the development of existing establishments far outweighs the two other components. From the more detailed material available the interesting fact emerges that the creation—closure rates practically match each other for services: some 21,000 openings versus some 19,500 closures. For manufacturing the figures are less spectacular. Once more, creation and closure of establishments, in spite of their small net effect, appear to be far more important than actual migration.

For *Rotterdam,* only data with respect to more recent periods are at our disposal. As far as the relations between the components of change are concerned, the picture they present is more or less identical with that of the other two towns. However, the economic depression of the last few years shows up in the fact that *in situ* growth, generally positive in the two other cities in the previous period, has now turned negative.

A small net change in total employment may disguise shifts of surprising amplitude in its components; that is true, for instance, of the components of the change in employment in the *Central Randstad* between 1960 and 1972. Firms existing there in 1960 experienced a heavy net employment loss in the period, viz. 30 per cent; on the other hand, 26 per cent of the average employment in the area was created during the same years by newcomers (8,800 jobs). Most of these (employing 7,600) represented complete moves; the remaining 1,200 jobs were the result of partial moves. Entirely new establishments were also quite important: with 7,400 employed they accounted for 12 per cent of total average employment in the area.

In the smaller areas outside the Randstad, migration appears a less important element of change than in areas in the vicinity of the major agglomerations in the west; from the further regional breakdown given for the provinces Noord-Brabant and Gelderland (by Grit, de Weert and Wever, 1977; and Grit, 1980) we know that such high figures, while valid for areas very close to a major expulsion area, are by no means attained in others: indeed, in areas outside the surroundings of the major cities in the west, the share of immigration in total employment tends to float around the figures given in the previous section.

Does movement of industry induce movement of persons?

In the previous sections we have considered the move of one job as the loss of one job to the region of origin and the gain of one to the region of destination. It is not clear however how far the move of jobs is accompanied by the physical move of employed persons.

For the Randstad some study results are available that indicate to what extent employees follow their firm when it moves. In the

Amsterdam area (SEO, UA 1978) approximately 70 per cent of employees appeared to stay with their employer after moving; for The Hague the figure was even more than 80 per cent. We find the same phenomenon on the other side of the migration balance: Ottens (1976) reports that in the Central Randstad about 60 per cent of the total staff of existing firms live in the municipality where the firm is located compared to 40 per cent of the employees of firms recently moved into the area. Buit (1981) observes, moreover, that the proportion of employees coming from the municipality where the firm has located tends to increase the longer ago is the immigration. Most moves within agglomerations being short-distance moves anyway, employers mostly can count on keeping their staff, who can be loyal to their company without having to make a residential as well as an occupational move. Staff members are not nearly so keen to follow their employer over longer distances; indeed, most inter-regional moves really involved the establishment of branch plants for a separate production line, for which staff were recruited locally.

The next question concerns the selective character of a move. As far as long-distance moves are concerned, there has been a filtering down of routine-type activities into the periphery rather than a loss of high-grade economic activity by the Randstad. Apparently the central area has managed to maintain its strong position in qualitative terms. The same applies much less to short-distance moves. From various studies the conclusion can be drawn that not only space-demanding manufacturing activities are suburbanising, but also some activities which appear to prefer the suburbs because their highly qualified staff want to live there. Indications of spatial segregation of quality work, still weak on the level of urban areas (thanks notably to the strong position of the CBDs (Central Business Districts) in various cities), are becoming clear on a somewhat higher regional level. A move of highly qualified jobs to areas in the Netherlands with pleasant residential surroundings (in particular in the intermediate zone) suggests that the Randstad is losing its hold on highly qualified employment, and that its industrial structure is weakening. The cause is not only industrial migration, but also, and possibly mostly, a higher rate of creation of new activities in these areas than in the traditional urban centres of the Randstad. As we have concluded elsewhere (Molle and Klaassen, 1980), the Randstad may eventually qualify for regional aid, next to the traditional periphery, if this tendency persists.

Policy implications

While many people advocate industrial movement for its beneficial effects on problem areas, an increasing number of others are now frowning upon it as a danger to the sound economic structure of the donor regions. As far as the dichotomy Randstad—Periphery is concerned, the most recent indications of development do indeed make it questionable whether continuation of a decentralisation policy is justified, now that the Randstad appears to have far greater problems than the traditional development areas. With respect to the dichotomy urban core—urban fringe, the situation may be judged somewhat differently however. Faster movement of people than of jobs has led to an important and still increasing relative spatial concentration of economic activity in the agglomerations first, in their cores next, causing large commuting flows and increasing traffic problems. If for the time being we take the dispersion of persons as given, strengthening the suburbanising trend of jobs would contribute to a better spatial equilibrium. That is indeed the official policy of the Netherlands government, which it pursues with infrastructural measures. It should be carried out with caution, lest it adds to the spatial segregation of differently qualified jobs.

Conclusions and outlook

The preceding analysis has highlighted the need for policy makers to be well informed about the volume and character of industrial movement on all areal scales. The study has also indicated that much is yet to be done to acquire a satisfactory set of knowledge on the subject in the Netherlands. The various aspects of industrial movement need to be probed more deeply. Those which stand out are the following.

First, the relative importance of the various components of change: creation, closure, immigration—outmigration, etc. About newly created establishments we know next to nothing in the Netherlands, and about closures very little; yet the available studies indicate that these two components account for a very large part of the regional differences in employment growth.

For their study to be taken up successfully, however, the statistical base will have to be much improved first. Not until full information on all components of change, including migration, is available for more and smaller areas, shall we be able to understand better the spatial-economic dynamics of industrial development.

A further conclusion from the preceding analysis is that so far the emphasis has been on manufacturing sectors, though they are declining both in absolute and in relative terms, in contrast to the service sectors, very much on the make. Only for the major cities is sufficient information available for services and industry to be studied on practically the same footing.

Finally, the analysis has indicated that longer-distance moves are dwindling, industrial movement consisting now mainly of (often suburbanising) short-distance moves within the same agglomeration area.

The main concern with industrial movement can thus be shifted from regional to urban planning. Indeed, in the continuous process of spatial adjustment within large urban agglomerations, the movement of industry may still be an important planning instrument to achieve the spatial equilibrium aimed at within the total urban area. On the other hand, regional policy makers are apt to find themselves bereft of their classical instrument of regional growth: enticing industries from the central areas to the assisted ones. Their hope now seems to lie in attracting new industries at an early stage of development, industries that, it is hoped, are numerous enough and vital enough to create progressive employment in the region.

References

AIV (1969), 'Kort verslag van een enquête gehouden door de Amsterdamse industrievereniging onder 275 geselecteerde industriële bedrijven in de binnenstad van Amsterdam', Amsterdam.

Beumer, L., van Holst, B. and Molle, W. (1979), 'De ruimtelijke dynamiek van economische activiteiten: bedrijfsverplaatsingen in Nederland', NEI, Rotterdam.

Boeckhout, I.J. and Molle, W.T.M. (1981), 'Some forces underlying the change in the Dutch urban system', in L.H. Klaassen, W.T.M. Molle and J.H.P. Paelinck (eds), 'Dynamics of Urban Development', Gower Press, Farnborough.

BSGA (1970), 'Onderzoek naar de reden van vertrek bij naar de agglomeratie vertrokken bedrijven met 10 en meer werkzame personen', Op grond van cijfers 7/2 Amsterdam.

Buit, J. (1981), Bedrijfsverplaatsingen naar Zuid-Hollands open Middengebied in het licht van streekplandoelstellingen, V.U. Amsterdam.

Buunk, F.B. and Elderman, P.C. (1982), 'De dynamiek in het bedrijven bestand in Rijnmond', ESB, pp. 1286—1290.

Graaf, B.V. de (1978), 'Bedrijfsmigratie naar West Brabant' Notitie Rijks Planologische Dienst, Den Haag.

Grit, S. (1980), 'De dynamiek in een regionaal industriële structuur: Gelderland 1955—1976', Geografisch Tijdschrift 1980—4, pp. 294—307.

Grit, S., de Weert, H. and Wever, E. (1977), 'Industriële bedrijfsverplaatsing in Overijssel en Noord-Brabant', Nijmeegse Geografische Cahiers.

Grit, S. and de Weert, H. (1977/1978), 'Industriële Mobiliteit in Noord-Brabant', *Tijdschrift Noord-Brabant* (ETIN) 1977, no. 5, pp. 281–97, 1978, no. 1, pp. 5–19 and 1978 no. 2, pp. 65/81.

Kemper, N.I., Kroeske, S. and Stynenbosch, M.H. (1975, *Struktuur in bedrijf*, deel II Hfdst, 4, GTUU Utrecht.

Kemper, N.I. and de Smidt, M. (1980), 'Foreign Manufacturing Establishments: in the Netherlands', *Tijdschrift voor Economische en Sociale Geografie*, 71 no. 1, pp. 21–40.

Klok, J. (1979), *'Werkgelegenheidsontwikkelingen en bedrijfsmigratie in de Zaanstreek'*, GIRUG 1979, Groningen.

Kruyt, B. (1979), 'The changing spatial pattern of firms in Amsterdam: empirical evidence', *Tijdschrift voor economische en sociale geographie*, pp. 144–56.

Lierop, A.F.J. van (1978), *'De industriële bedrijfsmigratie in Friesland in de periode 1960–1976'*, ETI Friesland rapport no. 842, Leeuwarden.

Linden, J. van de (1977), (Dienst S.O. Den Haag) *'Onderzoek migratiemotieven bedrijven 's-Gravenhage 1969–1974'*, Conceptrapport + bijlagen boek, Den Haag.

Molle, W.T.M. (1977), 'Industrial Mobility, A review of empirical studies and an analysis of the migration of industry from the city of Amsterdam', *Regional Studies,* vol. 11, pp. 323–35.

Molle, W.T.M. and Klaassen, L.H. (1980), 'Doelmatige rechtvaardigheid: regionale onevenwichtigheden, uitgangspunten voor een regionaal beleid', *Paper RSA,* Rotterdam.

Molle, W.T.M. and Vianen J.G. (1982), 'Het vertrek van bedrijven uit Amsterdam, ESB pp. 608–613.

Nozeman, E.F. (1980), 'Bedrijfsverplaatsingsonderzoek, terugblik en vooruitzicht', *Tijdschrift voor Stedebouw en Volkshuisvesting,* pp. 349–59.

Ottens, H.F.L. (1976), *'Het groene hart binnen de Randstad. Een beeld van de suburbanisatie binnen West Nederland'*, Assen.

Pellenbarg, P.H. (1977), *'Bedrijfsmigratie in Nederland, een onderzoek naar de migratiemotieven en hun betekenis voor de regionale ontwikkeling'*, Deel I Terreinverkenning, Deel II Onderzoekresultaten, SNHN/ICHN, Groningen.

Pellenbarg, P.H. (1979), 'Bedrijfsmigraties, praktijk en theorie', in *Vestigingstendenzen en bedrijfsmobiliteit,* KNAG, Utrecht.

Poolman, F.S., Potters, A.L.M. and Wever, E. (1978), 'Industriële bedrijfsmigratie naar en binnen Noord-Brabant', *Geografisch en Planologisch Instituut,* Publikatie no. 2, Vakgroep Economische Geografie Nijmegen.

Puffelen van, E.A. (1979), 'Migratieonderzoek Amsterdamse bedrijven' in *Vestigingstendenzen en bedrijfsmobiliteit,* KNAG, Utrecht.

RPD (1977) *Derde Nota over de Ruimtelyke Ordening*, deel 2d Regeringsbeslissing, Den Haag.

Schalk, P.P.J. (1971), Bedrijfsmigratie in de Provincie Utrecht, *Jaarverslag ETIU*, Utrecht.

SISWO (1967), *'Industriële bedrijfsmigratie in Nederland in de jaren 1950—1962; een onderzoek naar verplaatsingsfactoren'*. (a) Samenvattend rapport door Reinink; (b) Deelrapport 1, Een planologisch statistisch onderzoek naar verplaatsing van industriële bedrijven in Nederland in de jaren 1950—1962; (c) deelrapport 2: Een sociaalpsychologisch onderzoek naar verplaatsing van bedrijven in de jaren 1959—1962 in de bedrijfsklasse metaal, Amsterdam.

SEOUA Stichting Economisch Onderzoek (1978), *'Migratie onderzoek Amsterdamse bedrijven'*, Amsterdam.

Smidt, M. de (1968), 'Foreign Industrial Establishments located in the Netherlands', *Tijdschrift voor Economische en Sociale Geografie* 57 no. 1, pp. 1—19.

Vijverberg, C.H.T. (1980), 'Small scale enterprise: some economic and social aspects of the size of firms in the Netherlands', *NEI/FEER* 12 Rotterdam.

Weert de, H. (1980), 'Industriële Structuurverandering in Limburg', *GPIN publicatie no. 19*, Nijmegen.

Wever, E. (1978), 'Industriële suburbanisatie: enkele gegevens voor Overijssel en Noord-Brabant', *Geografisch Tijdschrift*, pp. 371—7.

Wever, E. (1981), 'Industriële suburbanisatie' in L.H. Klaassen, W.T.M. Molle and J.H.P. Paelinck (eds), *'De dynamiek van de stedelijke ontwikkeling in Nederland'*, NEI, Rotterdam.

9 Ireland
P. N. O'FARRELL

It is the objective of this chapter to review the published literature on industrial migration and mobility with respect to the Irish Republic and to concentrate particularly on the period since 1960. The volume of *internal* migration within Ireland by either indigenous controlled or overseas-owned manufacturing establishments has been negligible. Relocation of branch plants and transfers are rare phenomena confined almost exclusively to movement from the inner city area of Dublin to the surrounding suburban industrial estates and to nearby towns.[1] Therefore, the process which is of overwhelming importance in the Irish context is the choice of new 'green field' sites within the country by three major categories of enterprises — multinational branch plants, subsidiaries of Irish controlled multi-plant firms and single-plant Irish enterprises. Hence, the focus of this chapter will be the location patterns of these three groups of enterprise and upon the research which has been undertaken to explain these patterns. Attempts to understand the factors leading to the location of new foreign firms in Ireland have concentrated primarily on analysing their characteristics in order to deduce the reasons for their establishments; interview surveys concerning motives for investment, although less common, will also be reviewed.

General setting

National industrial development

Industrial development in Ireland should be viewed in the context of its relatively low level of prosperity compared with other EEC states: in 1977 it was the only Community nation with a GDP per capita of less than 50 per cent of the Community average. Successive Irish governments, therefore, have been confronted with the twin objectives of implementing strategies both to increase the rate of national economic growth while, simultaneously, attempting to stabilise and reduce spatial welfare disparities.

At the achievement of political independence in 1922 the industrial labour force was only some 100,000 representing about 7 per cent of those gainfully occupied (O'Malley, 1980, p. 3). The primary aim of industrial policy was to develop an indigenous industrial base to serve the domestic market, and foreign capital investment was not actively promoted. A large component of the indigenous manufacturing sector had its origins in the protectionist era which began in earnest in the 1930s and ended in the 1960s. The imposition of heavy tariffs and other trade barriers in this period was followed by quite rapid industrial growth with employment in industry more than doubling between 1931 and 1953 (O'Malley, 1980, p. 4). The majority of these firms were engaged in low value-added operations oriented towards the domestic market.

Persistently high levels of emigration, low economic growth and the small scale of the home market led to a radical change of policy from 1958. This new departure envisaged future economic growth as being dependent upon the creation of a modern export-oriented industrial structure primarily through the attraction into Ireland of foreign direct investment.

The rate of growth of industry since the end of the 1950s has exceeded that of GDP and the growing importance of industry in the Irish economy is illustrated by the fact that its share of GDP has risen from 28 per cent in 1960 to 38 per cent in 1979 while its share of employment has risen from 22 per cent to 29 per cent over the same period. It will be noted that the substantially higher manufacturing output growth rate from 1963–73 compared with 1953–63 was not accompanied by any significant rise in the growth rate of employment; indeed, when account is taken of changes in average hours, the growth of labour input was identical in the two periods (Kennedy and Foley, 1978, p. 88).

The output growth rate fell to 2 per cent per annum between 1973–76

Table 9.1

Annual growth rates in manufacturing (%)

Period	Volume of gross output	Employment	Man—hours	Gross output per capita	Gross output per man—hour
1953—63	4.2	1.6	1.5	2.5	2.7
1963—73	6.3	1.9	1.5	4.3	4.8
1974—76	2.0	−2.1	−2.6	4.2	4.6

Source: Kennedy and Foley, 1978, p. 89.

primarily because of the 1974—6 world depression (Table 9.1). Although gross output per man—hour rose at the same rate as between 1963—73, employment fell by 2 per cent per annum between 1974—76. To sum-marise the long-term employment trend, total employment in manu-facturing was 30,000 or one-sixth higher in 1976 than in 1953, repre-senting an annual average net gain of less than 1,500 per annum (Ken-nedy and Foley, 1978, p. 89). If the 1963—73 decade is examined (a period unaffected by serious depressions) the growth of manufacturing employment during this period was about 3,000 per annum, on average.

Kennedy and Foley (1978, pp. 90—2) have also produced evidence to show that the Verdoorn relationship — suggesting a strong positive association between the growth of output and both employment and labour productivity — has changed during the 1960s. Their analysis in-dicated that in the period 1953—63 to maintain the level of employ-ment (for unchanged weekly hours) required only an annual rise in output of 1.3 per cent; whereas in the period 1963—73 an annual rise of 3.6 per cent per annum was required (Kennedy and Foley, 1978, p. 92). The rise in labour productivity growth relative to output growth was strongly influenced by the accelerated growth of capital intensity. This will make it relatively more difficult to achieve manufacturing targets and full employment in the future.

External control

Under the New Industry (NI) programme of the Industrial Develop-ment Authority (IDA), foreign projects accounted for 56 per cent of employment and 60 per cent of exports in 1976. This must be viewed against the background of the NI share of total manufacturing gross output (52 per cent), exports (76 per cent) and employment (42 per cent) — shares which have increased dramatically since 1966 (see O'Farrell and O'Loughlin, 1980, p. 5). Between 1973 and 1976 employment in the grant-aided New Industry group displayed a net increase of 23,000 jobs while the rest of manufacturing declined by 35,000 (O'Farrell and O'Loughlin, 1980, p. 7).

At the end of 1978 it was estimated that about 30 per cent of employment in Irish manufacturing industry was controlled by foreign firms (Lyons, 1978, pp. 3 and 5) and, since this proportion is rising rapidly, it is reasonable to assume that by 1982 at least one-third of Ireland's industrial employment was externally controlled. This figure probably underestimates the full extent of external control because Sweeney (1973) found in 1972 that over 50 per cent of fixed assets of *Irish registered* industrial and service companies were owned by foreign enterprise and of these foreign-owned assets only just over 45 per cent were accounted for by IDA grant-aided firms. He also showed that two-thirds of Britain's 100 largest companies had Irish subsidiaries of which only 25 out of 310 had received New Industry grants and 70 had received re-equipment or adaptation grants. These findings imply considerable external involvement in older originally tariff-protected firms which are usually classified as 'domestic or Irish' (O'Malley, 1980, p. 35). The published information, therefore, makes it difficult to quantify precisely the degree of external control of Irish-based manufacturing. This taxonomic difficulty applies more to older (pre-1958) foreign firms; most of the research on foreign industry in Ireland is concerned with post-1958 arrivals.

Industrial incentives and regional planning

The system of investment incentives for industry in Ireland began in 1952 with the Undeveloped Areas Act. Cash grants of up to 50 per cent of the cost of plant and machinery and discretionary grants towards the cost of land and buildings were made available to firms establishing in the more depressed areas of the country. This was the first formal regional planning measure. Subsequent changes under the Industrial Grant Acts of 1956, 1959 and 1963 were aimed at encouraging increased investment in the economy as a whole. The effect of these policies was to weaken the differential between the original Undeveloped Areas and the rest of the country.

In 1967, the government re-introduced a substantial differential into the incentive scheme. Free depreciation of investment in plant and machinery was allowable in the Designated Areas (DA) against a 50 per cent initial allowance in the Non-Designated Areas (NDA) (see Map 9.1). A 20 per cent tax allowance was available in all areas for expenditure

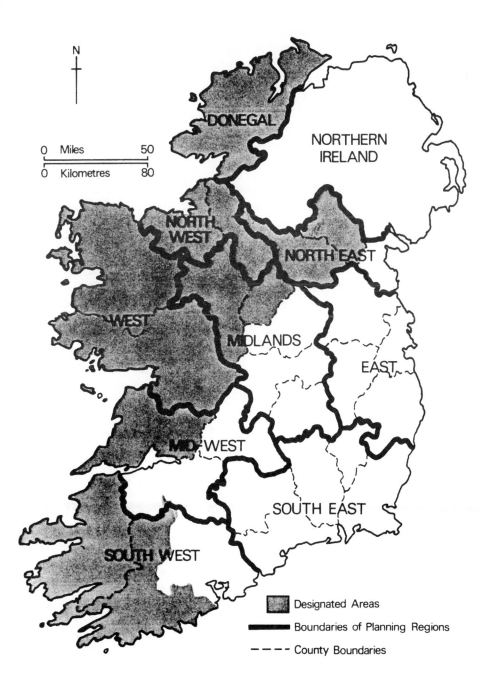

Map 9.1   Designated areas, counties and planning regions in Ireland

on industrial building and land. In 1969, a regionally structured investment grant scheme was introduced with the grant differential between DA and NDA set at 15 percentage points; a maximum of 60 per cent in DA and 45 per cent in NDA.

In 1971, free depreciation became available throughout the Republic and the 1975 Industrial Development Act maintained the DA/NDA grant differential with up to 50 per cent or £7,500 per job in DA, 35 per cent or £5,000 per job in NDA and 25 per cent or £4,000 per job in Dublin.[2] In 1977, the Dublin grant rates were increased to the level available in other parts of the NDA (i.e. 35 per cent) and the IDA began to actively promote the city as an industrial location.

The 1956 Finance Act introduced a major financial attraction to manufacturing firms by way of tax relief on profits from exports. The 1956 Act granted relief at 50 per cent from income tax and corporation profits tax on all profits earned on increases in export sales over their 1956 (or 1955) level. Firms newly established in Ireland, therefore, obtained tax relief in respect of all profits associated with exports. In 1958, the proportion of tax relief was raised from 50 to 100 per cent and, in 1960, the period of full tax relief was also extended from 10 to 15 years. This scheme is not available to firms commencing production after January 1981 but has been replaced by a uniform 10 per cent rate of corporation profits tax on all manufacturing firms over the period 1981–2000 inclusive.

Locational strategy

Initially no locational criteria were incorporated into the grants scheme but a growing body of opinion developed in favour of a growth centre policy from the late 1950s. The origin of the concept may be traced to Whitaker's seminal document on economic development in 1958 where he stated that 'a realistic appraisal indicates that if we are to have any hope of success . . . we must site our industries at, or convenient to, the larger centres of population' (Department of Finance, 1958, p. 160). These sentiments were endorsed both by a report in 1962 of the Committee of Industrial Organisation and the 1964 Report of the Committee on Development Centres and Industrial Estates.[3] The National Industrial and Economic Council (1965) upheld the views of the latter Committee and recommended that Galway and Waterford be designated as growth centres and added that there would only be a limited number, perhaps not more than six, outside Dublin and Cork. The government responded by establishing industrial estates at Galway and Waterford and, following consultants' reports upon Dublin and Limerick–Shannon, engaged a firm of consultants (Colin Buchanan and Partners) to draw up a development strategy.[4] The resultant study, known popularly as the 'Buchanan Report' (1969), sparked off more controversy than any other single issue in Irish regional strategy. It recommended a three-tier hierarchy of growth centres involving three national, six regional, and four local centres. It was proposed that 75 per cent of all new industrial jobs should be located in the eight national and regional centres in the period up to 1986. Such a high degree of spatial concentration was untenable for any Irish government and so it decided to further consider the issues. Finally, in May 1972, a brief statement of government regional policy was issued proposing that, although there would be some concentration of population into nine major centres, there would be substantial overall growth in other towns. An important component of this strategy was the endorsement by the government of the IDA's *Regional Industrial Plans, 1973—77* (1972) in which manufacturing job targets were specified for 177 towns, excluding the mid-west and the Gaeltacht.

This plan envisaged that 52 per cent of new industrial jobs would be located in the nine main industrial urban centres compared with the 75 per cent recommended by Buchanan. O'Neill (1973) argued that this represented a rejection of the growth centre approach and support for a policy of dispersion. It appears, however, that government and IDA strategy was more pragmatic for the IDA had recognised in its 1973—77 plan that dispersion and concentration were not mutually exclusive alternatives (*Regional Industrial Plans 1973—77*, p. 47). Conceptually, it was more realistic to conceive of a continuum of options ranging from extreme spatial concentration to dispersal between the two points of which lie a variety of alternative strategies (O'Farrell, 1974, p. 500). The IDA programme incorporated both elements of concentration and dispersal within their plans. A similar strategy has been adopted for the 1978—82 Plan.

Institutional framework

The Industrial Development Authority (IDA) was constituted in 1949 to promote the establishment of new industrial enterprises. Later, in 1952, An Foras Tionscail was set up to administer a scheme of cash grants designed to attract industrial investment to the underdeveloped areas west of the Shannon. The Industrial Development Act, 1969, provided for an amalgamation of the An Foras Tionscail (the grant-giving agency) and the IDA (the promotional agency) into one state-sponsored body. Section II of the 1969 Act assigned responsibility to the IDA, acting under the Minister for Industry and Commerce, for *national* and *regional* industrial development and, to this end, authorised it to provide and administer grants and other facilities for industry, and also to

307

acquire sites and develop, construct and administer industrial estates and advance factories (McAleese, 1977, p. 12).

The major job-creating activity of the IDA centres upon the *New Industries Programme* (NI) under which new domestic and overseas enterprises and major employment-creating expansions of existing undertakings are actively promoted. In addition to non-repayable cash grants, other incentives on offer include training grants, interest subsidies, loan guarantees, and research and development grants. Considerable steps have been taken to encourage the modernisation of existing Irish industry under the adaptation grants scheme, and, since 1969, the *Re-equipment Programme*. The *Small Industries Programme* was set up in 1967 to encourage the establishment of small-scale enterprises employing 50 persons or less. It includes grant incentives and advisory services.

Other features of the IDA's continually evolving industrial development programme include a *Joint Venture* programme started in 1973 to encourage the expansion of domestic firms through partnership arrangements with overseas companies and the Project Identification Unit established in 1975 to identify opportunities for supply from domestic sources of materials and components to new plants and to encourage import substitution (McAleese, 1977, p. 14). In 1974, the IDA introduced a *Service Industries Programme* to provide assistance to service industries wishing to export or engage in import substitution; the principal targets for this programme have been engineering, architectural consultancy and computer software firms. Since 1969, the IDA has been empowered to grant funds for R and D projects concerned with both product and process development. Finally, the *Enterprise Development Programme* was launched in 1978 to encourage Irish persons with technical, managerial and commercial skills to start their own manufacturing firms. The normal range of IDA incentives for new projects is supplemented under this programme by IDA guarantees for loans raised towards working capital requirements of the project and grants towards the reduction of interest payable on a loan raised to provide working capital.

The international location decision

Theoretical framework

The concept of the product life cycle model as an explanatory framework within which to analyse overseas manufacturing investment provides some tentative information as to the technological conditions which are desirable before a firm contemplates foreign investment. However, at an international level, the product life cycle model tells us little about the factors which influence the choice of foreign locations. The location decision may be viewed as an element in a set of investment decisions which reflect the firm's strategy for growth set in an international spatial framework (Thomas, 1980, p. 10). A firm's organisational structure may influence decisions with respect to the location of its foreign and domestic subsidiaries. It is clear that factors which may influence the choice of the host country (for example, political stability, access to markets, an oligopolistic response to a perceived competitive threat from European manufacturers) may be fundamentally different from those which affect the choice of location *within* the host country. Locational choice by, for example, US companies is a function of American managerial attitudes to, and perceptions of, the comparative attributes of several potential European host countries (Vernon, 1973, pp. 209–16).

Factors underlying inflow of foreign investment

It is important conceptually to define two spatial scales of decision making which any multinational will address when investing overseas: selection of country, and choice of location within the country. The factors influencing the location decision at these two scales are likely to differ substantially.

There is a consensus among researchers upon Irish industrial development that one of the most important incentives for overseas companies has been the 15 year tax holiday on profits earned from exports, although the evidence to support this assertion is largely anecdotal. The attractiveness of the Exports Profits Tax Relief[5] (EPTR) scheme and Irish tax relief, in general, to foreign investors is enhanced by double taxation agreements with all the major overseas investors — the USA, Germany, the UK, Japan and others — prohibiting or limiting taxes in their parent countries on profits of Irish branches of foreign companies. Apart from the incentives package itself, the country presented other inherent attractions for overseas investors: a location inside the EEC (since 1973); political stability; a Community attitude favourable towards foreign investment; a relatively (in the European context) low-cost and English-speaking labour force which, although not necessarily highly skilled, is well educated and flexible; and a highly effective and professional semi-state agency, the IDA, for promoting industrial development. The importance of relatively low labour costs and the EPTR is stressed particularly by Stanton (1979).

However, although Ireland's wage costs (and wage costs per unit output) are relatively low by mainland EEC standards, an increasing wage cost disadvantage due to the changing international division of labour has emerged relative to the newly industrial countries such as Taiwan, Brazil, Singapore and Hong Kong. It has been recognised by the IDA that these countries, with a combination of the technology of the multinational and very low labour costs, can undercut Irish firms in a growing range of products (*IDA Industrial Plan, 1979*, p. 32) although for certain standardised production processes an Irish location as a base for exporting behind EEC tariffs may have a comparative advantage (O'Farrell, 1980b, p. 12).

There are two questionnaire surveys of new foreign industries setting up in Ireland dating from the 1960s (Donaldson, 1965 and *Survey of Grant Aided Industry*, 1967). Both of these studies indicate that at the time no one factor was dominant; the *Survey* (1967) reported that 'availability of labour' was the most important single influence — named as the primary factor by firms employing 32 per cent of the labour force employed by respondent firms and as the secondary factor by those employing 27 per cent. 'Market accessibility' (24 per cent primary influence) was ranked second with 'grants' and 'EPTR' recording 12 per cent and 15 per cent, respectively, as the primary influence. Donaldson (1965), based upon a small sample of 34 firms, found that 20 considered EPTR a 'very important' factor influencing new investment in Ireland, compared with 22 for 'market, demand and access conditions' and 14 for both 'grants' and 'labour'. The relative importance of *individual* instruments and factors is difficult to evaluate accurately from these findings. A recent study published by the Allied Irish Banks (1981) reported that the most important factor influencing a final decision to locate in Ireland was the range of tax incentives and grant schemes with direct access to the EEC markets cited as the second-ranked 'factor'. Some 80 per cent of the 120 companies sampled evaluated the possibility of at least one other country as an alternative location before deciding upon Ireland. Of these competing countries, the UK was seriously considered by one-third of the sample, considerably more than Belgium and Spain.

In conclusion, it appears that a number of variables, in combination, have been important in attracting foreign direct investment (FDI) to Ireland. Factors such as political stability and a government and community attitude positively disposed to foreign enterprise have created favourable background conditions. Cheaper labour costs than for comparable workers in other Western European countries were probably of greater importance in the 1960s; during the past decade this comparative advantage has been partly eroded, in particular when compared with the UK. Yet this period has witnessed the greatest inflow of overseas manufacturing investment thereby suggesting that other factors have been more important than low labour costs. Clearly access to the EEC markets has been relevant since 1973 but it does not fully explain Ireland's better record in attracting overseas firms compared with other EEC countries, notably the UK which entered at the same time. The UK has not witnessed any growth in US investment after 1973, although it is more accessible to the major market centres of the EEC. It is apparent that the incentives package has been important but it is not a sufficient explanation for the large volume of FDI during the past decade for other regions of the EEC, notably the peripheral areas of the UK, were offering highly attractive incentives to foreign investment.[6] O'Malley (1980, p. 40) has suggested that cultural ties with the USA may have aided in promoting investment from that source but it would also seem that the expertise and efficiency of the IDA and its ability to administer all phases of an industrial investment from the project proposal stage through after-care services in an unbureaucratic and professional manner is a significant comparative advantage for Ireland over most other locations both in Europe and the newly industrial countries. The cultural links and a common language with the USA, political stability, a government and community attitude favourable to FDI, access to EEC markets, the extremely impressive profitability of existing US firms and the attractive grants package efficiently administered by the IDA have enabled this organisation to market Ireland successfully as a 'bridge' linking the US to the EEC markets.

Trends in overseas manufacturing investment

The inflow of foreign investment was unspectacular in the early 1960s, but received a boost from the 1965 Anglo-Irish Free Trade Agreement which granted duty-free access for Irish industry to the UK market (Walsh, 1979, p. 4). There has been a dramatic acceleration of overseas investment since the early 1970s. Of the 722 grant-aided overseas enterprises *in production* in Ireland at December 1980 (i.e. data include survivors only), some 390 (54 per cent) had opened in the seven years 1974–80 (inclusive).

The principal source of overseas investment has been the USA and through their 256 plants they controlled 38 per cent of all employment in foreign firms in 1976 (O'Farrell and O'Loughlin, 1980, p. 10); the 179 UK controlled plants employed 20 per cent of the labour force in foreign firms while the 106 German plants employed 13 per cent. The rate of US investment has been increasing rapidly: between 1973 and 1977 it grew at four times the rate for total US investment abroad (Walsh, 1979, p. 5) – a rate greater than in any other European country. This may be partly explained by the extremely high rate of return on capital achieved by US plants in Ireland between 1974–79 – an average of 29.4 per cent compared with 15.5 per cent for US subsidiaries throughout the EEC (US Dept of Commerce, 1980). Profits at this level would often in one or two years exceed the total IDA capital grant, so that grants could only explain a minor part of the returns of such enterprises (O'Malley, 1980, p. 39).

Characteristics of multinational branches in Ireland

Multinational enterprises may be defined by their industrial (extractive and manufacturing) action space (Vernon, 1973) or by their commercial action space (Labasse, 1975) which would include corporations producing in only one country but selling world-wide. The multinational is defined in this chapter as an enterprise which controls subsidiaries or branches in more than one country, as suggested by Vernon. The firm is usually characterised by a separation of ownership from control but the corporate organisation may differ significantly from one multinational to another and this may have an important influence upon their behaviour (McNee, 1960, p. 203). Although there is no research which has explored these organisational differences for multinationals located in Ireland, there is some evidence relating to the *consequences* of these differences in terms of the degree of autonomy granted to branch plants and the extent to which headquarter functions are decentralised to Irish-based branches.

Overseas enterprises tend to be highly export-oriented: the mean export–sales ratio for foreign plants in 1976 was 89.4 per cent (O'Farrell and O'Loughlin, 1980, p. 8). The median plant size of the New Industry (NI) group was 80 employees in 1976, an increase from a median of 55 in 1973 (O'Farrell, 1975, p. 4). The *mean* employment size of overseas plants is 168 – ranging from 176 for USA to 132 for UK controlled enterprises. The median employment size of multinational parent companies with Irish branches is 1,500 (mean 15,880) but the data suggest that there is a high degree of dispersion in terms of size. Nevertheless, most overseas investors are small by American standards. Foreign direct investment in Ireland has been compared with indigenous investment in order to test some of the postulates of the product life cycle model (O'Loughlin and O'Farrell, 1980). It was concluded that while overseas firms may be concentrated in sectors characterised by relatively high capital and technological intensity, they are not more capital and technology intensive than domestic firms when the sectoral effect is controlled; conversely, the production system used by overseas subsidiaries tends to be more standardised than that of Irish plants, as predicted by the product cycle model (O'Loughlin and O'Farrell, 1980, p. 180).

312

Overseas investment is becoming increasingly concentrated in potential high growth sectors, notably electronics, mechanical engineering, sports and leisure goods, photographic products, household appliances, pharmaceuticals, medical equipment and fine chemicals. Conversely, indigenous firms are relatively more concentrated in static or slow growth sectors such as good, painting, milling, textiles, wood and furniture and bakeries.

The location pattern within Ireland

Introduction

This section will review the research literature which has focused upon analysing the locational pattern of new enterprises in Ireland during the past 25 years. The nature of the enterprises studied means that most of the Irish research findings reviewed relate to the results of the locational behaviour of firms rather than to the underlying decision-making process. The locational patterns of multinationals and indigenous establishments are analysed with respect to three sets of regions: the core Dublin region and the rest of the country; Designated Areas (DA) and Non-Designated Areas (NDA); and the nine planning regions (Map 9.1). In addition, the size of settlement selected by both multinationals and indigenous Irish projects is analysed. The urban dimension to the analysis is important since a manufacturing plant may be foot-loose between a number of Irish regions but not footloose in its location with respect to town size: a company may be neutral regarding any of three regions providing it locates in an urban centre of, say, at least 40,000 population (O'Farrell, 1978, p. 135). Before summarising the major research findings, it is necessary to briefly review theoretical aspects of the location decision within a host country.

Theoretical aspects of location decision making within a host country

Theories of large enterprise behaviour in space are relatively unsophisticated (Watts, 1980, p. 21) but in recent years there has been a movement away from analysing manufacturing activity solely according to classes based upon the physical characteristics of either inputs or outputs towards taxonomies derived from ownership and organisational factors. The problem of locating a multinational branch in an Irish region must be viewed in the context of inter-relationships of existing sets of production facilities and service units and the strategy of the corporation and its interaction with state agencies.

313

The product life cycle model in an intra-national context is under-developed (Watts, 1980, p. 53); and Ireland is too small a country to expect regional differences in the location patterns of multinational branches according to whether, for example, they are at the growth or mature stage of the product life cycle.

Yannopoulos and Dunning (1976, p. 389) have argued that the choice of sites by foreign-based enterprises will be dominated by locational considerations different from those affecting similar choices by indigenous enterprises. One reason for expecting a contrast is that the foreign enterprise does not have, at least in the short term, a core region within its host country. In Ireland, they are overwhelmingly export-oriented (89.4 per cent of output exported in 1976) (O'Farrell and O'Loughlin, 1980, p. 8) whereas most indigenous firms at least start by producing for the domestic market. During the past decade there has been an increasingly polarised and inconclusive debate amongst academics and politicians focused on the role of multinational enterprises in exacerbating regional disequilibria in advanced Western economies. Some writers have asserted that the size and power of these large firms enables them to extract concessions from governments and to locate where they wish — that is, predominantly in the core regions of European countries (Watts, 1979, p. 71). Examinations of the locations of foreign-owned branch plants in the USA, Canada, the UK, France, Belgium and Ireland lead Blackbourn (1978, p. 125) to conclude that, in most cases, the core region has attracted a large percentage of the foreign-owned plants established in that country. Hamilton (1976, p. 273) has also stated that 'little doubt exists, however, that multinational firms — when left with open choices — have seriously sharpened inter-regional economic and social disparities within the present EEC member countries'. Other workers have cautioned against accepting these conclusions: Yannopoulos and Dunning (1976, p. 389) have suggested that it is unclear, both from existing literature and available statistical evidence, whether the investment location decisions of multinationals tend to strengthen the agglomeration tendencies prevailing in the spatial structure of market economies. In view of the politically sensitive nature of the foreign enterprises, they may be influenced by the need to maintain good relations with the state and its agencies which might suggest a greater willingness to locate in peripheral regions. Conversely, a foreign enterprise may place a premium upon access to an international airport to facilitate control (Hoare, 1975, p. 365). This would tend to act in the opposite direction. It does not seem unreasonable, therefore, to expect the locational patterns of foreign and indigenous enterprises to differ, but the direction and extent of those differences remains uncertain, and can be clarified only by reference to empirical evidence (Watts, 1980, p. 76). In short, the elements of enterprise structure and strategy interact in so many different ways that it is not possible to take any dogmatic position regarding the locational behaviour of foreign-based enterprises (Yannopoulos and Dunning, 1976, p. 398). The controversy has been prolonged by the patchy and unsatisfactory data sets which are available in most countries. There are a number of major questions arising from the research into the locational behaviour of multinationals in Ireland which are pertinent to this chapter. First, do multinationals reveal a greater tendency than indigenous manufacturing investors to locate their branch plants in the core (east) region of the Irish economy centred upon Dublin? Second, what factors influence the locational pattern of new plants — both indigenous and foreign at the level of the nine planning regions? In particular, within the multinational group, do specific national subsets of plants display varying propensities to locate in different regions? For example, in the Netherlands, de Smidt (1966, p. 15) has referred to 'psychological agglomeration' — a follow-the- leader effect — whereby firms from one country lead to others from the same nation locating in the same region.

Empirical findings

There are a number of studies which have analysed the locational patterns of new manufacturing establishments in Ireland and they have concentrated primarily upon grant-aided establishments set up during the past 25 years (see O'Neill, 1971, 1973; O'hUiginn, 1972; Blackbourn, 1972; O'Farrell, 1975, 1978 and 1980a; O'Farrell and Crouchley, 1979; and Walsh, 1979).

O'Neill examined the locational pattern of seven groups of manufacturing industry between 1921 and 1946, and 1946 and 1966, using trade directory data. She concluded that 'the pattern of industrial location throughout the whole island between 1926 and 1966 revealed a strong tendency towards clustering of manufacturing plants . . . The percentage of establishments located in small centres has decreased and the percentage located in larger centres has gone up significantly over the period'. She also observed that Dublin's share of the number of manufacturing and exporting establishments in the Republic rose over the period.

Blackbourn analysed the location pattern of foreign-owned manufacturing enterprises in Ireland over the period 1955—65. He suggested that 'the locations selected by investors differ according to the nationality of the parent corporation'. He tested the psychological agglomeration hypothesis. A nearest neighbour statistic, the coefficient of distribution, was calculated for German, UK, Dutch, and American plants.

315

No tendency towards clustering was observed. He also tested the related hypothesis that plants are distributed according to a spatial diffusion process in which neighbourhood effects are important. However, results suggested that for no nationality was there a regular process of expansion from an original settlement.

In a wide ranging study *O'hUiginn* surveyed 377 new manufacturing establishments grant-aided by the IDA between 1960 and 1970. A table which cross-classified town size location by region showed that the regions containing the four largest urban centres of Dublin, Cork, Limerick and Waterford attracted 62 per cent of the new projects; yet some 31 per cent of the population of new projects located in towns of less than 1,500 persons. He also argued that locational choice with respect to town size did not seem to have been heavily influenced by the size of establishment.

O'Farrell (1975) examined the locational patterns by town size and region of the 418 manufacturing enterprises assisted under the New Industries Programme of the IDA between 1960 and June 1973. Subsequent work (O'Farrell, 1978) tested a range of hypotheses relating to the regional and urban locational behaviour of these enterprises; and O'Farrell and Crouchley (1979) investigated the use of discriminant analysis as a technique for predicting industrial location. O'Farrell (1980a) has also analysed the locational behaviour of multinational enterprises at a number of spatial scales for the 1960–73 period, and this showed, *inter alia,* that foreign projects were marginally more likely than Irish ones to locate in peripheral Designated Areas.

The empirical analyses reported in this chapter all refer to industrial projects aided under the main job-creating scheme of the IDA, the New Industries Programme under which new domestic and overseas enterprises and major expansions of existing undertakings are actively promoted. In the locational studies undertaken by O'Farrell (1975, 1978 and 1980a) data on projects assisted under the New Industries Programme were made available from the internal files of the IDA and supplemented by information provided by the regional offices of the IDA and many individual companies.

The terms 'plant', 'establishment' and 'project' are used interchangeably and refer to a plant which has received a grant payment on any date between January 1960 and June 1973. A plant or establishment may be one of a number owned by a particular firm but is classified separately if it has a distinct plant and workforce at a particular location.

New industry location by size of urban community

During the past decade national economic growth has been associated
— as a consequence of regional industrial policies — with a relative dispersion of manufacturing employment into the regions and away from
the Dublin conurbation. Within the regions, on the other hand, sustained growth has been associated both with a degree of concentration
of activities into the larger centres *and* dispersion throughout the hierarchy (O'Farrell, 1979, p. 58). Between 1960 and 1973, of the 39,218
jobs created outside Dublin under the IDA's New Industry Programme,
42 per cent were generated in towns below 5,000 population and 18.6
per cent were located in the four towns of the 25,000—150,000 category (O'Farrell, 1975, p. 2).

The data in Table 9.2 also show quite clearly that the number of
industrial establishments per town is positively related in town size
group ranging from 0.28 for towns of below 1,500 population to
12.75 for the 25,000—150,000 group and 36 for Dublin. On the basis
of locational choices made between 1960 and 1973, a town in the
25,000—150,000 category had 45 times as great a probability of attracting a new plant as a town in the below 1,500 group, seven times as
great a probability as a town in the 1,500—5,000 group and five times
the probability of a town in the 5,000—10,000 category (O'Farrell,
1975, p. 31). Dublin had approximately three times as great a chance
of attracting a new plant as a town in the 25,000—150,000 population
group. These results refer to *all* New Industry projects, both indigenous
and overseas.

Table 9.2

Distribution of New Industry projects by town-size category, 1960—73

Town size group	No. of plants	Percent of total plants	Total employ-ment and per cent	No. of grant-aided establishments per town 1960—73
< 1,500	90 (105)	25.6	6,463 (14.4)	0.28
1,500—5,000	108 (132)	30.7	12,188 (27.2)	1.81
5,000—10,000	47 (52)	13.4	7,179 (16.0)	2.36
10,000—25,000	36 (42)	10.2	5,056 (11.3)	3.82
25,000—150,000	43 (51)	12.2	8,332 (18.6)	12.75
Dublin	28 (36)	8.0	5,604 (12.5)	36.00
Total	352 (418)		44,822	

Source: O'Farrell, 1975, pp. 25—30.
Note: Figures represent survivors: total in parentheses include survivors and closures.

Table 9.3

Location of foreign firms in Ireland, May 1977

Location	Approx. population	UK	West Germany	USA	Other[1]	Total
Dublin	900,000	25	1	27	19	72
Cork[2]	125,000	1	2	8	10	21
Limerick[3]	75,000	6	8	28	21	63
Waterford	35,000	7	5	5	9	26
Galway	30,000	1	3	10	3	17
Dundalk	25,000	4	–	3	0	7
Drogheda	25,000	4	1	4	5	14
Sligo	15,000	2	3	4	2	11
Athlone	15,000	1	–	–	3	4
Sub-total		51	23	89	72	235
Elsewhere		96	65	68	43	272
Total		147	88	157	115	507

[1] Including joint ventures
[2] Including Cork harbour area
[3] Including Shannon/Ennis

Source: Walsh, 1979.

Walsh (1979) has examined the location of foreign-owned establishments in May 1977 and the results show that 46 per cent of them located in the nine centres suggested originally by Buchanan (Table 9.3). The data also imply that there are variations in plant location with respect to nationality. Higher proportions of British (65 per cent) and German (74 per cent) plants located outside the nine major centres, compared with only 43 per cent of US establishments and 37 per cent of 'other' nationalities. It would be tempting but invalid to infer a causal relationship on the basis of these findings but, although the results are suggestive, statistical controls are necessary to isolate the independent effect of nationality, if any.

O'Farrell (1978 and 1980a) has analysed the locational pattern of the population of 418 new industrial projects[7] grant-aided between 1960 and June 1973 under the New Industries (NI) Programme of the IDA. Location was studied for individual establishments at three scales: the nine planning regions; Designated Areas (DA) and Non-Designated Areas (NDA) and town size group. The data used in the analysis were restricted to those recorded on the files for each plant by the IDA so that certain variables for which data were not available, such as proximity to inputs, could not be tested.

In conducting the analysis at all three scales the question of whether to control for variables which may be either obscuring a relationship or creating a spurious one was investigated. In the context of the town size analysis, a Kolmogovov–Smirnov test demonstrated that the frequency distribution of plants by town size group was not independent of DA/NDA location (P<0.001) and, furthermore, the relationship is not a weak one as evidenced by a Kendall's tau statistic of $r_c = 0.33$ (O'Farrell, 1978, p. 141). Therefore, a DA/NDA control is necessary when testing town size location hypotheses. Similarly, it is desirable to apply a binary town size control (above and below 25,000) in the *regional* level analysis. Further significance tests indicated that the relationship between organisational type (branch or independent) and nationality is significant and not weak.[8] Hence an Irish/non-Irish control is necessary in testing the effects of organisational type upon regional and town size location (Figure 9.1). Similarly, organisational type is significantly correlated with market orientation *and* with fixed assets/labour ratio. Finally, as expected, plants of a particular nationality market much of their output in their parent countries and this is supported by a substantial Goodman and Kruskal tau statistic ($r_b = 0.48$). Hence, in testing the nationality effect, there is a clear need to control for market orientation (Figure 9.1).

The results of the hypotheses tested at town size group level in both DA and NDA show that there are more significant relationships in DA than within NDA (Table 9.4). In the more prosperous NDA, manufacturing group is related to town size group location, but its association is a weak one: a knowledge of manufacturing group only reduces the proportional error in predicting town size location by 3.6 per cent. It is somewhat expected that within NDA, establishment size is unrelated to town size location and, furthermore, the location pattern of large plants (above 100 employees) with respect to urban size does not differ from that of small ones. It may be inferred that, in the context of the factors analysed, there is little systematic variation by town size group within NDA.

There is a significant but weak (r=0.22) relationship between log establishment size and log town size in DA: larger plants are more likely to locate in more populous urban centres; but only 5 per cent of the variation in town size location is accounted for by plant size. Manufacturing group is more strongly associated with town size location in DA than in NDA: there is a proportional reduction in error of 11.8 per cent in predicting town size location from a knowledge of manufacturing group. Statistical testing also reveals that the IDA has not been varying its percentage grant payments by town size in NDA but, conversely, it has paid a disproportionately large number of projects over 50 per cent grants in towns below 1,500 in DA. Also, within DA, non-Irish branch plants, when compared with independents, reveal a marked preference for larger towns, thereby strengthening existing agglomeration trends; but in the more prosperous and densely popu-

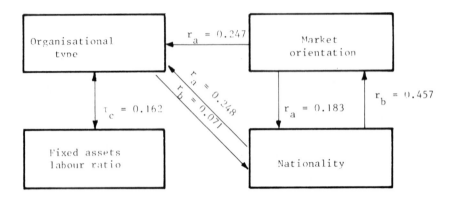

Figure 9.1   Independent variables: significant and strong relationships
Source: O'Farrell, 1978, p. 140.

lated NDA, no such preference relative to independents exists.

Blackbourn (1972, pp. 441–2) suggested that German-owned plants preferred locations in the small remote towns of south-western Ireland with populations of less than 1,500 and that 'British companies . . . were concentrated in Dublin'. These conclusions were based upon calculating the simple percentage of UK plants locating in Dublin and ignore the fact that in order to test the nationality effect, controls for both market orientation and DA/NDA are required (O'Farrell, 1978, p. 148). Separate significance tests for plants manufacturing in the UK, Europe and Ireland suggest that nationality is *not* related to town size location in either DA or NDA (Table 9.4). Various nationality groups do not display marked preferences for any town size category. The results suggest that even within DA the relationships are fairly weak which provides the IDA with the scope to influence location patterns, although not to the same degree as between town size groups in NDA.

Table 9.4

Town size group location patterns: summary of statistical results

Independent variable		DA	NDA
Establishment size		$r = 0.22$ ($P<0.01$)	$r = 0.106$ (NS)
Manufacturing group		$P<0.001$ ($r_b = 0.118$)	$P<0.02$ ($r_b = 0.036$)
Capital grant as a percentage of fixed assets		$P<0.012$ ($r_b = 0.108$)	NS
Percentage females employed		NS	NS
Organisational type	Irish	NS	NS
	Non-Irish	$P<0.05$ ($r_c = -0.230$)	NS
	UK market	NS	NS
	European market	NS	NS
	Irish market	NS	NS
Nationality	UK	NS	NS
	USA	NS	NS
	German	NS	NS
	Irish	NS	NS
Market orientation	Irish	NS	NS
Fixed assets/labour ratio	Irish	NS	NS
	Non-Irish	NS	NS

Source: O'Farrell, 1978, p. 170.

A binary town size group control above and below 25,000 population is necessary in analysing location patterns at regional level and the results of the hypotheses testing point to a number of general conclusions (Table 9.5). First, there are four variables — establishment size, percentage females employed, market orientation and fixed assets/labour ratio — which are not related to the regional location of plants in towns above and below 25,000 population.

Also, the size of the country is such that the market orientation of plants — even for those selling domestically — has not influenced their regional location. Second, for the plants in towns above 25,000 population (that is in regions east, south-east, south-west, mid-west and west) none of the independent variables tested is related to regional location. The inference is that, with regard to the factors analysed, plants — once they have decided to locate in centres above 25,000 population — are relatively indifferent as to their regional location. This apparent randomness in regional location behaviour provides the IDA with the opportunity — which it already exercises — to substantially influence regional location decisions. Third, the sectoral variable is only weakly associated with regional location in towns below 25,000 population: the Goodman and Kruskal tau statistic (r_b = 0.059) indicates that a knowledge of manufacturing group only reduces the probability of error in predicting its regional location by 5.9 per cent.

The test of the nationality effect for plants with a UK orientation in towns below 25,000 is significant and the contributions to chi-square suggest that German plants are over-represented in the south-west; that Irish plants selling to the UK are over-represented in the east/south-east and, logically in view of transport costs to Britain, are under-represented in the west/mid-west, and that, somewhat surprisingly, there are more UK establishments than expected in the west/mid-west and, equally unexpected, British plants marketing in the UK are under-represented in the east and south-east. It may be inferred that transport costs per unit output for British plants selling in the UK are not perceived as an important factor in regional location. The Goodman and Kruskal tau statistic suggests a weak association between nationality and regional location: a knowledge of nationality reduces the proportional probability of error in predicting regional location by only 3.7 per cent (O'Farrell, 1978, p. 149). Nationality does not influence the regional location of plants in towns below 25,000 population selling to the European or Irish markets. The analysis suggests that the four variables which are associated with regional location — in towns below 25,000 population — manufacturing group, organisational type (non-Irish plants), capital grants as a percentage of fixed assets and nationality (UK market orien-

Table 9.5

Regional location patterns: summary of statistical results

Independent variable		Regional location ($<$25,000 towns)	Regional location ($>$25,000 towns)
Establishment size		NS	NS
Manufacturing group		$P < 0.01$ ($r_b = 0.059$)	NS
Capital grant as percentage of fixed assets		$P < 0.001$ ($r_b = 0.020$)	NS
Percentage females employed		NS	NS
Organisational type	Irish	NS	NS
	Non-Irish	$P < 0.002$ ($r_b = 0.052$)	
Nationality	UK market	$P < 0.015$ ($r_b = 0.037$)	No test possible
	European market	NS	NS
	Irish market	NS	No test possible
Market orientation	UK	NS	No test possible
	USA	NS	No test possible
	German	NS	No test possible
	Irish	NS	No test possible
Fixed assets/labour ratio	Irish	NS	No test possible
	Non-Irish	NS	No test possible

Source: O'Farrell, 1978, p. 152.

323

tation only) — are only weakly related to regional location. The significance of the grants factor has helped to increase the chances of peripheral regions attracting investment. Establishments clearly display a high degree of randomness in choosing a regional location.

Discriminant analysis has been applied at regional level in order to predict industrial location patterns (O'Farrell, 1978 and O'Farrell and Crouchley, 1979). A four-fold regional division was used and the standardised discriminant function coefficients indicate that the manufacturing group 4 dummy (the wood, furniture and paper sector) makes the greatest relative contribution to differentiating the projects between the four regions; other important discriminators are percentage grants (x_{35}) and the manufacturing group 6 dummy (chemical and pharmaceutical plants). The regional locations of 40.1 per cent of the establishments are assigned correctly by the model but there is a considerable inter-regional variation in the ability of the model to predict location: it classifies 67.5 per cent of the mid-west and south-west plants correctly, 38.7 per cent of the east and south-west plants, 27.0 per cent of the Donegal, north-west and west establishments, but fails to accurately predict any of the north-east and midlands plants (Table 9.6). This suggests that there may be some variables not included in the model which might improve its predictive capability or, in terms of the variables analysed, there is little or no difference between certain regions in the characteristics of projects locating there. This inference is consistent with the cross classification analysis in showing that plants are relatively indifferent as to their regional location and that manufacturing group, nationality and percentage grants are — even in an additive model — fairly weakly associated with regional location. The characteristics of those plants which have located in the mid-west and south-west and which the model classifies as locating in this region with a high probability, are predominantly American branch plants with an average level of grant payment oriented towards the engineering and electrical machinery sector. The projects with a high probability of locating in the east and south-east are primarily of Irish, British or American origin, with a low level of grant payments which are producing for the wood, furniture, printing, chemical and pharmaceutical markets.

Location patterns by Designated Areas (DA) and Non-Designated Areas (NDA)

The DA and NDA do not constitute complete sets of regions: many of the nine regions cross the DA/NDA division and this justifies the case for an examination of location patterns at this level (Figure 9.1). The

324

results show that six of the eight independent variables are not related to DA/NDA location within any town size group (Table 9.7). Hence, size, sector, organisational classification, market orientation, fixed assets/labour ratio and percentage of females employed have not influenced location decisions at the scale of DA/NDA. Since the legal limit on percentage grants was always higher in DA than in NDA throughout the period of the analysis, it is of interest to examine which nationalities, if any, were most likely to take advantage of the extra grants. Blackbourn (1972, pp. 441–2) asserted that, in the Irish context, American and German plants preferred DAs while British establishments are under-represented in these areas. Having applied market orientation and town size group controls, the significance tests show that for plants selling in the UK, nationality is independent of DA/NDA location for both town size groups (Table 9.7). Similarly, for plants marketing primarily in Europe, nationality is independent of DA/NDA location (Table 9.7). There is, therefore, no tendency for German plants to prefer DA and British NDA when compared with other nationalities. In the case of projects marketing in Ireland only the test for 29 plants in the 1,500–5,000 town size category was significant ($P<0.05$). Hence, American branch plants are no more likely than British, German or Irish ones to locate in the DA. It is apparent that, in the context of the factors tested, new industry projects are highly indifferent as to whether they locate in DA or NDA. The evidence which shows that percentage grant is quite strongly associated with DA/NDA location for plants in all town size groups – except 10,000–25,000 – suggests that the differential grant system operated by the IDA and favouring DA has been the single most important factor influencing the pattern of location as between DA and NDA. Assuming that the capital grant proportion is a causal variable – and this seems very plausible at DA/NDA level – the results indicate that a tiered grants scheme has the ability to substantially influence locational behaviour within Ireland. This implies that a flexible policy of varying grant levels in different regions depending upon social and economic circumstances – already being operated to some extent by the IDA – can substantially affect, in conjunction with the organisation of itineraries and the provision of advanced factories, the regional distribution of new industry projects. There is some evidence of variation in the importance of different location factors between the regional scale, on the one hand, and the DA/NDA level, on the other. The variables, establishment size, percentage females employed, market orientation and fixed assets/labour ratio do not influence location patterns at either scale; but manufacturing group – although independent of DA/NDA location – is a significant factor at regional level for plants in towns below 25,000 population. The grants variable is significant at both spatial scales, but its influence – as ex-

Table 9.6

Discriminant analysis results for regional model

Variables	Unstand. discrim. function coeffs.	Stand. discrim. function coeffs.	Classification function coefficients			
			Region 1	Region 2	Region 3	Region 4
Percentage grant: x_{35}	-0.048	-0.765	0.120	0.153	0.143	0.184
Man. group 2: z_2	1.457	0.538	68.373	69.600	71.117	71.154
Man. group 4: z_4	5.994	1.513	71.963	74.087	81.133	76.441
Man. group 5: z_5	1.291	0.591	69.147	69.492	71.613	71.186
Man. group 6: z_6	1.815	0.607	68.921	69.787	72.229	71.675
Man. group 1, 3, 7: z_a	0.646	0.304	69.417	69.577	71.159	71.619
Nationality UK: s_1	-1.055	-0.415	2.479	1.321	1.309	2.201
Interaction $s_1 z_5$	2.012	0.351	-4.634	-1.682	-2.795	-4.513
Interaction $x_{35} z_4$	-0.108	-0.995	-0.098	-0.123	-0.255	-0.151
Constant			-38.306	-36.751	-38.295	-39.810

Discriminating power of discriminant functions

Number removed	Eigenvalue	Canonical correlation	Per cent of trace	Wilks' lambda	Chi-square	d.f.	Sig. level
0	0.198	0.407	78.5	0.791	81.008	27	0.000
1	0.044	0.205	17.3	0.948	18.451	16	0.298

One function used in analysis: centroids of groups in reduced space: region 1, −0.721; region 2, 0.124; region 3, 0.496; region 4, −0.374. A priori probabilities based upon group size: group 1, 0.179; group 2, 0.349; group 3, 0.301; group 4, 0.170.

Actual region	N	Predicted group membership				Percentage correctly classified
		1	2	3	4	
1	63	17	41	5	0	27.0
2	123	10	83	30	0	67.5
3	106	5	60	41	0	38.7
4	60	14	40	6	0	0
Total	352	46	224	81	0	40.1

Source: O'Farrell, 1978, p. 180.

Table 9.7

Designated Area and Non-Designated Area location patterns:
summary of statistical results

		DA/NDA location — Town size group control				
		$<1,500$	$1,500–5,000$	$5,000–10,000$	$10,000–25,000$	$25,000–150,000$
Establishment size		NS	NS	NS	NS	NS
Manufacturing group		NS	NS		NS	
Capital grant as a percentage of fixed assets		$P<0.001$ $r_c=-0.32$	$P<0.001$ $r_c=-0.38$	$P<0.001$ $r_c=-0.35$	NS	$P<0.01$ $r_c=-0.497$
Percentage females employed		NS	NS	NS	NS	NS
Organisational type	Irish	NS	NS	NS	NS	NS
	Non-Irish	NS	NS	NS		NS
Nationality	UK market		NS	NS		
	European market	NS		NS		NS
	Irish market	NS		NS		
Market orientation	UK	NS		$P<0.05$	NS	
	USA	NS			NS	
	Irish	NS	NS		NS	
Fixed assets/ labour ratio	Irish	NS	NS	NS	NS	NS
	Non-Irish	NS	NS			

Source: O'Farrell, 1978, p. 161.

328

Table 9.8

Number of grant-aided manufacturing establishments per town classified by town size group and by region

Town size group	Donegal/North-west	West	Mid-West	South West	South East	East	North East	Midlands	Mean
<1,500	0.45	0.31	0.14	0.33	0.23	0.16	0.60	0.10	0.28
1,500–5,000	1.40	1.25	1.33[1]	2.43	0.33	0.80	2.17	1.67	1.45
5,000–10,000	3.00	2.00	1.00	3.00	1.25	4.25	3.00	1.33	2.36
10,000–25,000	5.00	–	10.00*	4.00	2.00	2.00*	5.50	4.00*	4.40
25,000–150,000	–	16.00*	7.00*	11.00*	18.00*	–	–	–	13.00
>150,000	–	–	–	–	–	37.00*	–	–	37.00
Mean	0.67	0.83	0.57	0.93	0.70	1.11	1.12	0.52	0.82

[1]Shannon plants (23) excluded. If included, value rises to 1.78.
*Figure based upon one town only.

Friedman two-way ANOVA: $x^2 = 12.86$; d.f. = 7; NS. Test run on rows 1–3 x 8 cols ($n = 262$). Test re-run (pooling West and Mid-West) on rows 1–4 x 7 cols: $x^2 = 11.84$; d.f. = 6; NS.

Source: O'Farrell 1978, p. 171.

pected — is considerably stronger at DA/NDA level. The organisational structure of non-Irish plants (branch plant or independent) is related to regional location in towns below 25,000 but the association is a weak one. Nationality is a significant factor — but not a strong one — for plants marketing in the UK at regional level and for plants marketing in Ireland in towns between 5,000 and 10,000 at DA/NDA level.

Industrial location patterns: town size and regional effects

It is now appropriate to examine town size and regional location patterns *simultaneously*, and to test whether locational differentiation is greater by town size or region in the Irish context. The number of industrial establishments per town is cross classified by town size group and region in Table 9.8, and the fundamental question is whether the probability of a plant locating within a specific town size group varies significantly by region, or whether the inter-regional variations are simply the realisation of a stochastic process. Application of the Friedman two-way analysis of variance to test the null hypothesis that the column variable (region) has no effect, indicates significance at the 0.01 level specified. *It may be concluded that the number of plants per town by town size group is independent of region, suggesting that the probability of a town of a specific size group attracting a new industry project does not vary regionally.*

Application of two-way Analysis of Variance (ANOVA) to the data in Table 9.8 although not totally justified statistically (due to between cell heterogeneity of variances), does enable three hypotheses to be tested: (i) column (regional) means equal; (ii) row (town size group) means equal; (iii) additivity in population (no interaction). The interaction effect between town size and region is significant ($P<0.01$) and the non-additivity is produced by the 10,000—25,000 town size group. When the 10,000—25,000 group is excluded from the analysis, the test for interaction among the remaining categories below 10,000 population is insignificant (results in parenthesis, Table 9.9).

Assuming additivity in the model, the sums of squares due to interaction are thrown back into the error term to test hypothesis (i) and (ii). The two-way ANOVA run on seven columns (West and Mid-West pooled) and the four town size groups below 25,000 populations confirms that there is a highly significant town size group effect ($P<0.001$). When the 10,000—25,000 town size group is eliminated, the town size group effect is also highly significant ($P<0.001$) (Table 9.9). *There is little doubt that when we control for region by letting this factor explain all that it can of the variation in number of plants per town and then let town size group explain what it can of the remainder, there is*

Table 9.9

Two-way analysis of variance of number of grant-aided manufacturing establishments per town classified by town size group and by region[1]

Source of variation	Sums of squares	Degrees of freedom	Mean square	F	Sig. level
Total	127.04 (27.8)	27 (20)	4.71 (1.39)		
Between regions	14.20 (4.8)	6 (6)	2.37 (0.80)	1.04 (1.57)	NS (NS)
Between town size groups	71.71 (16.8)	3 (2)	23.90 (8.42)	10.47 (16.42)	$P < 0.001$ ($P < 0.001$)
Error	41.18 (6.2)	18 (12)	2.28 (0.51)		
Test for non-additivity Error	41.08 (6.2)	18 (12)	2.28 (0.51)		
Non-additivity	16.18 (2.18)	1 (1)	16.18 (2.18)	11.04 (6.05)	$P < 0.01$ (NS)
Remainder	24.90 (3.97)	17 (11)	1.47 (0.36)		

[1] Results in parentheses are for two-way ANOVA with 10,000–25,000 towns eliminated

Source: O'Farrell, 1978, p. 172.

a substantial relationship between town size group and number of plants per town. Hypothesis (ii) may be rejected. Conversely, the F test for the between region effect (hypothesis (i)), controlling for town size group, is not significant in both cases, which provides support for the Friedmann two-way ANOVA result of an insignificant regional effect.

Although towns throughout the urban hierarchy have attracted investment — notably 25.1 per cent of new projects have located in towns below 1,500 — the analysis clearly demonstrates the not unexpected finding that the degree of locational preference displayed by new industry plants varies positively with town size (O'Farrell, 1975, p. 31). *Locational discrimination by industrial investors in Ireland appears to be much greater with respect to town size than region and this is partly a consequence of the IDA's regionally differentiated incentive scheme and organisation of itineraries.* Although the level of incentives was constant throughout the DA, communities of a given size in more remote locations were no less likely to attract industrial projects than those more centrally located. These results might appear to contradict the earlier findings which indicate that four independent variables are related to town size group location in DA and only one in NDA. However, it is logical to interpret the results as implying that plants do discriminate by town size group but that this differentiation is only weakly related, with the exception of establishment size, in DA to any of the factors analysed. Most plants of all characteristics display preferences which are positively related to town size.

The relevant DA/NDA data are outlined in Table 9.10 and they reveal a somewhat unexpected pattern in that for every town size group there are more establishments per town in DA than NDA, even if the Shannon Industrial Estate plants are excluded. The assumption of additivity is supported by an insignificant F statistic (Table 9.11). Application of two-way ANOVA to the towns below 25,000 demonstrates that, as in the case of the regional analysis, the between-areas effect is not significant, whereas the between-town size effect is highly significant ($P < 0.01$). This analysis suggests, therefore, that even at the scale of DA/NDA industrialists exercise a greater degree of locational differentiation by town size than by the two large regions. It is reasonable to infer that the insignificant between-areas effect is largely a consequence of the more generous incentive available to investors in DA.

The results indicate that there are varying degrees of footlooseness within the Irish economy. It is clear that plants are considerably more footloose with respect to regional location than they are with respect to town size location. The location of an urban centre of specific size within the country — however peripheral — will not influence — assuming a continuation of DA/NDA grant differentials — the attractiveness of that centre for industrial investment: when town size is controlled,

Table 9.10

Number of grant-aided manufacturing establishments per town
classified by town size group and by Designated Area/Non-Designated Area

Town size group	Designated Area	Non-Designated Area	Mean
<1,500	0.406	0.164	0.28
1,500–5,000	2.03[1]	1.07	1.45
5,000–10,000	2.50	2.18	2.36
10,000–25,000	6.33	3.57	4.40
25,000–150,000	16.00[2]	12.00	13.00
>150,000	–	37[2]	–

[1]Shannon Industrial Estate excluded (2.71 if included).
[2]Figure based upon one town only.

Table 9.11

Two-way analysis of variance of number of grant-aided manufacturing
establishments per town classified by town size group and by area

Source of variation	Sum of squares	Degrees of freedom	Mean square	F	Sig. level
Total	27.64	7	3.95		
Between areas	2.29	1	2.29	3.34	NS
Between town size groups	23.29	3	7.76	11.31	$P<0.01$
Error	2.06	3	0.686		
Test for non-additivity Error	2.06	3	0.69		
Non-additivity	1.65	1	1.65	8.08	NS
Remainder	0.41	2	0.205		

Source: O'Farrell, 1978, p. 173.

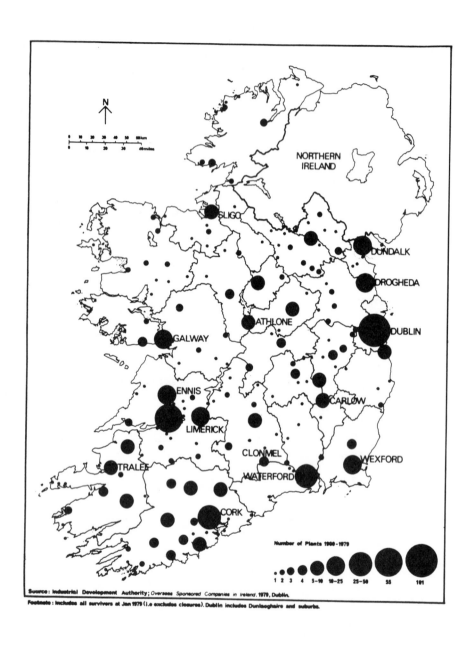

Map 9.2 Number of plants by area, created in the period 1960—79
(including all survivors at January 1979 (i.e. excludes closures). Dublin
includes Dunlaoghaire and suburbs).

the between region effect upon number of plants per town is insignificant.

Multinational enterprises and core region location

The bulk of the empirical evidence considered so far has been concerned with examining the locational patterns of plants — both indigenous and foreign — grant aided under the IDA New Industry programme. In this section, more attention will be directed towards the locational behaviour of overseas firms and their responsiveness to regional incentives (Map 9.2). Some writers have asserted that the power of these firms enables them to locate where they wish, that is predominantly in the core regions of European countries.

There is no obvious criterion against which to judge whether the proportion of overseas plants locating in core regions is 'high' or 'low'. Figures of the different percentages of foreign and indigenous plants locating in core regions might be conceived as a crude — although (as will be argued later) possibly misleading — criterion of the relative degree of responsiveness to regional incentives. Of the total population of foreign-owned plants established between January 1960 and June 1973, 17.8 per cent of them located in the East region while 19.5 per cent of indigenous Irish plants commenced operations in the East over the same period. *Hence, indigenous plants have shown a marginally greater tendency to concentrate in the core region* (O'Farrell, 1980a). Between 1960 and 1973, 59 per cent of foreign projects located in DA compared with 43 per cent of Irish ones — a marked differential suggesting greater responsiveness to regional incentives by foreign investors. However, this begs the question as to whether there is an underlying causal relationship between nationality and regional location.

A simple examination of the percentage of foreign-owned industrial plants locating in DA or a specific region may lead to incorrect inferences being drawn because there are interaction effects between market orientation and nationality; also, town size group is related to both region and DA/NDA. Therefore, appropriate statistical controls must be applied in analysing the effects of the nationality factor upon location. The analysis of the effect of nationality upon DA/NDA location reported earlier has shown that foreign plants marketing in the UK located in towns below 5,000 revealed a significantly greater tendency to locate in DA than indigenous ones. This includes about one-quarter of all grant-aided plants between 1960 and 1973 and is the one substantive relationship underlying the aggregate pattern of 59 per cent of multinationals in the DA compared with 43 per cent of Irish plants. Hence, foreign enterprises, far from exacerbating regional disequilibria, were more likely than Irish ones to locate in DA between 1960 and 1973 (O'Farrell, 1980a, p. 149).

It is now of interest to examine whether the locational choices of overseas companies have changed over time. The IDA list of overseas-sponsored companies in Ireland provides data on all new overseas-owned subsidiaries and branches which opened between 1960 and December 1980 and survived till the end of the period.[10] Of the overseas branches established between 1960 and 1973, 59 per cent located in the DA, 41 per cent in the NDA and, within the NDA, 15 per cent of the national total located in Dublin county. Between 1974 and 1980, the proportion of overseas firms locating in DAs dropped to 37.4 per cent, the corresponding NDA proportion rose to 62.6 per cent and the Dublin share of the national total remained constant at 15 per cent. Hence, there has been a strong relative shift between 1974 and 1980 in favour of the NDA outside Dublin county, which includes those parts of the East region which now constitute the outer Dublin suburbs and satellite towns. This is partly a consequence of the IDA promoting the Dublin region more vigorously, especially since 1977, and partly a result of the downgrading in importance of the DA/NDA division for the purposes of awarding grants. A more pragmatic attitude to grant levels has been adopted in recent years with the IDA varying its grant offers according to existing and predicted social and economic indices for specific locations or town groups.

The process of decision making

There are no behavioural studies of the locational decision-making process of new firms but O'hUiginn (1972) did ask managements whether, in the light of experiences with their present location, they would now prefer to relocate the plant. Of the 375 establishments which responded, 70.6 per cent reported that they would still prefer to remain at the same location, whereas 29.4 per cent said they would like to move to another location. Some 17 per cent of firms wishing to move indicated their preference for a location outside the Republic; they represented only 5 per cent of the total sample interviewed (O'hUiginn 1972, p. 31). There was above average desire for firms in Dublin to remain there and this was also true of plants in towns of 10,000–20,000 population. There was below-average desire to remain in towns of the 3,000–5,000 category while other size groups were about average or the samples were too small to draw valid conclusions.

At regional level, the proportion of plants which would not wish to relocate was highest in the East (81.5 per cent) compared with a national figure of 70.6 per cent (O'hUiginn, 1972, p. 33). The other above-average regions were Donegal (70.8 per cent) and the Midlands (72.2 per cent). Three regions, the West (64.6 per cent) Mid-West (64.7 per cent) and North-West (63.2 per cent) recorded the greatest degree of dissatisfaction with their regional location, although only slightly over one-third of plants would relocate elsewhere (O'hUiginn, 1972, p. 33). The largest number of relocations, if given the choice again, would be to Dublin, the East coast or a port location in order to improve transport costs and facilities (O'hUiginn, 1972, p. 43).

Effects upon donor and acceptor regions

Industrial closures

Since industrial migration *within* Ireland is such a rare phenomenon, this section is concerned with impacts of new investment upon acceptor (host) regions. O'Farrell (1975 and 1976) analysed the closures which occurred amongst New Industry projects in receipt of grant payments from the IDA between 1960 and 1973. Of the 418 new industrial establishments, 66 (16 per cent) had ceased production by June 1973; but these establishments accounted for only 6.9 per cent of grant payments and 4.6 per cent of employment. The mean annual closure rate for 1961—72 of 2.5 per cent is comparable with those observed by Townroe (1974, p. 291) up to the end of 1971 of between 2.2 and 4 per cent per annum for the total inter-regional moves in the UK between 1966—68.

In contrast to findings of other studies, an analysis of closure frequencies against number of years in operation before closure revealed that closure is *not* a time-dependent phenomenon: survival is independent of age (O'Farrell, 1976, p. 436). The level and range of incentives provided by the IDA is clearly sufficient to prevent higher closure rates in the early years of a plant's life.

Establishment size was weakly related to closure ($P < 0.05$); but the proportion of plants of below 75 employees which closed (20.3 per cent) was higher than that for plants employing 74 or more employees (10.5 per cent). The overall χ^2 value based upon the five degrees of freedom for the original six size categories was partitioned into three additive components and the results suggest significant differences between the proportions of closures among plants above and below 74 employees at the 0.01 level, but homogeneity within the two groups (Table 9.12). Furthermore, the χ^2 value due to regression suggests that

337

the increase in the chance of survival is a linear function of increasing size (O'Farrell, 1976, p. 440).

Table 9.12

Components of χ^2 for projected employment size

Component of χ^2 due to			Degrees of freedom	Significance level
(i)	Difference between 0—74 and >74	7.594	1	p<0.01
(ii)	Difference within 0—74	0.594	2	NS
(iii)	Difference within >74	0.977	2	NS
Overall χ^2		9.165	5	NS

Source: O'Farrell, 1976.

Subsequent analysis indicated that survival or closure of a grant-aided establishment was independent of sector, organisational type (branch or independent) and nationality. Survival or closure was also independent of town size location, regional location and DA/NDA location, although there are significant differences between the West and Mid-West and the rest of the country (O'Farrell, 1976, p. 444). McAleese (1977) reported evidence of an increase in closure rates between 1973 and 1975 — a period marked by a major economic recession. It is also notable that high closure rates, with a distinct increase since O'Farrell's data, were recorded by McAleese in textiles, clothing and footwear, and structural clay/glass and cement (McAleese, 1977, p. 78)

Job losses

Teeling (1975) found evidence of labour-saving investment among grant-aided firms up to the early 1970s in order to raise labour productivity. McAleese and Counahan (1979) examined employment in grant-aided foreign and domestic industry over the period 1973—77 in order to test whether overseas companies were more likely to close or cut back employment during a period covering a pre-recession employment peak and a post-recession recovery. They discovered that in 1975 (the worst year of the recession) employment in their sample of non-food multinational branches fell by 9.4 per cent while employment in the comparative sample of Irish firms declined at virtually the same rate (−9.1 per cent). However, multinational employment had recovered to its 1973 level by early 1977 whereas new domestic firms suffered continued job losses during 1976 (McAleese and Counahan, 1979, p. 350).

In analysing employment decline at the level of the individual multinational subsidiary, two factors emerged as statistically significant: plant size and degree of marketing autonomy. Large plants weathered the recession better than smaller ones; and multinationals with marketing autonomy experienced less severe job losses than those whose marketing functions were controlled from abroad (McAleese and Counahan, 1979, pp. 355−6). Multinationals located in the DAs did not record a greater rate of employment decline than those in NDAs (McAleese and Counahan, 1979, p. 354). The evidence suggests that multinationals are not an unstable element in the economy and this leads McAleese and Counahan (1979, p. 356) to conclude that 'the economic consequences of the nationality of ownership of a country's manufacturing sector may well be much less pronounced than is often believed'.

Job creation by town size group

It is clearly important to examine the *consequences* of the numerous location decisions made throughout the country for job provision. In Table 9.13 the actual number of jobs created under the New Industry Programme between 1960 and 1973 within specific town size groups is expressed per 1,000 urban population. As urban population and populations of hinterlands are highly correlated,[11] the results may be interpreted as a broad index of job creation performance with respect to the total population within journey-to-work areas. On the basis of this criterion, towns within the 1,500−5,000 group have benefited most from the New Industry job creation programme between 1960 and 1973 with 59.3 jobs per 1,000 urban population (Table 9.13). The 5,000−10,000 size category gained 47.2 jobs per 1,000 urban population and the ratio then falls to approximately 32 per 1,000 urban population for both the 10,000−25,000 and 25,000−150,000 categories. The one striking anomaly is the very low level of jobs created per 1,000 urban population (7.2) in Dublin. This partly reflects IDA policy in the pre-1973 period which was to divert as much new manufacturing investment as possible away from Dublin and into the regions. Hence, when assessed by the criterion of number of jobs created per

Table 9.13

Number of New Industry grant-aided establishments and employment created per 1,000 urban population by town size group, 1960—73

Town size[1]	Total urban population	No. of establishments per 1,000 urban population	Employment created[2] per 1,000 urban population
<1,500	197,557	0.43	32.7
1,500—5,000	205,550	0.64	59.3
5,000—10,000	152,243	0.34	47.2
10,000—25,000	159,211	0.26	31.8
25,000—150,000	260,483	0.20	31.9
>150,000	778,127	0.05	7.2

[1] The <1,500 group includes all towns as defined by the census.
[2] Actual employment January 1973.

Source: O'Farrell, 1979, p. 66.

1,000 urban population, policy has been most successful throughout the 73 small 1,500–5,000 towns with the 24 centres in the 5,000–10,000 category also benefiting from a high level of job creation. It is important to note that manufacturing employment creation per 1,000 urban population has been as high in the small towns and villages below 1,500 population as in the major regional growth centres of Cork, Waterford, Limerick and Galway.

Branch plant autonomy

It may be hypothesised that certain intra-firm factors – especially the internal division of labour within the firm – may constrain the innovative and adjustment potential of branches in peripheral regions. In a survey of 207 multi-plant firms, 62 of which were Irish-owned, O'hUiginn (1972, p. 18) showed that the proportion of plants with characteristic headquarter functions was low: almost two-thirds of the plants did not perform the marketing function and 78 per cent were dependent upon the parent organisation for research and development services. There are no data available to show the extent to which there are interregional variations in the degree of decentralisation of headquarter functions.

The degree of purchasing autonomy enjoyed by plants belonging to multi-plant companies is quite high: a total of 59 per cent of a sample of multinationals have complete raw material purchasing autonomy whilst only 12 have zero autonomy (O'Farrell and O'Loughlin, 1980, p. 40). The degree of freedom granted to branch plants in making decisions concerning the allocation of service expenditures is even greater with 88.7 per cent having complete autonomy from their parent company. The extent of parent company control over purchasing does not vary according to the nationality of the overseas company.

Some 88.9 per cent of New Industry plants use exclusively Irish resources for transport services. The independence of branch plants from their parents is most marked in the provision of repair and maintenance services: only four establishments rely to any degree on their parent company and almost 95 per cent of plants use either their own employees or outside Irish firms (O'Farrell and O'Loughlin, 1980, p. 41). A similar pattern of provision exists for auditing and accounting, advertising and publicity services with over 90 per cent using either their own employees or outside Irish firms.

It is apparent that multinationals largely provide certain key strategic services from abroad, but devolve responsibility upon the Irish branch to organise the more routine lower-order functions. The evidence suggests that external control has not been greatly detrimental to national or regional economies with respect to division of functions within the firm, except for those plants which process a high proportion of inputs from affiliates abroad.

Linkages

There is some evidence of the *direct* effects which new manufacturing investment – both indigenous and foreign – has had upon the national and regional economies through the mechanism of backward and forward linkages.

The New Industry sector purchased 59.5 per cent of its inputs in Ireland in 1976, although non-food plants obtained only 16.4 per cent of their materials and components from Irish sources (O'Farrell and O'Loughlin, 1980, p. 17, and 1981). However, these proportions have risen by 3.5 and 1.7 percentage points, respectively, since 1974. An econometric analysis of input purchasing at *national* level (the dependent variable was the proportion of total inputs purchased in Ireland) showed that there was a significant Irish nationality effect suggesting that Irish plants purchased 6.7 percentage points *more* of their inputs domestically than overseas firms, having controlled for the effects of other variables. There was no significant difference between the enterprises of *individual* overseas countries in their relative propensity to purchase in Ireland (O'Farrell and O'Loughlin, 1980, p. 22). Approximately 30 per cent of the total imported inputs of multinationals are supplied from within the company. The analysis has also shown that once the effects of the various plant level variables have been accounted for the location of a plant has no influence upon its propensity to obtain inputs in Ireland.

The analysis of input purchasing at *local* level (i.e. within a 20-mile radius of each plant) shows that the New Industry group purchased 26.2 per cent of total inputs (domestic plus imports) locally (4.6 per cent for non-food plants) and this represented 44.1 per cent of Irish expenditure (27.7 per cent for non-food manufacturers). An econometric model was calibrated to explain the between-plant variation in the proportion of total raw materials and components purchased in the local area (Table 9.14). The results show that there is no difference between independent and branch plants – both Irish and foreign – with respect to local area purchasing.[12] The analysis also suggests that multinationals which have been in production a decade longer obtain approximately 5 percentage points more of their inputs locally (O'Farrell and O'Loughlin, 1980, p. 27). A number of locational variables were tested and all were insignificant. This implies that, when the effects of other variables have been controlled, none of the locational factors

Table 9.14

Regression results for input purchasing at local area level
(t-ratios in parentheses)

Dependent variable (Y_2) = percentage of raw materials and components purchased in the local area	Intercept	Value/weight ratio of major output	Number of years in production	Independent variables			$\bar{R}^2$	F	Sig P<	S.E.E.
				Food sector dummy	Joint ventures and others dummy	Midlands region dummy				
		$\log X_{78}$	$\log X_{69}$	S_1	F_5	R_8				
All plants (n = 320)										
Equation 1	22.42	−8.65 (3.74)	—	31.40 (10.51)	13.04 (2.56)	−9.57 (2.54)	0.35	42.9	0.001	19.6
Beta coefficients										
Equation 1A	—	−0.17	—	0.49	0.12	0.12				
Multinational plants (n = 137)										
Equation 2	1.94	—	5.75 (1.96)	24.60 (5.57)	—	—	0.20	12.5	0.001	12.1
Irish multi-plant firms (n = 68)										
Equation 3	36.52	15.63 (3.03)	—	32.98 (5.68)	—	—	0.43	26.4	0.001	20.9

Source: O'Farrell and O'Loughlin, 1980.

343

tested influences *local* area purchasing, not even a Dublin location with its large and diversified range of suppliers. It appears that backward linkages for inputs are forged primarily both between individual urban centres in Ireland and, especially, these centres and other towns abroad rather than *within* the centre itself and its commuting hinterland.

A country such as Ireland with its advanced business service sector should be able to meet the demands of most manufacturing plants over a wide range of service needs and this is confirmed by the finding that 77.2 per cent of total expenditure on service and other inputs was allocated to Irish suppliers.[13] Domestic spending by the New Industry non-food plants on services was almost identical to their expenditure on Irish raw materials and components and, of the service expenditures which can be spatially disaggregated, 42 per cent were made to supply firms within the *local areas* of the plants (O'Farrell and O'Loughlin, 1980, p. 44). An analysis of the distribution of service payments with respect to the ten major urban centres in the country indicates that 82.6 per cent of all service expenditure which can be allocated spatially goes to the ten largest towns, and Dublin alone accounted for 52 per cent (O'Farrell and O'Loughlin, forthcoming).

The percentage of Irish service expenditures allocated to the local area economy was shown by the analysis to be dependent upon six factors: population of the largest town within a 20-mile radius; a Dublin location effect; distance to the nearest town of over 28,000 population; plant size and value/weight ratio of the major output. The three locational factors contribute most to explaining between-enterprise variations in local area service payments. A combination of a large town in the local area and close proximity to it would probably boost local area service payments by £32 thousand per plant (1976 prices). These results indicating significant locational influences upon the propensity to purchase services in local areas are in direct contrast to the findings for material and component inputs. The argument put forward by a number of economists in Ireland that the overseas element of the New Industry sector is not integrated into the domestic economy, while perhaps valid for input purchasing by many non-food firms, is certainly untenable when business service linkages and wage and salary payments are brought within the concept of backward linkage effects.

The impact of foreign industries upon the skill structure of the labour force does not appear to be very marked, although the scanty data available on this question make it impossible to draw anything other than tentative conclusions. 'Industrial' workers in the New Industry sector in 1973 comprised 81.5 per cent and clerical, administrative and managerial workers 18.5 per cent of their labour force — exactly the same proportion as the national average for all of industry (O'Malley, 1980, p. 48). Craftsmen and apprentices made up 17 per cent of

New Industry workers, and 84 per cent of managerial staff were of Irish nationality (McAleese, 1977, pp. 53—7). Hence, there is little *published* evidence to suggest that new grant-aided plants offer proportionately less skilled or lower-grade work to Irish people other than industry; but more research into this problem is required before any firm conclusions can be reached.

Finally, there is evidence from the US Department of Commerce (1980) that American subsidiaries reinvested 74 per cent of their profits in Ireland between 1974 and 1979 compared with an average figure of 50.8 per cent for the EEC. This implies a high degree of confidence by the US multinationals in an Irish location and a commitment to expand their investment.

Outlook

The IDA plan for the 1978—82 period envisages that almost half the job approvals (i.e. 14,000 jobs per annum) in grant-aided manufacturing will come from *new* overseas projects. The total annual approval target of 30,000 is much higher[14] than any year before 1978 and the *absolute* number of jobs sought from new overseas sources (70,000 during the plan) is higher than in previous years (*IDA Industrial Plan 1978—82*, p. 34). There would be no prospect of achieving the industrial employment targets in the less-developed regions without an inflow of overseas investment. In order to achieve these goals the basis of IDA strategy for the 1978—82 period has shifted towards products with high value added based upon quality and design aimed at specialist markets (*IDA Industrial Plan, 1978—82*, p. 5). This implies moving from unskilled and semi-skilled industries to human capital-intensive firms employing graduates and technicians, such as micro-electronics, health care and other technologically-based projects which are associated with high proportionate expenditures on R and D. The IDA has explicitly recognised that, with the changing international division of labour, Ireland is no longer a low labour cost producer when compared with the newly industrial countries. Therefore, it is logical to build upon its comparative advantages which lie in the well-developed business and institutional infrastructure and the high level of education of an English-speaking workforce.

Of the 75,000 *actual* manufacturing jobs to be created between 1978 and 1982 (in firms with an ultimate job potential of 150,000), 19,000 (25.5 per cent) will be located in the east region — an area which contained 42 per cent of the nation's manufacturing employment in 1978. The greatest relative expansion[15] of new grant-aided manufacturing employment between 1978 and 1982 is planned to occur in the four least developed regions — Donegal, North-West, West, and Midlands (*IDA Industrial Plan 1978–82,* p. 46). The major policy instruments which will be employed to influence the location of new projects will remain the regionally differentiated incentives scheme, the provisions of advance factories, and the organisation of itineraries by the IDA. These instruments proved highly successful in achieving most regional targets during the 1973–8 plan, but there are two reasons why there should be no complacency concerning the 1978–82 goals. First, the more technologically-based plants which the IDA is seeking to attract to a greater extent than heretofore may be less likely to locate in small towns in peripheral regions since they may require access to a range of business services and research institutions only available in metropolitan areas. Second, the trend which has emerged since 1973 for a higher proportion of overseas enterprises to establish their branch plants in the NDAs may imply that the DAs will have to rely more upon their slender indigenous resources for future manufacturing growth. These arguments suggest that the IDA may have to adopt more vigorous regional policies in order to meet job targets in peripheral regions. Experience in the past suggests that IDA policy instruments are capable of generating the new job openings where they are required; what is more problematic are the spatial distributions of closures and redundancies over which the IDA has much less influence.

The IDA is placing increasing emphasis upon the small firm sector in future policy and they are targeted to provide 6,000 of the 15,000 'domestic' job approvals per annum during the 1978–82 plan. The majority of job approvals in small firms are in firms under indigenous control. The intervention of government to stimulate industrial development has been significant through semi-state agencies such as the IDA[16] but state enterprise *per se* has not constituted a major element of development strategy. Recently the IDA has been given a new mandate to work with state companies in finding new development projects. This is consistent with the pragmatic attitude of successive Irish governments towards the role of state enterprise in the economy.

There is no evidence to suggest that inter-regional movement of industrial enterprises in Ireland — either branch plant relocations or transfers — is going to become an important element in the components of manufacturing employment change during the next decade. A minor degree of movement outwards to suburban sites is likely to continue in the Dublin agglomeration and, to a lesser degree, in Cork. It is explicit IDA policy to halt the outflow of firms from the inner city area of Dublin to the suburbs and to foster small to medium sized enterprises as the principal source of new enterprises in the inner city (*IDA Industrial Plan, 1978–82,* p. 69). The major components of manufacturing employment change in the medium term in Ireland are likely to be new openings by both indigenous and externally-controlled enterprises, *in situ* changes by existing enterprises, and closures and redundancies. This chapter has shown that there is much yet to be learnt concerning each of these processes and their differential impact upon regions, sub-regions and the urban system. In particular, most of the works reviewed have been static cross-sectional studies and there is, at the moment, little understanding of the spatial dynamics of Irish industrial development.

Notes

1 It has been estimated that only 1.4 per cent of manufacturing plants in Ireland relocated between 1973 and 1981 and the majority of these occurred within the Dublin conurbation area (O'Farrell, forthcoming).

2 These grant levels represent the 'administrative' limit for NI grants. Higher levels up to the legal maximum of 60 per cent can be awarded in exceptional circumstances.

3 For more comprehensive reviews of industrial and regional location policies see O'Farrell (1971 and 1974); Hughes (1975); and Walsh (1976).

4 It was realised that a planned programme of industrial development could only occur within the framework of long-term plans for physical development and this was provided by the Local Government (Planning and Development) Act, 1963.

5 The EPTR created opportunities for overseas companies to engage in transfer pricing, and, although there is no more firm evidence on how prevalent this is in Ireland, it would be naive to assume that it did not occur.

6 It is extremely difficult to compare incentive schemes between the UK regions and Ireland since the selective financial assistance available for many products in the UK, in addition to the regional grant, in some instances may exceed the level of incentives paid by the IDA.

7 A total of 273 of the 418 plants were overseas-owned enterprises.

8 Goodman and Kruskal (r_a = 0.248, i.e. a knowledge of nationality reduces the error in predicting organisational type by 24.8 per cent).

9 A town size group control is required in analysing location at DA/NDA level.

10 There was a total of 722 overseas-sponsored companies in Ireland at the end of 1980.

11 There is a coefficient of determination of r^2 = 0.90 between the

population of an urban centre and the external population served within its median hinterland in County Tipperary (see O'Farrell, 1969, p. 107).

12   Four factors influence input purchasing at local level: value/weight ratio of the major output; a food sector effect; an ownership type effect and a Midlands region effect (Table 9.14).

13   This includes expenditure on repair and maintenance, transport, advertising, auditing and accounting, security, cleaning and professional services together with other items such as rates, gas, electricity, insurance, bank interest charges, royalties and licences.

14   This approval target has been exceeded in both 1979 and 1980.

15   Target for new grant-aided jobs as a proportion of total manufacturing employment.

16   The IDA has also taken up equity capital in certain projects, primarily large-scale technologically-based enterprises.

References

Allied Irish Banks (1981), 'Ireland as a Manufacturing Base', *Allied Irish Banks Review*, vol. 24, April.
Ambrose, W. (1978), 'Ireland's Exports', *Ireland Today*, 1 December.
Blackbourn, A. (1972), 'The location of foreign-owned manufacturing plants in the Republic of Ireland', *Tijdschr. Econ. Soc. Geogr.*, vol. 63, 438–43.
Blackbourn, A. (1978), 'Multinational enterprises and regional development: a comment', *Regional Studies*, vol. 12, 125–7.
Colin Buchanan and Partners (1969), *Regional Studies in Ireland*, An Foras Forbartha, Dublin.
Committee on Industrial Organisation (1962), Fourth Interim Report, *Industrial Grants*, Pr. 6924, Stationery Office, Dublin.
Department of Finance (1958), *Economic Development*, Pr. 4803, Stationery Office, Dublin.
Donaldson, L. (1965), *Development Planning in Ireland*, Praeger, New York and London.
Hamilton, F.E.I. (1976), 'Multinational Enterprise and the EEC', *Tijd. voor Econ. en Soc. Geog.*, vol. 67, pp. 258–78.
Hoare, A.G. (1975), 'Foreign firms and air transport: the geographical effect of Heathrow Airport', *Regional Studies*, vol. 9, pp. 349–68.
Hughes, J.G. (1975), *Regional Policy in Ireland: A Review*, National Economic and Social Council, Report no. 4, The Stationery Office, Dublin.
Industrial Development Authority (1972), *Regional Industrial Plans 1973–77*, Industrial Development Authority, Dublin.

Industrial Development Authority (1979), *IDA Industrial Plans 1978–82,* Industrial Development Authority, Dublin.

Kennedy, K.A. and Foley, A. (1978), 'Industrial Development' in Dowling, B.R. and Durkan, J. (eds), *Irish Economic Policy: A Review of Major Issues,* Economic and Social Research Institute, Dublin.

Labasse, J. (1975), 'The Geographical Space of Big Companies', *Geoforum,* vol. 6, pp. 113–24.

Lyons, J. (1978), 'Ireland's Industrial Development Authority', *Ireland Today,* 15 November.

McAleese, D. (1977), *A Profile of Grant-aided Industry in Ireland,* Industrial Development Authority, Publication Series Paper 5, Dublin.

McAleese, D. and Counahan, M. (1979), 'Stickers or Snatchers? Employment in Multinational Corporations during the Recession', *Oxford Bull. Econ. and Stat.,* vol. 41, no. 4, pp. 345–58.

McNee, R.B. (1960), 'Towards a more humanistic economic geography: the geography of enterprise' *Tijd. voor Econ. en Soc. Geog.,* vol. 51, pp. 201–5.

National Industrial Economic Council (1965), *Comments on the Report of Committee on Development Centres and Industrial Estate,* Pr. 8476, The Stationery Office, Dublin.

O'Farrell, P.N. (1969), 'Continuous regularities and discontinuities in the Central Place System', *Geografiska Annaler,* vol. 52B, pp. 104–14.

O'Farrell, P.N. (1971), 'The regional problem in Ireland: some reflections upon development strategy', *Econ. and Soc. Rev.,* vol. 2(4), pp. 453–80.

O'Farrell, P.N. (1974), 'Regional planning in Ireland – the case for concentration: a reappraisal', *Econ. and Soc. Rev.,* vol. 5(4), pp. 499–514.

O'Farrell, P.N. (1975), *Regional Industrial Development Trends in Ireland, 1960–73,* IDA, Dublin.

O'Farrell, P.N. (1976), 'An Analysis of industrial closures: Irish experience 1960–1973', *Regional Studies,* vol. 10, pp. 433–48.

O'Farrell, P.N. (1978), 'An Analysis of new industry locations: the Irish case', *Progress in Planning,* vol. 9, no. 3, Pergamon Press, Oxford, pp. 129–229.

O'Farrell, P.N. (1979), *Urbanisation and Regional Development in Ireland,* National Economic and Social Council, Report no. 45, Pr. 7716, The Stationery Office, Dublin.

O'Farrell, P.N. (1980a), 'Multinational enterprises and regional development: Irish evidence', *Regional Studies,* vol. 14, pp. 141–50.

O'Farrell, P.N. (1980b), 'The mobilisation of indigenous potential: towards a complementary regional strategy', *Papers in Planning Research,* no. 9, Department of Town Planning, UWIST, Cardiff.

O'Farrell, P.N. (forthcoming), 'Manufacturing Employment change in

Ireland: A Component's Approach.'

O'Farrell, P.N. and Crouchley, R. (1979), 'The locational pattern of new manufacturing establishments: an application of discriminant analysis', *Regional Studies,* vol. 13, pp. 39—59.

O'Farrell, P.N. and O'Loughlin, B. (1980), *An Analysis of New Industry Linkages in Ireland,* Industrial Development Authority, Publication Series, Dublin.

O'Farrell, P.N. and O'Loughlin, B. (1981), 'New industry input linkages in Ireland: an econometric analysis', *Environ. and Plan. A,* vol. 13, pp. 285—308.

O'Farrell, P.N. and O'Loughlin, B. (forthcoming), 'Environmental adaption of New Industry Enterprises: an analysis of service linkages', *Regional Studies.*

O'hUiginn, P. (1972), *Regional Development and Industrial Location in Ireland,* An Foras Forbartha, Dublin.

O'Loughlin, B. and O'Farrell, P.N. (1980), 'Foreign direct investment in Ireland: empirical evidence and theoretical implications', *Econ. and Soc. Rev.,* vol. 11(3), pp. 155—85.

O'Malley, E.J. (1980), *Industrial Policy and Development: A Survey of Literature from the Early 1960s,* National Economic and Social Council, Report no. 56, The Stationery Office, Dublin.

O'Neill, H. (1971), *Spatial Planning in the Small Economy: A Case Study of Ireland,* Praeger, New York and London.

O'Neill, H. (1973), 'Regional planning in Ireland: the case for concentration', *Irish Banking Review,* September, pp. 9—20.

Report of the Committee on Development Centres and Industrial Estates (1964), Pr. 8461, The Stationery Office, Dublin.

Smidt, de M. (1966), 'Foreign industrial establishments located in the Netherlands', *Tijd. voor Econ. en Soc. Geog.,* vol. 57, pp. 1—19.

Stanton, R. (1979), 'Foreign investment and host country politics: the Irish case', in Seers, D., Schaffer and Kiljunen (eds), *Underdeveloped Europe: Studies in Core-Periphery Relations,* Hassocks, Harvester Press.

Survey of Grant-aided Industry (1967), Survey Team's Report to the Industrial Development Authority, Prl. 117, The Stationery Office, Dublin.

Sweeney, J. (1973), 'Foreign Companies in Ireland', *Studies LXII,* Autumn/Winter, pp. 273—86.

Teeling, J. (1975), *The Evolution of Off-shore Investment,* D.B.A. thesis, Harvard University.

Thomas, M.D. (1980), 'Explanatory frameworks for growth and change in multi-regional firms', *Econ. Geog.,* vol. 56(1), p. 177.

Townroe, P.M. (1974), 'Post move stability and the location decision' in Hamilton, F.E.I. (ed.), *Spatial Perspectives on Industrial Organisation and Decision-Making*, John Wiley, London and New York.

USA Dept. of Commerce (1980), *Survey of Current Business*, Aι

Vernon, R. (1973), *Sovereignty at Bay: the Multinational Spread oʃ US Enterprises*, Pelican, London.

Walsh, F. (1976), 'The growth centre concept in Irish regional policy', *Maynooth Review*, vol. 2(1), pp. 22–41.

Walsh, F. (1979), 'Foreign direct investment and regional planning in the Irish Republic', paper read to Commission on Industrial Systems, I.G.U. Symposium, Rotterdam.

Watts, H.D. (1979), 'Large firms, multinationals and regional development: some new evidence from the United Kingdom', *Envir. and Plan. A.,* vol. 11, pp. 71–81.

Watts, H.D. (1980), *The Large Industrial Enterprise: Some Spatial Perspectives*, Croom Helm, London.

Yannopoulos, G.N. and Dunning, J.H. (1976), 'Multinational enterprises and regional development: an exploratory paper', *Reg. Studies,* vol. 10, pp. 389–99.

Three clear lessons stand out from the research studies which investigated the movement of industry in the UK over the first 25 years after
the Second World War. The first was that the total volume or flow of
industrial moves in the manufacturing sector depends upon the rate
of growth of industrial production. The second was that a high level
of aggregate demand in the economy, giving low rates of unemployment in the labour force nationally, makes labour supply one of the
most important determinants of the choice of new locations for mobile companies. The third was that policies of regional economic development and of planned urban growth can significantly influence the
spatial pattern of industrial movement. Each of these lessons remained
valid in the 1970s but their importance for understanding the national
picture of industrial movement in the UK has been weakened by changing economic circumstances. Old lessons will now need to be accompanied by new analyses to anticipate developments in the 1980s.

This chapter summarises the accumulated understanding of the processes of industrial movement in the UK. The focus is on manufacturing industry. 'Movement' is taken to mean the opening of factories in
locations new to the company concerned. The volume of research findings on the movement of manufacturing industry defined in this way is
very large. This chapter does not attempt to systematically review this
literature. The findings of the principal academic and government studies up to 1978 have already been brought together, (Townroe, 1979).
We will take advantage of the documentation in that book and focus
on the highlights of the literature only. At the same time some of the

352

statistics will be updated and consideration will be given to the two questions of whether an era of industrial movement in the UK has now passed, and whether new priorities in the geography of industrial activity are now emerging.

The general setting

Discussion and analysis of industrial movement in the UK over the past three decades has been heavily conditioned by the availability of data and by the framework of a particular policy context. In both of these respects, industrial movement as an area of study is like many other areas of the social sciences. A restricted data base reduces flexibility and comprehensiveness in the analyses undertaken while the given policy context narrows perceptions of what were the important questions and issues in the recent past.

The data base

Industrial movement studies in the UK have concentrated on the manufacturing sectors of industry, usually ignoring the smallest units and the very short distance moves. The key units of analysis have been the *transfer* and the *branch*. A transfer is an opening of a plant in new or existing premises which are new to the company concerned and is associated with the closure by the company of an existing plant elsewhere. This corresponds approximately to the definition of migration as given in Chapter 1. A transfer is therefore in general more characteristic of a single-plant company. A branch is an opening at premises new to the company concerned that is in addition to the existing plants of the company. This corresponds approximately to the partial move defined in Chapter 1. A branch move is not usually of a headquarters or controlling unit. This two-way classification of moves was the basis on which statistics were collected by the British government up to 1965. The publication of an analysis of the industrial movement between the sub-regions of the UK from 1945 to 1965 by R.S. Howard (1968) using this 'Record of Movement' was a critical landmark in industrial movement studies in Britain. The published information in that study, and the further unpublished figures made available to academics and researchers, were used for further studies which were both descriptive and analytical. In these studies there was a heavy emphasis on the longer distance moves to the Assisted Areas, those parts of the nation where companies were eligible for regional financial incentives.

The 'Record of Movement (ROM) used by Howard was not able to make next to transfers and branches the distinction between openings and closures of units. The 'Record of Openings and Closures' maintained by the Department of Industry regional offices since 1965 now allows these changes to be included, adding the category 'Enterprises New to Manufacturing'. This new record (ROC) also extends the coverage to smaller units and shorter-distance moves. This extension makes comparisons with earlier years of the total volume of industrial moves a little ambiguous. There has also been an ambiguity attached to the notion of a branch plant unit, especially when the new unit is a subsidiary company of its parent rather than just a production only factory. The 'origin' of the branch in the ROM was taken as the operating headquarters of the parent company. In the ROC, if there is no evidence to the contrary, the nearest unit of the parent company producing an identical or similar product range is taken as the origin.[1] Neither record makes any distinction by ownership (state, quoted public, private) except by overseas and domestic. Foreign-owned investments have 'overseas' as an origin, except where the new plant is owned by a foreign corporation already operating in the UK. In the ROC, since 1972, a transfer has to cross the boundary of a local government district to be included. Previously, in the ROM, 50 sub-regions were used. Between 1966 and 1972, travel to work areas were used (Nunn, 1980). Use of the district boundaries means that more short distance moves are included. In Scotland the boundaries of the Scotish regions are used. Northern Ireland is treated as a single entity.

The Record of Moves to 1965 was based on lists of employers kept by the Department of Employment and on information available in the then Board of Trade arising out of the administration of the industrial development certificate (idc) policy and the policy of regional investment grants. In 1972 the minimum limit for an idc was raised to 10,000 square feet from 5,000 and the requirement was dropped in the Development Areas. This modified the criteria for an 'opening' in the ROC to 10,000 square feet for new industrial premises or those changing their use into manufacturing. The criteria for counting as an opening have been based on a minimum employment level. The Annual Censuses of Employment and of Production both serve as sources of information for the ROC. A summary of the ROC is now published annually in *Regional Statistics*.

Both the ROM and the ROC have provided estimates of the employment involved in the mobile industrial units. Although a company will usually have an employment figure in mind when a new location for part of its operations is chosen, that figure may easily be hopelessly inaccurate. But when will a new plant in a new location be 'mature' in terms of the build-up of the workforce in the plant? How much employment growth should be allocated to the move itself; and how much to subsequent expansion? At the risk of introducing considerable distortions, the 1968 Howard analysis used an end-1966 employment figure for all the 1945—65 moves, ignoring the different lifespans, just as it ignored openings which then closed again in the period. The published summaries of the 1966 to 1977 openings treat survival and employment growth in a similar manner (to end-1977). However, the employment growth profiles of the new industrial plants are available on the record and have been used to adjust the published totals for the growth of employment to 'maturity' in the new plant (Nunn, 1980). These adjusted totals for inter-regional moves will be used below.

The ROC provides the only picture of industrial movement across the UK as a whole. It does however tend seriously to under-record short-distance moves and moves of small plants. Lloyd and Mason (1979) show this in their checks against their data bank for North-West England. There is no generally available source like the Dun and Bradstreet data which are now being used so successfully for industrial location research in the USA (e.g. by Struyk and James, 1975; or Schmenner, 1978). Access to the Regional Office Information System is restricted under the Statistics of Trade Act, although special analyses are available from the Department of Industry. Locally, researchers wishing to study the push and pull factors in industrial migration have in the past had to use industrial directories and information from town planning departments in local governments to build up a sampling frame for their surveys. In only three parts of Britain have comprehensive registers of industrial establishments been built up for the purposes of examining trends in industrial location: in Glasgow, in the Manchester and Merseyside conurbations in North-West England, and in the East Midlands.[2] Elsewhere, changes in employment have had to serve. Specially prepared registers make it possible to monitor very small moves, very local moves, and moves outside the manufacturing sector.

The policy context

For 25 years or so after the end of the Second World War interest in industrial movement in the UK has been set against two major areas of spatial policy concern: regional economic development and metropolitan decentralisation. Over the past ten years a third relevant policy focus has developed: the economic decline of parts of the inner areas of major British cities. All three of these policy areas have in turn to be seen against the changing fortunes and circumstances of the national economy (see Map 10.1).

Regional economic development policy in the UK has its origins in

355

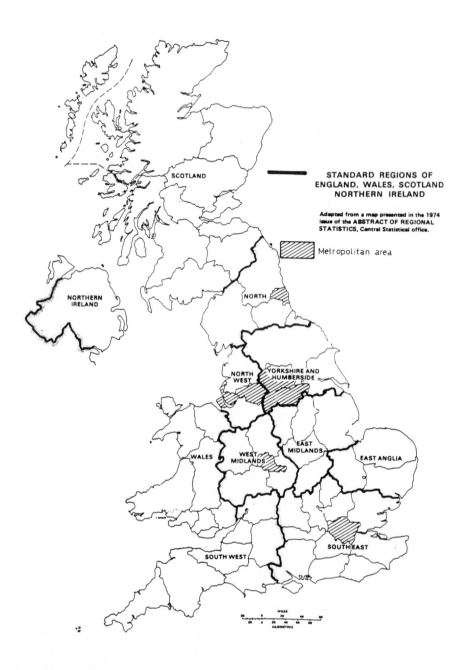

Map 10.1 Regions and urban areas in the UK

the intensity with which the inter-war industrial depression hit many of the towns and regions which had been the cradle of the industrial revolution a century or so before. Limited measures of financial assistance to private enterprise and selective public infrastructure investments were introduced in four 'Special Areas' in the 1930s. The attraction of industrial investments from the more prosperous and fast-growing parts of the country was an early priority. Public sector factory estates were seen as a way of attracting new types of manufacturing activity to these areas. Greater recognition of the importance of the problem came in 1940 with the report of the Royal Commission on the Distribution of the Industrial Population which argued forcibly for strong national action to influence the geographical distribution of industry.

Memories of the pre-war levels of unemployment led to legislation in 1945 to designate new Development Areas and to expand the industrial estate programme along with grants and loans to private industry. An industrial building licence system was also introduced. These principal features of regional economic development policy remain to this day, although there have been many reappraisals and modifications.[3]

The great pressure of industrial development in the immediate postwar period encouraged many firms to move to those regions of the country which had suffered from industrial depression. These 'peripheral regions' to the North and West of the nation could offer both surplus labour and surplus war-time ordnance factories, industrial inputs then in short supply. The flow of industrial moves from the South-East and the two Midlands regions was strong. Unemployment in these regions was kept low. By the middle of the 1950s, the government could play down the priority given to the peripheral regions and rather encourage industrial movement for a different purpose: metropolitan decentralisation. Employment in inter-regional moves fell away.

Bombing and lack of investment in housing in the war years exacerbated housing shortages from the 1930s and for 20 years or so from 1945 house construction was one of the major priorities of all British governments. Residential densities in the older areas of major cities were very high; the quality of the housing stock was very low. Along with the clearance of slums and rebuilding on the same sites, major public investments were made in housing estates on the edges of major cities, continuing a pre-war policy. In addition, a long campaign against high densities and the geographical separation of work and home, and against the environmental bleakness and monotony of the early public housing estates, resulted in two important pieces of legislation, both of which significantly influenced the geographical pattern of industrial movement up until the early 1970s. The New Towns Act was passed in 1946 and the Town Development Act in 1952.[4] Both provided for the development of industrial sites and factories, together with housing,

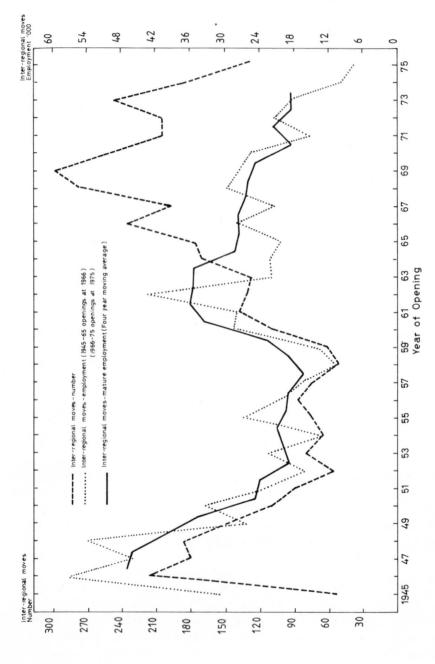

Graph 10.1 Inter-regional movement of manufacturing industry 1945–75   Source: Nunn, 1980.

in towns and cities around the major conurbations, thereby encouraging industry to decentralise from the urban cores to areas beyond the suburbs. Outside the Development Areas, there were no financial incentives to lure companies to these towns but new factory buildings on spacious sites and new houses for their workers were attraction enough. By the end of 1974 the 11 New Towns in South-East England receiving new firms largely from London had built 1,130 factories employing over 120,000 in the manufacturing sectors of industry. A further 1,021 factories employing over 80,000 had been built in the 24 smaller towns growing with the sponsorship of the Greater London Council under the Town Development Act (Keeble, 1976, p. 249).

At the end of the 1950s regional policy in the UK received a renewed emphasis. The old staple industries were facing strong foreign competition and the demand for coal started to fall. Unemployment rates in the peripheral regions began to rise, although by historical standards the economy was growing strongly and the national unemployment rate was low. New policy measures and a search for supplies of labour increased the flow of mobile industry to the Development Areas ('Assisted Areas') once again. By 1968, with approximately 20 per cent of the national population, these Areas were receiving some 45 per cent of the national investment in manufacturing. Many of the research studies we now have on the choice of new locations by firms refer to moves undertaken at this time, in the middle and late 1960s. The strong flow of moves did not continue, however. Because of the rate of increase in labour productivity, as the growth rate of the national economy slowed in the early seventies, the growth in demand for additional labour in manufacturing industry slowed even more. In many sectors and in an increasing number of geographical areas the numbers working in manufacturing started to fall. Difficulty in finding supplies of adequate labour ceased to be so important as a factor encouraging a firm to move from an existing site or neighbourhood. The flow of longer-distance industrial moves fell and the number of jobs provided by inter-regional moves returned to levels of the mid-1950s and below, as shown in Graph 10.1.

In the mid-1960s, rising birth rates had given rise to the expectation of a large increase in the population of the UK by the end of the century. Plans were made and strategies were prepared to accommodate the increase. In many of these documents movement of industry was seen as a key variable susceptible to the influence of policy. It was thought that the distribution of population in a very densely populated island could be improved by a spatial policy for employment rather than by leaving industrial location to market forces. Today, some 15 years on, the population of the country has stabilised rather than grown. The expected increases have not materialised, and confidence in the desirability of influencing the geographical distribution of both population and manufacturing investment at a national scale has eroded. With higher unemployment rates across the whole country in the 1970s, the attention given by local politicians and urban planners to promoting local economic development is much more geographically widespread than in the 1960s. Increased competition for a declining pool of manufacturing industry has led to a realisation that policy needs to focus on fostering the development of existing industry in a locality as well as seeking new investment from elsewhere. Nowhere has this been clearer than in those areas meriting maximum policy concern at a national level as well as a local level: the inner areas of the large conurbations.

The whole inner urban areas debate in the UK has limited relevance for a review of industrial movement except in one important respect. Politicians and planners responsible for the economic health of the major cities have long voiced criticisms of both the regional economic development policies and the metropolitan decentralisation policies, claiming that these interventions were draining away the economic life-blood of urban centres. Investment was seen as being 'exported' away from the conurbations, thereby damaging their economic prospects. Criticism of the operation of the industrial development certificate (idc) requirement was particularly strong. Subsequent research has shown that plant deaths and a failure of other plants to expand rather than out-migrations have been far more important in accounting for the declines in employment in manufacturing in those inner urban areas.[5] The idc policy was perhaps less important in promoting declines than in preventing the entry into these areas of new and expanding sectors of manufacturing. But these areas have been declining in attractiveness as an environment for manufacturing for other reasons also, a phenomenon shared with other large cities in developed countries. (A scarcity of sites and premises up to modern standards has been a particular problem.) The concentration of public attention on inner city unemployment and poverty has therefore been a further factor weakening the enthusiasm of national politicians for regional policies and town expansion policies which rely on industry from the 'seed beds' of the conurbations. It has also become clear that early approaches to the inner city problem in terms of generally attracting any available manufacturing industry back in were doomed to failure. Lloyd and Mason (1979) for example show how migrant firms coming into the North-West set up in the suburban periphery or in the new towns and not in the inner areas of the conurbations. The future employment base of these areas has to rest on non-manufacturing activities and on particular specialised sectors within manufacturing, building on what is already there with selective but limited inmigration of new enterprises where possible.

Spatial policies can only operate within the framework of national economic policy. The volume of moving industry in any one period of time is heavily dependent upon the growth of the economy as a whole and upon the growth of output within the manufacturing sector. This growth not only translates into a need for more factory floor space by the leading companies but also into a tight labour market for a company seeking additional workers. Both of these factors have been shown in interview surveys to be leading reasons for industrial movement (Townroe, 1979, Chapters 3 and 4). The success of national economic policy in the UK through the 1950s and 1960s kept unemployment low and the growth rate of output up close to the trend rate of growth of industrial capacity, (although this growth was slow by the standards of competitor nations). Under such circumstances movement was the course of action necessary for many firms to achieve higher output and lower costs. Underlying growth rates have since slowed. In the ten years to 1979, the Gross Domestic Product increased by 21.5 per cent, while the output of manufacturing industry increased by only 6.5 per cent. Employment in manufacturing fell from 36.9 per cent to 31.4 per cent of the employed labour force in the UK. Unemployment rates have since increased; from 2.6 per cent in 1970 to about 10 per cent today (1981). Between 1945 and 1969 the national annual unemployment rate only rose above 2.5 per cent in one year, 1963, in the UK. These two changes have removed much of the necessity for movement in many industrial companies.

Patterns of industrial movement

The total flow of industrial moves between the 11 regions of the UK between 1945 and 1965 is shown in Map 10.2. As has already been suggested, both the number of units involved and the employment created have been heavily influenced by regional economic development policies and by the growth rate of the national economy. The idc policy was operated with some severity in the South-East and the East and West Midlands regions by the 1964—70 Labour government. This helps to explain the peaking of the number of moves in 1968, with more small plants moving to the Assisted Areas than before or since. The moving average of 'mature' employment in Figure 10.1 has been calculated by Nunn (1980) to allow for the expansion of the labour force of the new plants up to full strength.

The geographical pattern of the major flows of moves, 1945 to 1965, are shown in Maps 10.2 and 10.3, taken from Sant (1975). Greater London is clearly the dominant source of moves, although, per thousand employees in manufacturing, the West Midlands Conurbation was actually providing more moves to Assisted Areas in the early 1960s. A high proportion of the large outflows from the Greater London area

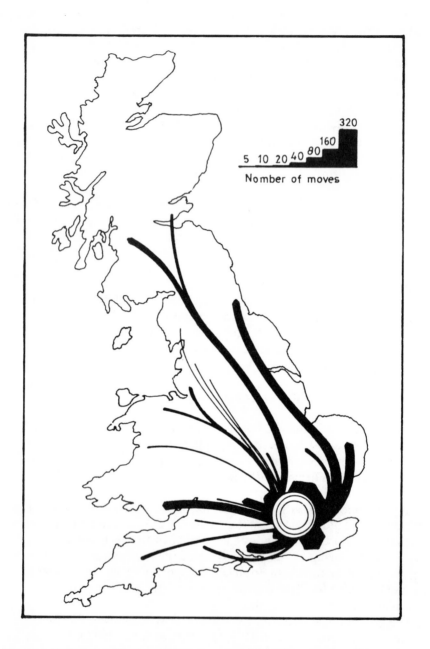

Map 10.2 Flows of industrial movement from Greater London,
1945—65.
Source: Sant, 1975 (reproduced by permission, Pergamon Press Ltd)

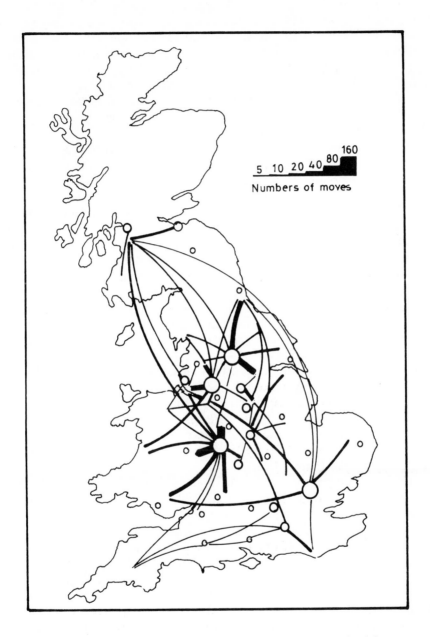

Map 10.3 Major flows of industrial movement from provincial sources, 1945–65

Source: Sant, 1975 (reproduced by permission, Pergamon Press Ltd)

are of course to the ring of New Towns within the South-East region. Behind these flows lies a clear distance decay effect, modified by regional policies, giving rise to what Keeble (1971) called the 'Dual Population Hypothesis'. This distinguishes short-distance overspill migration out of the major conurbations from the longer-distance movement, almost all from the South and Midlands to the Assisted Areas. Branch plants have been more important in the longer moves. Transfers move shorter distances to retain some or all of their existing labour force, and ties with other companies.

A summary of the movement flows between and within regions in the 1966—77 period is given in Table 10.1 for the UK. A feature in the decline in the volume of inter-regional moves compared with 1945 to 1965 has been a fall in the proportion of long-distance moves originating in the South-East and moving to destinations in the Development Areas. The Development Areas captured a smaller proportion of inter-regional moves 1966—75 (73 per cent) than in the early 1960s (83 per cent), and the number of jobs involved in these Areas fell from 21,000 per annum to 15,000 per annum. Relative to their employment base in manufacturing, the regions which have benefited most from inter-regional moves 1966 to 1975 have been Wales, East Anglia, Northern Ireland and the Northern region. Within each region more is now known about the more local moves because of the new ROC. Of 1,400 openings on average per annum 1966 to 1971, 347 took place within the same travel to work area, a further 174 took place between these areas but within the 50 planning sub-divisions, and a further 202 took place between sub-divisions but within regions. Only 19 per cent of the total were inter-regional moves. Forty-three units came from abroad and the final 26 per cent were units of enterprises new to manufacturing. The pattern between 1972 and 1975 with slightly different areal definitions was similar (Nunn, 1980).

The employment created by the inter-regional moves, the important focus of policy attention, is shown in Table 10.2. The rise and fall over time is clearly shown. The rate of employment build-up in moving firms has slowed over the years, and the proportion of transfer moves has increased in the 1970s, both factors leading to a smaller number of jobs per move. The 1960—65 figures were boosted by the establishment of four large motor vehicle factories in Scotland and on Merseyside.

The sectoral spread of mobile establishments is wide. In the 1945 to 1965 period, the electrical and mechanical engineering sectors were particularly important in the flow of movement because they were expanding sectors, looking for labour and for floor space. These sectors continued to be important between 1966 and 1975, providing 28 per cent of the employment generated in all moves in excess of 22 miles, even though nationally these sectors suffered a fall of 195,000 employees

Table 10.1

Origins and destinations of openings* of manufacturing units,
UK, 1966–71 and 1972–77[4] (number of units)

Origins		Destinations			
		'Assisted Areas'[1]	Other regions[2]	South-East	UK
Same region[5]	(a)	1019	1857	(1085)	2876
	(b)	984	1473	(788)	2457
'Assisted Areas'[1]	(a)	131	47	(29)	178
	(b)	87	64	(17)	151
Other regions[2]	(a)	357	444	(40)	801
	(b)	311	359	(26)	670
Abroad	(a)	90	79	(60)	169
	(b)	123	107	(60)	230
EEN[3]	(a)	549	1281	(910)	1830
	(b)	752	1130	(568)	1882
Totals	(a)	2146	3708	(2124)	5854
	(b)	2257	3133	(1459)	5390

Notes: 1 Wales, Scotland, Northern Ireland, North, North-West, Yorkshire and Humberside regions, excluding inter-regional moves.
2 South-East, South-West, East Anglia, East Midlands, West Midlands regions, excluding inter-regional moves.
3 Enterprises new to manufacturing.
4 Numbers surviving to the end of 1976 (1966–71 openings) and 1977 (1972–77 openings).
5 (a) = 1966 to 1971; (b) = 1972 to 1977

* Moves and new creations of enterprises new to manufacturing.

Sources: *Regional Trends*, HMSO, London, 1981. *Regional Statistics*, HMSO, London, 1980.

in the period. Other sectors important for movement were the food and drink industries (7.5 per cent of employment generated), textiles (8 per cent), and clothing and footwear (7 per cent).

Between 1945 and 1965, 258 foreign-owned manufacturing plants were included in the ROM. These plants provided 108,500 jobs by the end of 1966, and they were especially important for Scotland, the destination of one-third. Between 1966 and 1975, 334 foreign-owned plants were included in the ROC. These plants will generate 37,000 jobs at maturity, 17 per cent of all inter-regional moves. Scotland again was an important destination of these 'inmigrants', especially after 1970 as exploration for oil in the North Sea developed. These figures

Table 10.2

Jobs created in inter-regional moves in manufacturing

| | Total | Per move[1] | |
Year	Employment (p.a.)	ALL/plants[2]	Survivors
1945—51	38.9	274	448
1952—59	18.1	258	360
1960—65	34.3	239	259
1966—71 ·	24.6	99	124
1972—75	18.1	85	91

1 Employment to 1966 for 1945—65 moves; to 1975 for the 1966—75 moves.
2 Includes subsequent closures.

Source: Nunn, 1980, p. 17.

understate the importance of foreign capital to the total investment involved in industrial movement however, because they refer only to new plants owned by overseas firms with no existing UK plants.

More than half of all moves in the ROC 1966—75 were over distances of less than 22 miles. By employment, half of all moves covered distances of less than 12 miles. Seventy per cent of transfers move less than 12 miles. The longer-distance moves seem more prone to subsequent closure than short-distance moves. Many new plants are of course quite small. For example, 22 per cent of 1966—71 openings employed 11—19 people by 1975; and a further 50 per cent employed 20—99 people.[6] About one-quarter of the 1945 to 1965 inter-regional moves had closed by the end of 1965. This annual rate of 1.9 per cent of the stock of moves closing per annum rose in the 1966—75 period to vary between 2 and 5 per cent. The relative performance of the Development Area regions in closures worsened in this period.

The high numbers of moves that take place over short distances is frequently associated with a desire for a suburban site by a firm with a plant in or near the city centre. The trend towards the suburbanisation of manufacturing employment is deep-seated, and observable in many countries. In aggregate, the trend is much more the result of the pattern of plant closures and plant births and of relative rates of expansion than of intra-urban industrial movement.[7] However, the work of Keeble (1968) and Economic Consultants (1971) in London, and of Cameron

(1973) in Glasgow does show a general trend of radial decentralisation by plants moving within the urban area. Industry by industry, the new plants tend to replicate the locational pattern of the parent industry, and the larger the plant the further the probable decentralisation will be. This pattern is only modified by the cross-movement of certain sectors to retain or enhance the advantages of external economies. (The same trends have been found in the USA and Canada, see Townroe, 1979, p. 39—41.)

The volume of this local movement relative to the stock of establishments has been estimated at about 3 per cent per annum for the metal trade industries in the West Midlands Conurbation (Smith, 1970). Plants opening during 1972—77 and surviving at 1977 (5,390 units) accounted for 3.9 per cent of the 1977 employment in manufacturing. It should be remembered however that many locational changes in manufacturing companies do not come about because of changes in locational circumstances alone. Hamilton (1978) for example, in his study of 1,486 UK companies, found that 43 per cent had been involved in acquisition or merger activity between 1960 and 1971. Only 14 per cent of his firms did *not* make explicit locational changes in production or office jobs through closures, relocations or new facilities, and 95 per cent of the firms claimed that they had altered the relative importance or functions of their existing units.

Information on the movement of the service sectors of industry in the UK is much less complete than the detail provided by the ROC for manufacturing. Much of the movement in the service sector is associated with retail outlets and small offices and is over short distances. The offices of large organisations however are much more like the factories of manufacturing industry, being influenced in their choice of locations by both city-wide economic forces and by regional market and factor supply considerations. The major institutional difference in the office sector is that in the UK premises are typically leased rather than purchased outright. This makes a move easier but it also makes it more difficult to influence movement by government policy than in the manufacturing sector.

The only indication of the scale of movement in the office sector comes from the operation of the Location of Offices Bureau, a government-sponsored agency charged with promoting the decentralisation of offices out of central London. Between 1963 and 1975, 1,761 office firms known to the Bureau had moved or were in the process of moving within or out of Greater London. Forty per cent of the moves were within the GLC area, a radius of 8 to 10 miles from the centre; and two-thirds were within 40 miles. Only 13 per cent of the moves and 19 per cent of the total of 141,000 jobs involved were in moves of over 80 miles. Eighty per cent of all of these firms employed less than 100 people. Much of the movement was to suburban office complexes, such as those at Croydon and Romford and Hounslow, a type of movement not found in other large UK cities. A number of towns in the South-East region have developed as important office employment centres, such as Southend-on-Sea, Worthing, Reading and Guildford. The amount of longer-distance movement of offices from London to the Development Areas has been minimal, apart from selected offices and departments of the central government pushed to those Areas as part of the regional development policy.[8]

One of the changes in the industrial geography of the USA in the 1970s has been that the suburbs of the metropolitan areas are no longer the fastest-growing areas for employment or for population. Most rapid growth is now occurring in non-metropolitan counties in the hinterlands of the metropolitan areas (Beale, 1976). There are signs that a similar change in emphasis has occurred in the UK, although the switch from increasing population concentration in metropolitan areas is less clear-cut.[9] Keeble (1980) has examined the growth of manufacturing employment by county 1971 to 1976. He identified a clear urban to rural shift, operating independently of the initial structure of manufacturing in the two types of area. It is not clear how far industrial movement is an important or dominant contributor to this shift. Fothergill and Gudgin (1981) discount movement as a significant factor overall, although it is clear that movement has been a major source of net employment growth in many rural sub-regions. The shift does appear to be independent of the regional policy incentives (which are available of course in the rural parts of the Development Areas). Keeble (1980) argues that the regional incentives were anyway having a much reduced impact on the changing spatial patterns of manufacturing employment by the mid-1970s. He links the shift to rural areas to increasing diseconomies of agglomeration in the major industrial centres and to the availability of low cost and less unionised female labour.

Factors in the choice of new industrial locations

The decision to move comes as the result of the management of a company balancing two sets of forces, one internal and the other external. Table 10.3 is taken from the largest survey so far commissioned of firms establishing plants in new locations in the UK: 531 firms in the period 1964–67. This government survey remains the prime source of locational factor information, even though it will be argued below that the relative importance of these factors has been changing in the 1970s. The table shows the dominance of internal forces in the reasons for

Table 10.3

'What caused you to consider opening a new plant
in a new location?'

	Percentage of all respondent firms		
	Major reason	Minor reason	Outstanding single reason
1 To permit an expansion of output	83	8	20
2 Inadequate existing premises or site	50	11	8
3 Unsatisfactory labour supply at existing location	40	11	15
4 Inducements and facilities made available by official bodies	27	14	2
5 Opportunity to purchase or rent premises or site at new location	20	8	3
6 Too far from established or potential markets	19	1	9
7 Refusal or expected refusal of idc	12	4	5
8 Town planning difficulties	11	3	4
9 Lease or former premises fell in, or good offer received	5	2	3
10 Desire to be in more attractive surroundings	4	8	1
11 Too far from supplies, actual or prospective, of materials or services	3	2	1
12 More profitable to operate elsewhere, no other postulated reason being major	1	—	1
13 No one outstanding reason	—	—	28

Questions 1—12 were asked of 531 firms.
Question 13 was asked of 492 firms, having been added after some interviews had taken place.

Source: Department of Trade and Industry, Inquiry into Location Attitudes and Experience, *Memorandum submitted to the Expenditure Committee (Trade and Industry Sub-committee) on Regional Development Incentives.* (Session 1973—4) p. 532, HC 85 - 1, HMSO, London.

Table 10.4

Probabilities of locational choice for prospectively moving plants, based on surveys of firms that actually moved in manufacturing in the UK and USA

Company and plant characteristics	Alternative locations, which are:				with:					
	Close by existing	Sub-urban	Non-metro-politan	New region	Large labour pool	Good transport access	Finan-cial in-centive	Avail-able buildings	High residen-tial amenity	Same industry already present
1 Company										
Public	1	1	2	3	3	3	3	2	( )	—
Private	2	2	3	2	2	2	1	3	3	—
Single-plant	2	2	3	2	2	2	1	3	3	—
Multiplant	1	1	2	3	3	3	3	2	1	—
2 Plant										
Transfer	3	2	3	1	2	2	1	3	3	—
Production unit	1	1	2	3	3	3	3	3	1	—
Subsidiary company	1	1	1	3	2	2	3	2	( )	—
< 50 employees	3	3	2	1	3	2	1	3	3	—
50–500	1	2	3	2	3	2	2	3	2	—
> 500 employees	1	1	2	3	3	3	3	1	1	—
Urgent	3	3	2	3	2	2	1	3	3	—
Non-urgent	1	2	3	3	2	3	2	2	3	—
3 Process										
New technology	2	2	3	1	2	3	2	3	3	1
Old technology	1	1	2	3	3	2	3	2	1	2
High skill level	2	2	3	1	2	2	1	2	3	2

Low skill level	1	2	3	3	2	3	3	1	—
Capital-intensive	1	2	3	1	3	3	1	1	2
Labour-intensive	2	2	3	3	2	3	3	2	—
Need to retain existing local linkages	3	2	1	1	3	1	2	1	—
Need new local linkages	1	2	2	( )	3	( )	2	1	3

4 Product

New market sought	1	1	3	2	3	1	2	1	—
High transport cost	1	2	3	2	3	2	1	1	2
Made to order	3	2	1	2	2	1	2	2	3
Batch production	2	3	2	2	3	2	2	2	—
Mass production	1	2	3	3	3	3	1	1	—

5 Reasons for moving

Need more space	2	3	2	1	2	2	3	2	—
Competition for labour	1	2	3	2	1	3	2	1	2
Government restrictions	1	2	3	2	2	3	3	2	—
Compulsory purchase	3	2	1	1	1	1	3	2	—
Review of locational costs	1	3	3	2	3	3	2	3	—
Desire to improve environment	1	3	2	1	2	1	2	3	—

Notes: 3 = high
  2 = average
  1 = low
  ( ) = uncertainty about scoring
  — = no relevant link identified

Source: Townroe, 1979, pp. 149–50.

industrial migration: the desire to serve new markets or to expand output, and the inadequacies of existing premises. However, external forces are also important. The available labour supply may change or new labour requirements may not be able to be met. A lease may fall in. Investment incentives are available elsewhere. Town planning rules or compulsory purchase orders make it difficult to remain at the existing site. These factors may also initiate a move.

At the risk of over-generalising we may say that the external pressures are likely to be more important for transfer moves. These moves are also short-distance moves. It is also clear that in the ten years since this survey was undertaken many of the external pressures on firms to move out the largest urban areas have been muted. Public authorities in those areas are now actively seeking to provide land and premises for industrial expansion, as well as to remove or restrain the levers of planning controls, compulsory purchase orders and idcs. A similar table for the (smaller number of) moves in 1980 might well rank amenity reasons and labour reasons higher, and reasons connected with premises and expansion as relatively less important.

In making comparisons with other countries here, it should be remembered that town planning regulations in the UK make a change of use of a plot of urban land difficult for an existing owner to achieve. Therefore reaping the profit on the rising value of urban land for non-industrial uses is not as common a reason for industrial movement as it might be in other countries.

There have been numerous postal and interview questionnaire studies investigating the important factors in the choice of new industrial locations in the UK. They have been reviewed by this author (Townroe, 1979), with a parallel consideration of American surveys. Table 10.4 has been drawn from that review as an informal but subjective summary of the results of the various studies. The table is expressed in terms of three probabilities of both the location chosen and the factors which are important in that choice, differentiated by company, plant, process and product characteristics and by the chief reasons for moving. The pattern of probabilities given in this table can only be approximate. One of the chief findings of location surveys is the great variety of experience and of motivation in locational choice for any given category of firms or plants. Generalisations are therefore necessarily broad.

Several features of the table stand out, remembering that it is based on experience in the 1960s. First, access to labour and transportation facilities (principally highways) are near universally important except for some short-distance and inter-urban moves. Available buildings also are important, except for the largest plants and for very capital-intensive operations. Financial incentives are important to long-distance moves to Assisted Areas, normally branch units of multi-unit publicly quoted

Table 10.5

Percentage of a sample of firms moving to the Assisted Areas, 1972–76, indicating whether the listed factors played a major, minor or no part

Factor	(1) Major	(2) (ILAG)	(3) Minor	(4) No part	(5) Numbers*
Labour availability	69	(80)	25	7	353
Regional incentives	64	(81)	25	12	354
Local authority aid	42	(37)	36	22	346
Transport facilities	42	(33)	31	28	356
Access to markets	32	(24)	25	43	349
Non-government factory	24	(22)	10	66	327
Management needs	22	(12)	18	61	345
Idc considerations	21	(50)	23	57	328
Site characteristics	19	(21)	23	58	343
Scarce skills	18	—	33	49	346
Environment	17	(27)	33	50	350
Access to supplies	15	(11)	26	59	347
Public utilities	7	—	13	80	351

*For each of the possible location factors, differing numbers of respondents declined or failed to check off one or other of the three levels of influence.

Source: Evidence to the Expenditure Committee (TISC) 1972–3 and F. Herron, 'Industrial Movement into the Assisted Areas of Great Britain' (1976) (unpublished monograph).

companies. Residential amenity is important to transfer or complete moves, to privately owned companies, to small units, often those with a new technology and high skill requirements of the workforce. The presence of the same industry in the new location is unimportant for most categories of move, being limited to products which have a high transport cost or which are made in individual units to order (such as moulds or tools for machine tools). The evidence in general in both the USA and the UK is that local linkages, or inter-industry transactions, are not an important location factor to the large majority of migrant units (Pred, 1976). The UK economy is sufficiently geographically compact for linkages to be maintained after movement with previous suppliers and customers by all but the smaller companies in the electrical and mechanical engineering and metal-working industries and in certain service-type manufacturing operations such as printing. Variations in local property and other taxes were not and are not a significant location factor in the UK.

From the discussion in this chapter so far there must be an expectation that the location factors of the 1970s will be ranked a little differently to the location factors of the 1960s. Higher unemployment levels and slower growth rates of manufacturing output in general put less of a premium on labour availability as a factor. The idc policy has been operated more leniently with less spatial discrimination, so it is less important, and factory buildings and public utilities are more widely and uniformly available across the country.[10] The expectation of these changes is borne out in Table 10.5, which refers only to moves to the Assisted Areas. Comparisons with the earlier government survey are made in column 2. What is perhaps unexpected about this table is the rise in importance of transport facilities, and the high numbers of respondents saying that access to markets (43 per cent), to suppliers (59 per cent) and to services (80 per cent) played no part in their choice of new location. The rise in the proportion quoting aid from local authorities as a factor reflects the increased proportional activity by local governments to attract industry. The new category in this table of 'scarce skills' is important, highlighting the point that although labour in general may be widely available, labour with the specific skills required by individual companies in manufacturing may not be. It is also unexpected that the factor of 'environment' is lower in this table. This is contrary to the findings of other studies, which suggest that as improved infrastructures and transportation facilities erode spatial cost differences, then the psychic costs of entrepreneurs combined with a sound managerial consideration of the residential preferences of their labour force will become progressively more important in industrial location decisions (e.g. Henderson, 1980, p. 221).

The importance of regional incentives as a location factor for new plants in the Assisted Areas may not be unexpected in replies to a questionnaire survey. It is however supported by regression models and shift share analyses which have tried to analyse the forces determining the share of inter-regional industrial moves going to the Assisted Areas. Although there is not full agreement on the specification of the most appropriate model to be used, one set of results suggests that regional incentives induced (via diversion and generation) some 165,000 jobs between 1960 and 1971 in the Assisted Area (Rhodes and Moore, 1976) from industrial movement.[11]

There are four important considerations to bear in mind when comparing the results of location factor surveys. The first is that a necessary condition for a location to be chosen is not a sufficient condition. When necessary conditions can be met in many locations, as is now the case in the UK, then it is factors of relative intensity (such as prices, size of labour pool, value of incentives) which are listed as of major importance, rather than factors like level sites, utilities, access to highways etc. which constitute near absolute preconditions. Second, locational search for all but short-distance moves tends to work down the spatial scale, from region to city to site. Clearly, different factors are evaluated at each scale. It may be difficult for respondents to weigh, say, a site factor against a choice of region factor. This suggests a further worry: the ambiguity of rankings when the ranking given by the respondent may actually have been different for the different sites considered. Some factors may enter the decision calculus as critical only in the sense of tipping the balance one way or another between two or three very similar and viable alternatives.

Location decision making in the firm

Relatively little is known about how location decisions are made within the firm. What evidence we have suggests a pattern of behaviour that is as may be expected *ex ante*, once it is realised that choosing a new location occurs very infrequently for the majority of individual companies or industrial managers. In other words, the behaviour pattern observed follows from the managers concerned having a lack of precedent to follow and from not having well defined objectives other than the need to get into production at the new site as quickly as possible. Locational criteria are unclear; the source and status of relevant information is unknown or uncertain. Problems and issues are not fully foreseen. The locational element in the overall sequence and series of decisions about the new investment (size, technology, provision for expansion, product mix, flexibility, etc.) is frequently played down. Lack of past experience in opening a new plant in a new location can lead to over-simplification and neglect in the analysis and evaluation of locational alternatives.

The above remarks do not, of course, apply to the largest companies, in which there is a fund of experience in these matters to draw upon. These issues are not very important to local migrants, moving within a well known locality, retaining an existing labour force or recruiting in the same labour market, and using known suppliers of services etc. But for intermediate and longer-distance moves by all but the largest companies, the following generalised pattern of decision-making emerges (Townroe, 1976, Chapter 10; and Townroe, 1979, Chapter 6).

The first decision in the sequence is clearly the decision whether a move is the best way of solving the current problem set in which the company finds itself. The managers or directors of the company have to consider other options (takeover, shift work, delay, new equipment, etc.). However, the decision to move seems to be taken quickly in most companies, with only half undertaking a systematic evaluation of other alternatives. In a few cases in this author's 1969 survey, the option not to move was only considered in detail after the search for a new site had commenced and the full realisation of what was involved in a move had begun to hit the management.

The second decision is the choice between a transfer move and the opening of a branch plant unit. This choice appears self-evident to the majority of companies. Transfers are usually forced on the company, and many branch units are established away from the parent unit with reluctance. However, a significant minority of UK transfer moves start as a branch move; then, as cash flows permit, and encouraged by experience in the new location, the rest of the company follows. In the USA, Schmenner (1978, Table 3.3) found in his survey that a branch plant strategy is preferred if the problems of the parent plant are those of product proliferation, labour availability and of meeting expected future growth. Relocation or 'complete move' is preferred if the push factors are associated with the layout of the existing plant, materials handling, new technology, production and inventory control, and insufficient managerial capacity to run two sites; as well as the lease falling in or the issuing of a compulsory purchase order.[12]

The more urgent the need for a new site, the more the search and the decision is delegated, often to the chairman or managing director in a small company or to a senior executive in a larger company. It is rare for this individual to be allocated to the task full-time. The board of directors is typically not involved in evaluating alternatives.

Search procedures seem to follow one of two broad approaches: either drawing up in advance a list of desirable locational attributes for the given project and then searching for a site which has the attributes; or proceeding by visiting locations which seem attractive *a priori* and eliminating those which do not meet requirements. In the UK government survey, 50 per cent of 466 respondents followed the first approach, 32 per cent the second (and 18 per cent could not say). Search either proceeds concentrically from base, modified by major axes of communication; or by focusing indirectly on a given region chosen for its markets or its incentive package. Eighty per cent of firms in the above survey sought alternatives, 58 per cent in more than one region.

The information used in the search comes from a wide variety of sources. The public sector is of paramount importance for all but the short-distance moves as a data resource, and as the force behind much of the advertising and promotion of regions and towns. The private sector is more important at the level of individual sites and buildings. Personal visits are a prerequisite to the elevation of a given location to the status of a 'serious possibility' for the majority of firms.

376

The evaluation of alternatives proceeds at two or three levels. At level one, areas are ruled out of consideration before individual sites are sought. Reasons such as distance to the parent company, transport costs or inadequate supplies of available labour remove areas from consideration. More subjective judgements about the attitudes in the labour force or the quality of the residential environment have a role here also. At a second level, a more detailed look at a limited number of areas is undertaken, with visits and data collection. Then at a final level a short (3.5 on average) list of alternatives is subjected to detailed evaluation. At this level, other members of the company not previously involved may be brought in, together with outside advisers. In contrast with some other countries, however, it is rare for UK companies to use consultants for locational search.

Comparative cost analysis is not undertaken in the majority of companies. For example, in a study of 98 firms by Cooper (1975, p. 88), 71 per cent 'selected their location on the basis of whether or not the site and/or buildings were suitable for the proposed project. Only 29 per cent made comparisons of costs, labour supplies, accessibility, or similar factors'. It is very rare for cost factors to be set against non-costable items. It seems that for many companies costings and financial projections offer a spurious accuracy. The important attributes about a new location such as labour force attitudes and productivity are difficult to predict, and so do not fit easily into the usual financial appraisal used by the firm in considering new investments. Strong uncertainty is present. This uncertainty is seen in the willingness of company managers to talk to executives in other recently moved companies to learn by their experience, especially for longer-distance moves. It is also evident in follow-my-leader patterns of movement, linking origins and destinations and accounting in part for sectoral concentrations of new openings in particular areas.

An important issue for the modelling of industrial location decisions is whether companies seek a feasible rather than an optimal alternative in choosing a new location. The evidence from two UK surveys suggests that many companies are essentially satisficers rather than maximisers. Cooper's (1975, p. 87) results show 55 per cent of his sample of firms choosing a first satisfactory site, with only a minority looking further. Large companies were more likely to compare alternative satisfactory sites than small companies. In this author's 1969 survey, 17 of 57 firms chose the first possible answer for their particular situation. A further 23 made a 'sub-optimum' choice, finding a site that was not only possible (i.e. met minimum requirements) but was satisfactory. Only 17 continued to generate alternatives before coming back to one considered earlier. These firms may be considered to have exhibited optimising behaviour, in continuing search until diminishing returns were identified.

It is clear that both the ingredients to the industrial location decision and the procedures followed are heavily influenced by the size and the corporate style and structure of the company involved. Ideally, a locational choice needs to be seen as part of an investment decision, which in turn is part of a corporate strategy in which locational change is only one potential policy instrument. Recent studies, emphasising the locational impacts of what are essentially non-locational choices, have tried to bring together the market and institutional contexts at the company level for multi plant firms with locational changes at the margin of the individual branch plant or subsidiary company (Massey and Meegan, 1979).

The impact of industrial movement on regional development

Table 10.2 showed the employment in inter-regional industrial moves in manufacturing in the UK over the 30-year period, 1945 to 1975. As the discussion in the second and third sections of this chapter suggested, the impact of these flows of jobs was considerable, especially for the new and expanding town developments and for the objectives of regional economic growth in the Assisted Areas. Industrial movement has not only modified the spatial distribution of manufacturing in the UK but it has also reduced inter-regional inequalities in incomes and in employment opportunities. By 1976 the personal disposable income per head in the regions of the UK ranged from 109.6 per cent of the national average in the South-East region to 84 per cent in Northern Ireland, with all of the remaining nine regions falling between 93.4 per cent and 98.8 per cent. In the Assisted Areas in particular the industrial structure of the local economies has been widened, particularly in job opportunities for women, and a measure of improved stability in the face of cyclical downturns in the national economy has been achieved. The infrastructure investments, made in utilities and transport and in industrial sites and factories as well as in social investments such as hospitals, schools and colleges in part to attract industry, have brought provision closer to a common national standard. Industry was a key weapon in UK 'lagging region' policy and it has most certainly been used successfully to improve economic conditions in those regions and to reduce regional differences.

The overall economic impact of using incentives and prohibitions to encourage and force a movement of industry that would not otherwise have taken place is less clear. Although an active regional economic development policy can bring about gains to national wealth and industrial output by bringing into play unused or under-used resources (principally unemployed labour), the total effects of the exchequer cost involved are difficult to estimate, and an active location of industry policy can impose locational inefficiencies on companies which they would otherwise avoid.

To keep a sense of perspective on exchequer cost, it may be useful to remember that the direct government budget outlay cost (i.e. not allowing for multiplier effects and for new tax revenues generated) of regional development policy in the UK has always been smaller than aid to agriculture, a sector now only employing 2 per cent of the labour force. Remembering that regional incentives in the UK are not directed at industry alone (and less so now than in the past), a recent careful assessment of the costs and benefits in the macro-economic impact of regional policy came to the following conclusion (Marquand, 1980, p. ix):

> In the short to medium term, regional incentives may compare unfavourably in their effects upon GDP and employment with a Public Sector Borrowing Requirement equivalent use of other fiscal instruments. However, regional incentives are designed to operate directly upon investment rather than employment, and to provide a stream of benefit over a long period. When attempts are made to take this into account, the PSBR costs per job/year associated with regional incentives appear on balance to be comparable, or even to compare favourably, with those associated with changes in direct or indirect taxation, or in government of current goods and services. But to assume precision in the estimates underlying any of these judgements would be spurious.

In the literature on industrial movement in the UK a number of other issues related to the impact of incoming firms on a local area have been raised (Townroe, 1979). One early area of interest and concern was the impact of factory work habit requirements on a labour force previously engaged in mining or agriculture (or housework). Even for people formerly engaged in older industries such as ship building and heavy engineering the change to new and expanding light industries was often difficult. Managers in some of the incoming plants were not prepared for the labour attitudes which came with the new workforce from its previous occupations. This led to some adjustment problems. A study by Oakey (1979) for example details how the product and process technologies in newly locating plants in the instruments industry were the source of a range of labour problems for the managers. However, factory culture is now so widespread across the country that this adjustment problem is largely restricted to new entrants into the labour force.

One further aspect of the impact of new industry which has received considerable attention is the issue of the extent to which the economic benefits to a region of 'in-migrant' branch plants are muted if those plants lack higher-order occupations in their labour force and if they lack any managerial autonomy from their parent units elsewhere, (e.g. Lloyd and Mason, 1979). While production-only branch plants may hold back career opportunities locally in a region, there is little evidence that external control is harmful to a region. The related belief that branch plants are more prone to closure in the Assisted Areas than indigenous local firms has been shown not to be true (Townroe, 1979, p. 190). The effective impact of external control depends very much on the corporate strategy and organisational structure of each company in the area. It does not follow that local growth is lost if the local managers in a unit of a multiplant company are unable to take significant investment decisions themselves (Dicken, 1976). Foreign control of inmigrant companies (and of acquisitions and new expansions) seems to be a positive advantage to an Assisted Area in most respects, as shown for example in Forsyth's (1972) study of American companies in Scotland. Only in the area of research and development expenditures and in the provision of higher-order corporate functions have the Assisted Areas suffered relative to the rest of the country in investments by foreign-owned firms (Dicken and Lloyd, 1980). But in these matters foreign firms are not very different in their spatial behaviour from UK-owned firms.

One hope behind regional development policies directed at moving industry was that the new plants would develop local inter-industry linkages, thereby raising income and employment multipliers in an expanding growth pole system.[13] There is little evidence that this has happened (Pred, 1976; Townroe, 1979, pp. 193—6). Policy has not however actively sought either to combine interlinked industries locationally, or to foster actively local linkages once a move has taken place.

Outlook

Industrial migration, as the term is used in this book, refers to just one component of the aggregate of changes in the location of economic activity. These locational changes are in turn a response by productive organisations, companies, to three sets of forces. The first set comes from within the company itself. It is comprised of strategies and policies pursued by the management of that company, both to improve the profit and the growth rate in the face of a given external environment; but also to respond to changes in that environment. These changes form the second two sets of forces. One set comes from changes in aggregate or macro-economic conditions, conditions which influence the overall behaviour of companies in all sectors or in specific sectors or markets only. The other set is really a sub-set: changes in the external environment of the company with a specifically locational orientation. As has already been suggested, considerable change and turbulence is taking place in this external environment for companies operating in the UK at present. The resulting locational outcomes will have a lot more to do with decline and closure than with growth and expansion in the short and medium term.

Today, the UK economy is experiencing its most severe industrial depression since the 1930s. Industrial production is falling, there is a severe crisis of confidence among investors in manufacturing industry, and unemployment is at a record post-war high. Plant closures and bankruptcies have never occurred at a more rapid rate in the post-war period. Increased competition in manufactured products has come from the accession of the UK to the EEC in 1973, and from the development of industrial capacity in Third World nations. This competition is not just in export markets but, very seriously, in domestic markets also. A high exchange rate for sterling is holding back the benefits previously expected for an economy about to become self-sufficient in oil. The short-term outlook for industrial movement in the UK therefore has to be for only a small number of projects.

In the longer term a return to overall numbers of projects establishing in new locations similar to those of the mid-1970s seems possible, and likely. The employment involved will be less than before, however. No government of any UK political party can continue to allow present industrial trends to continue. Indeed, with inflation in single figures and a positive balance of payments, there is little justification for keeping interest rates high and for continuing to cut non-welfare public expenditure, thereby deflating the economy. An incomes policy, import controls, a change in the form of monetary policy, or greater direction to investment flows may each or all allow strong economic growth to take place in the UK economy in the second half of the 1980s on the back of its strong energy resource position, developments in the world economy permitting. However, the spatial impact of that growth may be rather differently distributed than in the last period of strong expansion in the 1960s.

Regional economic development policies will not be as significant a factor as in the past. The problems which called forth such policies in the past are now more evenly spread across the nation, being in evidence in parts of every region: unemployment, low female activity rates, presence of declining industrial sectors, relative socio-economic deprivation of households. At the same time, communications between regions have greatly improved, and inequity in the provision of industrial and social infrastructures is much reduced. The present government has already considerably reduced both the areas eligible for regional aid, and the forms in which that aid can be given.(It must, however, be remembered that aid for projects from the EEC Regional Fund is now a further source of investment finance in the Assisted Area regions partly replacing direct UK government financing but also adding to the aid in reducing interest charges on infrastructure projects.)

Government aid to industry has become increasingly sectoral in its emphasis over the last 15 years. The UK public sector extends into the motor car industry, ships, computers, aero-engines, machine tools and chemicals as well as the principal utilities, steel and the transport sectors. Current reappraisal of the systems by which investment in UK manufacturing is financed seem likely to result in greater differentiation between manufacturing sectors; as well as renewed efforts to coordinate the patterns of investment within the public sector. It seems doubtful that a significant spatial policy element will be allowed to intervene in any new strategies, other than the regional development policies already in place, even though significant differences in the spatial distribution of any growth in manufacturing jobs are likely to persist.

To the degree that industrial movement follows population movement, urban expansion will be less of a factor in industrial location decisions than in the past. The new town and town expansion programme is not being extended. The national population total is static. However, the trend towards ex-urban and rural living is likely to continue. Car ownership rates continue to rise along with home ownership rates. The UK labour force therefore is now better able to respond to new industrial locations by commuting or by moving house than was the case 15 years ago. This improvement will continue as real incomes rise, perhaps exacerbating the social and economic problems of inner urban areas, and leading to renewed efforts to use moving industry as part of the solution.

The great unknown about the period up to the end of this century for industrial movement in the UK is the changing relationship between industrial investment and employment. Within the manufacturing sector and those service sectors containing large essentially routine office functions there is a widespread expectation in the UK that the microprocessor will have a fairly dramatic effect on labour productivity. Therefore, in the absence of higher rates of investment and growing demands for the output of these sectors, employment therein will fall. The employment that is left will be of a new skill mix. If the other sectors of the economy expand, unemployment will not be permanently at a higher level. Job sharing, a shorter work week, further education and earlier retirement could all be factors reducing the numbers of people looking for work. However, these changes do point to a reduced role for manufacturing in influencing the location of employment; and conversely to a reduced role of the location of employees for the location of manufacturing.

Notes

1 The status of subsidiary units is particularly difficult to classify in UK manufacturing. The ownership structure is very oligopolistic with extensive vertical and horizontal integration, as well as holding company type relationships between technologically and market unrelated activities.

2 The Glasgow data bank has now been extended into SCOMER (Scottish Manufacturing Establishments Record) held by the Scottish Office. For details, see the *Scottish Economic Bulletin*, vol. 13, 1977. For details of the Glasgow data, see Firn and Swales (1978); for Manchester, Lloyd and Mason (1978); and for the East Midlands, see Gudgin (1978).

3 The history of legislation has recently been reviewed by McCallum (1979).

4 The history of the New Towns and the Town Development schemes is summarised in Cullingworth (1975).

5 Manufacturing employment fell in the eight largest conurbations of the UK by 13.4 per cent between 1971 and 1976. Dennis (1978) examines the London case. Region-wide, Tyler (1980) examines similar accusations of regional policy made in the West Midlands; and finds manufacturing jobs lost in the region not to be a consequence of regional policy.

6 This closely matches the size distribution of all manufacturing establishments in the UK employing more than ten.

7 See Gripaios (1977) on London, and Henderson (1980) and Bull (1978) on Glasgow.

8 Examples include the Department of Health and Social Security offices in Newcastle-upon-Tyne, part of the Ministry of Defence to Glasgow, the Post Office Savings Bank offices to Durham, and the Vehicle Licensing Centre to Swansea. The whole issue of office location and movement is reviewed very thoroughly by Daniels (1977).

9 Also in other European nations see e.g. Hall and Hay, (1980) and Klaassen, Molle, Paelinck (1981).

10 Henderson's study (1980) of immigrant industry into Scotland shows how the supply of land and suitable factory buildings has been a key factor in attracting industry, even to districts with poor physical and social environments. However, the supply is now large, making the

availability of suitable factory space a necessary but not sufficient condition for a locality to attract mobile industry.

11 A later paper with a different model by Ashcroft and Taylor (1977) reduced this estimate to 90,000 jobs. These studies have recently been reviewed by Ashcroft (1980) and Marquand (1980).

12 See also Schmenner (1980).

13 Typical values of income multipliers calculated for UK regions range from 1.1 to 1.7. Marquand argues for a medium-term employment multiplier of 1.4 in calculating the effects of regional policy, rising to 1.7 in the long term (1980, pp. 51–5).

References

Ashcroft, B. (1980), 'The Evaluation of Regional Policy', *Studies in Public Policy No. 12,* Centre for the Study of Public Policy, University of Strathclyde, Glasgow.

Ashcroft, B. and Taylor, J. (1977), 'The movement of manufacturing industry and the effect of regional policy', *Oxford Economic Papers,* vol. 29, no. 1, pp. 84–99.

Beale, C. (1976), 'A further look at non-metropolitan population growth since 1970', *American Journal of Agricultural Economics,* vol. 58, no. 5, pp. 953–8.

Bull, P.J. (1978), 'The spatial components of intra-urban manufacturing change: Sub-urbanisation in Clydeside 1958–68', *Transactions of the Institute of British Geographers* New Series, vol. 3, no. 1, pp. 92–100.

Cameron, G.C. (1973), 'Intra-urban location and the new plant', *Papers and Proceedings,* Regional Science Association, vol. 29, pp. 1–16.

Cooper, M.J.M. (1975), 'The Industrial Location Decision Making Process', Occasional Paper no. 34, Centre for Urban and Regional Studies, University of Birmingham.

Cullingworth, J.B. (1975), *Town and Country Planning in Britain,* Allen and Unwin, London.

Daniels, P. (1977), 'Office location in the British Conurbations: trends and strategies', *Urban Studies,* vol. 14, no. 3, pp. 261–74.

Dennis, R. (1978), 'The decline of manufacturing employment in Greater London: 1966–74', *Urban Studies,* vol. 15, no. 1, pp. 63–74.

Dicken, P. (1976), 'The multiplant business enterprise and geographical space: some issues in the study of external control and regional development', *Regional Studies,* vol. 11, pp. 181–98.

Dicken, P. and Lloyd, P.E. (1980), 'Patterns and processes of change in the spatial distribution of foreign-controlled manufacturing employment in the United Kingdom, 1963–1975', *Environment and Planning,* vol. 12, pp. 1405–26.

Economic Consultants Ltd (1971), Strategic Plan for the South East: Studies volume 5, HMSO, London.

Firn, J.R. and Swales, J.K. (1978), 'The formation of new manufacturing establishments in the Central Clydeside and West Midlands conurbations 1963–72: a comparative analysis, *Regional Studies,* vol. 12, no. 2, pp. 199–214.

Forsyth, D.J.C. (1972), *United States Investment in Scotland,* Praeger, New York.

Fothergill, S. and Gudgin, G. (1979), 'Regional Employment Change: A Subregional Explanation', *Progress in Planning,* vol. 12, no. 3, pp. 155–219.

Fothergill, S. and Gudgin, G. (1981), *Unequal Growth: Postwar Employment Change in UK Cities and Regions,* Heinemann, London.

Gripaios, P. (1977), 'The closure of firms in the inner city: the South East London case 1970–75, *Regional Studies',* vol. 11, no. 1, pp. 1–6.

Gudgin, G. (1978), *Industrial Location Processes and Regional Development Growth,* Saxon House, Farnborough.

Hamilton, F.E.I. (1978),'Aspects of industrial mobility in the British economy', *Regional Studies,* vol. 12, no. 2, pp. 153–66.

Hall, P. and Hay, D. (1980), *Growth Centres in the European Urban System,* Heinemann, London.

Howard, R.S. (1968), *The Movement of Manufacturing Industry in the United Kingdom, 1945–65,* HMSO for the Board of Trade, London.

Henderson, R.A. (1980) 'An analysis of closures amongst Scottish manufacturing plants between 1966 and 1975', *Scottish Journal of Political Economy,* vol. 27, no. 2, pp. 152–74.

Henderson, R.A. (1980), 'The location of immigrant industry within a UK Assisted Area: the Scottish experience', *Progress in Planning,* vol. 14, no. 2, pp. 151–222.

Keeble, D.E. (1968), 'Industrial decentralisation and the metropolis; the North West London case', Transactions of the Institute of British Geographers, vol. 44, pp. 1–54.

Keeble, D.E. (1971), 'Industrial mobility in Britain', Chapter 2 in M. Chisholm and G. Manners (eds), *Spatial Problems of the British Economy,* Cambridge University Press, Cambridge.

Keeble, D.E. (1976), *Industrial Location and Planning in Britain,* Methuen, London.

Keeble, D.E. (1980), 'Industrial decline, regional policy and the urban-rural manufacturing shift in the United Kingdom', *Environment and Planning,* vol. 12, pp. 945–62.

Klaassen, L.H., Molle, W.T.M. and Paelinck, J.H.P. (eds) (1981), *Dynamics of Urban Development,* Gower Press, Farnborough.

Lloyd, P.E. and Mason, L.M. (1978), 'Manufacturing industry in the inner city: a case study of Greater Manchester', *Transactions, Institute of British Geographers,* vol. 3, no. 1, pp. 66—90.

Lloyd, P.E. and Mason, L.M. (1979), 'Industrial Movement in North West England: 1966—75', *Environment and Planning,* vol. 11, pp. 1367—85.

Marquand, J. (1980), 'Measuring the effects and costs of regional incentives', Government Economic Service Working Paper no. 32.

Massey, D. and Meegan, R.A. (1979), 'The geography of industrial reorganisation', *Progress in Planning,* vol. 10, no. 3, pp. 155—237.

McCallum, F.D. (1973), 'UK regional policy 1964—1972' in G.C. Cameron and L. Wingo (eds) Cities, Regional and Public Policy, Oliver and Boyd, Edinburgh.

Nunn, S. (1980), 'The opening and closure of manufacturing units in the United Kingdom, 1966—75', Government Economic Service Working Paper, no. 36.

Oakey, R.P. (1979), 'Labour and the location of mobile industry: observations from the instruments industry', *Environment and Planning,* vol. 11, pp. 1231—40.

Pred, A.R. (1976), 'The interurban transmission of growth in advanced economies: empirical findings versus regional planning assumptions', *Regional Studies,* vol. 10, no. 2, pp. 151—72.

Rhodes, J. and Moore, B.C. (1976), 'Regional economic policy and the movement of manufacturing firms to Development Areas', *Economica,* vol. 43, pp. 17—31.

Sant, M.E.C. (1975), *Industrial Movement and Regional Development: The British Case,* Pergamon Press, Oxford.

Schmenner, R.W. (1978), *The Manufacturing Location Decision: Evidence from Cincinnati and New England,* Economic Development Research Report, US Department of Commerce, Washington, DC.

Schmenner, R.W. (1980), 'Choosing new industrial capacity: on-site expansion, branching, and relocation', *Quarterly Journal of Economics,* vol. 95, no. 1, pp. 103—19.

Smith, B.M.D. (1970), 'Industrial overspill in theory and practice: the case of the West Midlands', *Urban Studies,* vol. 7, no. 2, pp. 189—204.

Struyk, R.J. and James, F.R. (1975), *Intra Metropolitan Industrial Location,* Lexington Books, Lexington, Mass.

Townroe, P.M. (1976), *Planning Industrial Location,* Leonard Hill, London.

Townroe, P.M. (1979), *Industrial Movement: Experience in the US and the UK,* Saxon House, Farnborough.

Tyler, P. (1980), 'The impact of regional policy on a prosperous region: the experience of the West Midlands', *Oxford Economic Papers,* vol. 32, no. 1, pp. 151—62.

11 Belgium
N. VANHOVE

Introduction: available data

However important the phenomenon of industrial movement, the researcher hardly finds any information on the subject in Belgium permitting him to draw up much of a picture. Therefore, the present chapter will not, like many others, be based on a review of empirical studies; instead, we have carried out original inquiries to obtain a quantitative basis for our analysis. Thanks to the co-operation of the Regional Development Authorities (that is, the Provincial Economic Councils, institutionalised since 1975) it has been possible to get an idea of industrial movement in Flanders. As to Wallonia, the lack of continuity of the institutions means that the information supplied by the Regional Development Authority was so scarce that we had to leave that part of the country out of consideration.

The inquiry covered the period 1955–80 and was limited to industrial companies (omitting building and transport) employing 20 or more people. The time available did not allow us to go into the employment aspect of industrial movement.

The inquiry focused on the following four aspects, to be treated in succession:

1 international industrial migrations;
2 inter-provincial industrial migrations;
3 intra-provincial initiatives and relocations;
4 intra-agglomeration relocations.

First, however, we will recall briefly the aspects of regional economic development and regional policy, and some institutional aspects. The contribution will be rounded off with some conclusions and an outlook towards the future.

The spatial and policy setting

Regional development and policy

At the end of the 1950s, Belgium had the lowest growth rate among the countries of the European Community of the Six, and a relatively high unemployment figure. In that context, the then prime minister, Mr G. Eyskens, took the initiative to the general and regional expansion legislation laid down in the laws of 17 and 18 July 1959. These laws, recognising the regional problems in Belgium, have had an undeniable influence on long-phase economic growth.

In the last two decades the industrial map of Belgium could be observed to alter considerably. Table 11.1 gives an idea of the regional spread of industrial companies and employment in 1960, 1974 and 1979 (by province).

The geographical situation of the provinces is given in Map. 11.1. The table shows that in the course of the last two decades, the share of the four northern provinces — roughly identical with the Flemish region, except Flemish Brabant — increased considerably, both in number of companies and in employment, at the expense of the province of Brabant (divided into the Capital of Brussels, and Flemish Brabant) and the four southern provinces, roughly coinciding with the Wallonia region. The process was already far advanced before the economic crisis of 1974.

To understand industrial movement in Belgium one should realise that regional problems in Belgium can mainly be traced back to two factors. First, various parts of the country had long suffered from negative labour market balances, which in the late 1950s showed up in the form of high unemployment figures, commuting (particularly to Brussels and some other agglomerations), seasonal work and frontier work. Especially in the Flemish part of the country the problems were serious. Second, the recession in the mining industry in Wallonia and Limburg and the textile industry in Flanders had left certain areas in Wallonia and Flanders 'stranded'.

The general objective of the regional expansion legislation, however, was not only to decrease unemployment but also to level out differ-

388

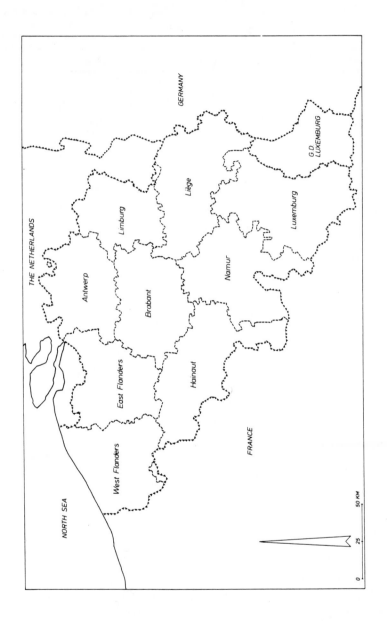

Map 11.1   Administrative division of Belgium

Table 11.1

The evolution of the number of industrial firms and employment by region,
1960—79 (mining excluded)

	Number of establishments on June 30			Total employment		
	1960	1974	1979	1960	1974	1979
Antwerp	15.8	17.1	17.4	17.8	19.1	20.4
East Flanders	14.9	15.3	15.4	15.4	14.7	14.4
West Flanders[a]	13.2	13.8	14.9	9.9	12.3	12.3
Limburg	3.2	5.5	6.0	1.9	6.0	6.9
(North)	(47.1)	(51.7)	(53.7)	(45.0)	(52.1)	(54.0)
Hainaut	10.4	9.9	9.3	14.0	13.4	12.7
Liège	10.1	9.8	9.6	13.7	11.2	10.7
Luxemburg	1.7	1.7	1.8	0.5	0.8	0.7
Namur	3.1	3.2	3.1	2.6	2.5	2.6
(South)	(25.3)	(24.6)	(23.2)	(30.8)	(27.9)	(26.7)
Brabant	27.6	23.7	22.5	24.2	20.0	19.3
Country	100.0	100.0	100.0	100.0	100.0	100.0

[a]After frontier readjustment.

Table 11.2

Unemployment rate and income level by province, 1955—57

Unemployment rate (Belgium 1957 = 100)		Income per inhabitant (Belgium 1955 = 100)	
	Low (<85)	Medium	High (>115)
High (>115)	West Flanders 78 (148) East Flanders 81 (159)	Antwerp 109 (130)	
Medium	—	—	—
Low (<85)	Limburg 72 (80) Luxemburg 84 (61)	Hainaut 100 (65) Liège 108 (65) Namur 95 (59)	Brabant 125 (70)

ences in income.

In the 1950s, the unemployment figure and income per capita were the only indices of a region's prosperity; from them the economically weak provinces in the mid-1950s can be identified. The relevant figures are given in Table 11.2.

In the mid-1950s West and East Flanders were the two provinces with the lowest level of prosperity (the first figure gives for each province the income level in relation to Belgium, while the figure in parentheses stands for the unemployment level in relation to Belgium). By their level of income, Limburg and Luxemburg should be added to the weak regions.

However, such a method of appreciation leaves out of account the discrepancy that can be expected between the supply of and the demand for labour resulting from the population growth and/or the recession in traditional activities.

In Belgium, the problem of congestion or excessive industrial concentration had never been raised officially; indeed, there had never been explicit attempts at decentralising the economic activities of certain agglomerations to development areas. In Belgium, there are no conurbations comparable to Greater London, Paris, the Dutch Randstad, etc., and there was no reason for the government to introduce such negative incentives as the industrial development certificate in the UK or the building licence cum special taxes in France (Vanhove and Klaassen, 1980). Yet in various circles the necessity to limit the growth of the Brussels and Antwerp agglomerations with their high operating costs had often been pointed out. The Flemish wish to slow down or even neutralise the further growth of the Brussels agglomeration would instantly have given rise to political problems and was, therefore, not an attainable proposition, while the port of Antwerp constituted an important trump card in the industrialisation of Flanders.

The economic and social motivations of regional policy in Belgium implicitly included the decentralisation of companies from the Brussels area to other parts of the country. Indeed, two of its objectives being the optimum use of production factors (surplus on the employment balance in certain areas and deficit in others) and considerable reduction of anti-social commuting (and the high transport costs involved, appearing from the deficits of the National Railway Company), regional policy perforce had to try to decentralise companies from areas with a shortage of labour, in particular the Brussels agglomeration.

Awakening regional consciousness in Belgium, and the importance of Provincial Economic Councils in Flanders

In the gradual awakening to the regional economic problems of certain areas and the growing willingness to do something about them, the part played by the Provincial Economic Councils and the Regional Councils — including the Economic Council for Flanders and the Conseil Economique Wallon — deserves to be underlined.

The first institution for economic regional development in Belgium was founded in 1945 in Wallonia under the name of 'Conseil Economique Wallon' (CEW); its foundation was largely inspired by the difficulties arising in the classical industrial sectors of Wallonia between 1930 and 1940 and the lack of a specific approach by the central government. The decline of the larger companies, particularly the coal-mining companies, and the movement of industry towards the north of the country in search of better access to the sea, were striking facts. In the Wallonia part of Belgium the CEW created provincial groups for Hainaut, Namur, Liège, and Luxemburg. Moreover, a number of provincial services were created on the initiative of the provincial government, for example in Brabant and Namur.

Action in Flanders started a little later and the initiatives there came from the provincial authorities. The central point of interest was not so much the general economic development of Flanders as the stimulation of industry in distressed areas. The action for a concrete attack on regional economic problems in Flanders was preceded by a stage of study. Governors, permanent deputations and the provincial councils finally stimulated the installation of Provincial Economic Councils (PEC) in Flanders between 1951 and 1956; the Economic Council for Flanders was founded in 1951. Although there were no hierarchic ties between the Provincial Economic Councils and the Economic Council for Flanders, they have always consulted one another and forged a tie through their management commissions. The PEC's function was fourfold: study, conception, promotion, and co-ordination; that it was difficult for a PEC to proceed to implementation of its own accord became apparent quite soon. The promotional task of the Provincial Economic Councils had several aspects, one of them being the attraction of new industrial plants from inland and abroad. To that end, industrial estates were required; inter-municipal associations were founded — often on the initiative of the Provincial Economic Councils — for the specific purpose of making new industrial land available. The new industrial estates were designated not only for new companies but also for the relocation of existing companies so far established in agglomerations and cities. Indeed, in the post-war period many companies located in city centres; and finding themselves unable to realise necessary modernisations and economies of scale in their original locations, were obliged to move.

Patterns of movements in Flanders

The international moves

In the post-war period a great number of foreign companies set up plants in Flanders, a movement that started at the end of the 1950s, thus coinciding with the creation of the Common Market. Several companies, especially American multinationals, who were interested in establishing a production unit in the EEC, were induced by various factors to locate their plants in Flanders. The geo-economic situation was the first factor. According to Clark, Wilson, and Bradley (1969) the economic potential of Flanders in the total area of north-west Europe was very high in comparison with other regions with similar socio-economic structures. In the second place, Flanders had three important seaports: Antwerp, Gent, and Zeebrugge, an essential factor in view of the change-over from European to non-European raw materials. The third factor in favour of Flanders was its ample labour market and good social climate, the latter favouring Flanders above Wallonia, which had lost much of its attraction for new plants by the persistent strikes of 1961. As the Common Market was activating economic growth, the number of EEC regions with a shortage of labour increased. Several companies were thus induced to look for other regions to set up branch units; that explains the interest of German and Dutch companies in Flanders in the 1960s.

In the fourth place, Belgium in general and Flanders in particular were highly praised for their good general investment climate. This was promoted by the general expansion legislation and the regional expansion legislation, providing important financial incentives mostly in the form of interest subsidies.

Table 11.3 surveys international industrial migration towards Flanders in the period 1955–80; it refers to 509 plants, which means that 509 plants which moved in from abroad during the period considered were operational in Flanders in 1980, companies which closed down again in the meantime have not been taken into account.

What are the conclusions to be drawn from this table?

1　The greater part of foreign plants come from the USA, the Netherlands, and Western Germany; they account for about three-quarters of the new companies. The UK ranks fourth with 27 new firms; the number of companies from France (17) and Japan (11) was rather small. From remaining countries, the plants from Scandinavia, Switzerland, and Canada should be mentioned.

Table 11.3

International industrial movement towards Flanders by country of origin and sector, 1955–80[1,2]

Country of origin	USA						Germany					
Industrial sector	W[3]	O	A	V	L	F	W	O	A	V	L	F
Metal industries	5	16	19	4	9	53	5	3	1	2	8	19
Textile	2	2	—	—	—	4	—	1	—	—	2	3
Clothing	3	2	1	—	3	9	3	2	—	—	2	7
Food	1	—	3	—	—	4	—	1	—	—	—	1
Wood and wood products	—	—	—	—	—	—	1	1	1	—	1	4
Chemicals	—	18	23	1	10	52	1	4	4	—	3	12
Other	3	11	2	—	3	19	—	2	—	—	—	2
Total	14	49	48	5	25	141	10	14	6	2	16	48

[1] The new firms which have been closed down are not taken into account, except for the province of Antwerp.
For the Vlaams–Brabant region only the firms on industrial sites are considered.

[2] Joint ventures included.

[3] W = West-Vlaanderen province.
O = Oost-Vlaanderen province.
A = Antwerp province.
V = Vlaams–Brabant.
L = Limburg province.
F = Total Flanders

[4] Joint ventures of the province of Antwerp are classified in the group 'other countries'.

Source: Inquiry with Regional Development Authorities in Flanders.

Netherlands						Other						Total					
W	O	A	V	L	F	W	O	A	V	L	F	W	O	A	V	L	F
4	7	10	2	21	44	3	18	19^4	1	4	45	17	44	49^4	9	42	161
—	4	2	—	3	9	—	4	1	—	2	7	2	11	3	—	7	23
5	3	26	1	28	63	—	1	3	—	—	4	11	8	30	1	33	83
2	1	6	1	7	17	1	1	4	—	2	8	4	3	13	1	9	30
—	0	1	—	5	6	—	1	2	1	—	4	1	2	4	1	6	14
—	6	6	—	5	17	—	14	24	1	6	45	1	42	57	2	24	126
—	3	8	1	13	25	—	12	8	—	6	26	3	28	18	1	22	72
11	24	59	5	82	181	4	51	61	3	20	139	39	138	174	15	143	509

2 Three sectors have contributed in particular to international migration: metal products (including electronics), chemicals, and clothing; together they account for 73 per cent of the plants.
3 The lion's share (89 per cent) of the foreign companies in Flanders settled in the provinces of Antwerp, Limburg, and East Flanders, distance apparently playing an important role. More than other provinces, Limburg attracted projects from Western Germany and the Netherlands; the province of Antwerp also includes a great number of Dutch companies.
4 One-third of the Dutch plants settled in Flanders belong to the clothing sector, which clearly demonstrates how Dutch projects in the clothing sector were attracted by the availability of female labour in the Antwerp Campines and the province of Limburg.
5 The many projects in the chemical sector indicate how important was the industrial land available in the port areas of Antwerp and Gent.

The inter-regional moves

In this section attention will be focused on the relocation of production units from other provinces in Belgium to any of the Flemish provinces. Its location and socio-economic structure — in particular its labour availability — have proved quite attractive to many firms. The attractive elements of the Flemish location profile emerged clearly from the evaluation of the location factors of industrial firms in Flanders undertaken in 1971; in that research project, known as 'The development of the Flemish economy in the international perspective', 900 out of 4,000 approached firms with a minimum of 20 workers actively co-operated. All of them were asked to answer the following question:

If you had to make a decision regarding the location of your firm in 1971, how would you appreciate the various factors: dominant influence, very important, important, less important, no importance at all?

To measure the relative importance of the different factors, a scale was elaborated for each factor (running from 400 to 0 points). From Table 11.4, the availability of labour is the most important among location factors. Of course, we must not generalise; for certain industrial sectors — the steel industry and oil refineries are good examples — the traditional factors are still the most important.

Availability of labour together with the desire of some companies to re-establish themselves outside the Brussels agglomeration or, to a

Table 11.4

A general estimation of the location factors (maximum 400 points, minimum 0 points)

Category	Location factors	Points
Labour (193)	Availability of unskilled and trained male workers	220
	Availability of unskilled and trained female workers	140
	Availability of skilled male workers	210
	Availability of skilled female workers	99
	Availability of staff	176
	Wage level	199
	The faithfulness of labour to the firm	253
	The social climate in the region	250
Infrastructure (112)	Availability of good water connections	83
	Availability of good railway connections	85
	Availability of good road connections	255
	Situated at a highway	163
	Nearness to a seaport	75
	Nearness to an airport	34
	Possibilities of pipeline connections	30
	Availability of equipped industrial sites	148
	Availability of equipped industrial sites at a canal	53
	Price per m^2 of industrial sites	195
Input (108)	Availability of raw materials in the region	123
	Low transport costs on raw materials and components	198
	Availability of cooling water	87
	Availability of processing water	121
	Possibility of avoiding waste water	109
	Nearness of similar firms	56
	Nearness of other industries	69
	Presence of annex firms (backward linkage)	97
Output (138)	Presence of annex firms (forward linkage)	116
	Local market (in the region)	162
	Access to the Belgian market	227
	Nearness of the German market	115
	Nearness of the Dutch market	144
	Nearness of the French market	130
	Nearness of the UK market	72
	Central position in Europe	137
Environment (133)	Availability of social and cultural amenities in the region	127
	Nearness of a big town	122
	Suitable housing accommodation for workers	156
	Presence of auxiliary firms	139
	Nearness of financial firms	145
	Easy contact — personal or by telephone — with suppliers and the demand	225
	Nearness of an attractive recreation area	64
	Nearness of the headquarters of the firm	96
	Living habits in the region	126
Regional financial aids (215)	Financial stimulus in the framework of regional expansion laws in favour of firms setting up in an under-developed region	215

Source: Vanhove and Klaassen, 1980, pp. 133–4.

lesser extent, outside the Antwerp area, explain the inter-regional industrial moves contained in Tables 11.5 and 11.6. Although no inquiries were made among the companies, cost factors (transportation costs, land, and particularly labour) are likely to have played an important role in these inter-regional moves.

As Tables 11.5 and 11.6 illustrate, in the period 1955–80 the Flemish areas attracted 120 companies in all. The inter-regional moves represent 3 per cent of the total number of firms with 20 or more employed. Indeed, the proportion of migrations was rather low in all sectors. Table 11.5 should be read as follows: 11 plants relocated out of West Flanders into East Flanders. From Table 11.6 we learn that 2 out of 12 relocations belong to the metal sector. Mark that 40 per cent of these originate from Brussels and about one in four from the province of Antwerp. Most of these plants moved towards the province of East Flanders; the moves from the capital (Brussels) to the sub-region of Aalst and those from the Antwerp area to the Land van Waas are worth mentioning in particular (distance 15 to 30 km). Flemish Brabant, too, benefited from migration out of Brussels. In that context the study by Dablaere and Stappaerts (1978) on the industrial estates in Halle–Vilvoorde may be cited; this study refers to all industrial plants that were established there up to 1977. It states: 'Economic activity on the industrial estates of Halle–Vilvoorde is continuously increasing. On the 16 estates taken into consideration, 15,800 people are employed by 235 companies, that is 12.5 per cent of the overall number of employees registered with social security in the district.'

The results of the analysis of the companies settled on the estates of Halle–Vilvoorde can be summarised as follows:

1 Most striking is the predominance of companies from Brussels that moved completely or in part: over 63 per cent of all companies considered. Twenty-four per cent of the moves come from other areas; consequently, only 13 per cent of the moves concern first or new plants.
2 Neither in the number of companies nor in the number of people employed is the secondary sector leading. The greater part of the companies (79 per cent) and of the employed (84 per cent) belong to the tertiary sector; especially storage and related distribution activities are well represented, with administrative, commercial, and industrial development projects, transport, storage, and hotel business adding to the tertiary activities.

Table 11.5

Inter-regional industrial movement, 1955—80

Destination Origin	West Flanders	East Flanders	Antwerp	Flemish Brabant[a]	Limburg	Total
West Flanders	—	11	—	—	2	13
East Flanders	4	—	—	—	3	7
Antwerp	4	17	—	—	3	29
Flemish Brabant	—	8	2	—	3	13
Limburg	1	1	—	—	—	2
Brussels Capital	3	27	4	12	3	49
Wallonia	—	3	—	3	1	7
Total	12	67	6	15	20	120

[a]Only firms on industrial sites have been considered.

Source: Inquiry among Regional Development Authorities in Flanders.

Table 11.6

Inter-regional industrial movement in Flanders by sector, 1955—80

Sector	West Flanders	East Flanders	Antwerp	Flemish Brabant	Limburg	Total	%[a]
Metal industries	2	25	1	6	6	40	4.4
Textile	4	11	—	—	1	16	3.1
Clothing	2	—	1	1	—	4	0.8
Food	1	11	—	1	3	16	3.6
Wood and wood products	1	3	—	2	4	10	2.6
Chemicals	1	3	—	2	4	10	2.6
Other	1	13	2	3	5	24	1.3
Total	12	67	6	15	20	120	3.0

[a]Total moves in percentage points of total number of firms with 20 or more employed in 1979. 9.

The present section will deal with initiatives for setting up new industrial activities taken by firms or persons indigenous to the province, and to a lesser extent present some general ideas about relocation within a province.

In the study period, many new activities were initiated in the various regions of Flanders. Because creation, though not strictly a migration phenomenon, yet is an important element of total industrial dynamics, these initiatives merit some attention. Table 11.7 surveys new industrial plants in the various regions, including intra-regional relocations, and the establishment of branch units. According to data supplied by the Flemish RDAs and the Regional Economic Council for Brabant, 360 new plants were established in Flanders in the study period, a small portion of them being relocations.

Table 11.7

Intra-regional industrial migration and creation of new firms
by sector and province, 1955–80[a]

Sector	West Flanders	East Flanders	Antwerp	Flemish Brabant[b]	Limburg	Total
Metal industries	14	22	29	4	48	117
Textile	12	8	1	–	6	27
Clothing	2	3	4	1	11	21
Food	11	10	7	1	14	43
Wood and wood products	8	10	11	1	19	49
Chemicals	7	10	11	3	14	45
Other	5	7	13	4	29	58
Total	59	70	76	14	141	360

[a] Probably some firms do not employ 20 persons.
[b] Only the firms on industrial sites.

Source: Inquiry among Regional Development Authorities in Flanders.

Table 11.7 should be read as follows: in West Flanders 59 new industrial establishments and/or relocations other than inter-agglomeration were undertaken (each involving at least 20 employed people), 14 among them belonging to the sector of metal industries. Two main points emerging from this survey are:

1 A great number of plants were set up in the province of Limburg.
2 The metal industries sector dominates with about one-third of
the total number.

Intra-agglomeration migrations on industrial estates

In the post-war period many Flemish companies were forced to look
for new locations within their agglomeration, city, or municipality; in
most cases they moved from the core of the city or agglomeration to a
new industrial site, often in the suburbs. Most of the moves involved
were undertaken for one or some of the following three reasons:

1 Modernisation of the company;
2 Scaling-up of the company;
3 Town planning and ecological factors within the framework of
physical planning.

By their policy of actively promoting the creation of industrial estates, the Regional Development Authorities and inter-municipal associations have considerably contributed towards that development. Some
figures on migration within agglomerations are given in Table 11.8.

Table 11.8

Intra-agglomeration (intra-urban) industrial migration
on industrial sites by sector and province, 1955−80

Sector	West Flanders	East Flanders	Antwerp	Flemish Brabant	Limburg	Total
Metal industries	37	28	27	4	7	103
Textile	10	13	1	−	−	24
Clothing	12	12	3	−	−	27
Food	8	8	12	1	4	33
Wood and wood products	25	11	10	1	1	48
Chemicals	7	5	9	−	4	25
Other	18	20	15	5	2	60
Total	117	97	77	11	18	320

Source: Inquiry among Regional Development Authorities in Flanders.

401

The figures in Table 11.8 represent only a portion of all relocations, because they do not include the smaller companies (fewer than 20 employees), nor the companies from the building, transport, and tertiary sectors.

In Flanders, 320 intra-city relocations of industrial companies on industrial estates were registered in the period 1955–80, which can certainly be considered a great many. The migration phenomenon was especially marked in the province of West Flanders: over one in three intra-city migrations were effected in that province. Indeed, 117 firms in West Flanders moved from their previous locations to an industrial estate in the suburban areas. Moreover, the economic growth of that province was largely based on the dynamic management of a great number of local companies.

Especially in the area of Kortrijk, the inter-municipal institution of Leiedal made great efforts to offer possibilities for modernisation and expansion to existent companies. Up to 1980 there were no fewer than 37 relocations of industrial plants employing more than 20 people on the eight industrial estates of Leiedal. A striking fact is that all companies involved had relocated within a radius of less than 5 km from their original location. That small distance between original and new plants is due to two factors. In the first place entrepreneurs try to minimise distance on behalf of the people employed; in the second place managers of small and medium-sized companies prefer to have their own residences as near as possible to the plant to keep it under their direct control.

Conclusions and outlook

This limited contribution has revealed a surprisingly large number of industrial migrations. The absence of essential data demonstrates how much this phenomenon has been neglected in regional analyses. The topic is interesting enough to be investigated thoroughly.

Forecasting the future is difficult; one point is clear, however. Although we have not made a time breakdown in the tables, we know that industrial moves were less important in the 1970s than in the 1960s; indeed, the economic growth of the 'golden 1960s' lasted until 1973. The economic recession, which may last for several years more, will be a prohibitive restriction on industrial movements in Belgium during the 1980s. Furthermore, even without economic recession, we cannot expect Belgium or Flanders to become again as attractive to foreign investors as they were in the 1960s and early 1970s. The international division of employment has changed and there are now many new competitors on the market for projects of multinationals. Strained relations between the North and South of Belgium put another restriction on industrial movement: moves between Flanders and Wallonia, already limited in the past, will probably be diminished further by the present aggravated situation.

A possible economic revival in the late 1980s will most probably affect first of all the fourth group of moves, namely, the intra-agglomeration moves. For the other groups a revival is expected to need much more time to take effect.

References

Clark, C., Wilson, F., Bradley, J., (1969), Industrial Location and Economic potential in Western Europe, *Regional Studies,* vol. 2.

Deblaere, G., en Stappaerts, M., (1978), De industrieparken in het arrondissement Leuven en hun betekenis voor de tewerkstelling, *Eco Brabant,* no. 20.

Vanhove, N., and Klaassen, L.H., (1980), *Regional Policy, a European Approach,* Gower Press, London.

Vlassenbroek, W., (1975), Industriële dynamiek in Oost en West Vlaanderen, het effect van nieuwe vestigingen op het spreidingspatroon 1952–1972, *Tijdschrift voor economische en sociale geographie,* no. 1.

12 Past Experience and Future Prospects: A European Synopsis

W. T. M. MOLLE and L. H. KLAASSEN

In the previous chapters, various authors have reviewed the empirical knowledge accumulated in their countries, thus together providing a fairly complete picture of industrial migration and mobility in the whole European Community. That as such is a valuable result of the present study.

However, the book aims beyond the mere collection of results of national studies; its further purpose is to draw general lessons from these results. In the following sections we will attempt such a synthesis; in doing so we shall often refer back to the general aspects of industrial movement discussed in Chapter 1.

First we shall give a short appreciation from a European point of view of the various topics discussed in the national studies; this section provides the basis for subsequent generalisations.

Next, we shall turn to the spatial patterns of movement in Europe; it will be interesting to see the overall picture that emerges as the country sketches are mounted in a European frame.

The motives for movement, the manner in which firms decide to relocate, and the different types of moves will be the next objects of our attempts at synthesis.

The methods used in the analysis are particularly interesting and we shall devote a whole section to the model aspects of industrial movement, trying to classify all models by their basic approach and drawing some general conclusions as to their quantified results.

We shall also pay some attention to the workers directly affected by industrial movement, an aspect that tends to be overlooked.

Most of the studies on industrial movement have been made in relation to some conception of regional development; a discussion of the effects of movement on donor and acceptor regions is, therefore, a logical step in the study.

Finally, we shall speculate about the future. Indeed, with economic conditions drastically changed, we may expect that the role of industrial movement will differ from the one it has played in the past; a better definition of that future role is immediately relevant to future policy making.

Coverage and context

The studies reported on in the previous chapters vary widely as to area, type of industry, time period, definition, etc. They have made it clear that the information available on industrial movement differs much from one European country to another. In some, a wealth of studies has been carried out (the UK, Ireland); in others, a fair number of researchers have tackled the problem, covering a satisfactory part of the total area (France, Germany, Denmark, the Netherlands); in some (Greece, Belgium, Italy) information is scanty.

From the foregoing chapters, the empirical analysis of industrial movement in the EC seems to have been conditioned largely by each country's policy context and probably even more by the availability of data — the latter of course being not independent of the former. In countries where a good data basis was accessible to researchers, many studies have been made. An example is the UK where the publication of the so-called Howard report sparked off a large number of studies. The UK government's efforts to solve the acute problems of certain regions by inciting industry to move there have no doubt given an additional push to the study of industrial movement. Still, the impression remains that the main reason why one country abounds in analyses while in others the attention has remained below par, lies in the availability or absence of an adequate data base. The cases of Greece and Italy, where in spite of very grave problems of imbalanced regional growth relevant research is very limited, sustain that impression. The lack of attention to industrial movement in Italy may also have had something to do with the fact that the problem of the Mezzogiorno was thought of not as one that could be solved by persuading industry to move but rather as a very general development problem, requiring the simultaneous application of a wide array of instruments.

The influence of policy needs on data availability is also evident. At one end of the scale we find Ireland. This country, very keen on stimu-

405

lating the influx of companies for national and regional development, has made one single organisation, the IDA, responsible for monitoring the migration process as well as for collecting data. Researchers have been able to acquire much empirical knowledge from IDA. At the other end of the scale we find countries like Greece and Belgium, where political problems make it unlikely that the results of inquiries into the transfer of activities from one region to another will be implemented and used in practical policy.

Data availability and policy interest in the other countries of Europe are somewhere between these extremes. Policy makers in France, Germany, the Netherlands and Denmark, who show considerable concern about problems of regional development, apparently feel that the movement of industries could do a great deal towards their solution. Data bases have been set up in these countries, usually outside the regular statistical offices; the data they contain have been studied with some thoroughness.

The policy situation in the various countries tends to determine not only the scope of the work on industrial movement but also its orientation. The centralised structure of the French spatial economic system makes it hardly surprising that many studies carried out in France reflect a concern for the balance between Paris and 'la province'. To a lesser extent the same applies to Denmark, and even in the Netherlands the equilibrium concept is accepted to some degree, although the polynuclear structure of its central region (the Randstad) makes it less applicable there. In Germany finally, a country which historically and thanks to its post-war federal structure enjoys a fair regional balance, the accent is on the overall balance between cities and development regions rather than on specific flows from certain centres to certain assisted areas.

Let us now turn our attention more specifically to the data situation in the light of the theoretical basis of the study. As pointed out at some length in Chapter 1, the movement of industry ought always to be studied in relation to the other components of the change in total economic activity, i.e. new indigenous industry, closures, and *in situ* growth. For that kind of study a good data base is essential. Strikingly, in no single country of Europe has the study of movement been based on such regularly collected statistical data as Censuses of Establishments, or on the changes reported by the Central Register of Establishments of the Statistical Offices; the sources used were regional industrialisation offices, labour exchanges, and other private, semi-public, or public files.

Next, concentrating on the policy orientation of the studies, we find that numerous studies on a regional scale have been made for the purpose of testing a number of hypotheses on regional and urban development. Some are 'urban' studies, concerned in particular with changes in intra-metropolitan location patterns; others are 'rural' studies, concerned with the distribution of growth within an acceptor region. Both types of studies seem again greatly dependent on the availability of data.

What with the data limitations and the tendency of studies to focus on one particular aspect, total coverage of the EC was hard to achieve. Coverage is better for some aspects than for others, so let us take a closer look at the coverage by subject before we go on to draw general conclusions.

1 Most studies deal almost exclusively with *manufacturing*; only a few studies are reported to deal with offices, the decentralisation of government services, and such service sectors as wholesale and transportation. Recently, service sectors have become a more important source of migrant industry than manufacturing, and by consequence have been getting more attention.

2 Of all the components of change — migration or transfer (closure + new opening), branch plant (creation with contraction), closure with expansion, etc. — the *growth* aspect seems to have drawn the most attention. (The definition of these concepts was introduced in Chapter 1.) Most studies focus on the creation of new plants (divided into the categories: newly created indigenous plants, branch plants, and complete move) as seen from the point of view of acceptor regions, rather than on the closure aspect of migrated plants, let alone the closure and contraction aspect.

3 The sources from which data are drawn give little information about the *quantitative importance of industrial movement* in general. Unfortunately, in no country can one be sure that the information is exhaustive; moreover the delineation of the components of change (migration, branch plants, closures, etc.) is in most cases far from clear. Therefore, assessing the relative importance of movement for acceptor and donor regions requires careful consideration. Movement is difficult to measure; the results of the individual chapters give an idea just how difficult it is. However, they have also shown that the concepts proposed in Chapter 1 are very generally applicable and may serve as a good common denominator of all the concepts used in the widely varying data bases of the country studies.

4 The *motives* for movement have been studied in quite a few countries, though not always in relation with inquiries into movement patterns. Still, the motive studies seem sufficiently numerous, detailed, and comparable for a general evaluation.

5 That *theoretical considerations* have not been developed far in the country chapters is not surprising: their emphasis is on empirical knowledge. Probably the lack of theoretical developments is the reason why the difference between factors determining migration and mobility has largely escaped attention. We shall take up that point again when discussing sectoral aspects.

6 The *distance of the move* appeared an important criterion by which to distinguish different types of moves. As far as international moves are concerned, this criterion was given a good deal of attention in Ireland and some in the Netherlands, Belgium, and France. All the relevant studies focus on arrivals and give no information whatsoever on international departures; further analysis of the closures in each country would probably reveal such information.

Studies of long-distance moves, often associated with regional policy problems, have been made in the UK, Germany, France, and the smaller countries Denmark and the Netherlands; together they may provide sufficient material for a total picture of long-distance movement in Europe.

In some countries attention has also been given to short-distance moves, often associated with urban developments; a fair basis for generalisation seems to exist. Indeed, even if Europe is not completely covered, there is hope that the observed patterns are general enough to justify their application to the whole area.

Patterns of movement

The previous chapters have shown some remarkable points of resemblance in the patterns of movement observed in the various countries, in particular as far as the *spatial* patterns of movement are concerned. In all countries the distinction between inter-regional moves characterised by deconcentration and intra-metropolitan moves characterised by suburbanisation was relevant. For international moves the results are less clear-cut. Let us review the general European patterns and some specific points in some more detail.

The information on *inter-regional moves* shows in general an outward movement from the major conurbation, a pattern that remains stable for the whole period 1955–75. In the UK there was movement from the London area to most other parts of the country. In France, industries moved radially away from Paris. In the Netherlands, the flows went mainly from the major cities of the Randstad to all other provinces. In Flanders moves originated primarily in the Brussels and Antwerp areas, and were directed towards the provinces of Flanders. In Denmark the same picture emerges: industry tended to move outwards from Copenhagen, favouring counties at short distances from the capital. For Germany the picture is not quite so clear, but a decentralisation trend away from the Rhein/Ruhr/Neckar conurbation can nevertheless be observed. A comparable picture for Italy has to be more intuitive. Most probably, the industrial triangle of the north-west has been the origin of most moves, all other regions benefiting to varying degrees.

The general picture for the EC is shown in Map 12.1. The centrifugal forces that have been at work in Europe as far as the community members are concerned, are clearly visible. Greece, on the other hand, seems to have gone counter to the general trend, a number of plants still appearing to concentrate in Athens and Thessaloniki.

Map 12.1 gives only the major flows from the major centres. Of course, there have also been quite important flows from other centres, for instance the Midlands in the UK and many cities in Germany; indeed they show similar patterns on a smaller scale. Because these flows tend to be less well documented and smaller than those from the main centres, we have refrained from indicating them on the map.

A comparative study of the reports of those countries that have given evidence of empirical studies of *intra-metropolitan moves* also shows very distinct common European features. Indeed, the spatial adjustment patterns emerging from them all highlight the influence of distance: most of the establishments that moved out resettled in areas quite close to the city centres they had left (compare Paris, London, Amsterdam, Turin); there is little evidence of sectoral specificity. The indications in these urban studies of a strong suburbanisation trend in industrial movement are general enough to be applied to all Europe.

International moves (studied in the Netherlands, Belgium, and Ireland) were in all countries found to be in some sense associated with the creation or the existence of the Common Market. Moves to the Netherlands appeared also inspired by the — at first — low cost of labour and the central situation in the EC, in particular for port-oriented developments. The latter factor has also played a role for Belgium, overriding the high initial cost of labour there. Ireland seems to have been chosen as a location for industry for its combination of low labour cost, English speaking population, attractive package of incentives, and favourable organisational aspects. The overall information is too scarce, however, for a quantitative pattern for the whole of Europe to be distilled from it.

No clear common patterns of movement among *sectors* emerged from the international comparison. The information available on sectoral aspects is scanty and relates to Germany and Denmark, and to a lesser extent to the Netherlands, the UK, and Belgium. Sectoral move-

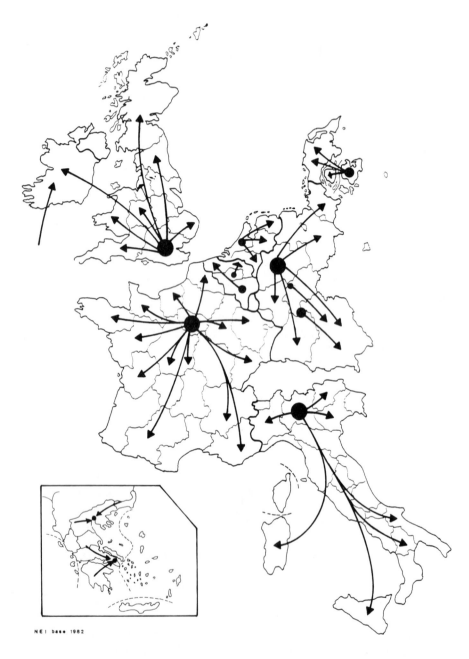

Map 12.1 Industrial migration patterns in the European Community
1955–75

410

ment patterns are expected to be closely related to the concepts of mobility and external factors (see Chapter 1). Sectors like the steel industry, characterised by high investment in equipment, would be expected to be less mobile than sectors like the clothing industry, which need hardly any fixed capital at all.

Other factors, such as growth, already referred to in Chapter 1, may also determine differences in mobility among sectors. The two factors work out differently in a European comparison. Indeed, high per capita investment of sectors is likely to lead to the same picture of movement all over Europe; sectoral growth, on the contrary, may differ from country to country, and from period to period, resulting in different sectoral movement patterns, but all under the same influence. We have tried to reorganise the material available on sectoral movement in Europe, but the picture remains very difficult to interpret. That, after all, is not so surprising, what with the diversity of sectoral groupings, areal scales, etc., used in the various studies, and the intricate interplay of external factors and mobility determinants. For a further analysis, much more research would be necessary, the more so as the basic theoretical concept of mobility as defined in Chapter 1 was not consistently adhered to in the various country analyses.

Analysis of the *temporal* aspect of movement has shown that in all countries studied the growth of the economy as a whole has determined to a very large extent the number of moves.

Motives, processes and strategies

In many countries surveys have been conducted to find out why entrepreneurs had taken certain location decisions, and more specifically, *why they had moved.* The common characteristic of the surveys mentioned in the country chapters is that they are all based on interviews or postal questionnaires. Some surveys used pre-coded questions, others open questions, still others worked with a fairly broad checklist of points to be discussed with entrepreneurs.

Before trying to synthetise the relevant analyses, let us draw attention to a few points that should be taken into account in interpreting the results.

First, in the fairly long period of some thirty years, important changes have occurred in the conditions external to the firms; therefore, the general environment in which the survey was taken has to be taken into account.

Choosing a new location occurs only a few times in a company's lifetime. Most firms have gone about relocating in a fairly unsystematic way, which implies that the reasons they give are often not the real ones; managers tend to rationalise *ex post* their decisions, and to produce answers they think will be acceptable to the interviewer. Moreover, if some time has elapsed between the move and the questioning, the wrong reason may be given because the persons responsible for the choice cannot be traced any more, or because they tend to refer to the firm's present situation rather than to the situation at the time when the decision was taken.

The reasons for a particular choice are perceived in different ways. To some firms, certain requirements for production are so obvious that they do not even mention them when asked why they have made a certain choice. They rather tend to stress in their answers the problems that formed a bottleneck in their operations, or took particularly long to solve.

Different people, with different perceptions, will give different answers to questions about, for instance, the successive stages of decision associated with area and site selection; even more detailed questionnaires cannot entirely eliminate that fact. Moreover, the reality with which entrepreneurs are confronted is probably too diverse for them to attach specific weights to all the factors.

On the above considerations, there is evidently little sense in trying to rank, on the available evidence, the factors relevant to industrial movement. A better proposition is probably to try to combine the reasons for a firm's leaving one site and choosing another with an evaluation of the firm's general environment and the strategies open to it. In that connection a closer look at the relevant (re)location factors may reveal the factors *ultimately* responsible for the move. What are, for instance, the ultimate reasons behind such often mentioned factors as 'space' and 'accessibility'? They may vary widely. Perhaps a firm has outgrown its industrial site because it has extended its activities or wishes to start a new production process requiring more space than the old one, or the firm intends to replace its fleet of lorries with larger ones which cannot park and be handled at the present site. Poor accessibility, especially in urban areas, may be the result of increasing private traffic; in that case the ultimate cause of the firm's relocation is exogenous.

Figure 12.1 shows these examples. The upper elements of the diagram represent changes in the size of the market, technological changes, and changes in traffic volume, to be considered the ultimate reasons for the relocation. The first two are supposed to result in an increase of the firm's activity level, for which additional space is required. The discrepancy between available space and required space may lead to a relocating decision; this discrepancy is then the first reason. Similar reasoning applies to accessibility: the ultimate reason is the increase in traffic,

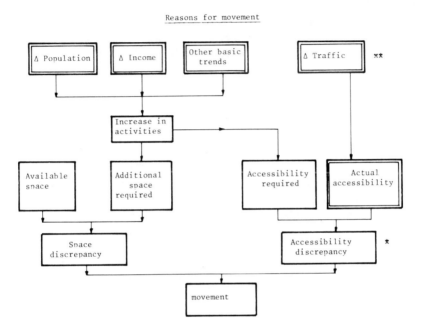

Reasons for movement

* Prima causae.

** Ultima causae

Figure 12.1 Reasons for movement

413

the first reason the discrepancy between required and actual accessibility.

Interesting as the first reasons may be, from an analytical point of view the ultimate reasons are far more intriguing. However, they are unlikely to emerge clearly from surveys.

The first point to be stressed, then, is that almost all questionnaires were made in a period of growth, and that for most entrepreneurs the major impetus to consider a move was that existing facilities were inadequate to cope with the new situation. The second point is that in the period 1960–74 there was near-full employment in almost the entire EC. As discussed in Chapter 1, in such a growth situation a firm is likely to rank its locational options as follows:

1 Extension on the existing site;
2 Establishment of a branch plant;
3 Complete transfer.

No wonder then that in most surveys one finds among the motives for choosing option 2 or 3 the reason why option 1 was out: inadequate facilities on the existing site, no labour available, no space available, bad layout, obsolete capital, unfavourable traffic conditions, etc. Other items from the list of external factors given in Chapter 1 (the section on external factors and impulses) are also often mentioned in surveys. What strikes us, however, is the consistency with which 'lack of labour' and 'lack of space' recur as prominent factors. Apparently, for a long period the production and distribution technology prevailing in Europe required a mix of production factors whose relative costs were such that it was more profitable to look for the necessary production factors elsewhere than to step up productivity on the existing site, or replace current production factors with others. Now the European evidence shows that firms requiring additional labour tend to spread out from the central areas, mostly by establishing branch plants. That strategy has the advantage of low cost and managerial ease, routine activities being gradually shifted while the firm's other functions are kept intact as much and as long as possible. Availability and cost of labour are mentioned as the basic reasons for the location of such branch plants; such elements as infrastructure, accommodating local authorities, and regional aid may further make one site preferable to others. The tendency of companies to move from the centres, generally characterised by congestion and high cost, to areas where labour was still fairly abundant and relatively cheap, dominated for several decades the movement of industry in Europe. Not surprisingly, however, many a national report indicates that with the change in economic conditions beginning in 1974, that type of movement largely came to an end.

414

Industries for which not the cost and availability of labour were the dominant factors, but such external conditions as space and traffic, tended to follow a different strategy. In line with the theoretical considerations of Chapter 1 they mostly moved out completely to resettle on a site meeting their new functioning conditions, but preferably close to the old site so as to disturb as little as possible existing ties with staff, business relations, etc. These industries tend to give as the most important reasons for choosing a certain new location: available space, low rent, good accessibility, parking area, etc. Co-operation of local authorities, incentives, and some other factors are mentioned as well, but evidently carry less weight. This type of movement continued also after the crisis.

Models

The problems associated with surveys have induced some authors to try to establish the relevance of certain factors behind industrial movement by other means. The alternative they chose was the explanatory model. An inventory of all modelling approaches referred to in the various country chapters showed that the use of models has been almost entirely confined to the UK; outside the UK only two studies in Germany and one in the Netherlands could be traced. Data availability seems to be the key factor here; indeed we have already seen in previous sections that the UK is privileged on that score. The existing models vary with the specific objectives they were built for and the kind of data available. To make an attempt at classification, we shall first divide the models into geographical and sectoral ones, the former intended to explain spatial patterns of movement, the latter the different rates of movement among sectors. Most models are easy to classify in that way, but one model, which integrates the sectoral and spatial approaches, will be put in a category by itself. Within the group of 'geographical' models we can distinguish those that explain the number of arrivals in a certain area, and others setting out to explain the number of moves towards certain areas.

After this broad grouping by purpose, the models may be divided further by the method they use: while all the models inventoried use ordinary least square techniques for estimation, some apply them to cross-section data and others to time-series.

Besides models using in some way or other aggregate data (number of moves, etc.), modelling work has also been done on the level of individual plants, the technique used being one specially adapted to the work, namely discriminant analysis.

Table 12.1

Survey of models of industrial movement

					Period
I	Geographical models				
	A	Generation models			
		(a)	Time series		
			1	Ashcroft and Taylor	(1979)	1945–71
			2	Spanger and Treuner	(1975)	1955–71
		(b)	Cross section		
			1	Sant	(1975)	1945–51
						1951–59
						1960–61
						1966–71
	B	Arrival models			
		(a)	Time series models		
			1	Beacham and Osborn	(1970)	1945–65
			2	Sant	(1975)	1945–65
			3	Moore and Rhodes	(1976)	1945–71
			4	Ashcroft and Taylor	(1979)	1945–71
		(b)	Cross section models		
			1	Keeble	(1970)	1945–65
			2	Townsend and Gault	(1972)	1945–65
			3	Keeble	(1972)	1945–65
			4	Sant	(1975)	1945–51
						1952–59
						1960–65
						1966–71
			5	Spanger and Treuner	(1975)	1955–71
			6	Molle	(1979)	1967–73
II	Sectoral models				
		(b)	Cross section		
			1	Townroe	(1973)	1945–65
			2	Molle	(1979)	1966–73
III	Combined models				
			1	Bade	(1979)	1964–77
IV	Locational models – discriminant analysis				
			1	O'Farrell	(1978)	1960–73
			2	O'Farrell and Crouchley	(1979)	

416

Area	Dependent variable
UK	Number of moves in the UK
FRG	Number of moves in the FRG
UK	Number of moves from each region of UK
UK	Moves to all peripheral areas
UK	Moves to each of the 10 regions of UK
UK	Moves to all peripheral areas
UK	{ Moves to 4 regions of UK
	Total moves to all development areas
UK	{ Moves from South West to all other UK areas
	Moves from West Midlands to all other UK areas
UK	{ Moves from South East to rest of UK
	Jobs from South East to rest of UK
UK	See Keeble 1972
UK	Moves to each of the regions of UK
FRG	Moves to types of municipalities in Nordrhein/Westfalen
Netherlands	Moves to municipalities in the area of Amsterdam
UK	Number of moves ± 30 branches
Netherlands	Number of moves ± 20 branches
FRG	Number of moves in the FRG
Ireland	Individual plant level regional and urban location choices

In Table 12.1, all studies with model approaches are arranged according to the above division. The first column mentions the authors of the study, the others give the period and area to which it applies, and briefly indicate the dependent variables.

Two models explain the *number of moves generated* by means of time-series analysis. According to Ashcroft and Taylor (1979), the total number of inter-regional moves generated in the UK depends on growth (change in the level of manufacturing production and investment), the spare capacity still available, and the strength of restrictive policies in the central areas (measured by the number of industrial development certificates). Spanger and Treuner (1975) found the number of moves to be closely related to the business cycle (activity levels).

Sant (1975), in his cross-section model, of course finds spatial rather than general economic factors as determinants; the level of urbanisation, the new town programme, and some modified gravity measure all showed themselves important variables in his analysis.

Among the *arrival models,* those based on time series may be expected to feature national factors; generation and arrival models represent indeed two sides of the same models, and if the figures of total departures equal those of total arrivals, they even give identical elaborations. That is true of the Beacham—Osborn (1970) model, which features two dominant factors: labour-market tension on the one hand, and the government's restrictive policy in the South-East on the other. In the contributions by Moore—Rhodes (1976) and Ashcroft—Taylor (1979), next to overall pressure of demand for products, the different policy variables that succeeded one another in the course of time (investment incentives, regional employment premiums, special development area status, Local Employment Act, and industrial development certificates) seem to play an overwhelming role in explaining why the number of moves varies from one year to another. Sant (1975) comes up with slightly different results: over and above the economic variables already cited, he has found some spatial attraction factors, such as housing in new towns, town expansion schemes, etc.

Cross-section models, into which the distance function was introduced at an early stage, are more consistent in their results; the number of moves was invariably found to be a positive function of an attraction factor and a negative function of distance (Keeble 1970, 1972, Townsend and Gault 1972). The authors developing these models defined their attraction factors in different ways, although availability of labour was in general measured by unemployment. Sant (1975) also found regional policy, female activity rates, and urbanisation as important factors; Spanger and Treuner (1975) made a composite indicator of attractiveness, accounting for a large number of infrastructure and amenity elements. On the smaller scale of the agglomeration, Molle (1979) on the contrary found the availability of industrial sites, accessibility, and amenities to be essential factors.

The two *sectoral models* showed up as explanatory factors of differences in movement: growth of activity, size of establishments, female employment rate, and transportation cost on the regional scale (Townroe, 1973), and size of establishment and transport intensity on the urban level (Molle, 1979). Admittedly, the European countries do not show very consistent patterns as far as the spread of moves among sectors is concerned. We do find in both models some of the factors that in Chapter 1 were considered to determine a plant's mobility, but also some elements that do not very well fit our theoretical framework. The general impression is that sectoral models, as indeed the whole concept of sectoral mobility, need to be developed further.

Next we come to the *combined* models. Bade (1979) has shown that a combination of sectoral aspects (growth rates, proportion of female labour, etc.) and locational characteristics (proportion of plants located in agglomerations, etc.) could explain the total number of moves by sector. Bade's approach indeed integrates external impulses and mobility aspects in an attempt to explain the differences in movement ratios by sector.

Finally, the *individual plant and site models* (O'Farrell, 1978) form a category by themselves. These discriminant models were used to predict the distribution of indigenous and foreign plants by size among regions and towns in Ireland. Similar techniques, if less elaborate, have been used in many other studies beside O'Farrell's.

We could only make a very short analysis of the available models, most of which would have warranted a much more detailed discussion. Still, this brief analysis suffices to show that the model results corroborate in many respects those of theoretical and questionnaire-type analyses. Indeed, we had encountered all the explanatory factors before, if perhaps in a slightly different form. That means on the one hand that the results obtained with models in a specific country, like those acquired otherwise, may be generalised to other countries, and on the other, that a modelling approach would be feasible in other countries as well, to the extent that the data can be made available.

One last comparison to be made is that between the empirical models treated in this section and the theoretical model presented in Chapter 1. The latter, a geographical model, resembles most the cross-section models referred to above. It contains a mobility coefficient, distance, and a set of attraction factors. The arrival models actually tested all contain some elements of the theoretical model, some of them even quite a few, but none arrives at testing the whole set of coefficients presented in our theoretical model. Apparently, there is still ample scope for improvement, both in theory and in practice.

The consequences of industrial migration for the workers

Industrial migration should be seen as part of a far more general process of regions adapting to new opportunities or changing prospects. The consequences for firms, and in particular the people they employ, should receive considerably more attention than they have so far. Indeed, when speaking of industrial migration, we have been referring to workplaces rather than workers; yet, from a social as well as an economic point of view, the migration of workers in association with the migration of workplaces is extremely important.

How many workers move with the establishment in which they are employed? How does the distance over which the establishment moves affect their number? How many workplaces are actually filled after arrival at the new location? How does industrial migration affect the unemployment figures in donor regions? Did the migration of the establishment go hand in hand with a change in the production process, requiring a different skill mix of workers? Obviously, to answer all those questions, one would have to monitor the establishment for some time, from before the move until well afterwards. From the few longitudinal studies made, some indications do emerge. From a study of short-distance moves from towns to suburbs, a very high proportion (about 75 per cent) of the staff appears to stick with the establishment when it moves. About long-distance moves far fewer data are available, but what information there is points to much lower percentages. The former high percentage can be explained by the fact that employees need not move house, but can go on (or start) commuting; indeed, the commuting distance may even have become shorter. Indeed, it is hardly surprising that more workers leave the company as the move is farther: commuting becomes more difficult and moving house will often prove impossible. The family situation and the situation in the labour market as well as the housing market have great influence.

One effect of industrial moves is that of *segregation:* establishments are moving *outward from the cities* and most highly skilled employees are already living in the suburbs, so essentially the low skilled workers living in the towns find themselves with a choice of commuting, or give up and find another job — or join the army of unemployed. Especially the weaker groups on the labour market (young people, women, low skilled workers) will have problems. A division of work seems to ensue, the higher qualified jobs being performed in the suburbs, leaving the lower grade work and the excluded lower skilled people behind in the central large towns, where the already serious problems will only get worse as a consequence. There are indications, indeed, that the flow of highly skilled commuters from suburbs to towns is decreasing, while that of low skilled workers from town centres to suburbs is increasing.

420

Apart from such indicative results, quite a few questions remain largely unanswered, such as: what happened to the firm itself; was there a general modernisation of administration, bookkeeping and management? Can one say that industrial migration generally coincides with modernisation? Does that imply a modernisation of the acceptor regions? From the Italian report and a number of other indications (decrease of disparities, for instance) one would be tempted to answer these questions in the affirmative, but for a detailed and thorough reply the necessary statistical and other material is still lacking. There is no doubt that closer investigation of the matter would deepen our insight into the consequences of industrial migration, and thus would make us better judges of its significance and desirability.

Effects on donor and acceptor regions

Industrial movement affects in many ways the regional equilibrium of a country. A major effect is the quantitative change of employment that is due to movement. For a long time regional policy has stimulated movement so as to improve the employment situation in acceptor regions and ease the strain on donor regions.

From the evidence available, the migration aspect of movement clearly has made on the whole little impact on total employment distribution. Other categories of change, in particular *in situ* growth and the balance of closures and new openings, were mostly more important. However, as the delineation of the various components is very uncertain, such conclusions should be interpreted with some caution. On the one hand, the movement aspect of many new creations is difficult to grasp, especially in international cases; on the other, there is much confusion about the measurement of subsequent growth of plants that have moved in. Taking proper account of these aspects one finds that for quite a number of regions, especially peripheral agricultural ones, the whole industrial base consists of plants that, by migration or creation, 'moved' to the area. There is also evidence that many immigrant plants, small at the moment of moving, have subsequently grown considerably.

The impact of industrial movement on employment redistribution is greater at the urban level (especially that of large cities) than at the regional level. The loss of employment in central cores is substantial, while plants settling in the suburbs account for the majority of jobs created in the suburbs. The same holds for the smaller agricultural areas, where a large portion of the new employment is due to immigration.

Apart from the quantitative effect, there are some qualitative effects of movement that call for some further discussion, in particular the effects that the movement of firms has on the industrial structure of the donor and acceptor regions and the quality of employment. The 1960s were the era of debates on the nature of the process of industrial movement. This process was felt to be highly selective, high grade jobs with a low sensitivity to cyclical movements keeping to the central areas, which thus could get an ever firmer hold on the total economy, while low grade jobs, so vulnerable to cyclical movements, changes in corporate policy, and market conditions, were consigned to (peripheral) acceptor regions. Although not irrelevant, the picture seems to exaggerate the negative effects on the acceptor regions. Indeed, from some country reports employment in moved establishments does not appear more vulnerable to outside changes than local employment. Moreover, the industry created in regions that at the end of the war were virtually without any industrial base at all, dependent as it may have been on extra-regional decision centres and even if it did employ only low skilled labour, still introduced a certain industrial 'culture', opening the way to the gradual upgrading of skills and the take-off of local initiatives. As a consequence, the sectoral composition of the economy came to be more and more equal. The phenomenon is general all over Europe (Molle et al., 1980).

In the central, donor, areas the industrial base has been more and more eroded. Initially, the erosion process was welcomed as it strengthened the control functions and the specialisation in high technology high skill labour. Recently it has become apparent, however, that it has made these areas, particularly as far as control and other high grade functions are concerned, increasingly vulnerable to changes in locational trends, and that for labour market reasons a more balanced industrial development would have been preferable.

That aspect gets even more relief on the intra-urban level. Many areas in central cities have lost practically all manufacturing to the suburbs or towns even farther away. However, because many of the workers have stayed behind and new low skilled labour (often foreigners) have moved in, these areas now face the difficult task of adapting their economic base to the labour force available; actually, they might even welcome a return of some industrial activity.

Regional policy

In the previous chapters, regional policy has occasionally been referred to.

Indeed, from the information that could be used for a European comparison, movement studies like the one in hand seem relevant on

422

the following three points:

1 Knowledge of the migration of establishments within urban agglomerations, its contribution to suburbanisation processes, and its influence on traffic patterns (in particular journey-to-work patterns) is of eminent importance for the study of urban agglomerations and the policy to be pursued there.
2 When high technology sectors — requiring highly skilled manpower — migrate from urban to non-urban regions, the urban regions and the quality of employment there as well as the non-urban regions and the structure of their labour force will feel the effects.
3 Knowledge of the basic forces behind international migration (notably from the USA to Western Europe, but also from Europe to the Far East, or within Europe, for instance from central countries to such peripheral countries as Ireland and the Mediterranean states) is essential for understanding why the competitive position of developed countries in respect of developing nations changes in a certain way.

All three points are relevant to policy makers: the first on the level of agglomerations, the second on the (inter)regional level, and the third on the international level. With that in mind, we can understand why policy makers stimulate movement studies.

For some time industrial movement has been considered the major vehicle for regional policy in many countries, e.g. the UK, Ireland, France, and Germany. In Italy the influence of government-controlled organisations on industrial movement was quite important. Regional policy has used all kinds of instruments, both to induce plants to leave certain regions (controls, levies), and to get them to settle in certain others (e.g. financial incentives) (see Allen et al., 1981).

Another instrument of regional policy mentioned in Chapter 1, namely, the movement of government agencies, has been widely used in some countries (UK, NL), but the existing literature does not say much about it.

We do not want to probe too deeply into the relations between movement and policy; for a general discussion of regional policy in Europe we may refer to Molle (1983), and notably Vanhove and Klaassen (1979). The whole scenario for regional policy has changed lately. As the employment problem became general, and the flows of industrial movement dwindled, regional policy began to reorient itself towards the regions' indigenous growth potential. Or, in terms of the matrix of component change presented in Chapter 1, regional policy began to try to influence the components birth and death, and, in another way, *in situ* growth, rather than migration. The set of instruments to be tested for that purpose has not yet crystallised out.

Outlook

In view of the wealth of information contained in the country reports on the motives for migration, the direction of industrial movement, the influence of distance, and the relation between industrial movement and general economic growth, the question arises to what extent we shall be able to predict the future role of industrial migration. Obviously, regional developments are intimately linked to general societal developments, but that consideration does not bring us much farther; indeed, forecasting the future is not what it used to be!

> Thinking in scenarios is the most recent form of shaping the future: interfutures is a case in point. Scenarios are schematic representations, consistent to some extent, of future developments that can be envisaged; they are concerned mostly with certain sub-areas of society. Scenarios have the advantage of presenting alternative developments revealing a whole spectrum of situations for which to prepare oneself; the draw-back is that, the future being unknown, the spectrum may become so broad as to make no sense. Moreover, politicians sometimes seem to think that the government can simply choose one out of a fan of scenarios, and then, just by operating the right instruments, make the future of that scenario come true. It is that alleged control of the future that makes it so difficult, if not impossible, to respond flexibly to other than planned developments.
>
> Of course, a government can wield certain tools and exert some influence, but it is highly doubtful that it can thus control the fundamental developments of society. Who can say how things will evolve on the political plan (perhaps the most uncontrollable?). Who knows if the present more and more childless society will not invoke forces that lead to the return of larger families? What solutions may suddenly present themselves for the energy problem? What medical innovation may lead to an essential prolongation of human life, resulting in the failure of all pension funds? No government can answer such questions, let alone control the events they refer to. Yet it is such developments that will change our future, as they have done in the past (Klaassen and Pawlowski, 1980).

However, let us formulate some speculations with respect to the future on the strength of past trends, speculations that may, or may not come true.

1 There will be growth in the more sophisticated industrial sectors, and decline in conventional industry.
2 Future sophisticated sectors will need highly skilled workers who want good living conditions in pleasant surroundings, and perhaps also close to centres of knowledge, such as universities and other large research institutions.
3 A considerable amount of research will focus on alternative sources of energy, which will gradually provide energy for domestic heating, manufacturing industries, and transportation.
4 In spite of 3, we must reckon with increasing energy prices and hence transport prices, leading to a general decline of potential output and supply markets and potential labour markets.
5 The EC will expand gradually, Spain and Portugal entering first. This will affect not only labour markets in the traditional member countries, but also production prospects in the new ones.

As said before, such factors will influence general developments and through them regional developments, but to what extent these and other factors will work out on the regional level is not easy to say.

The outlook for industrial movement as a whole depends also on the future development of the components into which total change has been broken down in the analysis. Quite possibly, movement in the sense of branch creation and complete transfer (migration) will in future play a much smaller role than creation and closure, first of all because of the general economic environment. The previous chapters largely agreed on the most common factors inducing movement: output growth, the curb on development at existing locations, and the attractiveness of some new locations. All three have lately shown trends different from the past, trends that are likely to persist. In general, the growth potential of the European economy for the coming decade is considered rather weak and in some sectors completely absent. A downward development is expected for many activities, in particular the more traditional ones. The difference in wage level between 'cheap labour' countries in Europe and Third World countries has become so great that many establishments are looking for cheap labour outside Europe. That would imply a speed-up of international emigration, showing up in European statistics as closures.

Drastic changes have also occurred in the balance between central and peripheral areas, changes that are likely to persist. They have a locational and a political aspect. In the past, there was lack of labour and government checks on development in the central areas, while in the peripheral areas there were large reservoirs of labour and government incentives. Now the general economic developments and the locational trends have brought about a new equilibrium: the centres have as much labour available as the peripheral parts, or even more, and the differences in cost have dwindled at the same time. Moreover, the government's policy is now to withdraw gradually both the stimulants in the periphery and the controls in the centre. Such levelling tendencies are likely to reduce movement, or migration, of industry. Some movement-inducing factors will remain, however.

The first is the technology push. From inventions and innovations, a number of new activities are springing up, for instance in the information sector and in the fields of micro-electronics and biochemicals. Most of these activities have a very high technology content, and need highly skilled manpower partial to pleasant living surroundings and wanting contact with research and development units of the industry itself and their counterparts in the educational sector: universities etc. For some time, such activities will continue to 'spark off' from the central areas, where 'central' activities are at home. An inter-regional and an intra-regional effect may be distinguished; within regions, there is a growing imbalance between pleasant residential areas, inner city areas, and the older industrial restructuring areas (see Klaassen, Molle and Paelinck, 1981). There are many such trends, too many to be gone into here. We will indulge, however, in some speculations as to the future inter-regional movement patterns. In the UK, France, and Germany, there will probably be a trek towards the southern regions, where living conditions are pleasanter than in the north. In Italy, where the north is probably as well endowed as the Mezzogiorno, tendencies will be less clear; an adapted version of the movement pattern of the 1960s may obtain in the 1980s: while in the 1960s the availability of cheap, often female, labour was the leading motive, in the 1980s highly skilled key staff forms the main factor of attraction.

Some regions that are particularly well provided with the locational advantages of the future, such as universities, laboratories, climate, sports facilities, environment, urban infrastructure, are likely to become the new economic strongholds. Within these new regions, adaption processes are probable. The demand for new products may rise steeply, that for older products vanish rapidly, with corresponding spatial effects. One may presume, indeed, that these will become the areas sparking off new growth instead of the old centres, and from where some diffusion processes will start. For the older areas and those newly developed ones not quite so richly endowed the future looks rather bleak; production processes, ripening faster than they used to, may pass them by and move straight to Third World countries.

426

The consequences for regional policy are grave. Not only do we have a new category of problem regions — the urban areas — on our backs, but we cannot count any more on one of the strong growth mechanisms either. That is why full weight should be given — as has been done for some time in southern Italy — to the indigenous growth potential of the regions themselves, attention being shifted from the migration of industry to openings for new industries.

The above considerations all reflect a concern with the long-distance (growth- and labour market-oriented) part of industrial migration. A group of movements with entirely different dynamics is, as we have seen, that of short-distance intra-metropolitan moves. Such moves, mostly initiated because the old location is badly matched to new technological, policy or other developments, are likely to continue in the future. Indeed, Molle and Vianen (1982) have shown that in Amsterdam the number of moves in seven years since the oil crisis has remained stable. For this type of move the external conditions have hardly or not at all changed, nor are they expected to in the future. If cities are not to be left completely behind in development, a renewal programme is imperative, and consequently the push to move will remain. Moreover, rising energy costs may well make industries move towards suburban workers, thus enabling them to cut down on transportation time and cost. Finally, new technologies coming on the market will compel some entrepreneurs to adapt their production capacity to new needs, and to that end change their locations.

The important question is: will spatial rearrangement manage to bring about the internal restructuration of the central regions' productive capacity needed to cope with the problems of unemployment and outmigration ahead? Once more, much attention should be paid to the conditions that foster indigenous growth.

The new tendencies we have just sketched will call for research into spatial-adjustment processes and the possibilities of intervention available to governments. One attempt at grasping the new relations between technology, employment, and location has been made in Molle (1982). Many researchers have already started to work along these lines on the basis of national experiences. Now for this new type of studies to succeed, new data will be badly needed. The previous analysis has clearly shown how dependent policy is on research, and the latter on data. The data most needed for the future will probably be those on the birth and death of establishments. Certainly, if national and local statistical offices concentrated more on the components of change in industrial growth and decline and on their systematic registration, the field of valuable and policy-relevant research would be considerably widened, and oriented to future needs. As long as the thoughts developed in this book have managed to draw attention to that rather unexplored field of spatial economic research, and if better statistics emerge as a result, the authors consider their efforts rewarded.

References

Allen, K. et al. (1981), 'Regional Incentives in the European Community; a Comparative Study', Commission of the EC, Brussels, *Regional Policy Series*, no. 15.

Ashcroft, B., and Taylor, J. (1979), 'The Effect of Regional Policy on the Movement of Industry in Great Britain', in D. MacLennan and J.B. Parr (eds), *Regional Policy, Past Experience, New Directions*, Oxford.

Bade, F.J. (1979), *Die Mobilität von Industriebetrieben*, Hahn, Meisenhelm am Glau.

Beacham, A. and Osborn, W.T. (1970), 'The Movement of Manufacturing Industry', *Regional Studies*, pp. 41–7.

Keeble, D.E. (1970), 'The Movement of Manufacturing Industry', Comment, *Regional Studies*, vol. 4, pp. 395–7.

Keeble, D.E. (1972), 'Industrial Movement and Regional Development in the UK', *Town Planning Review*, 43(1), pp. 163–88.

Klaassen, L.H. and Pawlowski, Z. (1980–1), 'Long-term Forecasting; Meditations of Two Pitfall Collectors', Netherlands Economic Institute, Rotterdam, Series: *Foundations of Empirical Economic Research*.

Klaassen, L.H., Molle, W.T.M. and Paelinck, J.H.P. (eds) (1981), *Dynamics of Urban Development*, Gower Press, Aldershot.

Molle, W.T.M. (1979), 'Industrial Mobility, a Review of Empirical Studies and an Analysis of the Migration of Industry from the City of Amsterdam, *Regional Studies*, vol. 11, pp. 323–35.

Molle, W.T.M., with the collaboration of Holst, B. van, and Smit, H., (1980), *Regional Disparity and Economic Development in the European Community*, Saxon House, Farnborough.

Molle, W.T.M. (1982), 'Prospects of Regional Employment and Scanning of Technological Options (PRESTO) in the European Community', Commission EC, Brussels.

Molle, W.T.M. (1983), 'Regional Policy' in: P. Coffey (ed.), 'Main Economic Policy Areas in the EC', Nijhoff, The Hague.

Molle, W.T.M., and Vianen, J.G. (1982), 'Het vertrek van bedrijven uit Amsterdam, *ESB*, pp. 608–13.

Moore, B., and Rhodes, J. (1976), 'Regional Economic Policy and the Movement of Manufacturing Firms to Development Areas, *Economica*, vol. 43, pp. 17–31.

O'Farrell, P.N., (1978), 'An Analysis of New Industry Locations, The Irish Case', *Progress in Planning,* vol. 9, no. 3, Pergamon, Oxford.

O'Farrell, P.N., and Crouchley, R. (1979), 'The Locational Pattern of New Manufacturing Establishments; an Application of Discriminant Analysis', *Regional Studies,* vol. 13, pp. 39—59.

Sant, M., (1975), *Industrial Movement and Regional Development: The British Case,* Pergamon, Oxford.

Spanger, U., and Treuner, P. (1975), 'Statistical Analysis of Location Determinants, *Papers of the Regional Science Association,* vol. 35, pp. 143—56.

Townroe, P.M. (1973), 'The Supply of Mobile Industry, a Cross-sectional Analysis', *Regional and Urban Economics,* 2, pp. 71—86.

Townsend, A.R., and Gault, F.D. (1972), 'A National Model of Factory Movement and Resulting Employment', *Area* 4, pp. 94—8.

Vanhove, N. and Klaassen, L.H. (1979), 'Regional Policy: a European Approach', Saxon House, Farnborough.

Index

438